Applied Economics

in

Banking and Finance

APPLIED ECONOMICS
IN BANKING
AND FINANCE

H. CARTER
AND
I. PARTINGTON

OXFORD UNIVERSITY PRESS
1979

Oxford University Press, Walton Street, Oxford OX2 6DP

OXFORD LONDON GLASGOW
NEW YORK TORONTO MELBOURNE WELLINGTON
KUALA LUMPUR SINGAPORE JAKARTA HONG KONG TOKYO
DELHI BOMBAY CALCUTTA MADRAS KARACHI
NAIROBI DAR ES SALAAM CAPE TOWN

*Published in the United States by
Oxford University Press, New York*

© *H. Carter & I. Partington 1979*

British Library Cataloguing in Publication Data

Carter, H
  Applied economics in banking and finance.
  1. Finance – Great Britain
  I. Title   II. Partington, I
  332′.0941   HG186.G7   79-40405

ISBN 0-19-877108-8
ISBN 0-19-877109-6 PbK

Printed in Great Britain by
Fakenham Press Limited, Fakenham, Norfolk

Contents

1 THE FINANCIAL SYSTEM   1

1.1 Introduction 1.2 Finance and the 'circular flow' 1.3 The circular flow and the flow of funds 1.4 The U.K. accounts 1.5 The 'problem' of surpluses and deficits 1.5.1 A sector with a budget deficit 1.5.2 A sector with a budget surplus **1.6 Summary**

2 WEALTH, ASSETS, AND MONEY   18

2.1 Introduction 2.2 Forms of wealth 2.3 The growth of claims 2.4 Money 2.4.1 The functions of money *2.4.1.1 Medium of exchange 2.4.1.2 Store of value 2.4.1.3 Unit of account 2.4.1.4 Standard for deferred payments* 2.4.2 Money and money-substitutes 2.4.3. Money stock data **2.5 Summary**

3 FINANCIAL INTERMEDIATION   34

3.1 Introduction 3.2 The nature of financial intermediation 3.2.1 Financial intermediaries 3.2.2 The need for financial intermediation 3.2.3 The process of financial intermediation 3.2.4 The economic basis of financial intermediation **3.3 Financial intermediaries and the economy** 3.3.1 Saving and investment **3.4 Bank and non-bank financial intermediaries 3.5 Summary**

4 MAIN FINANCIAL INTERMEDIARIES   48

4.1 Introduction 4.2 Classification 4.3 Bank and non-bank financial intermediaries 4.3.1 Size of financial intermediaries **4.4 Financial intermediaries and their balance sheets** 4.4.1 Introduction 4.4.2 The primary banking sector *4.4.2.1 The clearing banks 4.4.2.2 The Bank of England Banking Department 4.4.2.3 The discount houses 4.4.2.4 The National Giro* **4.5 Secondary banking 4.6 Other deposit-taking firms** 4.6.1 Building societies 4.6.2 Trustee Savings Banks *4.6.2.1 National Savings Bank* 4.6.3 Finance houses 4.6.4 Other financial intermediaries *4.6.4.1 Insurance companies and pension funds 4.6.4.2 Investment trusts and unit trusts* **4.7 Secondary banking and the problem of supervision 4.8 Summary**

5 THE DEPOSIT BANKS   90

5.1 Early history 5.2 Operation of the primary banks 5.2.1 Services to customers 5.2.2 Banks and their balance sheets

5.2.2..1 London Clearing Bank assets   5.2.2.2 Asset structure of the London Clearing Banks   5.2.2.3 Deposits of the London Clearing Banks
5.3 Summary

6 THE STOCK OF MONEY   **113**

6.1 Introduction   6.2 The banks and the stock of money
6.2.1 Deposit creation   *6.2.1.1 The individual bank and the generation of bank deposits*   6.2.2 Constraints on the growth of bank deposits
6.3 The government and the stock of money   6.3.1 The cash nexus   *6.3.1.1 Government spending   6.3.1.2 Government receipts*
6.3.2 Government borrowing   **6.4 The balance of payments and the stock of money**   6.4.1 Bank of England operations and the foreign currency market   6.4.2 Domestic credit expansion
6.4.2.1 Definition and calculation   6.4.2.2 Uses of the D.C.E. calculation
6.5 The stock of money   6.6 Regulating the stock of money
6.6.1 Controversy   6.6.2 The basis for control   **6.7 Summary**

7 THE GOVERNMENT SECTOR AND THE FINANCIAL   **147**
   SYSTEM

7.1 Introduction   7.2 The Bank of England   7.2.1 Functions
7.2.2 Bank of England balance sheets   **7.3 The parallel money markets   7.4 Control of the banking system**   7.4.1 Competition and Credit Control   *7.4.1.1 Competition   7.4.1.2 Credit control*
7.4.2 Competition and Credit Control and its aftermath
7.5 Summary

8 OTHER FINANCIAL SYSTEMS   **177**

8.1 The American system   8.1.1 The major financial intermediaries   8.1.2 U.S. commercial banking   *8.1.2.1 Classification and structure of U.S. commercial banking   8.1.2.2 U.S. commercial bank balance sheets*   8.1.3 U.S. central banking and bank supervision
8.1.3.1 Structure of central banking   8.1.3.2 Central banking operations
8.1.4 Banking supervision   **8.2 Banking in the Federal Republic of Germany**   8.2.1 The major financial intermediaries   8.2.2 West German central banking   *8.2.2.1 Bundesbank operations*   **8.3 The European Economic Community and monetary union**
8.3.1 Meaning and implications of monetary union   8.3.2 E.E.C. financial systems and monetary union   **8.4 Summary**

9 THE GOVERNMENT ACCOUNTS   **206**

**9.1 The definition of public expenditure   9.2 The growth in public expenditure and its importance in the economy
9.3 Public expenditure by economic category, spending authority, and programme   9.4 The public sector accounts**

9.5 The central government accounts 9.6 Methods of
taxation 9.7 Principles of taxation 9.8 The financing of the
public sector borrowing requirement 9.9 Summary

10 THE NATIONAL DEBT   227

   10.1 The origins and growth of the national debt 10.2 Types of
   debt 10.3 The holders of the national debt 10.4 Debt
   management 10.5 The burden of the debt 10.6 Summary

11 THE BALANCE OF PAYMENTS   245

   11.1 The balance of payments accounts 11.1.1 The structure of
   the accounts 11.1.2 The sterling balances 11.2 The adjustment
   problem 11.2.1 Determinants of the current account balance
   11.2.2 Adjustment between regions 11.2.3 Adjustment between
   countries 11.2.4 The adjustment problem: some global
   considerations 11.3 Summary

12 THE BRETTON WOODS SYSTEM   266

   12.1 Exchange rate systems 12.2 The adjustable peg system
   12.2.1 Adjustment 12.2.2 Liquidity 12.2.3 Co-operation
   12.2.4 Operation in the 1940s and 1950s 12.2.5 The strains of the
   1960s 12.2.6 Breakdown in the 1970s 12.3 The World Bank
   12.4 Summary

13 MANAGED FLOATING   284

   13.1 The general operation of the system, 1973-1978
   13.1.1 Historical background 13.1.2 Adjustment
   13.1.3 Liquidity 13.1.4 Co-operation 13.2 U.K. experience
   13.3 Monetary union and the snake 13.4 Fixed versus floating
   exchange rates 13.5 Prospects for the future 13.6 The
   European Investment Bank 13.7 Summary.

14 A SIMPLE MACROECONOMIC MODEL   307

   14.1 Introduction 14.2 The basic model 14.3 The
   multiplier 14.4 Fiscal policy 14.5 Summary

15 MONEY AND ECONOMIC ACTIVITY   320

   15.1 The Quantity Theory 15.2 The Keynesian and
   monetarist views of the demand for money 15.3 The role of
   monetary policy 15.4 Summary

16 MACROECONOMIC MANAGEMENT 331

16.1 Macroeconomic objectives 16.2 The framework of macroeconomic management 16.3 The sensitivity of economic objectives to changes in target variables 16.4 The ability of the authorities to control target variables 16.5 Other complications 16.6 Monetary instruments (or techniques) 16.7 Summary

APPENDIX 351

ADDITIONAL READING 356

GLOSSARY 357

POSTSCRIPT 365

INDEX 367

I

The financial system

1.1 Introduction

We have begun this book with an elementary discussion of the financial system as a whole rather than a detailed consideration of its components. Our purpose is to allow the reader to construct a coherent if simple conception of what is in reality a complex structure, and thus provide a framework upon which subsequent discussion of parts of the system may be developed.

In a modern economy the efficient production and exchange of goods and services requires money (i.e. a rather special type of good) which can act as a means of payment and exchange, thus allowing the purchase of the finished product – for example, a motor car. Money is also required for intermediate payments and transactions: for example, the motor car assembly plants need to be able to purchase the various components which go into making the final product. However, this would be a limited view of the role of finance in a modern economy since, to continue with our illustration, the whole process of the production and sale of a motor car will require the *financial system,* and not just money, to play an important part. In fact, in the mass production of motor vehicles the initial and continuing expenditure of funds for the purchase of investment goods (machinery, tools, etc.) is vital if production is to commence at all, and also if later production is to incorporate technical improvements or changes in style of the final product. The provision of investible funds, therefore, is a key function in a financial system. This particular function is made the more important by the fact that modern methods of production often call for a volume of funds greater than those likely to be generated by the producing firm itself in its early stages of production. This situation usually obtains in those firms and industries which are highly capital-intensive, or where the production period is very lengthy, e.g. shipbuilding. A financial system must therefore meet the needs of such enterprises by locating, securing, and channelling funds for firms which wish to invest.

The need for financial provision relates not only to producers but also to consumers. Again, to refer to the sale and purchase of motor cars, there are few private consumers who have sufficient accumulated savings with which to buy a car outright. Consequently many people are only able to purchase by borrowing either from a commercial bank or from a finance company by the means of hire purchase. In this way, part of the current output of motor cars is purchased not from current income of consumers but from, in effect, the future income of consumers. Although there are no published figures which identify the amount of credit which the personal sector (individuals, sole traders, unincorporated businesses, and private non-profit-making bodies) obtains in order to purchase motor vehicles, it is possible to observe a relationship between *credit* obtained through various agencies by the personal sector, and consumer *spending* on new and second-hand motor cars. In general, a shift in such consumer spending is seen to be reflected in the volume of bank and hire-purchase finance. In other words, what is suggested in our illustration is that the close relationship between the changes in borrowing and changes in spending on new and second-hand cars indicates the importance of the provision of finance in this area of consumer spending. Without such financial provision it is probable that the volume of sales of such consumer goods would be lessened. Indeed it is likely that a considerable proportion of consumer expenditure on final output relies on external financing, i.e. funds provided by agencies other than the individual or firm which wishes to spend. For example, about one-third of total spending in the U.K. is on such items as house purchase, the buying of consumer durables (cars, televisions, refrigerators, etc.); much of this expenditure will require external financing and, accordingly, will rely on the financial system which enables such financing to take place. The point we are making in this introduction is that to consider money the means of payment, rather than money as part of the whole financial system, is to over-simplify the issue, and ignores the role played by the many financial agencies, agencies which provide a wide range of assets for savers and, in turn, the credit and funds which enable an economy to function more efficiently by enabling the output produced to ultimately be bought.

The remainder of the chapter will attempt to construct a simple but useful model of a financial system, illustrating not only financial relationships but also those relationships between the financial sector and economic activity which are primarily connected with the production of current output of goods and services other than financial services.

1.2 Finance and the 'circular flow'

We will begin this section by describing a 'circular flow model' of an economy and then expand it to include financial aspects to which we have alluded. Let us assume that we have only two major groups of economic unit in this simple economy, households and firms (there is no government or foreign trade). The households provide labour services to the firms, and the households are also the holders of the firms' equity capital. In return for such services the households are paid wages, salaries, and dividends each week which are used to buy the final output of the firms. The revenue which the firms receive from the sale of output is then used to generate next week's output through payments for the necessary inputs, including further labour services from the households. Thus the firms' revenue of one week generates the income of the households in the following week. For the sake of simplicity, let us make a rather unrealistic assumption that the firms have 'inherited' a given stock of capital equipment which is gradually wearing out and which the firms are at least initially doing nothing to remedy. *Table 1.1* and *Figure 1.1* illustrate such a situation.

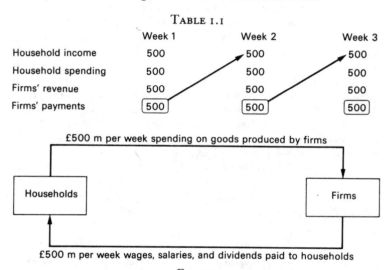

TABLE 1.1

	Week 1	Week 2	Week 3
Household income	500	500	500
Household spending	500	500	500
Firms' revenue	500	500	500
Firms' payments	500	500	500

£500 m per week spending on goods produced by firms

Households — Firms

£500 m per week wages, salaries, and dividends paid to households

FIG 1.1

Clearly many aspects of this simple economic model are remote from reality, but it is a useful model and does allow us to focus attention on two aspects of behaviour which have been assumed in the model. The first relates to the seemingly unrealistic behaviour of the households who, we have assumed, spend all their income and save nothing. In fact, there are clearly a number of very good reasons why households and individuals would wish to save a proportion of their disposable income (i.e. gross income minus deductions): as a means of planning future spending on expensive items, as a precaution against the need for unexpected future expenditures, to ensure adequate income during retirement, or simply from a desire to pass on wealth after one's death. Whatever the reasons it is clear that households are likely to save out of each week's flow of income they receive, and we must at some stage incorporate this into the model as well as examine its implications. The assumed behaviour of firms in the model also requires considerable qualification and , in particular, depends upon their attitude towards their capital stock. We had assumed earlier that the firms were using their existing capital stock without concern for its deterioration and its consequent decline in productivity. It would be much more reasonable to assume that firms will not only wish to maintain their equipment and buildings, etc., but also wish to add to their stock of capital equipment. Such expenditures would require funds which may be generated internally through corporate savings (by not distributing all the profits to shareholders) or obtained externally from the savings of others.

Table 1.2 indicate an alternative relationship between the two sectors. It will be seen that Week 4 represents no change on Week 3, but the figures have been broken down, showing that household income derives from the sale of labour services (£400 million) and the receipt of dividends (£100 million). However in Week 5 we have assumed that households wish to save £50 million out of that week's income and accordingly cut down their consumption spending to £450 million. If such a change occurred the firms producing consumer goods would find that they had unsold stocks of consumer goods to the extent of £50 million and would presumably reduce output. If they did this, there would be further consequences for households who would receive less income since firms would be employing less labour (provided by the households) and paying out less in dividends now that profits were lower as a result of reduced sales.

TABLE 1.2
(£m.)

	Week 4	Week 5	Week 5a
Household income	500	500	500
Consumption	500	450	450
Saving	0	50	50
Accumulated saving	0	50	50
Consumer good sales	500	450	450
Capital good sales	0	0	50
Firms total revenue	500	450	500
Firms borrowing	0	0	50
Wages	400	360	400
Dividends	100	90	100

= 450

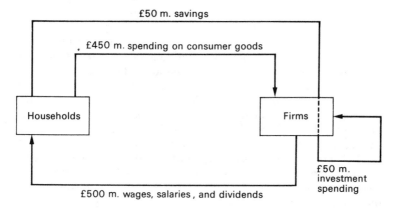

£50 m. savings

£450 m. spending on consumer goods

Households

Firms

£50 m.
investment
spending

£500 m. wages, salaries, and dividends

FIG 1.2

As an alternative course of events (*Figure 1.2*), in Week 5a we find that households plan to save £50 million from their income of that week and that firms *also wish to borrow £50 million in that week* in order to spend on capital goods. The result is that although the output of consumer goods has fallen to £450 million, this has just been offset by the new demand for £50 million capital goods. The firms are still obtaining receipts of £500 million and are thus able to sustain payments of £400 million for labour, together with £100 million in dividends to shareholders. Total firms' expenditure is maintained at £500 million and household income is also maintained at that level. If we continued the illustration on the assumption that households continued saving, we would observe the households accumulating wealth (their savings) each week.

Before modifying the simple circular flow model which has so far been outlined, we would draw attention to certain features which will be partially considered in this chapter and developed in later ones.

(a) The desire by households (and firms) to save poses the question as to the form such saving might take, or in other words the desire to save is likely to manifest itself as a *demand for some form of asset*. The form of asset chosen may be a tangible asset (gold sovereigns, jewellery, antiques), or the asset may be a financial asset – this type is sometimes referred to as a paper asset. In our illustration we assumed that households were prepared to hold the equity capital of the firms, i.e. financial assets. However, this may not be an acceptable assumption in reality since some households may be averse to the risk which is associated with this type of asset, i.e. the market value of shares can fall or rise. Furthermore, not all households have the same needs and preferences with respect to the form their accumulated savings or wealth should take: some households may wish to accumulate money balances, i.e. cash or bank deposits, whilst other households may prefer to hold, say, building society deposits, or other assets presenting different degrees of risk and return. It is also worth noting that our simple model (Table 1.2) shows the household sector accumulating financial wealth through saving. This raises the question of the form which savings may take when wealth is actually increasing. The increase in wealth itself may alter the preference regarding the sort of assets to be held, e.g. low wealth households in the U.K. may well hold a greater *proportion* of their wealth in the form of bank deposits than high wealth households (the latter perhaps wishing to hold more in the form of ordinary shares in commercial and industrial companies).

(b) The firms producing consumer goods in our simple model wished to spend in excess of its receipts (in Week 5a), i.e. to run a deficit of £50 million. If such firms are to obtain the additional funds, it follows that they must be capable of providing potential lenders with a financial asset suitable to the needs of the lenders. The requirement to meet the needs of potential lenders is probably one of the reasons for the *variety* of assets which companies may issue from time to time, e.g. ordinary shares, preference shares, debentures.

(c) The needs of both the *demanders* of assets (savers) and the *suppliers* of assets (the firms wishing to invest in capital goods) is likely to create a *market* for such assets to enable both sets of needs to be met. This development is analogous to the establishment of other markets, e.g. foodstuffs, raw materials, which in such cases meet the needs of consumers and producers. The development of product markets has resulted in the appearance of specialist firms operating in such markets, and in a similar way the development of financial markets has produced specialist firms, for example, the various types of bank.

(d) Table 1.2 shows that the accumulated wealth (assets) of the households is matched by the accumulated debt of the firms (Week 5a), and furthermore the accumulation of *financial* assets is paralleled by the production of *real* assets in the form of capital goods. One might therefore expect that a community's stock of financial assets will tend to grow as its stock of real capital grows.

(e) So far, the simple system we have constructed consists of three identifiable flows. There is the flow of spending on investment and consumer goods being produced and sold, and there is also the flow of saving taking place each week. In Week 5a, for example, the flow of spending on consumer goods is £450 million, the flow of spending on investment goods is £50 million, and the saving flow is £50 million. It is worth pointing out at this stage the difference between a 'flow' concept and a 'stock' concept; a distinction which is important in economics. If an individual is said to have an income of £100, this description will convey no meaning unless a *time* dimension is added. Thus an income of £100 per week, per month, per year, etc., does have meaning but only because the time-period has been specified. The use of the word 'flow' can perhaps be understood more clearly if one considers the flow of water through a pipe. Again, to say that the flow of water is 100 gallons has no meaning unless one adds the time dimension, e.g. 100 gallons per minute. On the other hand if an individual is said to have a total wealth holding of £100, this *does* have meaning and it is because wealth is a stock concept, i.e. a quantity which exists at a point in time. Thus one conceives of saving as a flow concept, e.g. £5 per week, whereas one's accumulated savings from the past constitute a stock concept since they are one's wealth. Similarly one's income is a flow concept, e.g. £50 per week, whereas the money which one has is a stock concept, e.g. £5 of currency held at 10.00 a.m. on Tuesday.

(f) All the transactions which we have identified in the model will require *money* to act as the final means of payment, regardless of whether it is goods or assets which are being traded. The simple economic system embodied in the model will therefore require a certain stock of money to enable the system to function and all the transactions to be made.

1.3 The circular flow and the flow of funds

In the previous section we identified two sectors which interacted with each other: households (the personal sector) and firms (the industrial and commercial sector). In practice, three other sectors can be identified: the public sector (central and local government and the public corporations), the financial sector (banks and other financial firms), and the overseas sector.[1]

First we shall establish in outline the relationships between the sectors (excluding the financial sector), showing the major transactions which the four sectors are likely to undertake. The personal sector, for example, obtains receipts in the form of an inflow of income and this is disbursed as the following: spending on

---

[1]This is rather less easy to define than the other sectors since it largely reflects changes in the balance of payments rather than a tangible area of activity. For this reason it will not be dealt with in any depth at this stage.

consumer goods, saving, and payment of taxes to the public sector. The industrial and commercial sector obtains *inflows* of receipts as a result of consumer spending (sales revenue), investment spending (firms making capital goods receive the spending of other firms who are wishing to invest, e.g. manufacturing industry buys steel girders from the steel industry in order to erect more factories), further receipts from the sales of exports, and finally the receipts from sales of goods and services to the public sector. The receipts of the industrial and commercial sector are disbursed as *outflows:* payments to households (wages and salaries, dividends), spending on imported goods and materials, and the payment of taxes to the public sector. It should be noted that the two lists of inflows and outflows are not intended to be comprehensive but illustrative of the major flows associated with each sector. Later chapters will provide much more detail, in particular relating to the public and overseas sectors (Chapters 9, 11). The various flows identified can be converted into a flow diagram (*Figure 1.3*).

The superficial resemblance between Figure 1.3 and a diagram showing a domestic water system is perhaps not inappropriate since it can be seen that the four sectors are linked to each other and the various flows feed into and out of each other. As with the earlier model (Figure 1.2), the personal sector (households) receives payments from the industrial and commercial sector (firms) and this income is disposed of in the form of three flows: consumer spending which goes

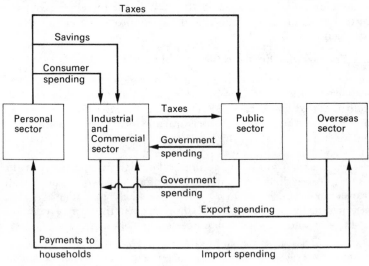

FIG 1.3

back to the firms, saving which is used by the firms, and taxes which flow to the public sector. Similarly, the public sector is linked with the personal and industrial sectors by the flow of tax payments, and government and other public sector spending. The overseas sector is connected to the industrial sector by virtue of import and export spending. We can make a number of general points about this model:

(i)   Figure 1.3 portrays a *closed system*.

(ii)   Since the inflows and outflows feed into each other within a closed system it follows that the *total* outflows from the sectors must be equal to the *total* inflows to the sectors.

(iii) Although *total* inflows must equal *total* outflows, for an individual sector this need not be the case.

(iv)   Clearly there are two important possibilities which could apply to the sectors. One is the total disposals of income by each sector is exactly equal to total income, and the other is that sectors may wish to spend more or less than their income. In the former situation each sector 'balances its budget', and in the latter, one or more sectors are in surplus whilst at least one other sector has a 'budget deficit'. *Table 1.3* and *Table 1.4* show each of the sector inflows and outflows identified in Figure 1.3 but with the addition of illustrative numerical values for each of the items.

In Table 1.3 each of the sector accounts have been divided into receipts and payments. Thus, for example, the industrial and commercial sector obtains receipts from three sources: sales of consumer goods to the personal sector (£10,000), export sales (£1,000 millon), and sales to the public sector (£1,500 million). Total receipts are £12,500 million and this is disbursed in payments to the personal sector – wages and dividends (£10,000 million), payments for imports (£1,000 million), and tax payments to the public sector – V.A.T. and corporation tax (£1,500 million); total payments are £12,500 million. Furthermore it is clear that *all* sectors have 'balanced budgets'[2] since no sector has a surplus or deficit.

However, in Table 1.4 we have assumed that sector behaviour has changed such that the personal sector has decided to reduce its consumer spending and save £1,000 million. This can be observed in the personal sector account which shows a fall in consumer spending from £10,000 million to £9,000 million. This spending, together with income tax payments of £1,500 million, accounts for the £10,500 disbursements by the personal sector in relation to receipts of £11,500 million, giving a 'budget surplus' of £1,000 million in the form of saving. Although the result of this is a reduced level of sales of

[2]The term 'balanced budget' in this context simply refers to a sector's accounts. It is not the same as a 'balanced Budget' which refers to the central government accounts.

TABLE 1.3
(£m.)

Personal sector		*Industrial and commercial sector*	
Income from employment	10,000[c]	Sales revenue (consumer goods)	10,000[b]
Government subsidies	1,500[e]	Exports	1,000
		Government spending	1,500[f]
	11,500		12,500
Consumer spending	10,000[a]	Payments to personal sector (factor earnings)	10,000[d]
Income tax	1,500	Imports	1,000
	11,500	V.A.T.	500
		Corporation tax	1,000
			12,500
Surplus/deficit:	nil		
		Surplus/deficit:	nil
Public sector			
Income tax	1,500		
Corporation tax	1,000		
V.A.T.	500	*Overseas sector*	
	3,000	Exports (foreign spending)	1,000
		Imports (foreign receipts)	1,000
Public spending	3,000[g]		
Surplus/deficit:	nil	Surplus/deficit:	nil

$a = b; c = d; e = f; e + f = g$

consumer goods by the industrial and commercial sector (sales obviously fall from £10,000 million to £9,000 million), a part of the industrial and commercial sector is intending to invest and accordingly requires funds to finance such investment. Such funds are available from the personal sector (savings), and the spending of these funds on investment offsets the decline of £1,000 million in consumer good output. This offsetting rise in investment spending allows the earnings of the personal sector derived from employment within the industrial and commercial sector to be sustained at £10,000 million. If the investment spending had not taken place as assumed, the industrial and commercial sector would, *in the short run*, have been

TABLE 1.4
(£m.)

Personal sector		Industrial and commercial sector	
Income from employment	10,000[c]	Sales revenue (consumer goods)	9,000[b]
Government subsidies	1,500	Exports	1,000
		Government spending	1,500
	11,500		11,500
		Investment	1,000
Consumer spending	9,000[a]		
Income tax	1,500	Payments to personal sector	
	10,500	(factor earnings)	10,000[d]
		Imports	1,000
		V.A.T.	500
Surplus (saving)	1,000	Corporation tax	1,000
			12,500
Public sector			
as for Table 1.3		Deficit (borrowing)	1,000

Overseas sector

as for Table 1.3

$a = b; c = d$

forced to borrow £1,000 million in order to finance the production and
holding of unsold consumer goods as a result of the reduced consumer
spending by the personal sector.

It is important to realize that the above exposition is not intended
to be a totally realistic account of the responses which would be likely
to take place in the sectors. Rather the intention is to show in a
rudimentary form the basic relationships between the sectors which
necessarily apply on the basis of the system shown in Figure 1.3 on
p. 8. In particular:

(i) The system *as a whole* cannot move into deficit or surplus.

(ii) A deficit/surplus in one sector must have an opposite
surplus/deficit change mirrored in another sector or sectors.
Thus if one sector chooses to move from a 'balanced budget'
position (as the personal sector did in Table 1.4) this alters the
spending flows between the sectors (a fall in receipts by the

TABLE 1.5
U.K. flow of funds accounts: income and expenditure, 1974
(£m.)

Personal sector		Company sector[b]	
Income from employment and trading	52,001	Income from trading and employment[c]	9,706
Other income	22,840	Other income	12,263
	74,841		21,969
Consumption	51,670	Investment	12,970
Investment[a]	3,006	Taxes and other payments	12,646
Taxes and other payments	15,918		25,616
	70,594		
		Deficit:	3,647
Surplus:	4,247		

Public sector		Overseas sector	
Taxes and other receipts	31,246	Exports and other receipts	18,688
Income from employment and trading	2,545	Imports and other payments	22,431
	33,791	Surplus[d]:	3,743
Consumption	16,641		
Investment	7,317		
Grants, subsidies and other payments	14,912		
	38,870		
Deficit:	5,079		

SURPLUS		DEFICIT	
Personal sector	4,247	Company sector	3,647
Overseas sector	3,743	Public sector	5,079
Error[e]	736		8,726
	8,726		

[a] The personal sector includes sole traders, partnerships, and unincorporated private businesses as well as individuals who will of course wish to invest.
[b] Including financial institutions.
[c] This is a net figure, i.e. after payment of wages, salaries, and other costs.
[d] This is a surplus for the overseas sector (foreign countries) and not for the U.K. This figure is in effect the U.K.'s balance of payments 'deficit'.
[e] This is the residual error in the national income accounts.

Source: Tables 20, 31/7, Bank of England Statistical Abstract, No. 2, 1975.

industrial and commercial sector) and also causes a *financial* repercussion. This repercussion took the form of borrowing by the industrial and commercial sector in our example.

1.4 The U.K. accounts

So far we have been using hypothetical data in the accounts to ensure simplicity so that we can concentrate our attention on the underlying ideas. Nevertheless appropriate data for the United Kingdom is published and *Table 1.5* is a condensed version of the figures for 1974. The presentation of the information in this table has been made comparable to the presentation of the hypothetical data used earlier in Tables 1.3 and 1.4. The summary of surpluses and deficits at the bottom of Table 1.5 illustrates two of the general points made earlier. First, the sum of the surpluses and the sum of the deficits cancel out, i.e. for the system as a whole there can be neither a surplus nor a deficit position; second, the surplus sectors match the deficit sectors (ignoring the compilation error of £736 million).

1.5 The 'problem' of surpluses and deficits

In our presentation of the sector accounts we have made only limited reference to the financial repercussions of a change in the behaviour of one or more of the sectors. We had considered the possibility of one sector (the personal sector) moving into surplus with an accommodating change in another sector (the industrial and commercial sector moving into deficit), but we had not fully examined the financial consequences of such changes. It is now appropriate to consider in slightly more detail these repercussions, and we can do so by examining the two basic changes: a sector moving into a budget deficit position and a sector moving into a budget surplus position.

1.5.1 A SECTOR WITH A BUDGET DEFICIT

It has already been established that if a sector moves into deficit then quite simply that sector is, for some reason, spending more than it is receiving. Why might this be so? Within the framework of the model which we have built, there could be two basic reasons. One is that a sector wishes to purchase more output from the economic system than that sector's income can sustain. Another reason could be that the sector wishes to buy financial assets, and when this form of spending is added to that sector's purchases of output, total spending exceeds the sector's receipts. An example of the first case might be where the personal sector decides to purchase consumer durables on a large scale such that for a period the personal sector's desired expenditure exceeds its income. Such a deficit would involve the personal sector in borrowing. In the second case, a sector or major group may for example anticipate a fall in interest rates and in accordance with this expectation decide to purchase financial assets which yield the *current* interest rate. In order to finance such purchases the sector borrows funds short-term at the current rate with the intention of re-negotiating the borrowing later when interest rates have fallen. The final result, after the change in interest rates, might be a situation where the sector is holding £x million additional securities which yield say, 10 per cent, and is indebted as a result of borrowing £x million with an interest cost of say, 8 per cent. A further illustration might be a situation where a sector anticipates a borrowing need in the future and expects that funds may be scarce at that future date. In these circumstances the sector may attempt to purchase short-term financial assets *now* by using medium-term borrowed funds, and at a later date when the funds are actually required the financial assets acquired earlier could then be sold.

Whatever the particular intentions or needs of the deficit sector, we can generalize about the way such a sector might move into deficit. Basically there are three possible methods: by selling assets which have been accumulated in past periods, which allows the sector to purchase a value of output in excess of current income; by creating liabilities against itself which a surplus sector is prepared to buy, and thus provide funds for the deficit sector; or by a combination of the two. Clearly a potential deficit sector will be able to move into deficit only if: it is capable of selling assets which it happens to have accumulated, i.e. some other sector is prepared to purchase such assets; or a surplus sector exists and is prepared to accept, willingly (or unwillingly)[3] the liabilities of the deficit sector. Furthermore, whichever method is used – sale of existing assets or production of new assets by the deficit sector – there will be an effect in financial markets where such assets are traded, not least on the prices of such assets.

[3] If I refuse to pay for goods which I have had delivered from a shop, then in effect the shopkeeper is – unwillingly – accepting a liability which I have created against myself.

1.5.2 A SECTOR WITH A BUDGET SURPLUS

A sector which intends to move into a surplus position is one which is intending to spend less than its income. Some of the reasons for such behaviour have already been considered (p. 3), which relate to the desire to save. Whatever the reasons, if a sector is intending to move into a surplus position it is faced with three possible courses of action: it might accumulate assets which it purchases from deficit sectors; it might pay off past debts (in effect eliminating liabilities incurred in the past by buying back its own assets); or a combination of both. Whichever method is used, the potential surplus sector moves into surplus by obtaining some form of financial asset.

It is arguable that the position of the potential surplus sector is more flexible than the potential deficit sector, since a sector which wishes to move into surplus can always do so, at least in the short run, whereas the potential deficit sector may not always be in such a position. One can clarify this by referring back to the budget deficit position already considered in Section 1.5.1. We showed that a deficit position could be achieved if that sector were able to sell assets. Obviously there are no reasons why such a possibility is *necessarily* open to such a sector; either it may not have accumulated assets from the past or it may be unable to sell the assets which it wishes to create (e.g. a company may be unable to issue more shares or sell debentures because the market finds such assets unacceptable). However, similar limitations are *not* faced by the potential surplus sector. Even if a potential surplus sector has no debts to pay off or financial assets are not available from asset markets, such a sector would be able to move into surplus by accumulating the one financial asset which will be available, and that financial asset is money itself. In other words a sector wishing to move into surplus can, in the last resort, always accumulate money balances.

Earlier in this chapter we noted that for 1974 the personal sector in the U.K. was in surplus to the extent of £4,247 million (Table 1.5) and this surplus made some provision towards the deficits of the public and company sectors. However, our discussion so far implies that the move towards deficit or surplus by a sector is unlikely to be a simple, single manoeuvre in the form of a collective decision. Indeed it would be surprising if this were the case since each sector is an aggregation of what is in reality hundreds or even millions of individual decisions. Thus it is feasible that *within* a surplus sector there may be some tendency towards the liquidation of existing assets, or sale of new assets, but nevertheless on balance the sector is accumulating assets consistent with its overall surplus position.

1.6 Summary
By using a simple model of an economic system this introductory chapter has tried to show that within modern economies, especially the so-called 'private enterprise' economies, a financial system is likely to be needed to ensure the smooth operation of that economy.

i.   Expenditure and income flows between sectors of the economy may be such that some sectors are in surplus and others in deficit. These flow 'imbalances' will involve these sectors in decisions regarding their *stocks* of assets and liabilities.

ii. Changes in the preferences of sectors with respect to their assets/liability positon (i.e. changes in their *stock* position) may have an effect on the *flows* of expenditures and income in the economy. For example, in 1974 the U.K. personal sector increased its deposits with 'other financial institutions' by £2,063 million and part of this increase would have accrued to building societies since their deposits increased by £1,993 million in that year. If we assume that the personal sector's preference for building society deposits (rather than bank deposits) had increased in 1974 by say £1,000 million, then we may visualize the following consequences. The rise in building society deposits would have allowed an increase in the volume of mortgage lending and, assuming spare capacity in the building industry, produced an increase in new housing starts and eventual house completions. Such increased activity would have raised employment and incomes in the building industry. Since the switch of bank deposits to building society deposits need not necessarily cause a decrease in the total volume of bank deposits (see Chapter 6), any reduction in bank lending caused by such a switch may not offset the overall stimulatory effect on the economy because of the rise in mortgage finance.

iii. Although deficits and surpluses of sectors sum to zero in aggregate, there is the problem of communication and transmission between those sectors which are in surplus or deficit. Funds are required to flow from surplus to deficit sectors and, corresponding to this flow, deficit sectors will find it necessary to produce liabilities which are acceptable assets to surplus sectors.

iv. If we assume that tendencies towards surplus and deficit reflect sector preferences[4] (i.e. the personal sector wishes to save and the industrial and commercial sector wishes to invest), then inadequate links between sectors in an economy may thwart the achievement of sector objectives, e.g. the personal sector may limit its savings or simply hoard money balances because of inadequate or unsatisfactory outlets for such funds.

[4]As opposed to *errors* of budgeting by a sector.

v. Although our analysis has so far been of a rudimentary nature, it is becoming evident that there are at least two possible functions which the financial sector can perform. One is to provide efficient transmission of funds between sectors by acting as an intermediary so as to ensure that surplus sectors (demanders of assets) obtain the assets they prefer, and that deficit sectors obtain the funds they require by generating the appropriate sort of liability. For example, insurance companies provide savings opportunities for the personal sector and at the same time such companies have considerable influence on the nature of the liabilities which they themselves hold. As we shall see in Chapter 7, the Bank of England is very obliging in providing government securities which suit the preferences of investment managers of insurance companies and other financial firms. The operation of banks and building societies are other examples of financial sector activity since they provide specialized methods by which those with surpluses can have such surpluses transmitted to those who wish to go into deficit. The other function of the financial sector is to produce the appropriate 'signals' (e.g. a market interest rate) which will allow potential transacting sectors to make correct decisions about their present or future borrowing or lending. The interplay of competition amongst borrowers and lenders, together with the rapid transmission of information in modern financial markets, are important elements in this production of financial 'signals'.

2
Wealth, assets, and money

2.1 Introduction

In Chapter 1 our primary intention was to develop a simple model of an economic system within which the role of a financial system could be outlined in a rudimentary way. In Chapter 2 we shall be considering the financial system in more detail by looking at the nature of the output of such a system. The 'output' of the financial system may be thought of as consisting of two kinds. On the one hand the various firms operating within the financial system provide their customers with a variety of services which use their specialist knowledge and skills – the modern operation of the banks is an obvious example of such a provision (see Chapter 5). On the other hand the financial firms and institutions within the system are involved in the production of a slightly less obvious form of output, and that is the production of *financial assets*. The existence in an economy of those who wish to borrow, and those who are willing and able to lend, in effect creates a market for financial claims (assets) of one kind or another. Such claims may pass from borrower to lender *directly*, as, for example, when a company makes a direct offer of further shares to existing shareholders; or the process may be *indirect*, for example when a company raises additional funds by engaging a merchant bank's services including the underwriting facility which usually attends such an arrangement. In the case of the latter example, if the ultimate lenders – e.g. institutional investors, the personal sector – are not prepared to purchase the shares offered them, then the underwriters will be obliged to provide the necessary funds to their client company.

As a result of such direct and indirect financial activity within the financial system, the total of financial claims in existence is very substantial. For example, the market value of U.K. company securities in March 1974 amounted to £154,570 million; company security value was almost 2⅓ times as great as national income. However this is only a small fraction of the total financial claims which exist, since it ignores many other forms of financial asset, such as government securities, bank deposits, assets of pension funds, and so on.

2.2 Forms of wealth

Financial assets represent part of the wealth of individuals and institutions which hold such assets. However such wealth is only one constituent of the total wealth of individuals and institutions since wealth can take a real (i.e. physical) form, for example, property, stocks of goods, raw materials, land, machines, etc. Therefore if one is asked to add up the value of one's own wealth, such things as a house, motor car, etc., should be included as well as the amount of money one has in a bank and also the shares one might own. Although it seems simple to identify and calculate the wealth of an individual in this way, it is not appropriate merely to extend the same approach when we are considering the wealth of the whole community. One of the reasons for this is that the asset of one individual or group may well be the liability of another. If this is the case, then the total or aggregate position is less clear since it can be argued that the *net* position should be taken when examining the wealth of the whole community. In other words, since 'every financial asset is someone else's liability', it can be assumed that when calculating the community's wealth (as opposed to the individual's wealth) it is legitimate to net out liabilities in order to obtain a more accurate picture. If one did not do this exercise it could be argued that there is double-counting, i.e. counting assets and liabilities as two separate identities whereas they are in effect two sides of the same coin.

2.3 The growth of claims

This section will examine briefly the growth of assets of various kinds. Using some early estimates made by J. Revell[1] as the basis of our account one can establish that the nominal growth of assets during the year's 1957–61 was substantial. The value of total assets (physical assets plus financial assets) in 1957 amounted to £174,000 million, of which £68,400 million consisted of physical assets and £105,700 million were financial assets, whereas in 1961 total assets amounted to £237,700 million of which £91,900 million were physical assets and £145,800 million were financial assets. Examining the ratio of financial assets to physical assets one finds that the ratio has not varied greatly during these five years. However, the ratio does indicate that in 1957, for example, the value of existing financial claims was 54 per cent *higher* than the value of physical assets. At first sight this does seem rather curious since the earlier analysis in Chapter 1 (Section 1.2) indicated that the growth of financial claims would rise with the growth of physical assets, e.g. investment goods, in the economy. In Chapter 1 we had assumed that the corporate sector would add to its capital stock by borrowing funds from the personal sector and in return provide the personal sector with some

[1] J. Revell, *The Wealth of the Nation* (Cambridge University Press, 1967).

form of financial claim or asset. Accordingly the issue of financial claims would match the growth of real assets. It is evident from the date to which we have referred in this section that the growth of financial claims is greater than the growth of physical assets and clearly we need to offer some explanation for this. Leaving aside the problem of the value of the different types of asset in an economy (since this in itself is likely to produce a discrepancy), we can suggest two reasons for the different valuations.

First, one can question the assumption that the issue of a financial claim will arise solely through the process of capital accumulation as was assumed in Chapter 1. Quite simply, many individuals, firms, and indeed governments, will go into debt for the purpose of adding to their level of consumption or current spending. If this occurs there will be the issue of a financial claim but no corresponding increase in the capital stock. To use a rather simple illustration, if one borrows in order to sustain day-to-day spending, then one is adding to the total of financial assets in the community (i.e. a liability to oneself but an asset to the person or institution which has provided the funds), but since the funds are being spent on consumer goods the financial asset/liability remains even though the consumer goods which have been bought (e.g. food) no longer exist. In a similar way, governments borrow in order to finance the purchase or production of goods and services which are consumed and cease to exist, although the debt nevertheless remains. Probably the best example of this would be when a government borrows in order to finance a war. In this case the purpose of the borrowing is to purchase goods, some of which will ultimately be destroyed by war activity. In 1939 the U.K. national debt amounted to about £7,000 million whereas by 1952 it had increased to almost £26,000 million; an almost fourfold increase which was largely a result of the borrowing during the war of 1939–45.

A second reason for the 'imbalance' between the value of financial claims and the value of physical assets in an economy is that the process of raising funds for use, say, by a firm may well result in several financial firms being involved in the provision of the funds and at different stages. However at each stage in the transmission of such funds there will be an entry in the balance sheet of each of the financial firms. Therefore if one adds up all the entries in the various balance sheets the result would be a figure in excess of the actual sum raised. This aspect of the behaviour of financial firms will be dealt with in more detail in Chapter 5.

2.4 Money

At the beginning of this chapter we suggested that the financial system produces output in the form of services and alongside this goes

[margin annotations: (1) Reasons for the imbalance between value of financial claims & the value of physical assets in the economy (2)]

the generation of financial claims of a variety of kinds. We can take this approach when we consider the source and nature of money itself. In Chapters 6 and 7 we will be examining in considerable detail the mechanics of money creation and regulation, but in this section our main purpose is to attempt to identify money, its source, functions, and primary properties within a modern economic system.

Having already conceived of the financial system as 'producing' output in the form of assets, let us continue with this approach and establish who are the producers of money in the economy. Part of the answer to this question is very straightforward if one is considering only cash, i.e. notes and coins in circulation. In the U.K. the origin of notes and coin is of course the central bank, the Bank of England. Notes and coin are unambiguously 'money' because they are *legally* the means by which we can settle our debts. Even though there are upper limits to the quantity of coins which constitute legal tender, this does not really alter the substance of the point which has been made. The community is prepared to use and hold notes and coin not only because these are the statutory means of settling debt but also because the general application and acceptability of this rule ensures that holders of notes and coin can, when required, convert such cash into goods and services. In other words cash represents instant purchasing power – the command over real resources.

Is cash an asset? The existence of money in the form of cash represents an asset to the whole community since it enables transactions to take place, production to continue, and thus allows members of the community to satisfy their various wants and needs. Cash can be thought of as a lubricant of the economic system, allowing production and exchange of goods and services to take place. This is not to say that such operations would not be possible without cash, but it certainly makes the whole process much easier and more efficient. The paper and metal which compose cash are of little intrinsic value, but it is nonetheless a valuable asset to the community.

In our enquiry into the source and nature of money, we would be taking a very limited view if we considered only cash. From one's own personal experience it is obvious that cash represents only the 'small change' of the system since the bulk of one's spending – rent or mortgage payments, insurance premiums, large household bills – is done by the use of bank deposits drawn on by the use of the cheque. With the growing use of credit cards such as the Barclaycard and Access, even the items of spending which used to be done by cash are frequently undertaken by the use of a credit card, and settlement is finally made by the use of a cheque drawn on a bank deposit.

Bank deposits represent the major component of the money stock in modern economies, and in comparison with cash such deposits differ significantly in that their source is *not* the central bank but the private sector, i.e. the so-called deposit banks, and in addition such deposits do not rank as legal tender. Yet these assets produced by the banking system are widely used as money and provide an immensely convenient way of conducting transactions. In this respect these bank deposits are an asset to the community in the same way as cash.

However the inclusion of bank deposits as part of our definition of the money stock of the community does raise some rather awkward problems. As we have already said, these deposits are not legal tender and are not issued with the authority of the government. Indeed they are the result of the business activity of private sector profit-making firms. Furthermore, one can observe a wide variety of 'bank deposits' originating from the private sector part of the financial system. So which deposits are part of the money stock and which are not? Where can one draw the dividing line? Clearly it is necessary to look more closely at which kind of asset from amongst the many types produced by the financial system we can define as money and which we cannot. The following sections will consider this particular problem.

2.4.1. THE FUNCTIONS OF MONEY

What one might term the 'traditional' approach to the problem of the nature of money is to consider money from the point of view of what it *does* rather than what it *is*. In other words, if one can isolate the primary functions which money performs in an economy (i.e. what money does), then the problem of deciding what money *is*, is solved, since anything which performs these functions is money by definition.[2] Using this approach, money can be said to have four basic functions: it can act as a medium of exchange, a store of value, a unit of account, and a standard for deferred payments.

2.4.1.1 *Medium of exchange*

This is the most important function which money performs in an economy. A non-monetary economy would be one in which economic transactions are performed by a process known as barter. Goods and services which are produced and intended for exchange can only be so traded by a simple swap. Goods and services are exchanged directly for goods and services. In anything other than a very primitive economy this arrangement would be immensely inconvenient and also likely to be inefficient. The basic problem with a barter system is that a successful swap rests on what is called the 'double coincidence of wants'. This is the necessity for the two parties to an exchange (if an

---

[2] A common analogy is that an elephant is defined by what it is, whereas an umbrella is defined by what it does. Both methods of identification are legitimate, of course.

exchange is to take place) to want what the other party is offering, i.e. if one produces food and requires shoes, then for a successful transaction to occur, someone else who produces shoes and requires food is needed – hence the reference to 'double coincidence'. If such a coincidence does not exist, then for trade to take place there would have to be probably several intermediate transactions, e.g. if A produces food and wants shoes and B produces shoes but wants clothes, then A or B must search around for another transactor C who, say, produces clothes and wants food. This would allow A to trade with C, and then for A to trade with B. Clearly barter is a clumsy basis for trade and unlikely to be a system which encourages economic development. However the use of money can solve the problem quite simply since goods can be traded for money and then money traded for goods. The requirement of the double coincidence of wants is obviated where money acts as a medium of exchange.

Although this advantage of using money is very obvious, the history of money shows that the successful use of money in its role as a medium of exchange rests on the substance used as money being *generally acceptable in the performance of that function.* Clearly an individual will only accept money as payment for goods or services if that individual is convinced that others will do likewise both now and in the future. Without such general acceptance the particular money-substance, whether it be a coin, banknote, or bank deposit, will function imperfectly or not at all. Once confidence in the money-substance is lost, even if that money-substance is deemed legal tender, individuals within that community will either find some alternative money-substance or will resort to barter. This type of change in people's attitude towards money is usually in modern times a result of rapid inflation. If inflation is proceeding very rapidly, then this will be reducing the value of money swiftly and noticeably. It is therefore possible that individuals will be reluctant to use money since any delay in using or obtaining money as payment will result in a significant loss of purchasing power when purchase is finally made. Under such circumstances one either abandons the use of money or increases the rate of spending and increases the rate at which one receives money income (paid by the hour for example).

2.4.1.2 Store of value

Money is a liquid store of value in that it provides individuals with a means of holding and accumulating their wealth in a form which can, at any time, be converted immediately into goods and services. When money is being used as a store of value it is effectively being treated by the holder as a substitute for an alternative financial asset. One is able to make this assertion since the alternative to holding money as a store of value would be to hold another form of financial asset, say a bond, or time-deposit in a bank, and both of these would provide an explicit yield to the holder in the form of interest payments as well as being a store of value. The holding of money, as an alternative to an interest-yielding asset, involves the holder in a sacrifice of the interest which would otherwise have been gained; but one can argue that the holding of money must provide an *implicit* yield rather than *explicit* yield. Two such implicit yields are that of convenience and certainty. Storing value in the form of money allows the holder to convert his asset into goods and services instantly and with the certainty that the money value, at least in nominal terms, has been retained. An untimely sale of a bond may result in having to sell at a capital loss, or the holding of a time deposit may be inconvenient if one is unable to convert that deposit into purchasing power when needed. On the other hand, we can say that money has the supreme quality of being absolutely liquid in the sense of providing instant purchasing power.

As with its function as a medium of exchange, the usefulness of money as a store of value depends upon the value of money remaining fairly stable or at least not declining too quickly. Under conditions of inflation, using money as a store of value involves not only the foregoing of an interest payment, but also the loss of *real value* as a result of rising prices between the time when the money balance was accumulated and the time when it is spent.

2.4.1.3 Unit of account

The role of money as a unit of account is linked with its being used as a medium of exchange. Even within an economy which uses barter as the means of trade there is likely to develop some method by which the commonly traded goods can be assigned a value. One can imagine the problems of trading many commodities in circumstances where there is not a common means by which the value of a commodity can be established so that the traders know the relative quantities of each commodity to be exchanged. To take as an example, let us suppose that there are four commodities which are traded in an economy. For traders to trade successfully they will have to know the value of all commodities in terms of each other (their relative prices) and therefore a collection of price ratios would need to be established, i.e. how much of one commodity is to be exchanged for another. Quite simply we can establish how many ratios would have to be worked out, by producing the possible combinations of the four commodities (*Table 2.1*).

Thus one would need to know how much A exchanges for so much B, how much A exchanges for so much C, and so on. The combinations which are in parentheses are those which have been included, but the

TABLE 2.1
Price ratios – commodities A, B, C, D; E, F.

AB	BC	CD	(DA)	(EA)	(FA)
AC	BD	(CA)	(DB)	(EB)	(FB)
AD	(BA)	(CB)	(DC)	(EC)	(FC)
AE	BE	CE	DE	(ED)	(FD)
AF	BF	CF	DF	EF	(FE)

opposite way round, i.e. A:B and B:A. It is clear from the above illustration that four commodities will require the working out (and remembering) of six price ratios. Now let us assume that another commodity, E, begins to be traded in the economy. We can see that this results in another *four* price ratios having to be established. If a further commodity, F were added this would result in an additional five ratios having to be worked out. The nature of the problem is clear since if there are four commodities the six price ratios are need, five commodities require ten ratios, six commodities require fifteen ratios, seven commodities require twenty-one ratios, and so on. Clearly any community which traded or wished to trade in more than, say, fifteen commodities would require so many price ratios to be worked out that trade would indeed be a tiresome business. However a barter economy can still function without the use of money if it decides (and this is likely to happen naturally rather than as a conscious, collective decision) to adopt a unit of account. To take our earlier illustration, let us suppose that commodity A is chosen as the unit of account. By this we mean that all price ratios will be established in terms of a single commodity. The result of this is to simplify greatly the problem of setting price ratios. Thus so much of commodity A would be treated as the basic accounting unit and all other commodities would be priced in terms of that unity. An example is set out in *Table 2.2*. Once such an arrangement has been established then the problem of working out the price ratios of the other goods is fairly simple. It is evident that 3 units of B will exchange for 2¼ units of E, and 4 units

TABLE 2.2

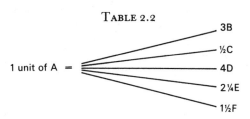

1 unit of A =
- 3B
- ½C
- 4D
- 2¼E
- 1½F

of D exchange for 1½ units of F. It will be noted in this example, that by introducing a unit of account (commodity A) the number of price ratios which have to be set and remembered is reduced from fifteen to five. For a barter economy the establishment of a unit of account would indeed represent a great leap forward since the limitations on trading a larger number of goods is eliminated. It is to be emphasized that commodity A is not used as a trading medium, i.e. the other commodities are not actually exchanged for commodity A, which is then used for purchasing other commodities, but rather commodity A is used to price the other goods which are then bartered for each other. However it would seem to be an obvious next step in the development of such an economy if it identifies a convenient commodity which could in fact be used as a medium of exchange. Such a change would then eliminate the need for the 'double coincidence of wants'.

2.4.1.4 Standard for deferred payments

A fourth function which is ascribed to money is that of being a standard for deferred payments. This function allows contracts to be made whereby a variety of transactions can take place in the present with payment being made at a later date. The sale and production of goods is made easier by money performing this function since goods can be provided through trade credit, labour and raw materials can be obtained by the producer, and the various parties will know the sums involved and payments to be made at a future date. Clearly this particular function of money is not essential for lending, borrowing, production, and distribution to take place, but it certainly makes such activities easier. During periods of very high inflation, money's performance of this function is inhibited since a deferred payment benefits the debtor and penalizes the creditor as a result of the decline in the purchasing power of money before payment is made. In such circumstances the period of deferred payment is likely to be reduced or an 'inflation clause' may be introduced so that the deferred payment takes into account the depreciation in the value of money. The introduction of inflation-proofed pensions and savings certificates whose value is linked to changes in the retail price index are examples of such arrangements.

We have now established the four basic functions which money is said to perform: medium of exchange, store of value, unit of account, and standard for deferred payments. However for something to be defined as money it is not necessary for the money-substance to perform all four functions. The only function which is essential for something to be called money is that of being a medium of exchange. Money may be an unsatisfactory store of value (e.g. in conditions of inflation) and other financial assets may be used to perform this function. Likewise, other commodities could be used as a unit of account. This might arise again under circumstances of high inflation rates where transactions are denominated not in money but in terms of another commodity, money being used only when final payment is made. For example, a sale of machinery could be valued in terms of say, gold, or barrels of oil, with final payment in money being made by establishing the value of the gold or oil at the time of payment.

2.4.2. MONEY AND MONEY-SUBSTITUTES

The approach to money outlined in Section 2.4.1 would seem to indicate that there is no real problem in identifying what money *is* (as opposed to what it does) since *anything* is money which performs a medium of exchange function. However this is a somewhat debatable contention since it can be argued that in a highly developed economy other media of exchange may arise, for example the use of trade credit. This is used on a very substantial scale[3] between producer, wholesaler, retailer, and customer; the granting of credit from one to the other enabling the process of trade and exchange to take place. Clearly, if one identifies the medium of exchange function as being simply the exchange of goods taking place without barter, *so long as there is confidence amongst the parties concerned that ultimately payment will be made*, many 'things' may act as a medium of exchange. Indeed it may not actually be of a tangible form, for example if a transaction is arranged between two individuals who have complete trust in each other, then *trust* itself may allow a transaction to occur; final payment taking place later. C. A. E. Goodhart,[4] amongst others, has therefore divided the essential qualities of money into the medium of exchange function, which is not unique to money, and the means of final payment function, which is. To refer back to our trade credit illustration, although trade credit acts as a medium of exchange it nevertheless cannot act as a final means of payment; only money can perform this function.

Earlier we made reference to the financial asset attribute which money possesses, and this is another source of difficulty when one is considering the identification of money in a modern economy. Although money possesses a unique property in being a means of payment, it is *not* unique as a financial asset since there are obviously many other forms of financial asset available. To illustrate the problem, let us take the analogy of an ordinary commodity, e.g. butter. There are obviously a number of substitutes for butter – margarine and other fats – and we can be sure that these are

[3]In 1973 trade credit between quoted companies amounted to £13,126 m. compared with £4,611 m. bank loans and overdrafts to such companies.
[4]C.A.E. Goodhart, *Money Information and Uncertainty*, (Macmillan. 1975), Chapter 1.

substitutes for butter because we can observe the response of consumers to changes in the price of such substitutes. If the price of margarine rises, then to some extent people will switch their buying away from margarine and towards butter; less margarine bought and more butter. Similarly a change in the price of butter will cause a change in the demand for butter substitutes. However if there are no substitutes for butter then a change in the price of butter will not result in a change in the demand for other commodities as a direct consequence of the change in the price of butter. People will either continue to buy the same quantity of butter or buy less if their income is insufficient to cover all other expenditures as well as maintaining their butter purchases. There would be no switching to other commodities. At the other extreme, if margarine and other fats are *very good substitutes* for butter then a relatively small rise in the price of butter will result in a substantial switch of demand away from butter towards the various substitutes. The concept which we are using here is known as the price-elasticity of demand[5] (price-responsiveness of demand), and the greater the price-elasticity (responsiveness) the greater will be the switch of demand in response to a relatively small change in the price of butter. It should now be clear that the size of this responsiveness to a price change is one way we can establish the degree of substitutability of butter for other fats. A high degree of responsiveness indicates that butter and other fats are good substitutes and a low degree of responsiveness suggests that they are not good substitutes.

We can use this approach when considering whether money can be uniquely identified or if there are in fact substitutes for money. In this case we shall use the rate of interest as our 'price', i.e. the means by which we shall test the existence of substitutes. Let us suppose we have four assets; cash, current account deposits, deposit account, building society deposits. Furthermore we will assume that the rate of interest paid on building society deposits rises substantially and the rate of interest on deposit accounts does not alter. What is likely to happen? It is probable that there will be a switch of funds from deposit accounts to building society accounts. In other words, building society deposits and bank deposits may be substitutes to some degree. Now let us suppose further that the rate on deposit accounts also rises. A possible consequence of this is that there would be some switching back of funds from the building societies, but apart from this possibility, what would be the effect on the size of current accounts? It may well be that individuals decide to prune their current accounts to the very minimum required, or indeed so to adjust the timing of their

[5]'Price-elasticity of demand' is both a concept and an analytical tool and the variant we are using here is termed 'cross-elasticity of demand'.

spending that individuals are able to reduce their current accounts and transfer funds to deposit accounts. It is also conceivable that individuals may even try to economize on their cash balances in order to take advantage of the higher interest rates. (Of course, if cash and current account balances are already at the absolute minimum then a change in interest rates will produce no effect on such balances.) This type of response by individuals to changes in interest rates, if it did occur in the way we have suggested, would be an indication that the four types of assets are in some degree substitutes. On analogy with our butter example, we can suggest that if the response to changes in interest rates is relatively large, i.e. a small change in interest rates results in a large switch in the holding of one form of asset for another, this indicates a high degree of substitutability between the assets. If a large change in interest rates produced only a small change in the holding of one form of asset, then this would suggest a low degree of substitutability.

There is some evidence that substitutability does exist between various types of deposit and it has been suggested therefore that attempting to identify definitively those assets which are unambiguously 'money' is a mistaken approach. Nevertheless one can accept the implications of the 'substitutability argument' and at the same time identify those assets which perform the function of means of payment in the U.K. Notes and coins in circulation are clearly means of payment since they are legal tender and current account deposits (demand deposits) are accepted extensively as a means of payment. Furthermore, current account and deposit accounts can be switched easily, i.e. one can use funds in the deposit account as part of one's current account, in effect, but with the penalty of loss of one week's interest. This facility or convention allows us, therefore, to combine the two types of deposit – at least for the purpose of defining money. Whether we can go beyond these assets is, as we have indicated, a debatable question and it is one to which we return in the next section.

2.4.3 MONEY STOCK DATA

Section 2.4.2 has shown that defining what money is within the context of a modern economy is rather difficult, at least it is difficult to draw a hard-and-fast line which is a totally reliable division. It is therefore not surprising that amongst economists this problem of definition is still a source of debate and controversy. There are some economists who take a 'narrow' view of what money is, and suggest that the means of payment function is *the* deciding factor and accordingly only cash and current account deposits fulfil this role. On the other hand another group of economists suggest that what one is

really concerned with is that collection of assets which shows the
closest relationship with changes in spending in the economy. This
latter approach is therefore a more 'broad' view of the definition of
money. The suggestion is made that if a group of such assets can be
identified, regardless of whether some or all can satisfactorily be
called 'money', then this group of assets is the one which economists
and the monetary authorities should focus their attention. The
possibility that such a group of assets may not satisfy in a thorough
way some theoretical requirement about the nature of money is
therefore regarded as largely irrelevant. However, the debate is not
settled, and neither the 'narrow definition' of money, as it is called,
nor the 'broad definition', is entirely satisfactory. The Bank of
England and other central banks therefore publish in their statistical
series different definitions of the money stock.

The Bank of England first published data on the money stock in
September 1970,[6] providing three choices of definition. The first,
narrow definition, known as M_1, consisted of notes and coin in
circulation with the public plus sterling current accounts held by the
private sector only. The public sector and the external sector holdings
were excluded from this definition. A somewhat broader definition,
M_2, was also devised and this included M_1 but with the addition of
private sector sterling deposit accounts with the deposit banks and
the discount houses. Finally, a broad definition, M_3, was also provided
which included M_2 plus all other deposits (sterling and non-sterling)
held with the U.K. banking sector without distinguishing between
public and private sector accounts. These definitions can be
illustrated by reference to *Table 2.3*.

In June 1972 the Bank ceased to calculate M_2, producing the series
for the narrow definition M_1 and the contrasting broad definition M_3.
As well as these changes the Bank has introduced certain differences
in definition, for example 'current accounts' has been replaced by
'sight deposits'.[7] One of the reasons for this is that 'sight deposits' is
an expression which has greater precision of meaning than simply
'current accounts'; 'sight deposits' refers to funds which are available
on demand. This is the notion really underlying the classification and
use of 'current accounts' but this particular terminology does exclude
funds placed 'at call' and which should really be included. The Bank
of England has also divided M_3 into a gross figure (M_3) and an M_3
calculation which is for sterling deposits. *Table 2.4* illustrates the
changes to which we have referred.

[6]*Bank of England Quarterly Bulletin*. vol. 10, No. 3 (September 1970), p.320
[7]In May 1969 the Bank presented data on 'Domestic Credit Expansion'. This concept
is dealt with in Chapter 6.

TABLE 2.3

U.K. money stock 1968–1971: March quarter
(£ m. unadjusted)

	1	2	3	4	5	6	7	8
	Notes & coin in circulation with the public	Sterling current accounts	M_1	Sterling deposit accounts	M_2	All other deposits (sterling & non-sterling; public & private sector)	M_3	Transit items
1968 March	2,851	5,726	7,965	4,686	12,651	1,852	14,503	612
1969 March	2,914	5,047	7,961	5,036	12,997	2,415	15,412	946
1970 March	3,040	4,996	8,036	5,035	13,071	2,619	15,690	1,178
1971 March	3,329	7,048	9,237	5,521	14,758	2,976	17,734	1,140

M_1 = Columns 1 + 2 − 8

M_2 = M_1 + Column 4

M_3 = M_2 + Column 6

Source: Bank of England Statistical Abstract, Nos. 1 and 2.

TABLE 2.4
U.K. money stock 1975 September and 1976 September[a]
(£ m. unadjusted)

	1	2		3	4	5	6	7	8
	Notes & coin in circulation with the public	U.K. private sector sterling sight deposits		M_1	U.K. private sector sterling time deposits	U.K. public sector sterling deposits	Sterling M_3	U.K. residents' deposits in other currencies	M_3
		Non-interest bearing	Interest bearing						
1975 September	5,482	9,466	1,825	16,773	19,368	691	36,832	2,779	39,611
1976 September	6,495	10,256	2,476	19,227	20,120	877	40,224	4,009	44,233

M_1 = Columns 1 + 2

Sterling M_3 = M_1 + Columns 4 + 5

M_3 = Sterling M_3 + Column 7

[a]Only two illustrative examples are given because of changes in the series May 1975.

Source: Bank of England *Quarterly Bulletin*, vol. 17, No. 2 (June 1977).

2.5 Summary

i. The financial system of a modern economy produces a variety of services which cater for the different needs of individuals and firms. This function of financial firms is one with which most people are familiar, but there is another, broader function which the financial system performs and that is the production of financial assets.

ii. Financial assets are part of the total wealth of an individual, the other type of wealth being real (i.e. tangible) assets. However, for the community as a whole financial assets may not really be part of the community's wealth since such assets have a corresponding liability. Thus the *net* position may be more appropriate: total assets minus total liabilities. If this is so, the net wealth of the community is virtually its physical assets since financial assets simply wash out when offset by financial liabilities.

iii. The growth of financial claims tends to exceed the growth of (physical) capital assets. Two reasons were put forward for this feature: one was that some claims arise because firms, individuals, and governments sometimes go into debt in order to finance current rather than capital expenditure. Additionally, the process of raising funds *indirectly* for use by industrial firms can result in a replication of financial assets/liabilities by virtue of the intermediate operation of financial firms.

iv. Money is the most liquid financial asset in the system which performs certain functions: medium of exchange, store of value, unit of account, and standard for deferred payments. However, the medium of exchange function can be identified as the most important since other financial assets may well perform the other three functions, and in certain circumstances (e.g. inflationary conditions) perform these other functions better than money.

v. Since money could be designated a financial asset, the possibility of there being substitute financial assets has to be considered. The sensitivity of money holding with respect to changes in the rate of interest on alternative assets was a possible means of detecting the degree or existence of money-substitutes.

vi. The problem of identifying money in a modern economy in an unambiguous way has resulted in the production of money stock data which covers both a narrow approach to money and a broad approach. The narrow approach usually identifies the means of payment function of money and limits the inclusion of assets to those which can be ascribed this role, whereas the broad definition includes other near-money assets, partly on the basis of the substitutability argument.

3
Financial intermediation

3.1 Introduction

We have so far considered only in passing the role and operation of financial firms within the economy. It is the purpose of Chapter 3 to delve into the basic operation of such firms and also provide the reader with an overview of their general functioning. Although in reality the range and variety of financial firms is considerable, fortunately it is possible to identify certain features which have general applicability.

3.2 The nature of financial intermediation

3.2.1 FINANCIAL INTERMEDIARIES

In the previous chapter we referred rather loosely to 'financial firms' without specifying the nature of their business which would justify a more precise description or name. Our intention in Chapter 3 is to provide a sharper picture of the sort of firms to which we have referred and the nature of their business operations. If one studies the financial columns of the newspapers or indeed merely looks down the 'High Street' of most towns, one would observe an almost bewildering array of competing firms: banks of different kinds, building societies, 'credit agencies', and so on. Fortunately we can simplify the situation by ascribing to these types of business the name and function of 'financial intermediary'. We are able to make this simplification because all these firms have a common, basic function which is to stand in between those who wish to lend and those who wish to borrow, or in the terminolgy used in Chapter 1, to stand in between those with budget surpluses and those who wish to run budget deficits. *Figure 3.1* illustrates in a simple fashion the contrasting possibilities.

The upper section of Figure 3.1 shows a situation where a financial intermediary does not enter the relationship between the borrower and lender. In this case there is a direct flow of funds between those with surpluses (lenders) and those intending to run deficits (borrowers). An example of this type of relationship might be where a saver decides to buy the new shares of a company which are offered for sale by advertisement in a newspaper. In the lower part of Figure 3.1 the primary (or ultimate) lender does not provide funds directly to the final (or ultimate) borrower but places funds with a financial

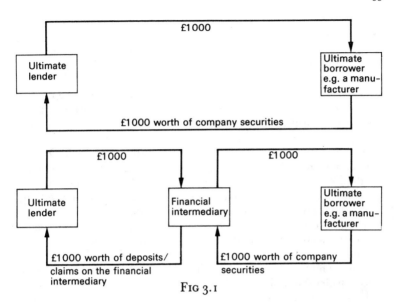

FIG 3.1

intermediary and in return has a deposit or claim on the financial intermediary. (Whether it is a deposit or another type of claim depends on the kind of financial intermediary. For example, if funds are placed with a bank the resulting claim on the bank is in the form of a bank deposit, whereas the payment of a life-insurance premium to an insurance company constitutes simply a claim on the company which may be 'presented' if death of the insured occurs or in the case of, say, an endowment policy, at the maturity date of the policy.) Having received the funds from the ultimate lender the financial intermediary is capable of on-lending such funds to the ultimate borrower who in turn provides security or securities which are held by the financial intermediary.

The reader at this stage might ask why it is necessary for a financial intermediary to stand in between the ultimate lender and the ultimate borrower. The next section of this chapter attempts to answer this and other questions.

3.2.2 THE NEED FOR FINANCIAL INTERMEDIATION

Perhaps the best way of examining this question is to consider the various circumstances and requirements which apply to lenders and borrowers.

(i) *Lenders.* One might ask what factors influence a lender's selection of the various outlets for his savings, thereby obtaining a claim or financial asset. (Note we are not considering here the much broader question why individuals *save*, in contrast with the decision to lend.) Obviously for different individuals there will be a different set of factors but in general it is likely that there are a number of common elements.

Most potential lenders would probably wish to minimize the risks which attend their lending. In these circumstances risk can take a number of forms: the risk of default, i.e. the borrower is unable to repay; the risk that the market value of the asset held by the lender may fall and thus reduce the wealth of the individual; the risk that the lender may need funds before the loan is due to be repaid, i.e. the term of the loan may in the event prove to have been too long; the risk associated with inadequately diversified assets. It is likely that a potential lender will consider two other aspects of the transaction: convenience and liquidity (these two are not unrelated to the question of risk). Lenders may have neither the time nor the inclination to examine in sufficient depth the opportunities for different forms of lending which may exist. Many lenders may be disinclined to study the considerable amount of material which is published by companies relating to their commercial and financial status; documentation which is relevant to the decision facing the lender/investor. Thus the existence of assets which eliminates or reduces this type of information gathering and analysis would be of benefit to such individuals. Perhaps most important of all, the lender is likely to be concerned about the liquidity of his investment. The term 'liquidity' is often given a variety of meaning but in this context we are considering a mix of qualities: the ease with which an asset can be sold and converted into money at the convenience of the holder and the certainty that the capital value of the asset will be maintained. Many lenders are likely to be very conscious of the uncertainty which attends their own future need for funds – a chance event may result in an individual's unexpected need for funds – and for many lenders, therefore, the liquidity characteristics of their investment will be very important. One expression of this concern may be a preference by lenders for relatively short-term lending.

(ii) *Borrowers.* In some respect the needs of the borrower are rather simpler to express than those of the lender. Fundamentally the borrower requires funds at a particular point in time, for a given period of time, and at the lowest cost. In exchange for such funds the borrower will provide the lender with some form of claim against himself. Such claims may take a variety of forms – shares, bills of exchange, bonds, etc. – but whatever the form, the claim must be acceptable to the lender otherwise the provision of funds cannot take place. In addition the borrower will require information about the markets for funds in order that successful borrowing takes place. Without such information the borrower may find that either insufficient funds are obtained or they are obtained at higher rates of interest than necessary.

There are at least two major risks which face the potential borrower. One is that the funds required at a particular time may not be available. This may be a result of an overall shortage of funds in the market or imperfect transmission of information within the market, i.e. a potential lender exists but is unaware of the existence of a suitable borrower. The other risk is that the lender may wish to terminate the loan at a time which is inconvenient to the borrower. This in turn may cause the borrower to re-borrow, perhaps at higher rates of interest – assuming of course that alternative funds are available. If re-borrowing is not possible, then the borrower may be forced to sell assets in order to meet the demand of the lender.

A great deal of borrowing by companies is for the purchase of capital equipment, and much capital equipment (machines, factory buildings, etc.) has a long life. Partly for this reason, a firm which wishes to borrow for the purchase of capital equipment may require the term of the loan to be lengthy so that there is opportunity for the capital equipment to generate sufficient funds to 'pay for itself' over the whole or part of its life.

From what we have discussed so far it is clear that lenders and borrowers are likely to have sets of needs which have to be satisfied before a financial transaction between the two parties can take place. The asset or claim which the borrower provides has to meet the various requirements of the lender – minimum risk, liquidity, etc. – but at the same time the needs or requirements of the lender must not be too demanding otherwise the potential borrower will be dissuaded from borrowing, and the potential lender will be deprived of an opportunity to make use of his spare funds. An alternative way of expressing the problem in the lender/borrower relationship is that the needs of the lender and borrower may not match. For example it may be the case that the majority of potential lenders prefer to lend for relatively *short* periods whereas the majority of borrowers prefer to borrow for *long* periods. Clearly if some lending and borrowing is to take place there will need to be some means by which the non-matching of needs is resolved. One way this may occur is through the market mechanism itself. Taking the previous example, the problem of short-term/long-term preferences may be resolved by the market if the rate of interest on long-term lending rose sufficiently relatively to short-term lending. Such a change in interest rate would tend to persuade some lenders to 'lend long' and some borrowers to 'borrow short', and thus both groups could be satisfied. However, changes in market interest rates are not the only means by which the incompatibility of requirements of lenders and borrowers can be resolved. Financial intermediation provides an additional way in which the needs of *both the lender and the borrower* can be met.

3.2.3 THE PROCESS OF FINANCIAL INTERMEDIATION

The previous section has shown that in the market for loans there is a problem of reconciling the needs of lenders and borrowers and it was suggested that the existence of financial intermediaries could help to overcome this problem. This section will examine more closely the operation of a financial intermediary and then show how such operation can help to satisfy both lenders and borrowers.

Figure 3.1 (p. 35) shows the financial intermediary receiving funds from the ultimate lender and then on-lending these funds to the ultimate borrower. At first sight this would seem to be little different to the direct provision of funds from lender to borrower. However, this is not the case since the financial intermediary has provided the ultimate lender with a *different kind of asset* than would have been the case with the direct provision of funds. Furthermore the financial intermediary has on-lent the funds in exchange for an asset which is less liquid than the corresponding liability in the balance sheet of the financial intermediary. Broadly speaking, the assets of financial intermediaries are less liquid than the corresponding liabilities. We can make this more clear by the use of a familiar institution – a deposit bank. Such banks as part of their ordinary course of business will receive funds which are deposited with them in the form of demand deposits (current account deposits) or savings deposits (deposit accounts). These funds are then used for the purchase of assets, the largest single category being lending to customers. The liabilities of the banks are their deposits, of which a large proportion are repayable on demand, i.e. for the holder of such deposits they are a very liquid asset since they can be converted into cash entirely at the convenience of the holder. However, the bulk of the assets held by the banks are much less liquid than this and cannot be converted into cash at the whim of the bank since many assets, e.g. certain loans to customers, government bond holdings[1], are for a period of years. A similar situation applies to an insurance company which has policy-holders who may make a claim (the liability of the insurance company) at any

---

[1]Although these assets may be sold on the stock market by banks and insurance companies they might be reluctant to do so because stock market prices of such securities could be at an unsatisfactorily low level. The decision to sell these assets might thus involve these intermediaries in the risk of capital loss.

moment, whereas the insurance company's assets, e.g. government bonds, ordinary shares, may not readily be encashed – they are less liquid than the insurance company's liabilities. Whatever the particular type of financial intermediary one is considering, all of them perform the function of creating assets (liabilities against themselves) which are more liquid than the assets which they themselves hold. Their operation is not merely that of being a middleman, i.e. simply passing on funds, but actually generating a new type of asset which is acceptable to the ultimate lender.

Having established this primary operation of financial intermediaries, we can now consider the way this function helps to satisfy the requirements of the ultimate lender *and* ultimate borrower. As before, we shall consider the lender and borrower separately.

(i) *Lenders*. The financial intermediary is able to offer the lender a more liquid asset than the asset obtained from the ultimate borrower by the financial intermediary. This allows the lender to satisfy more easily his need for liquidity and minimum risk associated with his lending. Without the operation of the financial intermediary the lender would have to buy either the less liquid asset offered by the ultimate borrower or not lend at all. By virtue of specialization the financial intermediary is able also to solve the lender's problem of information since the managers of the financial intermediary will accumulate skills associated with the use of funds and the purchase of assets. The lender simply has to decide which sort of financial intermediary suits his needs rather than which type of asset, from a wide range of assets, he wishes to purchase with his funds. Thus the lender has, for example, merely to decide whether to use a building society, deposit bank, Trustee Savings Bank, Post Office, etc., rather than having to choose from a very large range and variety of competing assets. The problem of choice is not eliminated by the existence of financial intermediaries but for many lenders the problem is made simpler. Furthermore the financial intermediary can act as a diversifying agent for the lender in a way which, say, the small lender would be unable to perform. Possibly the best illustration of this is the unit trust in which a lender is able to invest relatively small sums by buying units which are based on a spread of companies. (See Section 4.6.4.2.)

(ii) *Borrowers*. Some of the problems facing the borrower are also more easily overcome with the aid of financial intermediaries. The specialized nature of financial intermediaries and the scale of their operation does influence the overall provision of funds since the advantages they offer to potential lenders is likely to encourage the maximum volume of funds flowing from lenders. In addition the scale of operations of financial intermediaries may alleviate the problem of uncertainty of availability of funds for borrowers. This is because there is a greater likelihood that an unexpected reduction in funds flowing to the financial intermediary from one source is offset by additional funds from another. Finally, the existence of financial intermediaries is likely to result in a lower rate of interest paid by the borrower. Lenders will be prepared to accept a lower rate paid to them by the financial intermediary because part of the return lenders obtain is in the form of the liquidity quality of the asset created by the financial intermediary. Thus lenders are content with a lower rate of interest and, in turn, borrowers pay a lower rate. In the absence of financial intermediaries, risks would be greater for the individual lender and accordingly interest rates would have to be higher to compensate for this.

3.2.4 THE ECONOMIC BASIS OF FINANCIAL INTERMEDIATION

So far in this chapter we have described *in general* how all financial intermediaries behave, as well as outlining certain benefits from financial intermediation which may accrue to both the ultimate lender and the ultimate borrower. The purpose of this section is to explain *why* it is possible for financial intermediaries to operate in the way described.

Large-scale operation by financial intermediaries allows them to benefit from a phenomenon which is essentially statistical in nature, and probably the clearest example of this is to be found in the operation of insurance companies. We suggested earlier that the liability of an insurance company is its obligation to pay the policy-holder if the event which is the subject of the insurance agreement actually occurs. For example, the chances that a man aged 20 living in the U.K. will die within one year are approximately 12 in 10,000 whereas a man aged 75 has almost a 1 in 10 chance that he will die within one year. This type of datum is calculable for all age groups and is given in considerable detail – likely cause of death, etc. Since population data are also available it is a relatively easy matter to calculate how many people will die within a year, their age at death, and cause of death. An insurance company will have many policy-holders and as a group they will probably be representative of the population at large, and therefore each insurance company is able to calculate the likely claims which will be made in a given year, and the funds which the company will need to pay the claimants. In order that such claims can be met the insurance company will need to use the premiums it receives to purchase assets which either mature at the appropriate time or provide sufficient income to meet the likely claims. It is to be noted that the successful operation of the insurance company rests on having a large enough number of policy-holders who are typical of the population at large together with judicious investment of the premiums which flow into the company. If both these conditions are met, the insurance company will be able to operate successfully despite the fact that *its liabilities are more liquid than its assets*.

A deposit bank also relies on the same kind of statistical phenomenon illustrated in the case of the insurance company. However in this instance the problem relates to the likelihood of there being a net withdrawal of funds by depositors resulting in a change in total bank deposits. Observing the day-to-day operation of a bank we would notice that some depositors are withdrawing funds and at the same time other depositors are placing funds in their accounts. If the bank has a large number of accounts it is possible that at the same time as one depositor is withdrawing, say, £10, another depositor is depositing £10. The larger the number of accounts the more likely it is that this offsetting phenomenon is taking place. If a bank has a sufficient number of accounts for this offsetting flow of funds to occur, the bank will be able to purchase earning assets (with the funds on deposit) which are less liquid than the deposit liabilities of the bank, and yet not risk insolvency. However, it is unlikely that the offsetting flow of funds occurs in reality as satisfactorily as in our illustration. One cause of the lack of perfect offsetting is the seasonal variations in the need for cash and the transfer of funds. Nevertheless this problem can be resolved by a bank if it ensures that a proportion of its assets are very liquid, either holding cash itself or other assets which can be easily converted into cash without risk of capital loss. Experience gained over time will enable a bank to anticipate seasonal and other changes and therefore allow it to adjust its assets accordingly.

It is important to realize that in both our illustrations – the insurance company and the bank – the basic features of financial intermediaries' operations are the same:

    (a) the intermediaries rely on a sufficiently large scale of operation which will allow them to estimate the probability of changes in their liability position;

    (b) the known probabilities associated with their liabilities permit financial intermediaries to purchase assets which are less liquid than their liabilities, and yet to remain solvent;

    (c) the intermediaries do not merely pass on funds which have been deposited with them, but in addition create another type of financial asset which constitute their liabilities. It is this particular factor which differentiates the operation of financial intermediaries from that of middlemen or brokers whose function is simply to bring the lender and borrower together rather than to operate between them.

There is a further benefit from the large-scale operations of financial intermediaries which is that the risk of an individual investor (the lender) losing his money is reduced as the size of the intermediaries' operations increase. This reduction in risk for the lender arises for two reasons. One is that the financial intermediary will be able to diversify its assets, i.e. it will hold a *range of assets* of varying degrees of riskiness and return. (The unit trust was an example we used earlier.) The alternative facing an individual small lender may well be to 'put all his eggs in one basket' by placing his funds in a single form of investment. The other reason for the reduction in risk is simply a result of the scale of operations of the intermediary. To illustrate this point let us suppose that an individual lender wishes to invest £100, and there is a one in twenty chance that the borrower will default completely, i.e. at the end of the term of the loan the lender receives the whole of his money back or nothing at all. For simplicity we are ignoring the fact that the lender will receive a rate of interest. Now let us assume that instead of direct lending to the ultimate borrower the lender places his £100 with a financial intermediary which is also faced with a one in twenty chance that a borrower will be unable to repay. Furthermore let us assume that the financial intermediary has made 1,000 loans of £100 each, i.e. the total funds placed with the financial intermediary amounts to £100,000. Since one in twenty of these loans will not be repaid to the financial intermediary, the intermediary will therefore lose £5,000. However, returning to our individual lender who has placed £100 with the financial intermediary, we can see that he has exchanged a one in twenty chance that he will lose *all* his money if he lends directly to a borrower, for a near certainty that he will lose 5 per cent (one in twenty) of his investment as a result of the spreading of a loss of £5,000 over all investors in the financial intermediary. The opportunity to exchange the risk of losing *all* one's investment for a near certainty of losing a small fraction of that investment is one which many lenders are willing to take. Furthermore, the rate of interest charged by the financial intermediary can be adjusted so that in the long run the bad debts are covered. Many people cannot risk losing all their savings and for such individuals a financial intermediary offers considerable benefits.

3.3 Financial intermediaries and the economy

So far in this chapter we have emphasized the role and value of financial intermediaries to the individual lender and borrower. In this section we shall examine briefly the effect of financial intermediation in connection with the important activity of saving and investment.

3.3.1 SAVING AND INVESTMENT

We have already suggested that a large proportion of borrowing is needed to finance investment by firms in both the private and public sectors. The investment in new capital equipment is a means by which the community maintains and increases its stock of capital and this, together with technical improvements, permits productivity increase which in turn allows a rise in the community's standard of living. If firms wish to invest, and the productive capacity in the capital goods industries is sufficient to meet the demand, then clearly any means by which purely *financial* impediments are reduced or eliminated is of value. Financial intermediaries are important agencies which can help to remove two kinds of impediment. One such impediment is the possibility that potential lenders are unprepared to risk direct financing of firms. We have seen earlier in the chapter that a financial intermediary is able to reduce the risk facing the individual lender. By reducing risk to the ultimate lender, the financial intermediaries encourage the potential lender to lend and thus the total of funds available to firms who wish to invest is larger than would otherwise be the case. Another possible impediment to the flow of savings for investment is the lack of suitable assets for ultimate lenders which are issued by ultimate borrowers. For example, a firm may be engaged in a risky business venture – perhaps developing a new product – and therefore the assets which such a firm could offer in exchange for funds to invest in the venture would also be risky. Such assets may be unacceptable to many lenders and the firm may be unable to obtain the necessary funds. However, the intervention of a financial intermediary would allow the borrower to issue *the sort of assets which most suits the borrower* and yet obtain the funds required. As we have seen, the risk-spreading operations of financial intermediaries allow this to take place.

It is likely that the existence of financial intermediaries provides a general benefit to the community, whether such intermediaries are public or private sector firms, by aiding the transmission and growth of funds for investment and thereby meeting the needs of *both* lenders and borrowers.

3.4 Bank and non-bank financial intermediaries

We have so far suggested that *all* financial intermediaries have a common basis for their operation and the same role with respect to the lender/borrower relationship. However, there has developed over the years a controversy which concerns the difference or alleged difference between two groups of financial intermediary. These two groups are often termed 'bank financial intermediaries' and 'non-bank financial intermediaries', commonly abbreviated to B.F.I. and N.B.F.I. In this section we propose to take a brief look at the substance of this controversy.

It is probably accurate to suggest that both parties to the controversy would accept that all kinds of financial intermediary have the characteristics identified on p. 41. If this is so, where does the controversy lie? An important aspect of the controversy relates to the precise nature and use to which the liabilities of the financial intermediaries can be put. The reader will recall that by virtue of their intermediation all financial intermediaries *create* liabilities against themselves which are the assets held by the ultimate lender. It is suggested by some economists that the key feature which distinguishes B.F.I.s from N.B.F.I.s is that the liabilities created by the B.F.I.s are unique in that these liabilities are themselves 'spendable'. In other words, the liabilities of the deposit banks (e.g. Midland Bank) are used as money by the holders of the deposits whereas the liabilities of, say, a building society cannot be used in this way.

An alternative aspect of this controversy emphasizes the *creation* aspect to B.F.I. activities and the *transmission* activity of the N.B.F.I.s. B.F.I.s, it is argued, can actually increase the total volume of spending in the economy by their capacity to *add to* the stock of credit in existence, whereas the N.B.F.I.s are merely 'honest brokers' transmitting funds *which have been created elsewhere*, i.e. by the banking system. Essentially, therefore, this argument is suggesting that B.F.I.s can add to the stock of credit and N.B.F.I.s cannot. How accurate is this assertion? If by 'credit' we mean the availability of funds to an individual or firm which enables the individual or firm to spend in excess of current income, then one can argue that both B.F.I.s and N.B.F.I.s are able to perform this function. An illustration should help to make this point clear. Deposit bank liabilities, i.e. bank deposits, are the major component of the U.K. money stock. This was revealed in Chapter 2 (Table 2.4), where we saw that notes and coin amounted to about 33 per cent of M_1 and only 16 per cent of M_3. This accords with everyday experience in which the bulk of transactions (by value) are carried out through transfers of bank deposits and not notes and coin – notes and coin are indeed the small change of the system. This general acceptability of bank deposits as money has the consequence that a very high proportion of the liabilities of the deposit banking system are never presented to the banking system for redemption. It can be argued that this places the deposit banks in a very special position since the bulk of their liabilities is used as money. Thus a deposit bank which makes a loan to a customer can do so simply by crediting the customer's account by the amount of the loan, and the result of this is a matching rise in bank deposits (liabilities) and 'advances' (assets). Since the bank deposit is as spendable as notes and coin, the customer can obviously spend the bank deposit for the purpose the loan was made. The deposit bank (a B.F.I.) has added to the volume of credit and enabled additional spending to take place.

In contrast, it is difficult to conceive of an N.B.F.I. behaving in the same way. Take for example the operation of one of the most important N.B.F.I.s, the building society. The building society also lends to customers but in this case the funds which the building society provides the borrower are not the *creation* of the building society since such funds are either in the form of bank deposits or notes and coin. Thus the building society cannot spontaneously add to its liabilities and provide additional funds to borrowers[2]. On the basis of the discussion so far one could argue that there *is* a basic difference between the B.F.I. and N.B.F.I. and the two categories are justified. However one can envisage circumstances in which a N.B.F.I. is able to add to the volume of credit and enable additional spending to take place. To illustrate this, let us assume for simplicity that we have one deposit bank and one N.B.F.I. (a building society), and that the deposit bank liabilities consist of demand deposits, and savings deposits on which interest is paid by the deposit bank. Now let us assume that the building society raises the rate of interest offered to investors and this results in some customers of the deposit bank transferring part of their savings deposits to the building society. The building society, having received cheques drawn on the deposit bank, re-deposits these cheques in its own account with the deposit bank. Total deposit bank deposits remain unchanged – it is their character which has altered, there being less savings deposits and more demand deposits. Since the building society has now received additional funds, it is capable of *adding* to its mortgage lending, making such payments by drawing on its larger demand deposit with the deposit bank. In this illustration it would appear that the building society has added to the volume of credit and enabled additional spending (on house purchase) to take place. On the basis of this second argument presented it would seem that it is not legitimate to distinguish between B.F.I.s and N.B.F.I.s since both types of intermediary are capable of adding to the stock of credit and enable additional spending to occur.

A general conclusion might be that B.F.I.s and N.B.F.I.s have

[2]If building societies were able to do this, one would not observe the periodic appearance of 'mortgage famines'.

fundamental characteristics in common, i.e. both types of intermediary perform the basic role and function of financial intermediation, and that the differences are differences of degree rather than kind. In particular the type of financial assets which the B.F.I.s and N.B.F.I.s create for the ultimate lender (e.g. bank deposits by the deposit banks, and building society deposits by the building societies) have qualities in common but in different degrees – liquidity, convenience, risk, etc. can be ascribed to any financial asset, but the combination varies depending on the origin of the asset. It must be admitted that the liabilities created by the deposit banks do have the special quality of being used as money – the means of payment and exchange – whereas other financial assets created by other financial intermediaries do not. However, as one economist put it, 'there is nothing unique about being unique'. In other words, a bank deposit has the special quality of being used as the medium of exchange, but none the less the asset created by a building society (or other financial intermediary) for its depositors is also 'special' and different from other financial assets.

3.5 Summary

i.   Financial intermediaries interpose themselves between the ultimate lender and ultimate borrower.

ii. Financial intermediaries have flourished because the intermediation function allows them to satisfy the needs of *both* the lender and the borrower to their mutual benefit. Lenders obtain a more liquid and less risky asset and borrowers obtain greater certainty of funds in exchange for the kind of assets which the ultimate borrower would wish to make available to the lender. Without the intermediary it is possible that a lender may not lend because the asset offered by the borrower in exchange for funds has unacceptable qualities, e.g. it may be too risky or illiquid.

iii. All financial intermediaries have balance sheets which reveal that their assets are less liquid than their liabilities. This condition arises because the intermediary is attempting to satisfy the needs of both the lender and the borrower.

iv. The basis for successful financial intermediation is related to the scale of operation of the intermediaries. Large-scale operation allows the risk of default and other risks to be spread over a large number of investors, and also allows the intermediary to hold a more 'balanced' mix of assets than would be possible for the individual investor/lender. This 'balanced portfolio' helps to cut down the risk of loss through unbalanced investment in assets.

v.   The existence and growth of financial intermediaries probably aids the process of saving and investment in the economy. If this is so, financial intermediaries contribute to overall economic growth and the growth in the community's standard of living.

vi. Some economists suggest that one can divide financial intermediaries into two kinds: bank financial intermediaries (B.F.I.) and non-bank financial intermediaries (N.B.F.I.). The basis for this distinction is debatable. Although it is the case that the liabilities (deposits) of the B.F.I.s are used as *money* (medium of exchange and payment) in the economy whereas the liabilities of the N.B.F.I.s are not, it is nevertheless true that N.B.F.I.s are capable of adding to the volume of *credit* in the economy. *If* it is correct that changes in the amount of credit available has more effect on spending in the economy than changes in the money stock, then the distinction between B.F.I.s and N.B.F.I.s is relatively unimportant. Furthermore, *all* financial assets created by financial intermediaries have special, and possibly unique, qualities, and it may not be legitimate to single out the liabilities of the B.F.I.s for special mention – 'there is nothing unique about being unique'.

4
Main financial intermediaries

4.1 Introduction

The previous chapters have examined both the nature of a rudimentary financial system and the basic functioning of the intermediaries which operate within it. Chapter 4 is intended to look at the main types of intermediaries which have developed and are based within the United Kingdom, and in particular to consider the nature of their business operations.

Britain, and in particular the City of London, has long been known for its expertise in the field of finance, both domestic and international. The large number of financial firms which operate in London is a testimony to the pre-eminence of 'the City' in the whole area of money and trade. Not only British banks maintain their head offices in London, but almost two hundred foreign banks have established branches there. Such banks represent only a part of the whole financial sector in the U.K. comprising not only the domestic and international banks but also a whole range of other financial firms – discount houses, finance houses, savings banks, insurance companies, investment trusts, and so on. The list is extensive and the number of firms operating is considerable, in 1976 around 2,000 major firms with assets well in excess of an astonishing £200,000 million. However, this very large figure does obscure the fact that some of the financial intermediaries are very large and some are very small. For example, the main deposit banks have, on average, assets amounting to around £6,000 million, whereas over half the building societies have assets of less than £10 million.

4.2 Classification

The diversity of business activity and the range of size of these financial firms does raise the problem of how to classify and analyse them. Classifying the firms which compose the finance industry is not merely a manifestation of the economist's urge to be tidy, but is necessary in order to produce an orderly framework which makes analysis of the financial sector possible.

In general, there are several ways in which one may classify firms: the nature of the product, number of employees, value of turnover, capital structure, legal status, method of operations, etc. All of these approaches have been used to provide a framework for studying various industries, and one can, of course, choose several methods of classification and grouping for the same industry in order to produce a more complete picture. One question which arises is how one chooses a particular method of classification. Briefly, one will choose the approach which is likely to be most useful in the analysis of a particular industry or problem. For example, if one is concerned about the extent of monopoly in a certain industry, probably the most useful method of breakdown would be to classify the firms within that industry on the basis of their share of total output. By using such a procedure one would be able to establish whether a small number of firms held a dominant position (e.g. 2 per cent of firms producing 60 per cent of total output) and such analysis would be of some assistance in deciding the extent to which monopoly is present.

The 'finance industry' consists of many different types of firms producing a wide range of services, and this presents some difficulty in deciding how to classify them. This difficulty is partly the result of imperfect specialization by financial firms, i.e. many firms perform *several* kinds of function for their customers, and the distinguishing features may not be very clear from mere examination of their balance sheets. It may well be necessary to consider also who their customers are and the way in which they operate their businesses in order to differentiate and classify such firms – a good example of this would be the difference between a deposit bank and an acceptance house. Our approach will be to use, initially, the B.F.I. and N.B.F.I. classification.

4.3 Bank and non-bank financial intermediaries

Although we indicated in Chapter 3 that dividing financial intermediaries into 'bank' and 'non-bank' may be debatable, it is initially useful. This is because a major concern of this book is with those private sector financial firms whose liabilities act as medium of exchange and payment. However, deciding which of the present day financial intermediaries should be classified as B.F.I.s is not an easy matter, and this is because the function of medium of exchange and payment is not performed exclusively by a single group of firms. For example, demand deposit and cheque facilities are offered not only by the London Clearing Banks, but also by acceptance houses, foreign banks, savings banks, and the National Giro. However, the provision and service is not identical or uniform, and inevitably there is an arbitrary element in our proposed division of the various financial firms.

If one emphasizes the 'medium of exchange and payment' characteristic of bank deposits, the financial intermediaries which one identified as B.F.I.s would be limited to the clearing banks, the Banking Department of the Bank of England, the National Giro, and the Trustee Savings Banks, which provide some form of 'medium of exchange and payment' function. For most of the other financial firms, this side of their business is very small; the acceptance houses and overseas banks in London currently have little more than 2 per cent of their liabilities as demand deposits, for example. However, if one chooses to lay emphasis on the general business operation of

TABLE 4.1
Sterling deposit liabilities[a] of selected financial intermediaries (U.K.)
(21 July figures: £ m.)

Bank financial intermediaries (broad definition)	1956	1966	1976
London Clearing Banks	5,859	8,755	23,785
Scottish Clearing Banks	710	971	2,513
Northern Ireland banks	125	220	850[c]
Bank of England Banking Department	290	515	1,809
National Giro	—	10	171
Secondary banks	929	2,892	19,327
Discount houses	909	1,156	2,509
Total	8,822	14,519	50,964
Non-bank financial intermediaries			
Trustee Savings Banks[d]	1,055	2,149	4,060
Building societies	2,035	5,894	24,790
Finance houses	80[b]	648	420
Insurance and pension funds	3,617[b]	16,142	37,000
Investment and unit trusts	1,500[b]	3,586	8,435
Total	8,287	28,419	74,705
TOTAL	17,109	42,938	125,669

[a] In the case of insurance companies and pension funds, as well as investment and unit trusts, the concept of deposit liabilities is inappropriate and therefore figures for funds and assets have been used respectively.
[b] These figures are approximate.
[c] Exact figures are not available because of an industrial dispute in Northern Ireland.
[d] By 1976 part of the T.S.B. could be included under B.F.I.

Sources: Bank of England *Statistical Abstract, Nos.* 1 and 2; *Annual Abstract of Statistics* 1969, 1977.

financial intermediaries rather than the nature of their liabilities (i.e. whether they are money or not), then the financial intermediaries eligible for the B.F.I. classification would be increased. (In fact, this classification is very similar to the Bank of England's definition of the banking sector.) On this basis, the B.F.I. classification would comprise: clearing banks, Banking Department of the Bank of England, the National Giro, part of the Trustee Savings Banks' operations, the acceptance houses, other secondary banks, and the Discount Houses. The N.B.F.I.s would include the remaining financial intermediaries such as building societies, finance houses, and insurance companies. *Table 4.1* should help to clarify the various categories.

4.3.1 SIZE OF FINANCIAL INTERMEDIARIES

Before considering the various financial intermediaries in more detail, it would be both useful and interesting to examine the relative size of these firms as well as their growth in recent years. Table 4.1 shows the sterling deposit liabilities of the various intermediaries spanning a period of twenty years, and *Table 4.2* includes foreign currency deposits as well as sterling deposits for the same period. We must emphasize, however, that the figures quoted are intended only to give a broad indication of the changes which have taken place. This is because we have used only three years' figures from the available published data, and the latter are either incomplete or available in a form unsuitable for our purposes, so that we have had to adjust some of the published figures or make estimates. For example, the insurance companies, pensions funds, investment and unit trusts, are financial intermediaries but are not deposit-receiving institutions. We have therefore had to choose a substitute item for deposits, and in the case of the insurance companies we have used published figures for their funds. Furthermore, the published data in 1956 were far from adequate and figures for foreign currency deposits are unobtainable for that year. It is likely, however, that the value of foreign currency deposits for 1956 would have been very low. The figures for 1956 are therefore identical in Table 4.1 and Table 4.2. However, in spite of these problems it is possible to obtain a broad indication of changes and make some general comments about the two tables.

Sterling liabilities [1]

(i) The overall growth between 1956 and 1976 appears to be very substantial, rising from £17,109 million to £125,669 million, which represents an average annual (compound) growth of almost 10·5 per cent during the whole period. The most rapid growth seems to have

[1] See footnote *a* to Table 4.1.

TABLE 4.2

Sterling and foreign currency deposit liabilities[a] of selected financial intermediaries (U.K.)

(21 July figures: £ m.)

Bank financial intermediaries (broad definition)	1956	1966	1976
London Clearing Banks	5,859	8,755	28,319
Scottish Clearing Banks	710	971	3,036
Northern Ireland banks	125	220	870[c]
Bank of England Banking Department	290	515	1,809
National Giro	—	10	171
Secondary banks	929	6,807	115,641
Discount houses	909	1,156	2,649
Total	8,822	18,434	152,495
Non-bank financial intermediaries			
Trustee Savings Banks[d]	1,055	2,149	4,060
Building societies	2,035	5,894	24,790
Finance houses	80[b]	648	420
Insurance and pension funds	3,617[b]	16,142	37,000
Investment and unit trusts	1,500[b]	3,586	8,435
Total	8,287	28,419	74,705
TOTAL	17,109	46,853	227,200

[a]In the case of insurance companies and pension funds, as well as investment and unit trusts, the concept of deposit liabilities is inappropriate and therefore figures for funds and assets have been used respectively.

[b]These figures are approximate.

[c]Exact figures are not available because of an industrial dispute in Northern Ireland.

[d]By 1976 part of the T.S.B. could be included under B.F.I.

Sources: Bank of England *Statistical Abstract*, Nos. 1 and 2; *Annual Abstract of Statistics* 1969, 1977.

occurred during the second decade with 9·6 per cent average annual (compound) growth during 1956–66, and about 11·1 per cent annual average (compound) growth during 1966–76. It is likely that the more rapid growth in the second decade was influenced by the rising rate of inflation which would be associated with rising *money* value of bank deposits, etc., as well as with rising *money* incomes.

(ii) The relative position of B.F.I.s and N.B.F.I.s has changed over the years. In 1956 the two groups were about the same (B.F.I.s with £8,822 million and N.B.F.I.s having £8,287 million), whereas by 1966 the N.B.F.I.s were the dominant group (65 per cent of total liabilities) and this was sustained in 1976 (57 per cent of liabilities).

(iii) Within the B.F.I. group, it is interesting to note an apparent decline in importance of the main primary banks (London and Scottish Clearing Banks and the Northern Ireland banks). Although their total liabilities rose from £6,732 million in 1956 to £27,148 million in 1976, their share of B.F.I. liabilities fell sustantially from 76 per cent to 53 per cent.

(iv) A number of detailed items are worth highlighting:
(a) the very considerable growth in business of the secondary banks, rising from £929 million in 1956 to £19,327 million in 1976
(b) the substantial expansion of building society deposits from £2,035 million to £24,790 million in the 20-year period:
(c) the increasing importance of the insurance companies and pension funds is reflected in the growth of their funds: £3,617 million, in 1956 to about £37,000 million in 1976.

Sterling and foreign currency liabilities. [2]

(i) When we include the foreign currency liabilities with sterling liabilities, the apparent growth in business becomes even more rapid. Total liabilities in 1956 of £17,109 million rising to £227,200 million in 1976; an average annual (compound) growth of about 13·8 per cent. Between 1956 and 1966 the average annual (compound) growth was about 10·5 per cent, whereas between 1966 and 1976 the figure was nearer 17 per cent.

(ii) When the foreign currency liabilities of financial intermediaries are taken into account, we can see that the relationship between B.F.I.s and N.B.F.I.s is reversed, B.F.I. growth being the dominant element. Total liabilities of the B.F.I.s rose from £8,822 million in 1956 to £152,495 million in 1976 (average annual compound growth of 15·3 per cent).

(iii) Although the B.F.I. growth has exceeded that of N.B.F.I.s, within the B.F.I. group it is clear that the apparent decline of the primary banking business, the London and Scottish Clearing Banks and the Northern Ireland banks is much greater than when sterling liabilities alone were considered. In 1976 their share of total B.F.I. liabilities was only 21 per cent compared with 53 per cent when only sterling business was considered. The reason for this is the enormous growth in the foreign currency business of the secondary banks.

(iv) Additional features of Table 4.2 worth noting:

[2]See footnote *a* to Table 4.2

(a) in 1976 about 46 per cent of total liabilities was in foreign currencies;

(b) the dominance of the secondary banks in the foreign currency banking business – in 1976 they had over 90 per cent of the foreign currency deposits.

4.4 Financial intermediaries and their balance sheets

4.4.1 INTRODUCTION

At the end of Section 4.2 we suggested that another way of approaching the problem of classification was to examine *the nature of the liabilities and assets* of the various financial intermediaries, and group them accordingly. In this section we propose to make such a grouping, and also to consider more closely their business operations by means of an examination of their balance sheets. *Table 4.3* contains the proposed classification.

If we use financial intermediaries' liabilities (which is probably the most convenient presentation for the reader) as a basis for our classification, a natural grouping occurs in the form of the deposit

TABLE 4.3

(A) *Primary banking sector*[a]
   1. London Clearing Banks
   2. Scottish Clearing Banks
   3. Northern Ireland banks
   4. Bank of England Banking Department
   5. Discount houses
   6. National Giro

(B) *Secondary banking sector*
   1. Accepting houses
   2. Other British banks
   3. Overseas banks
   4. Consortium banks

(C) *Other deposit-taking institutions*
   1. Building societies
   2. Trustee Savings Banks
   3. Finance houses

(D) *Other financial intermediaries*
   1. Insurance companies and pension funds
   2. Investment trusts and unit trusts

[a] See p. 55, footnote 3.

banks, which include the London Clearing Banks, Scottish Clearing Banks, Northern Ireland banks, the Bank of England Banking Department, the discount houses, together with the National Giro.[3] The common element which binds this group is their important role in operating the payment mechanism (i.e. the economy's money transmission service). There are several common expressions used to refer to the banks which operate the payments mechanism: commercial banks, joint stock banks, as well as deposit banks. Probably the least ambiguous term is 'deposit banks' although in our view 'primary banking sector' is possibly the clearest description since this suggests their primary or basic function of managing the payments mechanism.

The other major group of banking firms, which, according to the Bank of England's classification, is part of the U.K. banking sector, are the so-called 'secondary banks'. These firms include the acceptance houses, other British banks, foreign banks in the U.K. and consortium banks. Although their asset structure bears some resemblance to that of the primary banking firms, their liabilities are very different in that they are almost entirely term deposits of which the bulk are denominated in foreign currencies. In other words, the deposit business of the secondary banks is not part of the U.K. payment mechanism

The remaining deposit-taking firms consist largely of the building societies, Trustee Savings Banks, and the finance houses. These three types of financial intermediary have two elements in common; they are all involved in relatively small-scale lending, and virtually all their business is within the U.K.

The financial institutions included in the final section of Table 4.3 are not strictly deposit-taking, but are nevertheless important financial intermediaries. These are the insurance companies, pension funds, investment trusts, and unit trusts.

The remainder of this chapter will examine the various groups of financial intermediaries more fully, although the study of the primary banking sector will be limited since this group is examined in some detail in subsequent chapters.

4.4.2 THE PRIMARY BANKING SECTOR

4.4.2.1 *The clearing banks*

These banks comprise some of the largest branch banks in the U.K. and to date consist of the London Clearing Banks: Barclays Bank

---

[3]Until mid-May 1975 the Bank of England classified the following banks as 'other deposit banks': Co-operative Bank Ltd., C. Hoare & Co., Isle of Man Bank Ltd., Lewis's Bank Ltd., and Yorkshire Bank Ltd. These banking firms should still be included as part of the payments mechanism.

Ltd., Coutts & Co., Lloyds Bank Ltd., Midland Bank Ltd., National Westminster Bank Ltd., and William & Glyn's Bank Ltd., all being members of the Committee of London Clearing Banks. There are also the Scottish Clearing Banks and the Northern Ireland banks which are very closely linked with the main London Clearing Banks. The commercial origins of most of these banks date from the eighteenth century or the early part of the nineteenth century, although their present establishment dates from about 1969 onwards, when a series of bank mergers occurred which reduced the number of London Clearing Banks from eleven to the present six.[4] Table 4.1 and Table 4.2 (p. 50, 52) show the value of deposits of the clearing banks including the Scottish and Northern Ireland banks. It is clear that the London Clearing Banks dominate this area of banking, having about 88 per cent of total deposits, and this is the case whether one is using the figures for total deposits or just sterling deposits. For our purposes it is legitimate to group the Northern Ireland and Scottish banks with the London Clearing Banks because (a) the business operations and distribution of assets of the Scottish banks are extremely close to those of the London Clearing Banks; (b) not only is the total business of the Northern Ireland banks very small compared with the other banks, but also two of the Northern Ireland banks are subsidiaries of two London Clearing Banks; and (c) the structure of their liabilities is similar, i.e. a large proportion of their sterling deposits are demand deposits – between 40 and 50 per cent.

We shall examine the combined balance sheet and operations of these important banks more fully in Chapter 5, and at this stage we will merely highlight a number of operational features.

(i) Almost half their sterling deposits are demand deposits,[5] and of the remainder a high proportion are deposits on seven day notice, which by convention are withdrawable on demand, with the penalty of the loss of a week's interest. The true volume of demand deposits (even though they are not strictly 'sight deposits') is between 70 per cent and 80 per cent.[6] Such deposits are the principal component of the U.K. money supply and as such form the major element in the transmission of money and means of payment in the economy. This

[4]Coutts & Co. is in fact 100 per cent owned by the National Westminster Group, but is operated independently.
[5]In 1975 the Bank of England provided a new set of banking statistics based on common reporting dates and common definitions. The term subsequently used for demand deposit is 'sight deposit', i.e. balances, whether interest-bearing or not, which are transferable or withdrawable on demand without interest penalty or interest indemnity.
[6]Committe of London Clearing Bankers, *The London Clearing Banks* (Longman Group Ltd., 1978), p.51

particular function of these banks is also reflected in the fact that four-fifths of their deposits are in sterling.

(ii) Since these banks have a substantial obligation to repay their depositors on demand, the banks' assets must reflect this highly liquid obligation. Currently about one-third of their assets are in a highly liquid form, by virtue of being either short-term (e.g. repayable 'at call' or a few days) or highly marketable (e.g. certificates of deposit, three-month bills).

(iii) Of the remaining assets, approximately 60 per cent are in the form of advances. Such lending to the banks' customers is very wide-ranging, including loans to manufacturing industry, the government sector, retailing, agriculture, as well as personal loans to individuals. Such a diversity of lending is consistent with the need for considerable prudence in the light of the extreme liquidity of the banks' liabilities.

4.4.2.2 The Bank of England Banking Department

We have included the Bank of England Banking Department in our discussion of the primary banking sector because this Department is a very important element in the payments mechanism. It provides money transmission services for both the government and the public, including the deposit banks themselves. However, we have devoted Chapter 7 to a study of the functioning of the Bank of England, and at this stage we will make reference only to its operations which parallel the functioning of the deposit banks. *Table 4.4* shows the liabilities of the Banking Department as of 28 February 1977. The bulk of the

TABLE 4.4
Liabilities of the Bank of England Banking Department, 28 February 1977
(£ m.)

Capital	15
Reserves	173
Current liabilities:	
Public deposits	112
Special deposits	711
Bankers' deposits	372
Other accounts	361
Payable to the Treasury	3
	1,747

Source: Bank of England *Report and Accounts*, 28 February 1977.

Banking Department's liabilities are deposits, and the two types of deposit to which we shall restrict discussion are Public deposits and Bankers' deposits. The remainder of the Banking Department balance sheet will be examined in Chapter 7.

(i) *Public deposits.* The central government is spending and receiving very large sums of money each day – a rough daily average currently would be £150 million. To facilitate such transactions, the government requires a bank, and quite simply the Bank of England is the government's banker. All authorized payments and receipts of the central government must be paid into and come out of the Exchequer, which is the government's central cash account held at the Bank of England. Other deposits which are held at the Bank of England include those of the National Loans Fund (see Section 9.5), the National Debt Commissioners (see Chapter 10), the Paymaster General, and the Inland Revenue.

(ii) *Bankers' deposits.* About 97 per cent of these deposits are held by the London Clearing Banks. Bankers' deposits serve at least three main functions, and these we shall examine in turn.

(a) We have already seen that the bulk of transactions by value within the U.K. are undertaken by transferring bank deposits by cheque rather than by the use of notes and coins. The volume of payments by means of cheques is very substantial: for example, between January and May of 1977, the average monthly transfers were well in excess of £200,000 million. The means by which such vast sums are transferred from one account to another is the operation of the clearing system, or more precisely, the Bankers' Clearing House in London which is operated by the clearing banks. To explain the need for the Clearing House and its operation, we shall consider two sets of circumstances; one in which an individual makes payment by means of a cheque drawn on his account with, say, Midland Bank, payable to another individual who also has an account with the Midland Bank, but at a different branch; and the other circumstance in which an individual draws a cheque on his account with the Midland Bank made payable to an individual whose account is with Barclays Bank. How is settlement made in these two cases? In the former case, the debiting on one account and the crediting of the other will be accomplished through the head office of the Midland Bank, one branch's deposits falling by the amount in question, and the other branch's rising by the same sum. In the second case, however, the indebtedness of the Midland Bank (acting on behalf of its customer) to Barclays Bank may be settled by the transfer of funds from the Midland Bank's account at the Bank of England to Barclays Bank's account at the Bank of England.

TABLE 4.5

Barclays Bank customers	Midland Bank customers	Nat. West. Bank customers
(A) £10 m. cheques paid to Midland Bank customers	(C) £6 m. cheques paid to Barclays Bank customers	(E) £4 m. cheques paid to Barclays Bank customers
(B) £12 m. cheques paid to Nat. West. Bank customers	(D) £3 m. cheques paid to Nat. West. Bank customers	(F) £15 m. cheques paid to Midland Bank customers

Net position between the Banks

Barclays Bank 'owes' Midland Bank £4 m. (A minus C)

Barclays Bank 'owes' Nat. West. Bank £8 m. (B minus E)

Nat. Westminster Bank 'owes' Midland Bank £12 m. (F minus D)

In practice, there are millions of cheques and other transfers involved in the daily 'clearings' and it will be the net amount which will be settled by alteration in the banks' balances at the Bank of England. *Table 4.5* should make the position clearer. In the circumstances shown in the table, Barclays Bank's balance at the Bank of England would fall by a total of £12 million, the Midland Bank's balance would rise by £16 million (of which £4 million would be from Barclays Bank's account at the Bank of England, and £12 million from the National Westminster Bank's account at the Bank of England), and the National Westminster Bank's balance at the Bank of England would fall by £4 million. Clearly the existence of Bankers' deposits at the Bank of England is a vital facility in settling interbank indebtedness.

(b) A further use to which Bankers' deposits are put is the provision of notes and coin in sufficient quantity, variety, and quality (e.g. cleanliness of banknotes) to meet the needs of the public. The public's desire to hold and use notes and coin fluctuates with seasonal factors, e.g. the demand for notes and coin rises during the summer holiday period and also at Christmas. Furthermore it varies according to the public's total holding of bank deposits: as the volume of bank deposits changes, the demand for notes and coin also varies in the same direction. When the public wishes to increase its holdings of notes and coin, it can do so by drawing cheques for cash against demand deposits. It is likely that such a change will be spread over all the clearing banks who will thus find their till money declining. To offset such a change, the banks can convert some of their Bankers' deposits with the Bank of England as a means of replenishing their cash holdings.[7]

(c) Finally, the Bankers' deposits are the means by which financial transactions between the central government and the rest of the economy (a better expression to use here would be the 'non-government sector') can take place. When discussing *Public deposits* we emphasized that the central government is spending and receiving moneys on a very large scale, and since the central government does not have bank accounts with the deposit banks of any significant size, the only way in which the deposit banking system can make payments to the central government and receive payments from it is by variations in the item Bankers' deposits. We shall consider this in more detail in Chapter 6, but it is sufficient to state at this point that *net* payments by the non-government sector to the central government will result in a fall in Bankers' deposits as the banks make payment on behalf of customers, and a rise in Bankers' deposits if *net* payments are made by the government to the non-government sector. A simplified illustration will help to make this clear. Let us suppose that an individual is obliged to pay £100 capital gains tax. One method of making payment would be by drawing a cheque on his bank account at, say, Barclays Bank, using the Bank Giro system, to transfer £100 to the Inland Revenue's collection account at the Bank of England. The final settlement would be made at the Bank of England by *crediting* the Inland Revenue's account (part of the item, 'Public deposits') with £100, and *debiting* Barclays Bank's account at the Bank of England (part of the item, 'Bankers' deposits') by £100.

4.4.2.3 *The discount houses*

So far, our discussion of the primary banking section has been concerned largely with its role in the transmission of money: the payments mechanism. Similarly, our discussion of the discount houses will be limited to that aspect of their operations.

The discount houses are a specialized group of eleven firms (they are all now public companies) belonging to the London Discount Market Association. These eleven companies, together with two discount brokers and the money trading departments of five banks, form what is known as the discount market. It is arguable that the definition of the discount market should include certain other firms, money brokers and gilt-edged jobbers, but since their operations are different to the other firms in the market we shall not include them in

[7]This is a simplification of the procedure which is convenient at this stage; there are further repercussions which will be considered in Chapter 7.

the discussion. The commerical operations of the firms in the discount market are essentially quite simple: they seek out loanable funds, usually available on a very short-term basis, and then use such funds for the purchase of a variety of assets which includes Treasury bills, commercial bills, and gilt-edged securities. This is, of course, the basic operation of any financial intermediary, but the difference here lies in the relationship between the discount market, the deposit banks, and the Bank of England.

(i) The discount houses perform a useful role in smoothing out the ebb and flow of funds between the clearing banks which result from transactions *within* the non-government sector. We may use an earlier example contained in *Table 4.5* as a means of making this clear. However, before we do so it is necessary to provide an additional assumption (albeit in a somewhat simplified form) which is that the Clearing Banks maintain a desired level of *cash* reserves at the Bank of England. If a particular bank's level falls, we assume that the bank will attempt to rebuild such reserves, and if the level rises, that the bank will attempt to reduce such reserves since they yield no return. Such reserves are needed, not least because of the Clearing Banks' obligations towards their customers in respect of the drawing of cash. The cash must always be available, should customers wish to convert their bank deposits into cash. We can now trace the consequences of the inter-bank indebtedness which was to be found in the illustration in Table 4.5 The net position we established was the Barclays' reserves would fall by £12 million, Midland Bank reserves would rise by £16 million, and National Westminster reserves would fall by £4 million. Barclays and National Westminster need to replenish their reserves by a total of £16 million, and this could be achieved by *calling in* £16 million of their loans to the discount market. However, the Midland Bank would have surplus reserves of £16 million which it would dispose of by *increasing* its lending to the discount market by £16 million. Thus the only change would be a change in the Bankers' deposits at the Bank of England, and the accounts of the discount houses would remain the same, by virtue of repaying and borrowing £16 million simultaneously. By this means, the settlement of inter-bank indebtedness, arising from the operation of the payments mechanism, can be undertaken in a smooth fashion by the preparedness of the discount market to absorb additional funds as well as repay on demand.[8]

(ii) The discount houses are also useful in respect of another type of

[8] This is by no means the end of the matter, but further examination will be left till Chapter 8.

smoothing operation, and that is one which arises from the transactions which take place between the *non-government* sector and the *government* sector. To refer again to the illustration in Table 4.5 we saw that there was simply a redistribution of Bankers' deposits between the various clearing banks, and the arithmetic of the example was such that the *total* of Banker's deposits remained unchanged. In practice it is unlikely that transfers between banks would cancel out. One reason for this is that individual persons and firms are not only making payments to each other *within* the non-government sector, but are also making payments to the government sector and receiving payments from the government sector. (Reference to this was made in Section 4.4.2.2 (i) and (ii)c.) It is conceivable, therefore, that at a particular time, the net payments between the non-government and the government sector may be such that Bankers' deposits rise (government sector paying out more than it is receiving from the non-government sector in taxes, etc.,) or Bankers' deposits fall (government sector receiving more than it is paying out to the non-government sector). In the first situation, the clearing banks will tend to have surplus funds which they will *lend to* the discount houses, and in the second instance, the clearing banks will be *calling in* their loans to the discount houses. By this mechanism the discount houses smooth out the ebb and flow of funds between the government and non-government sector, preventing unnecessary shortages or surpluses of reserves at the clearing banks.

4.4.2.4 *The National Giro*

The National Giro began its operations in the U.K. in October 1968, rather later than other European countries such as Austria (1883), Switzerland (1906), and France (1918). Indeed, most of Europe had established postal giro systems before the Second World War. What is remarkable about the U.K. situation is that the establishment of a National Giro should occur so late.

The giro systems which operate in many different countries have, understandably, a variety of practices, but the essentials of a giro system are that it provides a simple, swift, and economical money-transmission service through the agency of a single centre which maintains the records of customers' accounts. The prime virtue of a giro system is that it is economical and speedy and accordingly the development of modern giro systems can be linked to the development of communications systems, in particular the railways, postal services, electronic sorting, and finally the computer. On the face of it, the justification for setting up a postal giro system in the U.K. seems self-evident: the Post Office has more than 21,000 post offices (50 per cent more branches than the major banks) which are open six days in the week and for much longer hours than the banks, and since the Post Office is a single firm, it can clearly operate a central accounting system. Furthermore, the Post Office had operated a savings bank (now the National Savings Bank) since 1861 and a postal order service (i.e. a simple form of money transmission service) from the beginning of 1881. Both of these services had been a welcome innovation to that section of the community which did not use the banking system as a means of saving and money transfer.

A survey conducted in 1965 found that only about a quarter of the population over the age of sixteen had a current account, and this suggested that there was a very considerable potential market of 'unbanked' individuals who for a variety of reasons had no wish to use the traditional banking system. It was the weekly wage earner and those with relatively low incomes who, it was thought, would be the primary beneficiaries of the National Giro and would also be attracted to it by virtue of their familiarity with its parent, the Post Office and correspondingly, their unfamiliarity with, and possible aversion to, the relatively costly services of the Clearing Banks.

The mechanism of the National Giro is fairly simple from the point of view of the customer. Payments can be made to other Giro account holders by either Giro transfer forms or by standing order arrangement, for both of which services there is currently no charge. For payments to those who do not hold Giro accounts, the system provides cheques which are crossed or uncrossed – in the latter case, payment may be made at a Post Office after authentification at the Giro centre, and for such payments a service charge is levied. The deposit of money by a customer is free and simple, since cash can be deposited at any Post Office and cheques deposited by free post to the National Giro Centre at Bootle in Lancashire. Initially, withdrawals of cash could be made only from two designated Post Offices which were selected by the customer when a Giro account was opened. This rather limited facility has steadily been extended by the Giro by means of the cash card available to all those whose income is paid directly into a Giro account, and to other Giro account holders, in the light of the behaviour of their account.

Table 4.6 shows the changes in the business of the National Giro since its inception, measured by the growth in deposits.

Although the growth in total deposits of the National Giro seems substantial, £20 million in 1969 and around £240 million in 1977, it is likely that the National Giro accounts represent less than 1 per cent of current account business in the U.K. Reference back to the National Giro's ambitions and the White Paper on the Giro published in 1965 reveal the extent of the failure of the Giro to meet the target growth. The National Giro itself expected to have well over 1½ million

TABLE 4.6
National Giro: net deposits
(average of monthly figures, £ m.)

1969	20·2
1970	40·4
1971	55·8
1972	66·6
1973	81·3
1974	104·4
1975	131·3
1976	174·1
1977 (Aug.)	239·1

Source: Financial Statistics, September 1977.

accounts by 1973, and the White Paper set a more modest target of 1,200,000. In fact, by the middle of 1971 the growth of accounts had levelled off at around 450,000 and by the end of 1972 the number of accounts was a mere 467,000 – over half a million accounts short of the White Paper target. Furthermore, the Giro was, and is, heavily dependent on the public sector providing about half the deposits of the Giro.

There are a number of factors which contributed to the disappointing start to the National Giro. First, the survey conducted in 1965 showed that although there was a very large proportion of the working population who did not have current accounts, this group was largely indifferent or opposed to receiving their income by cheque or credit transfer. In other words a large proportion of the 'unbanked' population seemed content to remain so and receive their earnings in cash. Secondly, the Clearing Banks had not only been hostile to the setting up of the National Giro but were actively competing with it by the introduction of the bank giro. Furthermore, the introduction of the cheque card, Barclaycard, and Access in the mid-1960s must have represented a set-back for the National Giro if it had hoped to attract some business away from the Clearing Banks. The introduction of current accounts by the Trustee Savings Banks must also have deflected or retained business of a kind which might well have gone to the National Giro.

Following the General Election of 1970 the National Giro was the subject of an investigation in respect of its future commercial viability. After a considerable period, it was finally announced in November 1971 that the Post Office had been advised against closure and, with a number of changes (including an increase in charges), the National Giro was expected to cover its operating costs by July 1973 and to be fully viable by July 1977. As a result of these changes, the National Giro was covering its operating costs by March 1973, and by March 1977 had an overall surplus of £2·1 million. In April 1975 the National Giro acknowledged that it should provide a wider range of banking services and a capital reconstruction took place, effective from 1 April 1975, and involving the conversion of loans into public dividend capital. At the same time, the National Giro was set new objectives:

(i) to earn an average return over the period 1975–6 to 1977–8, on public dividend capital plus retained profits, of 12½% per annum.

(ii) to pay dividends over the period 1975–6 to 1979–80 at least equal to the interest that would have been paid on the loans that were converted to public dividend capital.

National Giro claims that its financial results to 1977 indicate that it is in line with the above targets. Some of the additional services provided by the Giro include personal loan service, travellers' cheques and foreign currency, overdrafts for certain personal account holders, a Giro guarantee card for cashing cheques at any post office, as well as international giro facilities, bridging loans, budget accounts, and personal deposit account services which are to be introduced in 1978.

The Giro is very conscious of the fact that its growth, particularly in the area of personal accounts, had not been particularly successful. Even in 1977 the number of accounts had only just topped the half-million mark. In its submission to the Committee to Review the Functioning of Financial Institutions,[9] the Giro has emphasized the following points:

(i) The cash payments of wages to around 15 million people is wasteful of resources and involves considerable risk and cost of insurance.

(ii) If wages were paid by Giro, Giro maintain that this would result in a greater use of savings facilities and an increase in unspent balances.

(iii) A more recent survey indicates that a high proportion of those receiving cash wages would not object to payment by Giro.

(iv) Giro experiences unfair competition from the clearing banks who, it is claimed, do not operate their money transmission services at prices (charges) which reflect their cost.

[9]This committee, under the chairmanship of Sir Harold Wilson, was set up by the Government in 1977 partly in response to the secondary banking collapse of 1974. The broad terms of reference of this committee include, for example, an assessment of the role, functioning, and value of financial institutions in the U.K.

Accordingly the Giro submission recommends that:

(i)   The government should legislate so that firms could make monthly payments by credit transfer to employees rather than weekly cash payments. This has been achieved in France where now only about one-sixth of French wage-earners are paid weekly.

(ii) There should be acknowledgement of the unfair competition which the Giro experiences, and especially of the highly economic nature of the Giro's money transmission service.

(iii) The Government should review its own banking and money transmission services. Implicit in this recommendation is that the Government is not making as much use of its own National Giro as it could, for example the payment of wages to government employees. The Giro is aware of the potential economies of scale from which it could benefit with a larger number of transactions.

4.5 Secondary banking

We have already referred to the secondary banks in Section 4.3 and we shall examine them now in more detail. One approach in defining the secondary banks in the U.K. is to use the classification provided by the Bank of England. The statistics currently provided by the Bank in its *Quarterly Bulletin* identifies the following banking groups:

Accepting houses
Other British banks
American banks
Japanese banks
Other overseas banks
Consortium banks

Table 4.7 identifies the sterling and foreign currency deposits of both the primary (deposit banking) and secondary banking sectors, as of 20 October 1976. The data are derived from the figures published by the Bank of England. A number of characteristics are identifiable from the table itself.

(i)   A substantial proportion (57) per cent of sterling deposits are held by the London Clearing Banks and the Scottish and Northern Ireland deposit banks. This fact, together with the high value of sterling deposits, as an average, held by each type of banking institution (£4,045 million for each of the six London Clearing banks, and £2,131 million for all thirteen), reveals the dominance of the British deposit banks in operating the payments mechanism within the U.K.

(ii) The foreign banks, by contrast, account only for about 18 per cent of sterling deposits, whereas the position is reversed in

TABLE 4.7

Sterling and foreign currency deposits of listed banks,[a]
20 October 1976
(£ m.)

	Total deposits	Sterling deposits	% share	Foreign currency deposits	% share	Average deposits		
						Sterling deposits	Foreign currency deposits	Total
British banks:								
London Clearing Banks (6)	29,305	24,270	49	5,035	4	4,045	839	4,884
Scottish Clearing Banks (3)	3,162	2,558	5	604	1	853	201	1,054
Northern Ireland banks (4)	901	876	2	25	<1	219	6	225
Total (13)	33,368	27,704	57	5,664	5	2,131	435	2,556
Acceptance houses (30)	6,332	2,755	6	3,577	3	92	119	211
Other British banks (70)	20,727	9,315	19	11,412	10	133	163	296
American banks (58)	47,284	5,096	10	42,188	37	88	727	815
Japanese banks (19)	16,486	463	1	16,023	14	24	843	867
Other overseas banks (107)	30,690	2,916	6	27,774	25	27	259	286
Consortium banks (28)	7,326	432	0·9	6,894	6	15	246	262
Total (325)								
TOTALS	162,213	48,681	100·0	113,532	100·0			

[a] 'Listed banks' are those banks which have agreed to maintain the minimum reserve ratio laid down by the Bank of England under *Competition and Credit Control* and which is currently 12½% per cent. This is dealt with more fully in Chapters 5 and 6.

Source: Bank of England *Quarterly Bulletin*, vol. 16, No. 4 (December 1976).

respect of foreign currency deposits, foreign banks holding 82 per cent of such deposits. Although the London Clearing Banks hold substantial amounts of deposits in foreign currency, with average deposits comparable with those of the foreign banks in the U.K., the Clearing Banks' share of the total is only 4 per cent.

(iii) The American banks (from the United States), together with the 'other overseas banks', account for 62 per cent of total foreign currency deposits, and 76 per cent of the foreign currency deposits held by foreign banks and consortium banks in the U.K.

(iv) The foreign currency deposits dominate the business of the *foreign* banks in the U.K. – about 91 per cent of their total deposits – in contrast to the *British* secondary banks (acceptance houses and 'other British banks') whose foreign currency deposits amount only to 55 per cent of their total deposits.

Obviously, the above points can only represent a partial view of the operation of the secondary banks, not least because we have observed only their liabilities, whereas, of course, other aspects of their operations are reflected in the assets side of their balance sheets. Additional features of secondary bank operation can be established by reference to their observed behaviour as well as by an examination of their overall balance sheets, and this is the next stage in our discussion.

A crucial feature of secondary bank operation, one which sharply differentiates it from the operation of the primary banks, is the fact that the number of depositors and the average size of deposit is very different from that of the primary banks. Calculating the number of accounts is rather a dubious exercise, but we can make a rough estimate on the basis of the size of deposits. We can do this by means of the known size of deposit acceptable to the secondary banks (£50,000–£100,000 minimum). On this basis the secondary banks held around 1 million to 2 million accounts whereas the primary banks had around fourteen million. This very substantial difference in the numbers of deposits[10] affects the operational behaviour of the secondary banks since they are unable to benefit from the 'economics of large numbers' which the primary banks can utilize (see Section 3.2.4) and must therefore structure their balance sheets on a rather different basis. Although secondary banks are required to observe the 12½ per cent reserve ratio (Section 5.2.2.2) which relates to sterling assets, the most significant aspect of their operation from the bank's

[10]The figures we have suggested are intended to give some idea of the order of magnitude rather than exact measurement.

point of view is the nature of the maturity relationship of their assets *and* liabilities. Since the number of deposits is relatively small and the size of the deposits is relatively large, the secondary banks attempt some *matching* of assets and liabilities in respect of their term to maturity. One reason for this simple objective may be understood if we consider a balance sheet which is perfectly matched. Under such circumstances (ignoring any risk of default) the bank would be operating so that its loans would be repaid at precisely the same time as its own liabilities fell due for repayment. In principle, there would be no need for such a bank to operate in terms of a liquidity principle in respect of the *assets side* of the balance sheet, as do the primary banks. This approach can be observed in the secondary banks' business in foreign currencies. *Table 4.8* illustrates how the secondary banks attempt this matching operation.

On the face of it, the matching of the assets and liabilities is far from perfect, although they are in fact correlated. There are three chief reasons for this lack of perfect matching: one is that such a matching is

TABLE 4.8
Maturity analysis of liabilities and claims of U.K. banks and certain other institutions, in foreign currencies.[a]
(18 May 1977: $m.)

Maturity	Liabilities	%	Claims	%	Net position
Less than 8 days	43,593	21	35,369	17	−8,324
8 days to less than 1 month	37,663	18	28,723	14	−8,940
1 month to less than 3 months	56,434	27	45,897	22	−10,537
3 months to less than 6 months	37,957	18	32,053	15	−5,904
6 months to less than 1 year	17,644	9	15,774	8	−1,870
1 year to less than 3 years	9,844	5	20,259	10	+10,415
3 years and over	3,640	2	29,187	14	+25,547
	206,775	100	207,162	100	+387

[a]These are gross figures and include some unlisted banks.

Source: Bank of England *Quarterly Bulletin,* vol 17, No. 5 (December 1977).

unlikely to be feasible since the demand and supply of funds is, overall, not symmetrical. Roughly speaking, there are likely to be more people and firms wishing to borrow 'long' than those people and firms who wish to lend 'long'. Accordingly, Table 4.8 shows that total claims for one year and over amounted to £49,446 million and total liabilities only £13,484 million. Another reason for mis-matching is that the bank itself may *choose* not to match as closely as is feasible. One explanation for this apparently imprudent attitude is that the bank may have firm expectations of interest rates falling in the future. In this case, it would be appropriate to increase its long-term lending (at current 'high' interest rates) and reduce its long-term borrowing at current rates. When interest rates fall, the bank would then attempt to improve the matching at the long end by increasing its longer-dated liabilities to match its claims at the long end. Finally, since long-term lending yields higher rates of return than short-term lending, the bank may choose to mis-match in order to benefit from higher profit margins, albeit at greater risk.

Finally we may observe the operations of the secondary banks by referring to their balance sheets, and in particular to the distribution and nature of their assets. *Table 4.9* represents a simplified balance sheet for the secondary banks operating in the U.K. and from it we can observe certain features which reflect the operation of all the secondary banks.

(i)   The reserve ratio is fairly high (15 per cent) in relation to the 12½ per cent minimum required. Indeed, some of the foreign secondary banks have very high reserve ratios; the 'other overseas banks', for example (accounting for almost 25 per cent of total business), had a reserve ratio of 18 per cent on that particular day. This reflects the point made earlier that these banks' operations are much less concerned with the 'liquidity' of their assets in the way the primary banks are. Furthermore, the reserve assets which the secondary banks hold are a much smaller proportion of their total assets than that of the primary banks, and this again reflects the different emphasis of their business operations.

(ii) The sterling and non-sterling assets and liabilities are very closely matched. Thus:

	Sterling	*Non-sterling*
Assets	£24,388 m.	£112,306 m.
Liabilities	£21,273 m.	£112,858 m.

(iii) In addition to the foreign currency overseas loans and deposits, £78,448 million and £76,916 million respectively, the U.K. banking sector is an important provider and recipient of funds. The bulk of its borrowing and lending is done by and from the banks themselves, most of it by secondary banks. These 'inter-bank deposits', as they are termed, are an important means by which an *individual bank* is able to match its assets and liabilities to the extent that it wishes. The development of this particular money market is discussed further in Chapter 8. Although this item of lending and

TABLE 4.9

Main categories of assets and deposit liabilities held by secondary banks in the U.K.

(18 May 1977: £ m.)

Assets

			% of total
(A)	*Sterling assets*		
	Reserve assets	1,971	1·4
	(average reserve ratio 15%)		
	Market loans (other than reserve assets)		
	Banks in U.K. and discount market	6,394	4·6
	U.K. local authorities	2,205	1·6
	Certificates of deposit	1,592	1·1
	Other	620	0·4
	Advances		
	U.K.	9,416	6·7
	Overseas	313	0·2
	Other assets	1,877	1·3
	Total	24,388	17·5
(B)	*Other currency assets*		
	Market loans and advances		
	Overseas	78,448	56·3
	Banks in U.K. and discount market	22,496	16·1
	U.K. private sector	6,354	4·6
	U.K. public sector	3,131	2·2
	Certificates of deposit	1,877	1·3
	Total	112,306	80·6
(C)	*Other sterling and other currency assets*	2,707	1·9
	TOTAL	139,411	100·0
	Acceptances	2,281	

(continued on p. 72)

TABLE 4.9 (continued)

Liabilities[a]

			% of total
(D) *Sterling deposits*			
	U.K. banking sector	7,854	5·8
	Other U.K.	8,521	6·3
	Overseas	2,370	1·8
	Certificates of deposit	2,524	1·9
	Total	21,273	15·9
	(of which sight deposits)	4,239	3·2
(E) *Other currency deposits*			
	U.K. banking sector	22,599	16·8
	Other U.K.	3,881	3·0
	Overseas	76,916	57·3
	Certificates of deposit	9,962	7·4
	Total	112,858	84·1
	TOTAL	134,131	100·0

[a]Capital and other liabilities have not been included and this explains the difference between the sum of the assets and liabilities.

Source: Bank of England *Quarterly Bulletin,* vol. 17 No. 4 (December 1977)

borrowing includes the discount market, it is unlikely that much more than 4 or 5 per cent of these funds flow in that direction.

(iv)   Consistent with the emphasis of the secondary banks on term deposits and term lending, the volume of sight deposits is correspondingly small – a mere 3·2 per cent of total deposits.

(v)   Although the secondary banks deal for the most part with foreign currency business, the size of their advances in sterling to U.K borrowers (£9,416 million) is by no means insignificant. The sterling advances made by the clearing banks at 18 May 1977 amounted to £15,667 million and the relationship between the two figures indicates the extent to which secondary banking has contributed to meeting the demand for term loans. It is perhaps not surprising that the clearing banks established secondary banking subsidiaries or took a share in secondary banks in order to participate in this expanding banking activity. Although the secondary banking subsidiaries of the clearing banks account for possibly 40 per cent to 50 per cent of the sterling advances made by the secondary banking sector, the share of sterling advances obtained by the other secondary banks is still fairly large and indicates their competitiveness in this field of banking business.

(vi) Table 4.9 shows that the secondary banks were holding a total of £3,469 million certificates of deposit as part of their assets, but had liabilities of £12,486 million certificates of deposit. In other words, the secondary banks are net issuers of certificates of deposit. Since the term of a certificate is flexible (see Chapter 7 for further discussion and glossary), the issuing of such certificates, as well as their purchase, does allow the secondary banks greater capacity to match their assets and liabilities.

(vii) Finally, we would draw attention to the secondary bank lending to U.K. local authorities. Although this asset is less important than previously (in 1970 this form of lending accounted for almost one quarter of secondary bank assets) it is nevertheless a substantial asset, and the role of the secondary banks in providing local authority finance is important. This topic will be dealt with further in Chapter 8.

Although the fundamental operations of the secondary banks are common to all, there are differences in their operations, which, in part, derive from their individual origins and development. In particular, the accepting houses are an interesting example of a group of firms whose original functions have been supplemented by others in response to the pressures of competition and change.

The traditional business of the accepting houses was the 'accepting' of bills of exchange, a process which effectively meant the addition of the good name and reputation of the accepting house to the bill (for a commission, of course), thus enhancing the marketability of the bill. The sale or 'discounting' of the bill would usually be arranged by the accepting house, and only in the case of default on the bill would the accepting house be liable to use its own resources to cover the bill. However, although the accepting houses are still heavily involved in this and similar business, it is relatively less important than other activities. For example, in 1954 the value of acceptances in relation to total assets amounted to about 60 per cent, whereas this ratio had fallen to around 18 per cent in 1977. Another activity of the accepting houses is to act as agents, mainly for U.K. companies, in the new issue market where they advise, arrange, and underwrite new capital issues. They have also extended their advisory activities in the direction of investment management, and especially in connection with pension funds. However, the major change in their activities has been the move towards full banking activity rather than mere agency work. A stimulus to such activity came with the development of the Euro-currency market and with this application of their expertise to the establishment and operation of the Euro-bond market. The growth of the inter-bank market has also provided additional opportunities. In the case of the other secondary banks, their establishment and development has been largely the result of response to one particular phenomenon: the growth of the Euro-currency, and in particular, the Euro-dollar market. The central role of London in this field has contributed to the rapid growth in the number of secondary banks.

4.6 Other deposit-taking firms

4.6.1 BUILDING SOCIETIES

Table 4.2 (p. 52) shows the importance of building societies as deposit-receiving institutions. Total sterling deposits are almost as large as the clearing banks, and second only to the insurance and pension funds within the category of non-bank financial intermediaries. Not only are the building societies important in terms of their total share of financial activity, but they are also highly specialized. Furthermore, their activity is of importance to a large proportion of the population since there are over 16 million investors in the societies, and well over 5 million borrowers. *Table4.10* provides the main items on the aggregate balance sheet. The difference between depositors and shareholders is largely a technical one in that

TABLE 4.10

Balance sheet of building societies in Great Britain, 1976
(end year: £ m.)

Liabilities		%	Assets		%
Shares and deposits	26,101	(92·8)	Mortgages	22,500	(80·0)
Official loans	20	(0·007)	British Government		
Accrued interest	340	(1·2)	securities	2,075	(7·4)
Reserves	970	(3·4)	Local authority		
Other liabilities	700	(2·6)	long-term debt	1,580	(5·6)
			Short-term assets	1,500	(5·3)
	28,131	(100·0)	Other assets	476	(1·7)
				28,131	(100·0)

Source: Financial Statistics, September 1977.

depositors are creditors of the society whereas the shareholders are 'members'; but since the societies are non-profit-making organizations, the shareholders are not shareholders in the commercial sense. The building societies are well established and trusted, so that it is not surprising that the value of deposits is small in relation to the value of shares which earn higher rates of interest than those on deposits. Further, the societies offer several kinds of savings opportunities to investors as a means of increasing the stability of funds deposited. Some shares are either for fixed terms or are in the form of contractual savings, and of course such shares offer higher rates of interest than the bulk of shares which are effectively withdrawable on demand (although technically the societies may demand notice of withdrawal, usually of one month). In 1974 the government made substantial loans of £300 million to offset a high rate of withdrawals, which would have triggered off a much greater rise in the rate of interest on mortgages than that which actually occurred. The item 'official loans' refers to the remaining balances from the government loan. The reserves which the societies have built up are used largely to maintain a mandatory minimum reserve ratio laid down by the Chief Registrar of Friendly Societies.

On the assets side of the balance sheet, the rather surprising feature is that 80 per cent of all assets takes the form of a single asset – mortgages (loans to borrowers for house purchase) which are nominally long-term, usually between 15 and 25 years. However, people change houses once every seven years on average and this means that on the sale of a house the mortgage is, albeit temporarily, repaid. The term of the societies' lending is in sharp contrast to the bulk of their liabilities which, though technically not repayable on demand, may be treated as such except in the case of fairly large sums. Indeed it is this aspect of building society shares which is a crucial element in ensuring an adequate flow of funds into the societies. Clearly the societies are in no way matching their assets and liabilities with respect to term, but are seemingly borrowing very short to lend long – a policy, which, on the face of it, could lead to insolvency. How do the societies survive? There are a number of explanations, but the following are the chief ones:

(i) House prices tend to keep pace with the rate of inflation and this ensures that the security for a mortgage (the house) is a very sound one.

(ii) The interest on shares and deposits is paid twice yearly, and almost invariably it is merely credited to the existing holding. This effectively provides additional funds for the societies since most depositors are prepared to leave the accrued interest in their accounts.

(iii) Existing mortgages are being repaid continuously in the form of principal, together with the interest payments. The societies are careful to check that potential borrowers are likely to be able to make regular payments to the societies out of income, with a minimum risk of default, and there is therefore a regular flow of funds from this source.

The investments which the societies hold are largely central and local government debt, and the composition of these investments is statutorily determined; the other assets represent the societies' premises and equipment. Finally, the item 'cash' accounts for till money and deposits held with the clearing banks which facilitate their day-to-day operations.

As a further safeguard to shareholders and depositors, the societies are obliged to maintain an additional asset ratio which is a minimum liquidity ratio of $7\frac{1}{2}$ per cent. This is calculated as the ratio of cash plus investments to total assets, and in practice the societies have been very cautious, maintaining a ratio of more than double the required ratio for many years.

4.6.2 TRUSTEE SAVINGS BANKS

Arguably the most dramatic change in the operation of U.K. financial institutions has concerned the Trustee Savings Banks, following the passing of the Trustee Savings Banks Act of 1976.

The T.S.B.s have been in existence since the early part of the nineteenth century and, like the building societies, are non-profit-making financial institutions. They differ from the building societies, however, in at least one respect, and that is that they are geographically localized whereas the larger building societies tend to have offices on a nationwide basis. The savings banks flourished during the nineteenth century since they provided both a valuable service and safe provision for the savings of the un-banked public – largely from the lower-income groups. The setting up of the Post Office Savings Bank in 1861 proved a setback to the savings banks, but the establishment of the Special Investment department in 1870 (a facility not provided by the Post Office savings bank until 1966) gave the remaining savings banks considerable impetus. The basic operations of the T.S.B.s prior to 1965, however, can be summarized by reference to the two departments into which they were divided, the Ordinary departments (providing savings accounts) and the Special Investment departments.

Deposits with the Ordinary department – a maximum of £10,000 – would earn a fixed rate of interest for the depositor, and the funds obtained would be transferred to the National Debt Commissioners to be invested in British Government securities. In turn, the T.S.B.s would receive the rate paid to depositors plus sufficient for management expenses, and a further sum for reserves. If an Ordinary department depositor had not less than £50 in that department, the customer could open an account in the Special Investment department. Funds obtained from this department by the T.S.B.s could then be invested in a range of public sector assets (central, local, and overseas governments) but with the approval of the National Debt Commissioners. The rate of interest received by a depositor in the Special Investment department would not, however, be uniform, since this would vary not only with the term of the deposit, but also with the maturity structure of the assets held by its Special Investment department.

In 1965 approval was given for the T.S.B.s to provide cheque and other current account services for customers.[11] However, the growth of the cheque accounts was not especially remarkable until full bank status has been accorded to the T.S.B.s in March 1976, when the Trustee Savings Banks Act, 1976, became operative and provided 'that each Trustee Savings Bank shall have power to carry on the business of banking'. This legislation followed the Page Committee's Report on National Savings which effectively recommended that the T.S.B.s should be freed from government control and allowed to develop full banking services. Not surprising, the condition for such freedom was that the T.S.B.s should amalgamate into much larger units. Within one year of the passing of the Trustee Savings Bank Act, the 72 T.S.B.s in existence at the time had been reduced to 20. The supervisory authority over the T.S.B.s is vested in a Trustee Savings Banks Central Board which has the necessary regulatory powers.

The T.S.B.s now provide a wide range of banking services: cheque cards, personal loans, overdraft facilities, term deposits, as well as the familiar savings and investment accounts. Prior to the Act of 1976, the T.S.B.s had already established the Central Trustee Savings Bank Ltd., which acts as banker to the T.S.B.s and, in particular, is a member of the Bankers Clearing House, acting for the T.S.B.s in the clearing of cheques. A further important service provided by the C.T.S.B. Ltd. is that of facilities and advice in respect of investments.

It is likely that with over 1,600 branches and the low handling charges to customers, together with the emphasis on the personal account, it is possible that the T.S.B.s – and other banking firms – might attract a considerable volume of business from the estimated 15 million income receivers who do not operate a cheque account.

[11]From 21 November 1976 *T.S.B.s* current accounts and Special Investment Departments were amalgamated to form the New Department.

4.6.2.1 National Savings Bank

Although the National Savings Bank, formerly the Post Office Savings Bank, is not a trustee savings bank (trustees are redundant since the National Savings Bank is operated by the State which, presumably, is trustworthy), it is nevertheless an organization very similar in character to the T.S.B.s prior to their emergence as proper banks in 1976. The N.S.B. provides both ordinary account and investment account facilities, and the funds so obtained are invested in British government securities. Although the ordinary and investment account facilities are the same as the T.S.B.s however, there are a number of differences between the T.S.B.s and the National Savings Bank

(i)   The number of accounts with the N.S.B. is very much higher than those with the T.S.B.s, but the average size of these accounts is very much less.

(ii)   The turnover of accounts in the ordinary departments of the T.S.B.s and the N.S.B. is very different. For example, in 1967 (the year prior to the setting up of the National Giro), the ratio of withdrawals to total balances for the T.S.B.s and the N.S.B. respectively was 1·28 and 0·37. In other words, only about one-third of the balances in the N.S.B. turned over during that year, whereas the whole balance in the T.S.B.s turned 1¼ times. The probable reason for this is the fairly low upper limit on deposits imposed by the Post Office, which is sufficient to prevent its use as a depository for wages and salaries. (On the grounds of cost of operation, the Post Office has resisted the use of its ordinary account as a *de facto* current account.)

(iii)   The much larger number of outlets for the N.S.B., i.e. every Post Office, provides a potential advantage to the N.S.B. over the T.S.B.s with their much smaller number of outlets.

4.6.3 FINANCE HOUSES

In 1965 there were 26 finance houses with assets of over £5 million but by 1972 the number had fallen to 14 as the result of a number of mergers. Of these 14, 5 were re-classified as banks, following the introduction of *Competition and Credit Control* (see Section 7.4.1) and currently there are 8 listed finance houses. It is evident from the heading of *Table 4.11* that the assets and liabilities shown are not a complete representation of finance house operations. Nevertheless, the official figures provide a broad indication of their business activities. It is clear from the main asset items that the major part of the business of the finance houses is the provision of funds for the hire

TABLE 4.11

Finance houses: holdings of selected assets and liabilities, Great Britain
(end 1975: £ m.)

Liabilities		Assets	
Deposits	415	Hire purchase debt	
Bills discounted with		outstanding	685
U.K. banks and discount		Other advances and	
houses	142	loans	153
Other borrowing	196	Securities other than	
Unearned finance		trade investments	32
charges	105	Trade investments	65
Issued capital and		Leased assets	264
reserves	215		
		Total	1,199
Total	1,073		

Source: Financial Statistics, September 1977.

purchase of various kinds of goods. This form of instalment credit is used by individuals and firms who wish to purchase consumer durables, machinery, and equipment. A considerable proportion of this £685 million provided by the finance houses flows to companies rather than individuals, because of the sustained and discriminatory pressure from the monetary authorities on consumer borrowing. In this way, the finance houses have moved to financing and competing for business in the company sector rather than the personal sector. Other advances and loans consist of finance to dealers in motor cars, for instance, in order to enable them to hold stocks, and this in turn provides a business outlet for the finance house when motor cars are sold at the retail end. The item 'trade investments' includes funds placed with the subsidiaries of the finance houses which specialize in factoring. Broadly speaking, this can involve the specialist company (the factor) taking over the debts of a company. One form of factoring, for example, involves the factor providing up to 80 per cent of the value of invoices, and clearly this could be of considerable advantage to a company since, for one thing, its cash situation would be eased. 'Leased Assets' represent the leasing business of the finance houses, which between 1966 and 1976 has grown five-fold. The leasing of assets such as ships, computers, aircraft, and other costly pieces of equipment is an alternative to hire purchase (which involves the option to purchase at the end of the hire period for a nominal figure) and other forms of credit, e.g. a term loan. Leasing, which lasts the length of life of the asset, may be advantageous to firms, and especially those which are not making profits, since the finance house can take advantage of the various tax allowances and incorporate this benefit in the rental charge. Leasing may also benefit a firm in time of credit shortage since the firm, in effect, is guaranteed the finance for the purpose intended, and for the period required. 'Securities other than trade investments' consist of relatively liquid assets, for example Treasury bills and other eligible reserve assets.

The first three items on the liabilities side of the balance sheet give some indication of the reliance which the finance houses place on the banking system as a source of funds. A high proportion of deposits are obtained from the secondary banking sector, as well as borrowing, by use of overdraft facilities. The finance houses compete for funds from the non-bank sector, and as far as the personal and company sector is concerned, such competition would have to be very strong indeed to attract depositors, since the alternatives, such as building society shares and other less risky forms of asset, are more attractive to many potential lenders, even though such assets may not offer as keen a set of interest rates as those offered by the more flexible finance houses.

4.6.4 OTHER FINANCIAL INTERMEDIARIES

This section is concerned with the other important financial organization which developed as part of the system of financial intermediation. These do not include a number of *ad hoc* bodies, established over the years – largely under the aegis of the government – which have a fairly specialized role: for example, the Industrial and Commercial Finance Corporation Ltd.,[12] the Finance Corporation for Industry Ltd.,[12] the National Enterprise Board. In relation to other financial intermediaries, the volume of business conducted by these *ad hoc* bodies is comparatively small.

4.6.4.1 Insurance companies and pension funds

Insurance companies and pension funds are linked in this section for two reasons. One reason is that a significant proportion of the pension fund business is done by the insurance companies, and the other reason is that the operation of a pension fund involves the same sort of approach as that of organizing life assurance. As Table 4.1 (p. 50) reveals, the volume of funds accounted for by the pension funds and the insurance companies in the form of life assurance funds (usually known as long-term funds) is very substantial.

Broadly speaking, the business of insurance, as the term implies, is

---

[12]These two firms have now been merged into a holding company, Finance for Industry Ltd., for the provision of short- and medium-term loans. Although agreement between the shareholding banks has been reached that up to £1,000 million may be provided, only a small fraction of this has been used so far.

with risks and, in particular, the spread of risks. In the case of life assurance, the insurance company is able to calculate a spread of the risk of death over time on the basis of the mortality figures available to the companies, and it is in this area of life assurance that about one-half of the insurance companies' business is concerned. The other forms of insurance which provide the companies' General Funds are associated with contingency risks, such as fire, theft, etc., The probability of such events occurring may be estimated and the risks spread over all those firms and individuals subject to such risks and wishing to obtain insurance cover.

The provision of pensions clearly is associated with the question of mortality and life-expectancy, and by virtue of their life assurance business, the insurance companies are experts in this particular area. They operate two principal services: one through a combination of an endowment policy, plus annuity[13] purchasable on maturity of the policy; the other; by the simple accumulation of funds sufficient to purchase an adequate annuity on retirement.

In order to meet such future obligations, the insurance companies and the pension funds need to make use of their existing funds, together with available new funds, in such a way as to ensure that when policies mature, or when retirement occurs, the companies have sufficient funds to meet these commitments. A fundamental problem facing insurance companies and pension funds is that the future financial obligation of the companies is calculated on the basis of a process of continual investment of received funds (premiums, etc.) which will yield a known dividend or rate of interest. The final obligation of the companies will be greater, therefore, than the funds received from policy-holders or potential pensioners. Thus the companies' current operations in the form of investment policy must take account of this, and accordingly the need to maximize current and future profits from investments will be of paramount importance. This objective must be consistent, however, with financial prudence, which in this case will require the firms to acknowledge two factors: (i) the need to adjust the maturity structure of their assets to take into account the long-term nature of their liabilities, and (ii) the need to adjust the composition of their assets so as to benefit (from the point of view of reducing risk) from asset diversification.

The different asset structures of the insurance companies and the pension funds do reflect the fact that pension funds are specialist institutions whose requirements are not precisely those of the insurance companies. In particular, the pension funds' obligations are related to the salaries of contributors at retirement. The

[13]An annuity is a series of payments in the future which are 'bought' by a payment of a lump-sum in the present.

implication here is that the pension funds need to ensure that their investments will rise, both in capital value and yield, in line with the general rise in incomes of the contributors to the pension schemes. Until recently, the purchase of ordinary shares was one way of ensuring that the value of an investment kept pace with the inflationary growth of incomes. Traditionally the pension funds hold a much higher proportion of their assets in the company sector (in particular, ordinary shares) than the insurance companies do. There are some similarities, however, between the insurance companies and the pension funds in that the bulk of their assets comprises a mixture of government and local authority securities, as well as company securities. The remainder is comprised largely of loans, mortgages, and investment in property, and only a small amount is invested in short-term assets (in view of the long-term nature of their commitments). The recent behaviour of insurance companies and pension funds, however, reveals their preparedness to adapt their investment of new funds to changing opportunities. The published figures for newly acquired assets during 1976 shows that for both groups there was very heavy investment in British Government securities, and reduced investment in loans, mortgages, and property. This switch no doubt reflected the expectations of falling interest rates and the associated capital gains, as well as the high level of yields on British government securities obtaining at the time. Uncertainty about the movements of company security prices no doubt contributed an additional factor of consideration.

Although the insurance companies and the pension funds appeared to switch fairly heavily to government securities in 1976, none the less both the insurance companies and the pension funds continue to dominate the provision of long-term capital for the company sector. For example, net *issues* of new securities of public companies in 1976 amounted to £1,080 million, whereas the total *purchases* of such securities by the insurance companies and the pension funds amounted to £1,356 million, i.e. other sectors were responsible for the net sale of company securities since the total purchased by the insurance companies and the pension funds *exceeded* the net issues in that year. Indeed, if we look back over the period 1971–6, we find that the purchases of company securities by the insurance companies and pension funds amounted to £6,613 million, whereas the new issues of securities during the same period amounted to £4,837 million. These two types of financial intermediary clearly are very important in absorbing new securities as well as helping to 'make a market' in existing securities on the Stock Exchange.

4.6.4.2 Investment trusts and unit trusts

The grouping of these two types of financial organization is founded on a major common element in their operation, and that is their capacity to spread risks on behalf of the individual investor. Furthermore, one aspect of their balance sheet suggests another common factor, and that is that the type of claims they hold are of the same kind as the claims which they create. Both points will become more apparent in the following account of the two types of organization. Investment trust companies are quantitatively more important than unit trusts, the market value of assets of unit trusts amounting only to £2,622 million as against the £6,066 million held by investment trusts in 1976.

Investment trusts. Although commonly designated as trusts, these firms are not proper trusts but are public companies whose funds are obtained in the normal way, i.e. by the issue of ordinary shares, etc. Funds thus obtained are then used to purchase other financial assets, and in 1976 almost 90 per cent were other companies' securities. The remaining investments were in short-term assets such as sterling certificates of deposits, local authority temporary debt, and British government securities. The share of this latter group of assets was only 8 per cent of total assets; £486 million out of a total £6,066 million.

The benefit of an investment trust company to the individual investor is that by the purchase of the assets issued by the company, he can obtain a 'share' in a *wide spread of assets* which are owned by the company. In other words, it allows the investor to avoid putting all his eggs in one basket. Furthermore, if the company is managed by experienced directors, then the individual benefits additionally from the investment skills embodied in the company. In order to divest oneself of a holding in such a company, it is necessary only to sell the asset, be it share or loan stock, through the normal channels. The price obtained will be that quoted on the Stock Exchange.

Unit trusts. These intermediaries offer similar benefits to the investor, but operate rather differently. In particular, the unit trusts are operated as trusts in that there is a company acting as trustee for the owners of units of the trust as well as another company which manages the trust and decides on its investment policy. The Department of Trade and Industry exercises close supervision of unit trusts in order to protect investors, most of whom are individual savers attracted both by the relative security of investing in this way and the tax advantages which obtain in connection with some of the methods by which units may be purchased. The purchase and sale of units in the trust is relatively simple: it does not involve the purchase or sale of *existing* securities (as with the investment trusts) but it involves the *creation* of new units or the *elimination* of units in response to the demand. Units are bought and sold from the trust itself and not through the Stock Exchange, as are the shares of investment trusts. When units are purchased, they are bought at a price which is geared to the total value of the trust, and when units are sold they, too, are re-purchased by the trust at a price which ensures that the total value of units corresponds directly with the value of the fund. This means that if the market value of the assets owned by the trust declines, then the buying and selling price of units also will decline. Accordingly, the value of units will vary as the market valuation of the assets of the fund varies. The calculation of the buying and selling price of units by the trust is determined by a formula laid down by the Department of Trade and Industry which sets a maximum offer price (the price of a unit when sold by the management company) and a minimum bid price (the price of a unit when bought by the management company). The difference between the two is partly accounted for by various expenses involved in buying and selling, e.g. brokerage charges and contract stamp, and also the profit, or 'turn', of the management company. Since the management company's profit from the unit trust depends on the number of units which are traded, it is in the interest of the management company to ensure that the trust is a successful, attractive, and expanding one. In this way, there is a built-in inducement for the managers of the fund to be as effective as is possible on behalf of the unit holders.

4.7 Secondary banking and the problem of supervision

Towards the end of 1973 a number of deposit-taking institutions on the fringe of the banking system experienced considerable withdrawals of their deposits. That is how the Bank of England introduced, in its Report for 1973–4, the problem of the collapse of a number of secondary banks. The first sign of a crisis was the collapse of London and County Securities, followed by Cedar Holdings and other firms. Possibly the most well-known name to be involved was Slater, Walker Ltd., the banking firm within the Slater, Walker Group.

What were the immediate causes of the failure of some firms and the acute liquidity difficulties of others?

One important factor was the very rapid rise in bank advances during 1972 and 1973, followed by a sharp response on the part of the authorities in the middle of 1973, which attempted to impose restraint. By the middle of 1974 such curbs on the banking system were appearing to have an affect. However, during the expansionary period between the end of 1971 and the middle of 1973 the banking system as a whole was comfortably above the minimum reserve ratio of 12½ per cent. The banks, both primary and secondary, increased their lending to one sector in particular – the financial sector. The share of total advances to this sector rose from 9 per cent in November 1971 to 16 per cent by November 1973, and within this general category of lending the amount which was loaned to property companies rose as a percentage share of total advances from 3 per cent to 6 per cent. The comparative figures in Table 4.12 give some idea of the amounts of money involved.

TABLE 4.12

Bank advances to manufacturing and property in Great Britain
(£ m.)

	November 1971	November 1973
Manufacturing	3,669	6,542
Property	499	2,094

Source: Bank of England *Statistical Abstract*, No. 2.

Heavily involved in this lending to property companies were secondary and fringe banks: lending by such banks rose more than six-fold during the two years. By November 1973 it was becoming evident that the authorities were determined to halt the rapid growth in credit, and one sign of their determination was the rise in interest rates during the second half of 1973. The Minimum Lending Rate rose from 7½ per cent in June 1973 to 13 per cent in November 1973. Other interest rates moved in step, including rates prevailing in the parallel money markets: these rates of interest are of particular significance to the secondary banks. The rise in interest rates was associated with, and accompanied by, a change in the fortunes of property companies who were experiencing falling property values due to the cut-back in the credit which had hitherto pushed up values. In this way, some of the secondary banks found themselves holding assets which were relatively long-term and in the form of loans to property companies, whereas the security for such loans was declining in value or nearly worthless. Their deposit liabilities, on the other hand, were of relatively short duration, and with the rapid change in monetary conditions (credit tightness) such deposits were being withdrawn. The banks which found themselves in this predicament were experiencing the classic circumstances associated with bank insolvency.

A more general explanation which can be put forward to explain the banking crisis during 1973 and 1974 is the lack of adequate supervision of the banking system at the time, as well as the uncertain demarcation of responsibility for supervision within the government.

So far in this book we have had little difficulty in defining and classifying those financial firms which we were considering. It was possible to distinguish them by virtue of their methods of operation and/or by the nature of their balance sheets. However at the more practical level of banking supervision, distinguishing characteristics need to be sharply defined in order to eliminate ambiguity and argument. Until the 1973–4 crisis, this problem of definition had never really been settled satisfactorily. Entry into the E.E.C. and the need to conform to the proposed harmonization of banking law, together with the crisis discussed above, forced the issue. The somewhat complicated situation can be summarized by reference to the relevant legislation which acknowledges the existence of 'banks' *by virtue of a particular function or purpose* – there is no *general* definition.

(i)   Under the Exchange Control Act, 1947, a number of banks are listed which are authorized to deal in foreign currency and to perform certain delegated functions. This type of bank is known as an 'authorised bank'.

(ii)   The Companies Act, 1948, provides for banks which are permitted to maintain hidden reserves: these are known as Schedule 8 banks. When the clearing banks were Schedule 8 banks (which they no longer are) this classification was probably the most 'gilt-edged'. The Registrar of Companies can be selective in the registration of this type of bank and thus can exclude the undesirable firms.

(iii)   The Protection of Depositors Act, 1963, establishes the conditions under which companies may advertise for deposits. Section 127 of the Companies Act of 1967 provides exemption to certain banks from the disclosure conditions of the Protection of Depositors Act, 1963. Under this same act, those banks not exempt (i.e. those firms which are not 'Section 127' banks), and who wish to advertise for deposits, are obliged to publish their accounts in a prescribed manner and at certain intervals. It is significant that the Department of Trade and Industry is not empowered to investigate or supervise the banks which it places on the exempt list.

(iv)   In 1966, what was then the Board of Trade assumed responsibility for deciding which 'banks' were banks from the point of view of their exemption from the provisions of the Money Lenders Act, 1900. If a 'bank' was granted this exemption, it was then able to reclaim loans even if it was not a licensed money lender or classified as a bank under previous definitions. Under Section 123 of the Companies Act, 1967, the Board of Trade (later to become the Department of Trade and Industry) was empowered to issue certificates establishing certain banks as *bona fide* banks, but *only in this limited sense* of their having the exemption qualification. The many banks which obtained this beneficial certificate became known as '123 banks'. It was the '123 banks' (or 'fringe' banks) which chiefly were involved in the crisis of 1973 and 1974. The granting of such a certification, however, was conditional on such firms fulfilling certain functional criteria laid down by the Board, but the Board did not have powers to supervise the business operation of the '123 banks'.

The Consumer Credit Act passed in 1974 will ensure that almost every firm involved in the general provision of credit will be required to obtain a licence from the Office of Fair Trading. The Office will be able to take into account the past behaviour of the applicant before deciding whether to grant a licence. This arrangement supersedes the Department of Trade and Industry Section 123 registration.

(v)   Under Section 54 of the Income and Corporation Taxes Act, 1970, the Inland Revenue is empowered to grant the appropriate 'bank' (identified under the same stipulations as '123 banks') the right to receive and pay interest gross of tax.

It is clear from the above classifications that the use of the word 'bank' by a deposit-receiving firm could mean that such a firm was the very symbol of financial probity and responsibility, or at the other extreme, that it was on the fringes of the banking world. Although a firm may use the word 'bank' on its letter headings, it could conceivably be far from competent in the handling of depositors' funds or its own assets.

The White Paper, 'The Licensing and Supervision of Deposit-taking Institutions', published in 1976, is likely to lead to a major change in the field of supervision. Even before the White Paper, the Bank of England had introduced changes in its operations in the area of supervision. In particular, the information obtained by the Bank is now broader and deeper than it used to be, in order that the Bank may obtain a truer picture of the operation of groups of banks as well as *individual* banks. The much more detailed information which the Bank can request includes such items as the size of capital and reserves and provisions and investments in fixed assets, as well as details concerning the items against which provisions have been made, details of large deposits and large advances, transactions with

associated companies, dealings with directors, as well as the maturity
analysis of deposits and lending in sterling (foreign currency details of
this kind are available already). These 'prudential returns' are
obtained in particular from 'fringe banks' and may be called for every
month, if required.[14]

The proposals contained in the White Paper include, amongst
others, the following:

(i)   Only a small number of institutions 'of the very highest
        probity and financial standing' will be permitted to use the
        term 'bank'. The remainder will be licensed deposit-takers
        and they will be able to operate with a licence only so long as
        they maintain the required standard of operation with
        respect to maturities and balance sheet ratios.

(ii)   *Individual* deposit-taking firms will have to satisfy the Bank of
        England that 'their management is honest, trustworthy, and
        suitably qualified to undertake the kind of business they
        intend to conduct'.

(iii)   Banks and licensed deposit-takers must participate in a fund
        managed by the Bank of England which will insure sterling
        deposits of up to £10,000.

The improvements in supervision which have been discussed,
however, occurred *after* the crisis of 1973. What did the Bank do at the
time? Its response was in fact very swift, once it was evident that a
significant number of fringe banks were in difficulties. On 21
December 1973, the Bank announced that, in order to sustain
confidence, a standing control committee of the Bank and the London
and Scottish Clearing Banks would be set up and would be chaired by
the Deputy Governor of the Bank. The committee would examine
applications and requests for financial support, and support would be
given if it seemed justified. Within a relatively short time, the
committee (the 'lifeboat' as it came to be known) had loaned £1,300
million to a number of firms, including Keyser Ullmann, United
Dominions Trust, and Mercantile Credit (later to be absorbed by
Barclays Bank). The Bank of England itself provided substantial help
to the Slater, Walker Group and in September 1977 the Bank
acquired from Slater, Walker Securities Ltd. its wholly-owned
subsidiary Slater, Walker Ltd. – an authorized bank. Interest is paid
on the loans provided by members of the committee although it is to
be noted that Bank Reports indicate that over £40 million has been set
aside to cover possible losses resulting from the Bank of England's
involvement in the support operation. The February 1978 Report

[14]For a much fuller account of the Bank's approach, see 'The Supervision of the U.K.
Banking System,' in the Bank of England *Quarterly Bulletin*, (June 1975), p.188. vol. 15,
No. 2

states that support lending was being extended to only four companies and the amount of support was around £600 million and expected to continue to fall steadily.

4.8 Summary

i.   The diversity of financial intermediaries within the U.K. provides the economist with a problem of classification. One basis for classification was that used in Chapter 3; the division into bank and non-bank financial intermediaries.

ii. The available data suggests that the non-bank financial intermediaries have grown more rapidly than bank financial intermediaries – particularly the building societies, insurance companies, and pension funds.

iii. The secondary banking sector has grown very rapidly compared with the primary banks, although it has to be noted that most primary banks have established secondary banking subsidiaries.

iv. It has become less easy to draw a sharp dividing line between the primary and the secondary banks in terms of their function. In particular, the primary banks have moved increasingly into those forms of business activity, e.g. term lending, which were the preserve of the secondary banks.

v.   Although we originally classified the Trustee Savings Banks as non-bank financial intermediaries, since 1976 they have taken on the full banking function and are extending their range of services which are competitive with the primary banks.

vi. Our survey of the existing legislation and regulations has shown that the definition of a 'bank' has been somewhat problematic – there has been no clear and consistent basis for defining such firms. The liquidity problems facing a number of secondary banks after 1973 highlighted the problem of definition as well as the lack of tight supervision over the business operations of deposit-taking firms. A White Paper related to this problem was published in 1976 and legislation is likely to stem from this document. By its own authority the Bank of England already has introduced changes in the methods and scope of banking supervision.

5
The deposit banks

5.1 Early history

As we saw in Chapter 1, financial intermediaries of all kinds exist because there is a *need* for the services and benefits which they provide. Likewise, British banking developed because the economic circumstances of the time were generating a need for new types of financial institutions. If one considers the basic services which a bank provides, one can find a clue to the reasons for the early development of banking. Banks can provide their customers with the safe custody of money and other assets but, more importantly, they can provide a means for the settlement of debt between different parties, i.e. a money transmission service or, in other words, the payments mechanism. The need for a developed payments mechanism is likely to grow as the economy of a country expands: its population grows, its manufacturing develops, agricultural innovation occurs, and with the improvements in the productivity of industry, trade becomes more important and the community's communications systems develop. Clearly the use of precious metals – gold and silver – can provide the means of payment, either in the form of bullion or of minted coins, without the need for a banking system, but a problem which may arise is that the quantity and quality of such metals may be inadequate 'to meet the needs of trade'. Under such circumstances trade and industry are inhibited and economic depression may ensue as, for example, occurred in the second half of the fourteenth century and the early part of the fifteenth century, when there was inadequate means of payments through shortages of gold and silver.

Trade, particularly the woollen trade, flourished in sixteenth-century England both domestically and internationally, and associated with this expansion were financial developments, in particular the growing use of the bill of exchange. However, it is in the seventeenth century when the most significant financial changes took place, and in particular after the restoration of the monarchy in 1660. Although the early part of the seventeenth century was fraught with civil war, economic development continued throughout the entire period with the development of the new industries which included coal mining, the expansion of shipbuilding, and glass manufacture. Nevertheless, the majority of the growing population was employed in agriculture, with manufacturing industry undergoing gradual change and expansion.

Although the seventeenth century was by no means a period of unremitting prosperity, it was none the less a time when financial developments were both propitious and beneficial. We can identify the main participants in these developments as the London goldsmiths.

The goldsmiths, by the nature of their original business operations, had facilities for the safe custody of coin, and the development of their business was initially that of custodian for their customers – receipts would be issued by the goldsmith for moneys deposited. The goldsmiths' function at this stage, however, was not that of a banker: the transition from goldsmith to banker was dependent upon the offer of interest on deposits, together with the goldsmiths' awareness that a certain proportion of deposited funds would not be called for repayment by customers, and thus a safe level of 'till-money' could be estimated. By 1660 the goldsmith bankers were in effect providing current account services to customers since *receipts* for deposits were being presented for *part* payment, in accordance with the needs of the customer, and the convenience of using the receipts as a means of *direct* payments (rather than encashing the receipt) had also become established. The use of these receipts, or promissory notes, marks an important step towards the proper banking function. Such notes were the precursor of the modern banknote, as the 'promise to pay' inscription on today's British bank notes reminds us. The middle of the seventeenth century also marks the origin of the cheque. Not only were the promissory notes of the goldsmith–banker in circulation, but 'drawn notes' also appeared which authorized the goldsmith to pay the creditor the appropriate sum due to him.

The goldsmith–bankers were not only of benefit to the private customer, but were also an integral part of government finance, since they either loaned funds to the government or discounted such claims on the government which were held by individuals. The security for such loans to the government would be tax revenues and other receipts which the monarch expected. In 1672 repayments of loans by the government to the goldsmith–bankers were suspended and this did considerable damage to the goldsmith–bankers who had committed themselves and their depositors' funds to financing the government. This unsatisfactory arrangement of State finances accounts for the establishment of the Bank of England in 1694. In return for £1,200,000 raised as a loan to the government to aid the prosecution of the war with France, the Bank received certain benefits, including the right to issue notes. The Charter of the Bank of England also prevented the setting up of joint-stock banks (other banks were forced to operate as private partnerships with a maximum of six members), and this, together with imperfect communications, limited banking largely to London. However, by the middle of the eighteenth century the needs of trade and the incipient industrial revolution was beginning to create the need for some form of banking facility outside London, not only as a means of operating a local payments mechanism, but also to channel funds and provide working and fixed capital for commerce and industry. Since the London goldsmith–bankers limited their activity to London, the private banks established in the provinces were often based on an existing commercial or industrial firm which issued its own notes. The growth of country banking is indicated by the following estimates of the number of English banks outside London:

1784	119
1797	230
1804	470
1808	800

Source: E. Nevin and E. W. Davis, *The London Clearing Banks* (Elek Books Ltd., 1970)

It is also estimated, however, that between 1750 and 1830 at least 343 self-styled banks failed through loss of confidence that the issued notes could be redeemed for coin, or through the over-issue of notes resulting either from incompetence or avarice. Most of the bank failures occurred at the end of the eighteenth century and the beginning of the nineteenth century: for example, 114 banks failed between 1814 and 1826. Such failures undoubtedly gave added momentum to the demand for joint-stock banking and for the removal of the restrictive element in the Bank of England's charter which had prevented their formation.

An act of 1826 effectively permitted joint-stock banking with the right of note issue, but imposed the restriction of unlimited liability and the proscription of business activity within a radius of 65 miles of London. This latter condition helped ensure the Bank of England's pre-eminence in London, while the act also allowed the Bank of England to open branches anywhere in England. Nevertheless, the new joint-stock banks withstood the competition both from the Bank of England and from the existing private banks, and by 1836 a hundred joint-stock banks had been established. Further, when the Bank of England's charter came up for renewal in 1833, a clause was inserted which allowed joint-stock banks to be established in London so long as they did not issue their own notes. In addition, the act established the legality of cheques drawn on these banks. Such was the opposition of the entrenched private banks in London, however, that it was not until 1854 that the joint-stock banks gained access to the London Bankers' Clearing House.

The Bank Charter Act of 1844 was an important development since its provisions allowed the eventual concentration of note issue in the hands of the Bank of England, together with certain restrictions on the operations of the joint-stock banks, allegedly in the interests of depositors. From the point of view of the development of deposit banking, the limitations on the rights of note issue by banks other than the Bank of England encouraged the use of the bank *deposit* as the medium of exchange and payment. Further legislation in the nineteenth century established the framework for the deposit banks by an act of 1858 which gave the option of limited liability, and another act of 1862 removed the awkward restriction which hitherto had required the substantial minimum share denomination in joint-stock banks to be £100.

The contrast between the early private banks and the later joint-stock banks can be summarized in the following way. For the private banks it was their right to issue notes which was their chief source of profit, whereas the joint-stock banks' objective was the attraction and use of deposits as the habit of banking spread. For the joint-stock banks, therefore, the extension of their activities through branch banking was a means of expanding their profit base. Furthermore, branch banking offered the customer greater security was well as the possibility of a wider range of services and expertise. It is not surprising, therefore, that the joint-stock banks ultimately became the dominant banks: by 1913 there were 43 such banks with almost 6,000 branches, and deposits of over £800 million. During the First World War, the amalgamation of joint-stock banks took place on such a scale that by 1918 the major banks amounted to five, controlling two-thirds of deposits. By 1936 the 'big five' primary banks – Midland, Barclays, Westminster, Lloyds, and National Provincial – held 87 per cent of total Clearing Bank deposit and it was not until the 1960s that further changes took place in the structure of deposit banking. In 1962 the National Provincial Bank acquired the District Bank and, following a report of the National Board for Prices and Incomes in 1967, which gave tacit encouragement to bank mergers, further mergers took place. National Provincial agreed to merge with the Westminster Bank in 1968 to form the National Westminster Bank, and the Three Banks Group merged with the National Commercial Bank of Scotland. A proposed merger of Barclays, Martins, and Lloyds was disallowed by the Monopolies Commission, although the merger of Barclays and Martins was permitted.

5.2 Operation of the primary banks

Although the modern primary banks appear to be very different from their seventeenth-century forbears, an examination of the functions and services of the modern bank would reveal many similarities; and it is the purpose of this section to examine the operations of the modern U.K. primary banks. These banks not only have responsibilities to customers, but also have profit objectives of their own, and it is by this distinction that we can examine their operations – their services to customers and the management of their balance sheets for the benefit of shareholders.

5.2.1 SERVICES TO CUSTOMERS

(i) We saw earlier that an attractive feature of the goldsmith–bankers was the fact that they could provide customers with the safekeeping of money and valuables. This is a function which the modern bank also performs, although in a slightly different way. Banks accept cash or deposits from customers which then represent a liability of the bank in the form of a sight deposit (current account) together with a cheque facility for the customer, or a time deposit (deposit account) which bears interest. These two types of account present for the customer a convenient and virtually risk-free form of holding wealth as well as a safe and useful means of settling debts by means of the cheque. The introduction of cheque cards, bank giro, Barclaycard, and Access, together with the convention by which time deposits may be used in effect as sight deposits, as well as the established probity of the primary banks, has meant that the deposits of the primary banks constitute the bulk of the U.K. money supply and the primary means of payment. The provision of other services such as the standing order and direct debt facilities further enhance the benefits to be derived from using this part of the banking system.

It is to be expected that the impact of competition between the banks (including the National Giro and Trustee Savings Banks), as well as the need to pay careful attention to costs, will produce further changes in the money transmission mechanism and ancillary services. For example, Barclays Bank have introduced a new self-service machine which at the time of writing (January 1978) provides a cash withdrawal facility (without the use of cheque or cash vouchers), the facility for depositing notes, cheques, and money orders, as well as providing personal bank statements.

(ii) An important service which banks provided very early in their development was the granting of loans to customers. Although the details regarding a particular loan facility may vary, one form is that of an overdraft, which allows the customer to draw cheques against his current account up to an agreed limit (interest charged on the actual amount overdrawn) and is therefore a flexible advance to a customer. Alternatively the bank may provide a loan of a given amount negotiated at an agreed term and interest rate, with repayments of interest and principal being made usually each month. In both cases the bank may require security to cover the amounts involved. Bank preference is usually for relatively short-term lending although the option or opportunity for a loan to be 'rolled over' – or overdraft facility renegotiated – does mean that much bank lending is, in effect at least, medium-term.

Apart from private individuals who may require loan finance for the purchase of consumer durables, or a bridging loan during house purchase, the major customers of the banks are industry (including the public corporations), the service sector, and the local authorities. One particularly important form of lending is for exports, and this is often based on insurance cover provided by the government's Export Credits Guarantee Department.

(iii) The banks provide their customers with a range of services which are largely concerned with using the financial expertise of the bank as well as its links with other financial firms. Of particular importance for many customers is the provision of advice in respect of investment and the use of savings. Advice on taxation matters, as well as executor and trustee services, are also available to the bank's customers.

5.2.2 BANKS AND THEIR BALANCE SHEETS

We have already observed that the primary banks are owned by shareholders who presumably intend their firms' operations to be profitable, even if they do not have the textbook objective of aiming for *maximum* profitability, and it is this aspect of the primary banks' operations that we shall now examine. A convenient approach is to look at the combined balance sheets of these banks and observe their structure and how this has changed over time. For this purpose, it is convenient to use the combined balance sheet of the London Clearing Banks. The omission of the Scottish Clearing Banks and the Northern Ireland banks does not distort the picture or affect our conclusions since these banks have very close links with the English banks as well as having balance sheet structures which are virtually identical to the London Clearing Banks. Furthermore, the Scottish and Northern Ireland banks are subject to the provisions of *Competition and Credit Control*, as are the London Clearing Banks.

TABLE 5.1
Sterling assets of the London Clearing Banks
(September figures: £ m.)

	I		II		III		IV		V — Sterling and Foreign Currency assets (Sept. 1977)		
	1952		1962		1971		1977				
Cash	503	(8·5)	623	(8·5)	847	(7·5)	1,050	(3·8)	(£) 1,050	(2·8)	
Money at call	539	(8·9)	692	(9·4)	1,391	(12·3)	1,214	(4·4)	(£) 1,214	(3·2)	
Bills:											
Treasury bills	1,231	(20·7)	968	(13·1)	191	(1·7)	472	(1·7)	(£) 472	(1·2)	
Other bills	64	(1·1)	276	(3·8)	1,063	(9·4)	700	(2·5)	(£) 700	(1·8)	
									(FC) 18	(0·04)	
Market loans:											
Banks in the U.K. and the discount market							2,944	(10·7)	(£) 2,944	(7·7)	
									(FC) 1,396	(3·7)	
Certificates of deposit							597	(2·2)	(£) 597	(1·6)	
									(FC) 117	(0·3)	
U.K. local authorities							336	(1·2)	(£) 336	(0·9)	
Other							145	(0·5)	(£) 145	(0·4)	

Investments:						
British Government securities	1,921 (32·4)	1,234 (16·7)	1,964 (17·3)	1,889 (7·0)	(£)	1,889 (5·2)
Other	1,688 (28·4)	3,428 (46·5)	5,877 (51·8)	970 (3·5)	(£)	970 (2·5)
Advances:						
U.K.				14,205 (51·5)	(£)	14,205 (37·3)
Overseas				2,406 (8·7)	(£)	2,406 (6·3)
					(FC)	(2,337) (6·1)[a]
Special and supplementary deposits	—	151 (2·0)	—	629 (2·3)	(£)	629 (1·6)
Other:						
Other foreign currency market loans and advances:						
U.K. public					(FC)	722 (1·9)
U.K. private					(FC)	766 (2·0)
Overseas					(FC)	2,455 (6·4)
Other investments and assets both £ and FC						5,036 (13·2)
TOTALS	5,937	7,372	11,333	27,557		38,067

[a] This figure is already included in other categories but it is useful to have it separate.

Source: Bank of England *Statistical Abstract*, Nos. 1 and 2; Bank of England *Quarterly Bulletin*, vol. 17, No. 4 (December 1977).

TABLE 5.2
London Clearing Bank deposits
(September figures: £ m.)

	1952	*1962*	*1971*
Current accounts	3,861	4,175	6,114
Deposit and other accounts	2,265	3,416	5,277
Totals	6,216	7,591	11,391

1977	
Sterling:	
(Sight deposits)	(12,147)
U.K. banking sector	1,332
Other U.K.	22,250
C.D.s	1,184
Total	26,143
Other currency deposits:	
U.K. banking sector	1,140
Other U.K.	527
C.D.s	313
Overseas	3,416
Total	5,396
Total deposits	31,539

Source: Bank of England *Quarterly Bulletin*, vol. 17, No. 4 (December 1977); Bank of England *Statistical Abstract*, Nos. 1 and 2.

Table 5.1 shows the composition of the assets of the London Clearing Banks for four selected years, which span a 25-year period.[1] Columns I–IV refer to the sterling assets held by the banks, and Column V includes the foreign currency assets. The figures in brackets show the percentage share of total assets in each category of asset. Reference has already been made in Chapter 4 to the problem of adequate banking data and the reforms introduced by the Bank of England; the increased detail in Columns V and VI reflect these improvements. The figures in Table 5.1 have not been structured on the basis of the obligatory asset ratios in existence at the time, but

[1] In 1969 the London Clearing Banks adopted different accounting procedures which prevent a completely accurate comparison of the figures in Tables 5.1 and 5.2. The points which are made in the text, however, are not invalidated by this problem of statistical comparability

rather to present the array of assets which the banks hold in the context of their risk, return, and liquidity qualities. *Table 5.2* shows the breakdown of the deposits of the London Clearing Banks for the same period.

During the 25-year period encompassed by the two tables, there have been significant changes in the banking behaviour of the London Clearing Banks – of their own volition as well as induced by the changing institutional arrangements introduced by the authorities. Because of these changes, it would be helpful to the reader if we identify the main items on the balance sheets embodied in the two tables, and then discuss the major changes which have taken place in banking behaviour.

5.2.2.1 London Clearing Bank assets

(i) *Cash.* The holdings of this asset by the banks can be divided into the cash balances required by the banks at their branches in the form of till money, and those balances held at the Bank of England which facilitate the clearing operations of the banks. Until September 1971, when the Bank of England introduced major changes, the mandatory cash ratio during the period was 8 per cent of gross deposits. The percentage figures in brackets in Table 5.1 are based on total assets, not total deposits, but nevertheless it is clear that the banks maintained almost exactly the required cash ratio. Clearly, holding cash in excess of the mandatory minimum ratio would be a practice in which the banks would not indulge since idle cash provides the banks with no income. Although it may seem that a cash ratio of 8 per cent is rather small in relation to the total sight liabilities of the banks, we shall see later that this relatively small holding of cash does not really reflect the flow of cash the banks are actually able to tap.

(ii) *Money at call.* In our earlier discussion of the discount houses in Chapter 4, we made reference to this item. The discount houses provide the banks with a useful means of utilising their spare cash since the banks can always lend such money, at call, to the discount houses. Prior to the September 1971 changes, about 70 per cent of such funds were borrowed by the discount houses, and the remainder flowed to a number of other financial firms who deal in bills and gilt-edged securities. Not only do the discount houses provide an outlet for surplus cash flowing into the London Clearing Banks, but day-to-day variations in the cash position of the banks can be adjusted by virtue of the money at call with the discount houses. Thus the banks' potential cash to hand is much greater in reality than the cash ratio alone would suggest. The discount houses and the call money arrangement is not, however, the only source of cash to the banks, as the next item will reveal.

(iii) *Bills.* Under this general heading there are a number of different assets which we shall examine in turn.

(a) *Treasury bills.* These bills, which were first introduced in 1877, are in effect an I.O.U. of the government to the holder of the bill. There is no rate of interest paid on these assets, but rather they are sold initially by tender at a discount by the Bank of England. The bills usually have a life of 91 days and the method of sale is for the Bank of England to announce the total offer of bills for the following week and invite tenders in large denominations, with a minimum acceptable tender of £50,000. On the Friday of the following week, the tenders are opened and the bills are allocated to the highest bidders. Thus the rate of interest obtained on such bills is the discount on the bill, i.e. an offer for £100 nominal may be, say, £98 which would yield an approximate *annual* rate of interest of 8 per cent. The banks do not bid directly for bills on their own account (although they will act on behalf of customers) but purchase such bills as they require them from the discount houses. The original purchaser of the bills can specify the day of the following week when the bills are to be purchased and from which the 91 days are to run. This arrangement allows the banks to purchase bills from the discount houses (who are important bidders for bills) in such a way that there is a steady stream of maturing bills. By this means, the banks are able to ensure a flow of cash, which allows them to meet *foreseeable* cash needs.

(b) *Other bills.* This item consists of commercial bills which the banks have discounted themselves directly from a customer, or which they have purchased from the discount houses. In Section 5.2.1 we referred to the important facility provided by the banks in conjunction with the Export Credit Guarantee Department of the Department of Trade and Industry. Bank credit provided under this scheme is included under this item 'other bills'. In addition, bills issued by a few of the larger local authorities may be held by the banks and included within this item in their balance sheets.

(c) *Market loans.* This category within the assets of the London Clearing Banks appeared after the new series of banking statistics was begun in May 1975. The use of the term 'market loans' is to emphasize that this category of lending by the banks is done through the existing markets and not by lending directly to their customers in the form of advances. Taking each of the categories:

(1) *Banks in the U.K. and the discount market.* This category of market lending includes balances and funds lent to listed banks and banks overseas, as well as funds used to discount bills of exchange

drawn by other banks. The lending to the discount market comprises loans which have been made to the discount houses, discount brokers, and the money trading departments of listed banks, but such funds are neither secured nor immediately callable. This is in contrast to the earlier item, 'money at call', which partly consists of loans to discount houses which *are* secured loans *and* callable.

(2) *Certificates of deposit*. The certificate of deposit, as its title suggests, is a certificate stating that a deposit of a certain amount has been placed with a particular bank for a given period and at a particular rate of interest. The certificate of deposit is a negotiable asset, so that depositors who hold this paper can, if they so wish, re-sell the certificate in a secondary market. The term of such deposits may be from between three months to five years, the term being fixed to suit the needs both of the depositor and the bank issuing the certificate. In principle, there are a number of advantages attached to this type of asset for both the issuing bank and the depositor. The arrangement provides the bank with a deposit for a fixed period and fixed rate of interest – the redemption date is known by the bank and obviously this can help in the planning of its use of the funds so obtained. Furthermore the bank is able to negotiate a rate on such deposits individually in order to attract these deposits (minimum amounts usually £50,000) without incurring the need to raise the *general level of rates* on its deposits. From the depositor's view point, the certificate received provides a satisfactory rate of return, but more especially it is a negotiable certificate and thus allows the depositor the possibility of re-selling the asset, should the need arise.

Such certificates have been issued in New York since 1961, but it was not until 1966 that Bank of England permission was given for the issue of dollar certificates of deposit in the U.K. These certificates were issued for terms varying from 30 days to two years, with a minimum deposit of $25,000. On the basis of the dollar C.D. experience, a market for sterling C.D.s was opened in October 1968 in London, such certificates being issued by the secondary banks and the secondary banking subsidiaries of the Clearing Banks, as well as the discount houses. After 1971 the London Clearing Banks began issuing sterling C.D.s in their own name.

(3) *U.K. local authorities*. Largely as a consequence of the restrictions on their borrowing of funds from the central government, especially during the years 1955–69, the local authorities have been very active borrowers at the short end of the market as well as raising longer term funds through mortgages and term loans. After 1971 the London Clearing Banks entered the

market, providing temporary loans to the local authorities.

(4) *Other*. This item is likely to include loans to listed money brokers as well as funds used to discount bills which have been drawn by overseas banks, including overseas offices of the London Clearing Banks themselves. The amounts involved are relatively small compared with the other assets of the London Clearing Banks.

(d) *Investments*. The London Clearing Banks have been reluctant to invest in the private sector of the economy through the take-up of new issues of company shares and stock, or by the purchase of existing company securities through the Stock Exchange. Such prudence on the part of the banks has meant that the bulk of their investments consists of holdings of gilt-edged securities (such holdings are free of the risk of default since they are either issued by or guaranteed by the government). The banks have preferred to provide finance for industry either directly through the cautious provision of advances to firms, indirectly through bank subsidiaries, or participation in such companies as Finance for Industry Ltd. Thus the item 'investments' consists very largely of stocks issued by the British Government and stocks of nationalized industries guaranteed by the British Government. Other investments consist of stocks and bonds issued by local authorities (except mortgage bonds which are included under advances) as well as some Commonwealth government bonds. The *new* series of banking statistics referred to earlier has meant that the item 'other investments' now includes investments in subsidiaries or associates of the London Clearing Banks as well as deposits with overseas offices which have been invested in fixed assets such as premises and equipment.

The term to maturity of British Government securities varies from the very short term (say, up to five years) to much longer terms extending to over thirty years, and there are even stocks which do not have a redemption date.[2] The banks are thus faced with the choice of selecting a suitable mixture of such assets. It is evident from the published figures that the banks have steadily reduced the average period to maturity of their holdings in British Government securities. In 1977 only about 10 per cent of their holdings had more than five years to run to maturity. A primary reason for this is that the trend of rising interest rates has meant that the possibility of capital loss on the premature sale of stock has increased.

Accordingly, the banks have moved towards the short end of the gilt-edged market. In addition, the banks have for many years

[2]Consult the Stock Market lists in the *Financial Times,* which will provide a list of most British Government securities which are available, together with their price, yield, and redemption dates.

adopted the policy of purchasing gilt-edged securities of varying maturities so that there is a steady stream of maturing securities. Not only does this provide the banks with greater flexibility in managing their assets, but it also provides them with a flow of cash as their accounts at the Bank of England are credited to the value of the maturing stock.

(e) *Advances.* This item is clearly now the largest single item, particularly if one considers only the sterling lending. Overdraft and loan facilities are included as well as lending under Department of Industry guarantee and E.C.G.D. arrangements, other than the amounts which have been re-financed by the Bank of England.[3] (It is the E.C.G.D. lending which is identified as advances overseas in Table 5.1, p. 96.) In 1977 the approximate proportion of advances to the various U.K. resident borrowers is shown in *Table 5.3*. Within each of the general headings in the Table there is a broad spread of lending and it is clear from the general headings that the banks do not emphasize one particular form of lending more than another. The principal of 'not putting all one's eggs in one basket' applies to banking as it does in other financial activities.

TABLE 5.3

Financial	13%
Services[a]	27%
Manufacturing	27%
Other production (i.e. extractive industries and construction)	14%
Persons	19%

[a]Service lending includes lending to exporters.

Source: Bank of England *Quarterly Bulletin,* vol. 18, No. 1 (March 1978).

(f) *Special and supplementary deposits.* These two items will be more fully discussed in Chapter 7, and the account below will therefore be brief.

(1) *Special deposits.* These deposits are held at the Bank of England and are called by the Bank usually when it wishes to exercise pressure on the lending policies of the banks. The Bank will usually inform the banks that a certain percentage of their gross deposits must be deposited with the Bank of England by a certain date (several weeks' notice is given). Broadly speaking, the call for special deposits tends to squeeze the 'liquidity' of the banks since such deposits do not qualify as part of the cash ratio or any other

[3]The re-financeable credits are included in the item 'bills discounted'.

ratio which the Bank may impose: such deposits are only released at the discretion of the Bank. Nevertheless, these deposits earn for the banks the current rate on Treasury bills, although on one occasion the Bank halved the rate in order to put further pressure on the banks to curb their lending.

(2) *Supplementary deposits.* The Supplementary Deposit scheme was introduced in December 1973 and is activated at the discretion of the Bank of England. Although the mechanics of its implementation are a little more complicated than the Special Deposit arrangement, the intention is largely the same – to restrict the growth of banks' business. When the scheme is operational, the size of the supplementary deposits which are to be placed with the Bank will vary from bank to bank, depending on how fast each bank has expanded its business in relation to the upper limit set by the Bank. The percentage of funds to be deposited is graduated so that the greater the deviation of a bank from the growth limit set by the Bank, the more the individual bank will have to deposit at the Bank of England. In contrast to the Special Deposit scheme, the supplementary deposits are non-interest bearing.

(g) *Other assets.* Prior to 1971 the business of receiving foreign currency deposits and utilizing such funds by lending was undertaken largely but not entirely by the secondary banking subsidiaries of the Clearing Banks. (We have already seen in Chapter 4 that the bulk of the secondary bank business is in foreign currencies.) However the 'other assets' in Table 5.1, Column V (p. 97), are denominated entirely in foreign currency and reveal the considerable volume of business which the London Clearing Banks undertake in their own names. Since 1971 the dividing line between the primary and secondary banks has, not surprisingly, been far more difficult to define clearly. With the new arrangements introduced by the Bank in 1971 (see Chapter 7), the Clearing Banks moved fairly quickly into other forms of business activity. Market loans, both sterling and non-sterling, have extended into the so-called parallel or complementary markets which include the inter-bank market and the Euro-dollar markets. Furthermore, it is clear from the comparison of foreign currency assets and liabilities, that the London Clearing banks – similar to the secondary banks – are largely providing an entrepôt[4] facility.

(h) *Other investments and assets, both sterling and foreign currency.* This collection of assets refers to: (1) items in suspense, e.g. debit balances

---

[4] An entrepôt facility is provided when, for example, goods are imported into a country's port and then are shipped abroad. The entrepôt acts as a central point for the redistribution of goods. The illustration in the text is referring to the inflow of foreign currencies into and out of London.

awaiting transfer to customers' accounts; (2) collections, i.e. cheques drawn on and in course of collection on banks and other institutions in the U.K. and debit items in transit between U.K. offices of an individual bank; collections on banks outside the U.K. and items in transit to overseas offices of an individual bank where the bank is acting as principal and not agent and where it has already given credit for the items; (3) assets leased, i.e. plant and equipment owned by a bank which have been leased out; (4) other assets remaining include gold bullion and gold coin, land, premises, and equipment owned by the bank.

5.2.2.2 Asset structure of the London Clearing Banks

Between 1951 and 1971 the London Clearing Banks were obliged to maintain two asset ratios. One was the 8 per cent cash ratio to which we have already referred. The other ratio was a liquid assets ratio which was informally established in 1951 by arrangement between the Bank and the London Clearing Banks. The required ratio was to be between 28 and 32 per cent of gross deposits. This effectively became a ratio of 30 per cent with any fall below this figure bringing disapproval from the Bank, although the ratio was subsequently reduced to 28 per cent in 1963. Furthermore, the 8 per cent cash ratio was part of the overall liquid assets ratio. The immediate problem which arises is the definition of 'liquid assets' since there are many assets in an advanced financial system which could be legitimately and with general acceptance be termed 'liquid'. The definition was not, however at the discretion of the banks because the Bank of England defined those types of asset which would be eligible for inclusion as part of the banks' liquid assets for the purposes of calculating the liquid assets ratio. The following list identifies the main liquid assets as laid down by the Bank:

    (a) Coin and notes (i.e. till money).
    (b) Balances with the Bank of England (excluding special deposits).
    (c) Money at call and short notice.
    (d) Bills discounted including:
        (i) British and N. Ireland Government Treasury bills;
        (ii) commercial bills.

In selecting the mix of liquid assets the banks would clearly keep their notes and coin plus balances at the Bank of England as close to the 8 per cent ratio as possible, and for the remainder the banks could choose the mix of assets which suited their particular needs. Although it may be argued that the imposition of these two ratios constituted a distortion of their business activity, it is fair to point out that the London Clearing banks had, prior to the imposition of the two ratios, voluntarily maintained very similar ratios between, for example, 1920 and 1939. In other words it appears that banking prudence had already established such ratios and the Bank's decision to make them mandatory in 1951 was merely a reinforcement of what the banks had already established.

Up to 1971 it is also evident that the London Clearing Banks were either choosing or being induced to alter the composition of their assets. British Government Treasury bills were of declining importance in the banks' asset. This was largely a result of the authorities' pursuing a policy of 'funding', i.e. reducing the volume of outstanding Treasury bills and replacing such assets with gilt-edged securities. As the banks' holdings of Treasury bills declined, however, there was a compensating growth in the importance of other bills, in particular commercial bills and re-financeable export credits. One of the reasons for the growth of commercial bill business was the use of the bill as a means of obtaining credit by a firm drawing a bill and then discounting it at a Clearing Bank. The periodic credit squeezes (i.e. a squeeze on bank *advances*) during the period as well as the expansion of world trade following the post-war recovery no doubt provided some stimulus to the use of the bill.

Money at call became an increasingly important liquid asset for the banks during the period, increasing both relatively and absolutely. A reason for this growth was the banks' need to find alternative liquid assets as the volume of Treasury bills declined (remember that the banks had to maintain their liquid assets ratio). Another reason was that this supply of funds to the discount houses allowed the discount market to purchase short-dated bonds, whereas if the banks had *directly* purchased such bonds these assets would not have counted as part of their liquid assets. By lending additional call money, however, which was then used to purchase such bonds the banks were able to sustain their liquid assets ratio whilst effectively financing the purchase of short-dated bonds.

It is very evident from the percentage figures calculated in Table 5.1 (p 96) that the banks ran down their holdings of investments, particularly their holding of British Government securities. At this stage we suggest two reasons for this change. One was that the long-run decline in prices of gilt-edged securities during the period (this was a corollary of the steady rise in interest rates) made gilt-edged securities rather less 'gilt-edged' than they used to be. Although it is correct to argue that if such assets are held to maturity there would be not risk of capital loss, nevertheless, there can be no certainty that liquidation of such assets prior to maturity would never be necessary and accordingly the holding of gilt-edged became riskier. A further reason for the run-down of gilt-edged was the preference of the banks to increase their advances at the expense of their gilt-edged holdings. The very substantial rise in advances by the London Clearing Banks is clear from Table 5.1, and by the end of the period about half their assets were in this form. Not only was such growth in lending meeting the needs of their customers, but the banks themselves preferred this readjustment of their assets since this particular asset is their most profitable. During periods of low demand for bank loans, the ratio of advances to other assets will fall and the alternative asset held by the banks would usually be gilt-edged securities.

After September 1971 the composition of the assets of the London Clearing Banks was subject to a further influence emanating from the Bank of England. This resulted from the implementation of proposals contained in a document entitled *Competition and Credit Control* (see Chapter 7) and these proposals were to extend to *all* banks and finance houses, with separate arrangements for the discount houses. In the context of this chapter we are concerned with the effect of such proposals on the deposit banks' asset structure.

Competition and Credit Control effectively abolished the cash ratio and the liquid assets ratio and replaced them with a reserve assets ratio. The list below contains the reserve assets which the banks would be expected to maintain as a ratio of 12½ per cent of their 'eligible liabilities' (this will be defined below).

Reserve assets

1. Balances held at the Bank of England[5] (head office and branches)
2. British Government and N. Ireland Treasury bills
3. Company tax reserve certificates
4. Money at call with the London money market which must be secured and callable with:
   (i)   Members of the London Discount Market Association.
   (ii)   Discount brokers and the money trading departments of certain banks.
   (iii) Certain firms directly connected with the overnight finance of the gilt-edged market, i.e. money brokers and jobbers on the London Stock Exchange. The money at call with jobbers has to be secured on British Government stocks or stocks guaranteed by the British government.
5. British Government stocks and nationalized industry stocks guaranteed by the British Government, with one year or less to maturity

---

[5] The London Clearing Banks agreed to maintain (day by day) a minimum of 1½ per cent of their eligible liabilities as cash at the Bank of England head office.

6. Local authority bills eligible for rediscount at the Bank of England

7. Commercial bills eligible for rediscount at the Bank of England, up to a maximum of 2 per cent of total eligible liabilities.

Eligible liabilities

1. All sterling deposits, of an original maturity of two years and under, from U.K. residents other than banks and from overseas residents other than overseas offices. All funds due to customers or third parties which are temporarily held in suspense accounts.

2. All sterling deposits – of whatever term – from banks in the U.K., less any sterling claims on such banks.

3. All sterling C.D.s issued – of whatever term – less any holdings of such certificates.

4. The bank's net deposit liability in sterling to its overseas office.

5. The bank's net liability in currencies other than sterling.

6. *Less* 60 per cent of the net value of transit items in the bank's balance sheet.

It is worth making a comparison between the liquid assets ratio and the new reserve ratio requirements in terms of the effect of the new arrangements on the assets of the London Clearing Banks.

(a) Cash in tills no longer represents a reserve asset. Thus surplus cash in tills provides the banks with no benefit from this point of view.

(b) Inter-bank lending is included no longer, nor are loans to stockbrokers and bullion brokers.

(c) Overseas government Treasury bills and commercial bills drawn on overseas residents are also excluded.

(d) U.K. commercial bills are eligible reserve assets, but to a limited extent. The 2 per cent limit was probably intended to prevent the credit squeeze avoidance which we mentioned earlier in this chapter (p. 106).

(e) The inclusion of gilt-edged securities with one year or less to maturity is a new item and was included no doubt partly because of the banks' expansion of money at call, some of which was used by the discount houses to purchase short-dated bonds. Since the banks hold short-dated gilt-edged as part of their investments which are arranged to provide a steady stream of maturities, it would be likely that the banks' preference for short-dated gilt-edged will be strengthened by the new arrangements. The banks will be able to utilize their investments to provide a steady flow of stocks which can be added to their reserve assets.

After the London Clearing Banks reconstructed their balance sheets in accordance with the new reserve ratio they found that the scheme was far from penal. In October 1971 their reserve ratio was 16·5 per cent – comfortably above the 12½ per cent minimum. On the basis of data published by the Bank of England, Clearing Banks appear to prefer a reserve ratio of around 13½ per cent – it would clearly be imprudent to be exactly on the 12½ per cent minimum figure since this would limit the banks' manoeuvrability – but they did not reach the preferred figure until the beginning of 1974. Not surprisingly, the arrangement provided the London Clearing Banks with considerable scope for an expansion in their business as a result of being well above the required minimum reserve ratio for nearly two years after the introduction of the scheme.

Our discussion so far in this section has emphasized the influence of the Bank of England on the composition of the assets of the London Clearing Banks. Although such influence clearly has an effect on their choice of assets and use of funds, we can none the less identify other factors which will influence their overall selection of assets and use of customers' funds.

More than half the liabilities of the London Clearing Banks are in effect sight deposits. The implication is that the banks must maintain an adequate reserve of assets which are easily realizable to accommodate any drain of funds. We have already pointed out that even before the Bank of England imposed a liquid assets ratio, the banks had adopted such a practice voluntarily. A substantial holding of encashable assets without risk of capital loss is vital for bank solvency. Hence the importance of money at call and Treasury bill holdings as well as the practice of arranging other assets to provide a stream of maturities.

In respect of their other assets, banking prudence requires a careful balancing of profitability and risk, and broadly speaking these two elements are directly related to each other. In other words the banks' most profitable assets tend also to be their most risky. A particularly good example is, of course, their advances to customers. Traditionally the banks have had a strong preference for lending which is self-liquidating, or, to use another well-known expression, 'seed-time to harvest' lending. For example, loans which provide firms with working capital, farmers to finance their next year's crop, rather than investment of bank funds in longer-term fixed capital projects. Although self-liquidating loans may be the preferred form of business of the banks, there has been growing pressure on the banks for many years to provide much longer-term finance for commerce and industry. Such business has expanded indirectly through lending by their secondary banking subsidiaries and also directly by the London Clearing Banks themselves. Undoubtedly one of the factors which has been an influence on banks' lending practices has been the very considerable and competitive expansion of term lending by the secondary banking system. The London Clearing Banks had either to respond to the needs of the market or acknowledge that the secondary banks would be obtaining an increasing share of a highly profitable business.

Since the new arrangements were introduced in 1971 the London Clearing Banks have abandoned their collective agreements on rates of interest offered on deposits. Prior to September 1971 (the introduction of *Competition and Credit Control*) the London Clearing banks exercised a collective agreement in respect of certain interest rates. The key rate of interest was Bank Rate and the banks agreed that the rate on deposits (deposit accounts) would be two percentage points below Bank Rate and lending rates on loans and overdrafts would range from one to five percentage points above Bank rate depending on such factors as the nature of the borrower, the use of the funds, size of the loan, and the lending capacity of the banks. The other agreed rate was the minimum lending rate to the discount houses which was fixed at 1·625 percentage points below Bank rate. Each bank now has a single 'base rate' which is not necessarily identical to the other banks, and the London Clearing Banks link their charges for advances and the discounting of bills to their declared base rate. Other rates will depend on the market conditions prevailing at the time. Furthermore, after December 1973 the London Clearing Banks stated that advances to certain customers would be geared to market rates rather than base rate. Between the end of 1971 and 1977 the London Clearing Banks have changed their base rates on approximately 36 occasions, or on average once every two months. Market rates of interest, however, vary daily in response to supply and demand and it has been possible at certain times to borrow from the banks and re-lend at a profit at market rates to other financial firms (including other banks). Thus the action of the banks in declaring that loans to certain customers would be at market rates and not geared to base rate was designed to eliminate the opportunity of profitable arbitrage operations by such customers. The impact of *Competition and Credit Control* on interest rates and competitiveness within the financial system will be discussed further in Chapter 7.

5.2.2.3 Deposits of the London Clearing Banks

Table 5.2 (p. 98) provides a breakdown of deposits into current and deposit accounts, with a more detailed analysis for 1977 resulting from the May 1975 improvement in banking statistics.

The current accounts of the clearing banks are the main source of the means of payment in the U.K. and in this field the clearing banks

TABLE 5.4

Source of deposits as a percentage of total deposits[a]

	March 1963	March 1975
Government	1·3	1·0
Local authorities	1·7	0·6
Public corporations	0·6	0·4
Financial institutions	2·9	4·8
Companies	20·7	15·6
Other	68·4	62·8
Overseas	4·4	13·6
C.D.s	—	1·2

[a]The two dates were selected on the basis of availability of the data.

Source: Bank of England *Statistical Abstract*, Nos. 1 and 2.

face very little competition except from each other; although, as we have discussed earlier, potential competition does lie with the Trustee Savings Banks and to a lesser extent the National Giro. The deposit accounts are a source of funds on which interest is paid, and need to be attractive in this respect since they are competitive with other financial institutions. The London Clearing Banks do offer their customers an additional benefit however, in their willingness to waive the notice requirement for withdrawal of these deposits, albeit with an interest penalty. The available published figures relating to the source of funds of the London Clearing Banks are not adequate and *Table 5.4* is an approximation since the data is derived from official figures which relate to all the deposit banks. Any distortion is likely to be small, however, since the London Clearing Banks' deposits comprise the greater proportion. There are a number of points which can be made on a comparative basis.

(a) The bulk of funds are derived from 'other', i.e. the personal sector, with the company sector ranking next. One would not be surprised at this since the London Clearing Banks are so important in operating the payments mechanism through the provision of current accounts as well as attracting customers through their other services.

(b) The increased significance of financial institutions as a source of funds is partly accounted for by the growing involvement of the London Clearing Banks with the inter-bank market as well as providing a convenient service to the secondary banks. In addition, part of the increased share of funds from financial institutions will also reflect the growing volume of business undertaken by the building societies and insurance companies.

(c) The substantial increase in funds from overseas reveals the direct involvement of the London Clearing Banks in the Euro-dollar market; an involvement to which we have already referred. Table 5.2 (p. 98) shows the considerable volume of funds which derive from the inter-bank market and also the Euro-dollar (and Euro-currency) markets.

(d) We can also observe in Table 5.2 the fact that the London Clearing Banks issue fairly substantial amounts of sterling C.Ds. (as well as holding C.D.s as part of their assets). This direct involvement in the C.D. and other markets has already been discussed and we emphasized that this growth of business stems from the introduction of *Competition and Credit Control* which was designed to provide and encourage a more competitive framework for the whole banking system.

5.3 Summary

i. The early part of the chapter briefly traced the development of English commercial banking, emphasizing the role of the goldsmiths in this process.

ii. We drew attention to the distinctive development of the private banks and the joint-stock banks and pointed out that the joint-stock banks based their growth on the spread of the banking habit and use of deposits. This contrasted with the private banks which had relied on their right to issue notes as their main source of profit.

iii. The primary banks, as private sector profit-making firms, provide a range of services for their customers.

iv. In the management of their own balance sheets, the banks have to balance the conflicting objectives of liquidity and profitability. In addition, the banks are very much constrained by the regulations laid down by the monetary authorities – the main instrument being the Bank of England.

v. The banks obtain funds from a range of sources, but it is the personal sector and the company sector which provide the bulk of their deposits. Overseas deposits and funds from other financial firms have, however, grown in importance.

6
The stock of money

6.1 Introduction

In Chapter 2, Section 2.4.3, we restated the problem of finding an adequate *definition* of the money stock from a theoretical point of view. The object of this chapter is to consider the components of the money stock and to deal with the question of how and why the money stock may *change*. Finally, we shall consider some basic ideas underlying the problem of regulating the money stock, and the nature of conditions necessary for this to be achieved. Since it is arguable that changes in the quantity of money in the economy affect the level of economic activity and therefore the standard of living of the community, one can understand why the last question is of considerable importance to economists and government policy-makers.

6.2 The banks and the stock of money

6.2.1 DEPOSIT CREATION

Whichever definition of money one chooses (see Chapter 2, Tables 2.3 and 2.4, p. 31 and p. 32), it is clear that the dominant component is bank deposits – regardless of whether one considers M_1 or M_3. Notes and coin in circulation with the public are a relatively small part of the total stock of money. It is crucially important, therefore, that we are able to explain the changes which take place in the volume of bank deposits, and it is the purpose of this section to provide a preliminary explanation. The type of banks with which we are mainly concerned are those banks whose liabilities are treated as a medium of exchange and payment.

It was pointed out in Chapter 5 that the primary banks (in particular the London Clearing Banks) voluntarily had adopted certain safe asset ratios in order to maintain the confidence of the public and to ensure bank solvency. Chapter 3, Section 3.2.4 was concerned with the economic basis for financial intermediation and used a deposit bank as an example. We suggested that a bank need not maintain a 100 per cent reserve ratio in order to remain solvent so long as it maintained a sufficient quantity of liquid assets (in our example, 'cash') to meet expected and unexpected net withdrawals (loss of deposits). This approach represents our starting-point in the more comprehensive discussion about changes in the volume of bank deposits. It is instructive to examine this topic from the viewpoint of the *individual* bank and also in terms of the banking system *as a whole*.

6.2.1.1 *The individual bank and the generation of bank deposits*

Let us assume for simplicity that a new bank is established and that this bank is the only bank operating in the financial system. Had we chosen to assume that there are several banks operating, this would not alter the conclusions at which we shall arrive but it would complicate the description unnecessarily. At the beginning, the bank's only assets are likely to be the funds provided by shareholders which are in part converted into bank premises. This source of funds is not, however, the prime source of profit for such a bank: its main task is to attract deposits from other sectors of the economy. Let us further assume that long banking experience has established that the bank requires a safe minimum cash ratio of 10 per cent of its deposit liabilities. In other words, for every £100 deposited with the bank, the bank will need to hold £10 in cash (notes and coin) in order to meet the day-to-day needs of its customers. A cash holding of less than 10 per cent would result, we presume, in the bank being unable to meet the daily *net* demand for cash brought about by customers converting their bank deposits into cash. (Remember that both cash withdrawals and cash deposits will be occurring each day and that it will be the net position which is of concern to the bank.) Since the bank will not need to hold cash in excess of 10 per cent of deposit liabilities, we may assume that the funds deposited in excess of the cash ratio requirement will be used eventually to purchase earning assets for the bank's own balance sheet. The balance sheet we have used in our first illustration displays a cash ratio in excess of 10 per cent (it is, in fact, 13 per cent) and we may presume for convenience that this bank has yet to exploit all the opportunities open to it. A simplified balance sheet might resemble, therefore, bank balance sheet (1).

Bank balance sheet (1)

Assets		Liabilities	
Cash	£1,300,000	£10,300,000	Customers' deposits
Other earning assets:			
Very liquid assets	3,000,000		
Less liquid assets	6,000,000		
	£10,300,000	£10,300,000	

This approach to changes in the volume of bank deposits suggests that the bank's role is a passive one – merely to await customers placing deposits with the bank and then to choose an array of assets which meet its own liquidity requirements. In terms of our discussion in Chapter 3, it would be difficult to distinguish such a bank from any other sort of financial intermediary whether it be, say, a building society or an investment trust, since the bank appears to be merely transmitting funds (deposits) which have appeared from elsewhere.

Such a view would be erroneous, at least in part, since the primary banks' deposit liabilities have a special property: they are generally acceptable as a means of payments and exchange,[1] i.e. *such deposits are money*. The implications of this are that the expansion of a bank's business is only partly dependent on *attracting* deposits since such a bank is capable of *creating* deposit liabilities against itself by virtue of the fact that its deposits are held and used as money. (Indeed, for many purposes the transfer of a bank deposit rather than cash as a means of payment is preferable, particularly where large sums of money are concerned, and for many it is simply more convenient than using cash.) This phenomenon allows such a bank to purchase earning assets by creating a corresponding liability against itself in the form of a bank deposit. Let us consider three examples.

(a) If the bank decides to renovate its premises and, assuming that the firm which undertakes the work has its account with the bank, on completion of the work payment can be made by the bank quite simply crediting the account of the firm with the appropriate sum.[2] Bank balance sheet (2) might represent such a transaction.

Bank balance sheet (2)

Assets		Liabilities	
Cash	£1,300,000	£10,300,000	Customers' deposits
Other earning assets:			
Very liquid assets	3,000,000		
Less liquid assets	6,000,000		
Premises	10,000	10,000	Additional customers' deposits (i.e. the firm which has worked on the premises)
	£10,310,000	£10,310,000	

[1] More precisely, sight deposits and that fraction of time deposits which, by convention, are treated as convertible into sight deposits by the holder of such deposits.
[2] It should be noted that this represents a simplification for illustrative purposes. The bank would in fact draw the funds from its own accounts.

(b) An alternative situation could occur where the bank receives a request for a loan or overdraft facility. The majority of firms or individuals who request this facility are unlikely to require the funds in the form of cash but would prefer to have their account credited with the loan (or to utilize their overdraft facility) in the form of a bank deposit. Bank balance sheet (3) illustrates the effect of granting a loan in the form of a bank deposit.

Bank balance sheet (3)

Assets			*Liabilities*
Cash	£1,300,000	£10,300,000	Customers' deposits
Other earning assets:			
Very liquid assets	3,000,000		
Less liquid assets	6,000,000		
Advances:			
Loan	10,000	10,000	Additional customers deposit (i.e. the bank has granted the loan by crediting the customer's account with a deposit)
	£10,310,000	£10,310,000	

It should be noted that in these two latter illustrations the bank remains solvent despite the increase in its liabilities. The crucial factor here is whether the bank's cash ratio is still adequate. Prior to the change in bank liabilities, the cash ratio was 13 per cent (£1,300,000/£10,300,000, i.e. the bank was maintaining a cash ratio in excess of the safe minimum) and after the change in bank liabilities, the cash ratio fell to 12·6 per cent (£1,300,000/£10,310,000). We have assumed that the safe cash ratio is 10 per cent and therefore in our examples the bank is sustaining an excessively high ratio, which leads us to consider the extent to which bank business may be expanded safely within the limits of this ratio. In other words, what is the maximum level of deposit liabilities which the bank can sustain with its existing holdings of cash? Since we know that bank cash must be no less than 10 per cent of deposit liabilities, we can express the problem symbolically:

$$C_b = \frac{10}{100} \cdot D$$

where C_b represents the amount of bank cash, and D represents deposit liabilities. We wish to know the maximum level of deposit liabilities (D) sustainable by a given volume of cash (C_b), and by rearranging the terms in the above expression, we have:

$$D = \frac{100}{10} \cdot C_b$$

The volume of bank cash is £1,300,000 and by substituting this in the above expression we can calculate the maximum level of D. In this case it is, of course, £13,000,000. Let us cross-check the answer. If deposits were at that level of £13,000,000, and bank cash holding was £1,300,000, what would be the size of the cash ratio? Obviously it would be 10 per cent, and we can conclude that at that level of deposit liabilities the bank would remain liquid. The numerical value which measures the volume of bank deposits sustainable by, in this case, a given volume of cash (or any other asset(s) used as reserves by the bank) is sometimes referred to as the 'deposit-multiplier'. Any further increase in the volume of bank deposits, however, may result in the bank's inability to meet day-to-day demands for cash by customers. For example, if deposits were £14,000,000 and bank cash was still £1,300,000, the cash ratio would have fallen to about 9 per cent and the implication of this – given our initial assumptions about the origin of the cash ratio – would be that for every £10 claims to cash (e.g. customers cashing cheques) the bank would have only £9 cash in its tills. Clearly the bank could not sustain such a situation and it would have either to increase its holdings of cash by some means or to reduce its liabilities. (These problems will be considered later.) The important point to realize at this stage is that the bank in our example could expand its deposits further – beyond £10,310,000 – through additional bank lending until the upper limit of £13,000,000 was reached. Thus the expansion of deposits may arise because the bank itself is *creating* deposits through its business activity and not merely as the result of customers placing deposits with the bank.

It is sometimes argued that an individual bank does not create money (i.e. deposits) by its activities since it can only lend what it has got – in other words, the suggestion is that banks merely transmit funds from depositor to borrower and do not *add to* the volume of bank money (deposits). Even if this proposition were accurate, we can show that a bank which only lends what it has got will none the less be part of a process of deposit creation. To illustrate this, let us assume that a bank receives deposits of *cash* and only lends *cash* – it does not lend by creating a deposit liability against itself. Let us assume also that the borrower of cash spends the money and that the recipient, e.g. a shopkeeper, deposits the cash in the bank. We will also maintain the assumption of a 10 per cent cash ratio. The sequence of balance sheets (4) and (5) could represent the process of deposit creation.

Bank balance sheet (4)

Assets		Liabilities	
Cash	£1,000,000	Deposit	£1,000,000
	£1,000,000		£1,000,000

Bank balance sheet (5)

Assets		Liabilities	
Cash	£100,000	Deposit	£1,000,000
Cash loan	900,000		
	£1,000,000		£1,000,000

Bank balance sheet (6)

Assets		Liabilities	
Cash	£100,000	Deposit	£1,000,000
New cash receipt	900,000	New Deposit	900,000
Cash loan (1)	900,000		
	£1,900,000		£1,900,000

Having made the loan of £900,000 in cash (i.e. the bank is only lending what it has got) the money is spent and received by others, e.g. shopkeepers, who eventually *deposit such receipts in their bank account*. The next stage may be seen in bank balance sheet (6). It should be noted that total bank deposits have risen and also that position (6) is one of excess cash holdings by the bank since its cash ratio is 52·6 per cent (£1,000,000/£1,900,000). The bank is now in a position to make further loans if the demand exists. Let us assume that there are customers who wish to borrow to the limit that the bank is capable of lending. Balance sheets (7), (8), and (9) illustrate what would be the result.

Bank balance sheet (7)

Assets		Liabilities	
Cash	£190,000	Deposits	£1,900,000
Cash loan (1)	900,000		
Cash loan (2)	810,000		
	£1,900,000		£1,900,000

Bank balance sheet (8)

Assets		Liabilities	
Cash	£190,000	Deposits	£1,900,000
New cash receipt	810,000	New deposit	810,000
Cash loan (1)	900,000		
Cash loan (2)	810,000		
	£2,710,000		£2,710,000

Bank balance sheet (9)

Assets		Liabilities	
Cash	£271,000	Deposits	£2,710,000
Cash loan (1)	900,000		
Cash loan (2)	810,000		
Cash loan (3)	729,000		
	£2,710,000		£2,710,000

Presuming that the second loan is spent and then later re-deposited with the bank, we would find the situation, in balance sheet (8). Under these circumstances, not only have total deposits risen again but the bank's cash ratio is once more in excess of the safe minimum, i.e. the cash ratio is 36·9 per cent (£1,000,000/£2,710,000). Thus the bank is still capable of making further cash loans without experiencing a shortage of cash. We will assume one further round of lending set out in balance sheet (9),[3] and then attempt to draw certain conclusions.

(i)   Although the bank is only lending what it has got, the volume of bank deposits is rising. This occurs because we have assumed that the recipients of the spent bank loans choose to place them in their own bank accounts.

(ii)   The capacity of the bank to make loans is diminishing. This is because the fixed amount of cash in the system – £1,000,000 – is becoming a smaller and smaller fraction of the rising volume of deposits (which are always potential claims on cash). The bank therefore has to make additions to its cash reserve before it considers further lending.

(iii)   The process of deposit expansion can continue so long as the cash loaned does *not* remain outside the bank, in the hands of the public.

(iv)   The process of lending can continue (so long as there is a demand for bank loans) until the bank's liabilities are related

[3] The reader should be able to repeat the sequences, showing that a substantial amount of additional lending is possible.

to bank cash holdings in the ratio of 1:10, i.e. the process of expansion of loans and deposits will cease only when the cash ratio has become 10 per cent. This will occur when total deposits are £10,000,000 and cash holdings are £1,000,000. Total lending by the bank will amount to £9,000,000 and yet the whole banking system will have adhered to the maxim of only lending what it has got.

(c) Finally, we should identify another means by which the volume of bank deposits may rise. This can come about through the bank's purchases of financial assets, either from its own customers or through existing financial markets. In the latter instance we must add the proviso that the financial assets sold to the bank are from the non-government sector. (We shall be dealing with this more fully in Section 6.2.2.) If a bank does purchase financial assets from the non-government sector (e.g. persons, industrial and financial companies, charities, etc.) the means of payment is most likely to be the creation and transfer of a bank deposit to the sellers and, as with the previous examples, the process of deposit expansion may take place in that way. Balance sheets (10) and (11) illustrate the point.

Bank balance sheet (10)

	Assets		*Liabilities*	
Cash	£1,000,000	Deposits		£1,000,000
	£1,000,000			£1,000,000

Bank balance sheet (11)

	Assets		*Liabilities*	
Cash	£1,000,000	Deposits		£1,000,000
Purchase of securities	9,000,000	New deposits (i.e. payments to those who have sold their securities to the bank)		9,000,000
	£10,000,000			£10,000,000

Although the above illustrations of deposit creation may seem rather artificial, they show nevertheless that the bank(s), by virtue of the special nature of their liabilities, can increase such liabilities without becoming illiquid. In the following section we shall be considering whether there are further limits to the process of deposit creation by the primary banks.

It would appear that there are two crucial factors which affect the volume of deposits, regardless of the approach we take to the mechanism of deposit creation. One is the volume of cash which the banks hold or to which they have easy access. If the total amount of cash available is fixed, then this acts as a constraint on bank activity. The other factor is the size of the cash ratio. In our examples we have assumed, for convenience, that the cash ratio is 10 per cent. This has implied that with a given quantity of cash as a reserve asset, the banks are able to support deposit liabilities by ten times the quantity of cash they hold. If the safe minimum cash ratio were 20 per cent, the capacity to support a given volume of deposit liabilities would halve, i.e. the deposit-multiplier would be 5 and not 10. On the other hand, a safe minimum cash ratio of 1 per cent would allow a given cash base to support deposit liabilities up to 100 times the volume of cash held by the bank.

6.2.2 CONSTRAINTS ON THE GROWTH OF BANK DEPOSITS

In the simple illustrations used so far we have seen that if the bank's cash reserves are fixed and if the safe minimum cash ratio is maintained, then our hypothetical bank would be able to expand the volume of deposits by a multiple of 10. This hypothetical *deposit-multiplier* would seem to be very powerful: £1 cash supporting £10 deposit money. (Chapter 5 contained reference to a cash ratio of 8 per cent which was maintained by the London Clearing Banks and, on the face of it, indicates that a London Clearing Bank would have been able to generate and support £12·50 deposit-money for every £1 cash held in its tills.) There are, however, a number of reasons why such a deposit-multiplier is unlikely to be so powerful in a realistic banking system. We shall identify three basic reasons.

(a) *Leakages*. A particularly important weakness of the preceding account is our assumption that the quantity of cash providing the cash base of the bank will remain unchanged as its deposits expand in the various ways described. There are several reasons why the cash base is unlikely to remain so conveniently stable.

(i) The non-government sector is likely to want to hold *cash* as well as bank deposits, and so far we have ignored this phenomenon. It appears that the public's demand for cash is fairly closely related to the volume of bank deposits the public holds (the relationship appears to be closer and more stable than say, the relationship between cash holdings and domestic expenditure). In other words, as additional bank deposits are held by the public, they will wish to convert part of that bank deposit into cash, either by reducing the flow of cash deposits into the banks or by cashing cheques. We must accept therefore that if a bank or banks expand their deposits and these deposits are held by the non-government sector, then the banks must expect a drain of cash as the public meets its desired ratio of cash to bank deposits. Thus the process of deposit expansion contains within itself the seeds of its own cessation: one is the rise in bank deposits which steadily reduces the cash ratio, and the other is the fact that the additional deposits created generate a demand for cash by the public which in turn reduces further the size of the cash ratio as cash is drawn from the banking system by the public. Our earlier illustrations of deposit creation ignored this probability. The bank's cash ratio and cash holdings were for encashment purposes for the bank's customers. As one customer withdrew cash, another customer would be depositing cash. The point we are making here is that the public is likely to have *a demand to hold cash*.

(ii) Our second point directs attention to a constraint which affects the individual bank. Let us alter our assumptions slightly and assume that the total cash held by the banking system is fixed, but that there are several banks in the system – not just one – which maintain the same cash ratio. If we now assume that *one* of the banks decides to expand deposits at a faster rate than the other banks, then this bank will experience the constraint of a cash shortage – a consequence of a movement of cash from its own reserves to the other banks. The reason for this is that deposits expansion through, say, an increase in bank advances will be associated with a transfer of some deposits to the *other banks*. The reason for such transfers is simply that some of the final recipients of the loaned funds (i.e. after the funds have been spent by the borrowers) are likely to have bank accounts with the other banks. Inter-bank indebtedness which will arise after cheque clearings will reveal a *net* indebtedness of the expansionary bank with the rest of the banking system. Settlement of such indebtedness is possible by cash transfers through the agency of the central bank. If the expansionary bank persists in deposit expansion which is out of line with the other banks, the decline in its cash base will put a break ultimately on such independent expansion.

(iii) Earlier in this section (p. 120) we emphasized that banks may add to the volume of deposits by the purchase of securities which are sold to them by the *non-government sector*. The reason for this stipulation is that if banks buy securities from the *government* sector, this will tend to reduce the volume of bank deposits. This surprising conclusion is based on the assumption that the government sector uses the central bank as its bank rather than the other banks which operate in the private sector. In other words, the British Government uses the Bank of England as its bank rather than, say, Barclays Bank. The following illustration should make the point clear.

Let us assume a bank does buy securities which are being sold by the Bank of England (via the Stock Exchange) on behalf of the Government and then examine the consequences. The crucial factor is that the method by which the banks make payment to the government is through their accounts held at the Bank of England (see Chapter 4, Section 4.4.2.2). If a bank is a net purchaser of government securities from the Bank of England, the result will be a fall in Bankers' deposits at the Bank of England, i.e. a fall in the cash holdings of the bank. Since bank liabilities will remain unchanged initially, the effect of the fall in the bank's cash base is to reduce the size of the cash ratio. If the bank was operating at a level of deposits whereby the minimum cash ratio was achieved, the fall in the volume of cash at the Bank of England clearly would push the cash ratio below the safe minimum. If this occurred and the bank was unable to obtain cash from alternative sources, the bank would have to take action to reduce its deposit liabilities until the required cash ratio was re-established. Hence our suggestion above that the consequence of banks buying securities from the government could be a possible reduction in the volume of deposits. Thus, to the extent that banks buy government securities from the government sector, this represents a leakage of cash from the banks. A further question which will be considered in Section 6.3 is whether the government spends the money raised through the sale of securities or allows it to lie idle as a balance at the Bank of England.

(iv) Individual banks are sensitive to the transfer of funds (deposits) by their customers to other financial intermediaries. They are sensitive because this represents a loss of funds which may well be in the form of time deposits – deposits which provide the banks with fairly cheap and profitable funds. A good example of such transfers is the movement of funds by customers from their time deposits into a share account with a building society. Such accounts offer the investor the advantages of a time deposit with a bank: very liquid and very safe, with the additional benefit, usually, of a higher rate of interest. Although this switching of funds is a phenomenon which the banks do not like, it is possible to argue that this 'leakage' is not quite of the same kind as the three we have identified so far. The reason is that the building societies hold working balances with the banks, i.e. a building society will have a sight deposit with a bank or several banks. The other working balance required by the building society will be cash in their branches to meet the cash withdrawals of their depositors and shareholders (see Section 4.6 which deals with building society accounts). Initially the funds transferred to the building society will be re-deposited by the building society with a bank and there would therefore be no loss of deposits by the banking system as a whole. The main qualification we need to make at this stage is that to the extent that the building societies will raise their cash holdings (they will need to do this since their own liabilities will have increased as a result of the transfer of funds to them), there will be a loss of cash from the banking system and a depressant effect on the cash ratio of the banking system.

Although such transfers may represent a large leakage to an individual bank, the net leakage to the whole banking system is likely to be much smaller: the actual size will depend on the reserve ratios of the building societies and the cash component of that ratio, i.e. how much cash the building societies drain from the banks. In reality the cash ratio of the building societies is very small – around 1 per cent – much smaller than the primary banks' ratio in the U.K. It is likely that the policy of the building societies towards the purchase of government securities is of greater significance to the banking system in respect of the potential cash drain. If the building societies used the additional funds deposited with them from the banks to purchase large amounts of government securities *from the government sector itself*, this would cause a more serious cash drain from the banking system than building society adjustments of their own cash ratio and cash holdings (see Section 6.3.1.2 below). Note that if the building societies – or any other type of financial intermediary – held all their working balances with the banks, the transfer of funds from the banks to such intermediaries would not result, of itself, in a reduction in the volume of bank deposits.

(b) *Demand for loans.* In our earlier account of the expansion of deposits through increased bank lending, we made no reference to the *demand* side for such loans. Implicitly we were assuming that if the banks were able to offer loans and overdrafts, the demand would be there. This assumption is not acceptable, however, since there is no reason to suppose that the demand for bank loans would match the supply at prevailing rates of interest on such loans. What then determines the demand for loans from the banks? This is a very broad question so we shall limit our discussion to the business sector. In Chapter 5 we saw, for example, that the primary banks in the U.K. lend to a wide range of business activity: industry of all kinds, commerce, and finance. The reasons behind such lending are likely to be varied and probably quite complex. We can suggest, nevertheless, that all the borrowers will have in mind the cost of such borrowing in relation to their expected return on the use of such funds and the risks associated with the intended use of the funds. For example, medium-term borrowing by manufacturing firms used for the purchase of capital equipment will be linked closely with the expected return on such investment which, in turn, will be geared to the current and expected demand for the products of that firm. If we generalize this, we can suggest that the borrowing by manufacturing firms is likely to be related to the state of the economy or, slightly more precisely, to the stage of the business cycle which the economy has reached and the course which it is likely to take. During periods when business activity is increasing it is probable that the demand for loans will rise (not least because firms will require additional working capital) and in times of contraction or business stagnation, the opposite will be the case. It is possible that the banks may have the capacity and inclination to expand their lending, but the demand for loans may be less than the potential supply. One factor may be that the demand for loans will be less than that which the banks wish to offer because the interest rate charged on such borrowing may be too high. (It will be remembered that we have suggested already that the demand and supply may not match at prevailing rates of interest.) If this is the case, the banks will be induced to lower their interest rates on loans in order to stimulate demand

(c) *Banks' lending policy.* We have emphasized repeatedly that the primary banks' obligations to depositors are such that the banks must be prudent in the management of their own assets. Since the largest single item is 'advances to customers' (of which only about one quarter represents personal borrowing) it is important that the banks are careful in the handling of this item. Part of the art of banking is the capacity to evaluate the risk of a potential loan and to judge the appropriate rate of interest and the term of the advance. A misjudgement in respect of these two features of the loan in periods when banks are eager to expand such business – when they are 'under-lent' – could result in the potential borrower changing his bank or requesting a loan from another bank. One problem which arises is that the risk factor of a particular project for which a loan is required is likely to vary with the course of the business cycle. In periods of low business activity many firms will be less profitable and this could be a factor influencing the bank's decision with regard to a loan, i.e. in times of business recession, banks will be less inclined to lend to firms which in past circumstances might have been regarded as a good risk. When a recession ends and there are clear indications that an upturn is beginning, the banks may change their view of the riskiness of loans and allow their lending to expand to certain types of business. The implication here is that the banks might tend to be fair-weather friends and are unlikely to be of assistance to firms at the very times when such assistance is desperately needed (for example, with the continuation or increase of overdraft facilities). Although our remarks so far suggest that bank preference may well be in favour of a high degree of caution, in practice a bank is likely to behave differently. If a bank takes the long-term view, it may realize that the ultra-safe lending strategy could result in the loss of custom: borrowers who have been refused or restricted in their borrowing, yet survive a business recession, are unlikely to maintain their custom with the bank which has been very limited in its assistance. Furthermore, a bank may be unable to extricate itself from commitments to borrowers if by withdrawing further support the result is bankruptcy of a business firm. In this way, a bank may be faced with the prospect either of providing additional funds to enable a firm to ride a rough period, or withdraw support and lose most of the funds that have already been lent.

For many years the banks have been subject to the criticism that their lending to industry has been far too cautious, in particular their lending to the small and medium-size firm, so that there has been a shortage of funds facing many firms. New and fast-growing firms have found the problem of adequate supplies of working capital particularly acute (these firms are prone to insolvency or bankruptcy partly as a result of their need for adequate and growing supplies of working capital), and firms which are hoping to invest in the production of high technology products, or firms using high technology equipment, often find finance a problem since the risk element may be relatively high for such ventures. Partly as a result of this kind of argument, a number of *ad hoc* bodies have been established.[4] It should be clear that bank lending policy, influenced by the bank's evaluation of risk and uncertainty in general as well as in particular cases, will influence the preparedness of the bank to expand advances and, therefore, its deposits. Our simple model used earlier in this chapter does not take these various elements into consideration.

6.3 The government and the stock of money

6.3.1 THE CASH NEXUS

We have observed earlier that financial dealings between the government and the non-government sector are ultimately transactions of a *cash* nature. Chapters 9 and 10 deal with the government's finances quite extensively and certainly in much more detail than is intended in this chapter. Our object here is to identify two aspects of the cash nexus between the government and the

---

[4]See glossary at the end of the book, p. 357

non-government sector and to consider the possible effects of this relationship on the stock of money.

6.3.1.1 Government spending

The reader is recommended to turn to Chapter 9, Section 9.3 for details of government spending and receipts. *Table 9.3* shows the items of spending for the financial year 1977–8 but it is important to realize that spending is taking place continuously throughout the financial year and is subject to variations during the year; it is not an even rate of spending. The government departments, not all of which are big spenders, have their accounts at the Bank of England (this is the item 'public deposits' in the balance sheet of the Bank of England). We can choose an item of government spending and trace its possible course from the government sector to the non-government sector, in particular to the banking sector. For simplicity, let us consider the payment of £1 million by the Ministry of Defence on completion of a military contract placed with a U.K. firm. The Ministry of Defence, having an account at the Bank of England, will draw a cheque on that account for £1 million, made payable to the supplying company. The firm receives the cheque for £1 million and deposits it with its bank – say, Barclays Bank. Barclays Bank, acting on behalf of the firm, will (a) credit the firm's account with £1 million so that Barclays Bank's deposits rise by £1 million, and (b) present the cheque for payment at the Bank of England (for simplicity we shall ignore any other financial transactions involving the Bank of England and Barclays Bank). The Bank of England will then make payment to Barclays Bank by crediting Barclays Bank account at the Bank with £1 million (Bankers' deposits rise by £1 million) and by debiting the Ministry of Defence's account by £1 million (public deposits fall by £1 million). This is not the end of the story, however, since Barclays Bank will find itself holding excess cash. If we assume, again for simplicity, that the cash ratio is 10 per cent, then Barclays Bank is holding excess cash to the tune of £900,000. It is £900,000 and not £1 million because Barclays Bank will need to retain 10 per cent of the extra deposits of £1 million as part of the extra cash needed to sustain the extra deposits. The cash is available to Barclays Bank since its total cash includes accounts at the Bank of England and these, as we have just seen, have risen by £1 million. It is clear that Barclays Bank is now in a position to expand its business on the basis of the inflated cash reserve. If we assume that Barclays Bank *retains* the additional £1 million cash as part of its reserve, it may be able to expand its deposits by increasing its assets up to a maximum level which will be determined by the size of the deposit-multiplier. This simple illustration allows us to draw certain conclusions.

(i)   Government spending can add to the volume of bank deposits directly (the firm in our example had increased its bank deposits by £1 million).

(ii)   Government spending can add to the cash base of a bank and the banking system.

(iii)   As a consequence of the addition to the cash base, the bank(s) are able to expand their business by virtue of their initially higher cash ratio, i.e. government spending provides a stimulus for the deposit-multiplier. *In this way the banks may increase their advances to customers or buy other financial assets.*

6.3.1.2 Government receipts

As with government spending we shall choose an illustrative receipt and trace its progress. Let us assume that an individual is liable for capital gains tax of £1,000. On receipt of the tax demand the individual will write a cheque for £1,000 payable to the Inland Revenue's account with the Bank of England. When the Inland Revenue receives the cheque, it will deposit it in its account at the Bank of England. The Bank of England will credit the Inland Revenue with £1,000 and present the cheque for payment by, say, Barclays Bank on behalf of its tax-paying customer. Barclays Bank is able to make payment by means of a reduction in its account with the Bank of England (Bankers' balances fall by £1,000) and Barclays Bank will then reduce their customer's deposit by £1,000. After these adjustments have been made it should be clear that Barclays Bank has experienced a drain of £1,000 cash from its cash reserve and a reduction in deposits by £1,000. The reduction in its cash reserve, however, may result in Barclays Bank's cash ratio falling below the required minimum figure since, if we maintain the assumption of a 10 per cent cash ratio, we can see that the loss of £1,000 *cash* reduces the capacity of Barclays Bank to sustain deposit liabilities of £10,000. Of this £10,000, £1,000 has disappeared as a result of reducing the customer's account by £1,000 after the payment of the capital gains tax, but this still leaves £9,000 deposits unsupported by sufficient cash. If we assume Barclays Bank are unable to replenish their cash reserve, the bank must make efforts to reduce its deposit liabilities by selling assets or by reducing advances by £9,000. Our illustration allows us to draw additional conclusions:

(i)   Government receipts can cause a fall in bank deposits directly (i.e. when the bank reduces the customer's deposit after paying the tax).

(ii)   Government receipts can reduce the cash base of a bank or the banking system.

(iii) As a consequence of the reduction of the cash base and the reduced cash ratio, the bank(s) are induced to cut back further their deposit liabilities, i.e. there is a *negative* deposit-multiplier. *Thus, the banks may have to reduce their advances to customers or sell other financial assets.*

Having examined the effects of government spending and receipts on the level of bank deposits, it should be clear that the effect of the government's spending and receipts on the banking system will depend on the *net* position. Each day the government is spending and receiving money: at times spending will exceed receipts and at others receipts will exceed spending. The final effect on the banking system will depend, therefore, on the net figure. For example, on a particular day the government may receive £90 million in taxes and other receipts, and spend £110 million, which in this case represents a net flow of £20 million from the government sector to the non-government sector, and as this feeds into the banking system there will tend to be an expansionary stimulus to bank deposit growth. It should be remembered that such a net outflow, when it finally reaches the banking system, will manifest itself as a *cash* flow from the Bank of England to the banking system. Thus:

(a) Government spending in excess of receipts leads to a net outflow of cash from the government sector, a stimulus to bank deposit growth, and an increase in the stock of money in the economy.

(b) Government spending which is less than receipts leads to a net outflow from the non-government sector to the government sector and a contractionary pressure on bank deposit growth, and therefore reduction of the stock of money in the economy.

(c) Expressing points (a) and (b) above in terms of the central government's budgetary situation, we can suggest that a budget deficit situation will tend to produce monetary expansion in the banking system, and a budget surplus situation will tend to produce monetary contraction.

6.3.2 GOVERNMENT BORROWING

In Section 6.31 we examined the implications for the banking system and stock of money of a change in the net position of government receipts and expenditure. For example, if government spending exceeded receipts, this would tend to be an expansionary factor influencing the banking system, but we ignored the implications of the net spending (i.e. the deficit) for government borrowing. We shall consider this question now.

If the government is to cover the deficit, it will need to borrow.[5] (See Chapter 10 for further discussion of government borrowing.) It is important to establish the consequences of government borrowing from the different sources within the economy, and these sources are as follows:

(i)　Borrowing from the non-bank public (i.e. persons, firms, non-bank financial intermediaries, etc.)

(ii)　Borrowing from the Bank of England (remember that the Bank of England is the government's banker).

(iii)　Borrowing from the banking system.

We would emphasize that the consequences of these three types of borrowing are not the same, and we shall examine therefore each of the sources.

(i) *Borrowing from the non-bank public.* In order to raise the necessary funds to cover its deficit, the government may attempt to sell a variety of suitable and acceptable securities to the non-bank public. Let us assume that the government's deficit in the period we are considering is £10 million and that the whole of this deficit is covered by sales of government bonds to the non-bank public. We can now trace the consequences of this sale. The non-bank public are likely to pay for the stock entirely by means of cheques drawn on their bank deposits made payable to the Bank of England – the Bank is responsible for arranging bond sales for the government. Thus £10 million of cheques drawn largely on the deposits of primary banks will be received by the Bank of England. The Bank will collect payment in the usual way by deducting £10 million from the primary banks' balances held at the Bank. The result of this sale of government stock will be initially that (a) Bankers' balances at the Bank of England (remember that these balances are part of the banks' cash base) will fall by £10 million, (b) the banks will deduct £10 million from their customers' deposits and therefore total bank deposits will fall by £10 million, and (c) the banks' cash base will have fallen and their cash ratio also will have fallen. If there are no alternative sources of cash and the banks are operating at the minimum cash ratio, the banks would be induced to contract their deposit-liabilities. Thus in the first instance sales of government bonds to finance a budget deficit will tend to put contractionary pressures on the banks if the stock is bought by the non-bank public. This is not the end of the matter, however, since we must take into account the fact that the government is borrowing *in*

---

[5] Obviously the deficit could be eliminated by raising government receipts or cutting spending. If we assume that these two possibilities are either impracticable in the short run or undesired by the government, then the only alternative is for the government to borrow.

order to spend in excess of its receipts from other sources. We must therefore further take into the account the consequences of such 'deficit spending'. In Section 6.3.1.1. we saw that government spending adds to the volume of bank cash and bank deposits by an amount equal to the amount spent. We can conclude, therefore, in this section that the act of spending the borrowed £10 million will recycle the cash which was drained from the banking system when settlement was made at the Bank of England. The cash will return to the banking sector and bank deposits will rise by £10 million when the recipients of government spending make deposits with their primary banks.

It is evident that we need to modify our earlier conclusion that government borrowing from the non-bank public produces contractionary pressure on the banking system. This effect does not occur because the volume of bank cash and bank deposits remains unchanged *so long as the government spends the funds raised through its borrowing*. An alternative view of this would be that budget deficits financed by asset sales to the non-bank public leaves the monetary base and the banking system unaffected in so far as there is no direct pressure on the deposit component of the money stock to change.

(ii) *Borrowing from the Bank of England*. If the government is unable to sell sufficient quantities of securities to the non-bank public, it may choose to sell securities to the Bank of England. Since the Bank of England is a state-owned body, there is no legal or technical problem: the Bank of England would have no option but to act in accordance with the government's wishes. The operation would involve the exchange of securities – printed by the government, of course – for deposits at the Bank of England. So if the government sells £10 million securities to the Bank of England, the Bank's assets (securities) will increase by £10 million and its liabilities (public deposits) will rise also by £10 million. If we assume that the government spends the whole of these additional funds in the non-government sector, the final effect will be (a) a rise in non-government sector deposits with the banks of £10 million, and (b) a rise in the cash base of the banking system also by £10 million. The banks, therefore, would be in a more liquid position since their cash ratio would have risen and they would be able to expand their business activities through the purchase of other assets and/or the expansion of advances through deposit creation (we gave an illustration of this in Section 6.3.1.1). It is clear that borrowing from the Bank of England produces an expansionary stimulus to the banking system as well as increasing the money stock. Borrowing from the central bank in the manner described is the modern equivalent of earlier governments' resorting to the printing press to meet their monetary needs.[6]

(iii) *Borrowing from the banking system.* We shall consider two means by which borrowing from the banking system occurs and the possible consequences of such forms of borrowing.

(a) Let us assume that a bank is maintaining a cash reserve in excess of the safe minimum and decides to purchase government securities which are being offered for sale by the Bank of England.[7] A bank which purchases, say, £5 million of such securities will make payment through its account at the Bank of England, i.e. Bankers' balances at the Bank of England will fall by £5 million. Since this represents a reduction of the cash reserve of the bank, the purchase of such securities will be revealed in the bank's balance sheet as a switch in the composition of its assets and there will be no change in its liabilities. The two balance sheets (12) and (13) indicate the situation before and after the purchase of £5 million government securities by the bank. In this illustration, the banks' cash ratio has fallen from 20 per cent in position (12) to 10 per cent at position (13) after the purchase of the securities. It would appear that government borrowing from the bank also has had the effect of changing the structure of the bank's assets. Let us continue the description and consider the use of the funds so obtained. First, the public deposits at the Bank of England will rise by £5 million as Bankers' deposits fall by £5 million, and secondly, the government presumably has borrowed the money in order to spend it. As with an earlier illustration, the act of spending by the government will recycle the cash back to the non-government sector and eventually back into the banking system. The banking system will once again have a cash ratio in excess of the safe minimum and will have, therefore, the capacity to expand its business. It should be noted that the preceding analysis assumed that the bank was able to purchase government securities with its surplus cash. If the bank had been maintaining the minimum cash ratio, then the bank would *not* have been able to purchase government securities since such purchases would have pushed the bank's cash ratio below the *minimum required.*

(b) The second method of borrowing from the banking system

---

[6] It is likely that additional notes and coin would need to be produced in these circumstances because the volume of bank deposits held by the non-government sector would rise and the cash needs of this sector would rise also. (See Section 6.22, sub-section (i))

[7] If the banks bought securities in exchange for bank deposits from the *non-bank public*, via the stock market, the effect would be to raise deposits and bank assets by the amount of the purchase.

Bank balance sheet (12)

Assets		*Liabilities*	
Cash in tills and at the			
Bank of England	£10,000,000	Deposits	£50,000,000
Other earning assets	40,000,000		
	£50,000,000		£50,000,000

Bank balance sheet (13)

Assets		*Liabilities*	
Cash in tills and at the			
Bank of England	£5,000,000	Deposits	£50,000,000
Other earning assets	40,000,000		
Government securities	5,000,000		
	£50,000,000		£50,000,000

which we identify occurs in rather a different way from the first. This method is connected with what is termed the 'residual financing role' of the banking system. Let us consider a situation in which the government wishes to finance a deficit, but in which the non-bank public is not prepared to purchase all the securities which the government wishes to sell. Under such circumstances the government initially will obtain the funds from the Bank of England (the government must never be short of the funds it needs even if this entails borrowing from its own bank) and such funds are then spent. The consequence of borrowing from the Bank is to add to the cash base of the banking system and this surplus cash in the banking system may well be used to add to banks' lending at call to the discount houses who, in turn, are likely to add to their holdings of government Treasury bills. Sufficient bills will be on offer from the Bank of England, both to finance the original deficit from the market, and to eliminate the direct borrowing of the government from the Bank of England. On receipt of the funds raised by sales of Treasury bills, the government will repay the Bank of England, thus reducing its direct borrowing from the Bank.

This mechanism which we have described reveals how the banking system automatically finances a government deficit through the provision of funds to the discount market, followed by the take-up of additional Treasury bills on offer. If the government cannot finance its deficit by the issue of securities (i.e. relatively illiquid government stock), the necessary funds are likely to be raised by the issue of highly liquid Treasury bills.[8]

The descriptive analysis we have used so far has utilized a budget deficit as the example to illustrate the main points. The reader should attempt to describe the reverse situation, i.e. the implications for the banking system if the government is operating with a budget surplus. It is a useful exercise to study the text – especially Section 6.3 – and re-work the illustrations on the assumption that the government receipts exceed government spending.

6.4 The balance of payments and the stock of money

This section considers the relationship between the balance of payments of a country and the domestic money stock. So far in this chapter it has been an implicit assumption that the monetary system under consideration was in a closed economy, i.e. neither international trade nor international capital movements. This is, of course, an unacceptable assumption, particularly for the U.K., and we now propose to study the consequences of changing the assumption to that of an 'open economy'.

6.4.1 BANK OF ENGLAND OPERATIONS AND THE FOREIGN CURRENCY MARKET

U.K. residents and overseas residents are involved in the buying and selling of goods and services (this causes changes in the flow of income and expenditure in both the U.K. and foreign countries through imports and exports changes) as well as the buying and selling of assets (this causes changes in the composition of the stock of wealth of U.K. residents and overseas residents). Both types of activity are likely to have consequences for the domestic money stock of the U.K. Before continuing with our discussion we need to adopt a definition of the money stock. In Chapter 2, Section 2.4.3, we saw that the definitions of money stock used by the Bank of England had been altered to take into account the sterling component. For example, the 1976 (September) unadjusted figures for the two M_3 calculations of the money stock were:

Sterling M_3	M_3
£40,224 million	£44,233 million

The difference between the two figures (£4,009 million) represented U.K. residents' deposits in other currencies than sterling. These deposits consist of foreign currency deposits permitted by the foreign exchange authorities to be held by such firms as oil companies, insurance companies, and other firms involved in international

[8]The implications of this will be considered more fully in Chapter 7.

operations and therefore requiring foreign currency balances. Capital funds approved for foreign investment and awaiting investment abroad are also included in this figure. The separation of sterling M_3 from the overall figure for M_3 recognizes that it is the sterling volume of deposits which is likely to be the more relevant variable when considering the behaviour of the banking system and the economy.

For several decades the Bank of England has operated in the foreign currency market. Since 1932 the Bank's instrument has been the Exchange Equalisation Account although technically control is vested with the Treasury. The major role of the E.E.A. in the foreign exchange markets is to act as a stabilising influence on the course of exchange rates, checking undue fluctuations. Between 1944 and 1972 the E.E.A.'s operations were within an international framework of fixed exchange rates and the operations of the E.E.A. had to comply with international agreement (via the International Monetary Fund) regarding the extent of permitted variations in exchange rates. After June 1972 the U.K. (and later, other countries) defected from the system of fixed exchange rates and instead allowed the market forces of supply and demand for currencies to exercise a dominant influence on exchange rates. The basic mechanics of the E.E.A. are crucial to our consideration of the impact of the balance of payments on the domestic money stock (sterling M_3) and it is these mechanics which we will now examine,[9] with the assumption that the E.E.A. is intending to maintain fixed exchange rates.

(a) *Balance of payments 'deficit'*.[10] Let us assume that U.K. residents are attempting to buy £100 million of overseas goods, services, and assets during a particular period, and overseas residents are attempting to buy £50 million of U.K. goods, services, and assets in the same period. Imports are greater than exports and there is a balance of payments deficit of £50 million in that period. The manifestation of this in the foreign exchange markets is that there is an excess of sterling being supplied by U.K. residents wishing to spend on overseas goods, services, etc. If the exchange rate between the pound sterling and other currencies was determined entirely by market forces, the effect would be for the pound sterling to depreciate in value in the foreign exchange market as a result of the £50 million excess

[9]The Bank of England has published a useful article on the E.E.A. and this should be consulted for further detailed descriptions of methods of operation of the E.E.A. following its inception in 1932. Our account in the text is an abstract of such detail and concentrates on the essential (if simplified) elements. See Bank of England *Quarterly Bulletin*, vol. 8, No. 4 (December 1968), p.337.
[10]The word 'deficit' is given in inverted commas because of some of the theoretical difficulties associated with the precise meaning of the word in the context of the overall balance of payments accounts; and, similarly, 'surplus'. See Chapter 11.

supply of pounds. If the object of the government and the Bank of England is to stabilize the exchange rate, then the Bank of England via the E.E.A. will have to supply foreign currency to U.K. residents (£50 million worth of foreign currency) and take up the £50 million sterling being offered by U.K. residents through their banks. By absorbing the excess supply of pounds and by supplying foreign currency at the desired exchange rate, the exchange rate will therefore be stabilized at that rate. We can offer a few additional facts and conclusions.

(i)   The E.E.A. obtains the foreign currency from the Official Reserves of holdings of gold and foreign currencies. The Official Reserves will therefore fall.

(ii)   The E.E.A. has an additional £50 million sterling and in practice this is used to buy U.K. government Treasury bills supplied by the Bank of England.

(iii) U.K. residents make payment for the foreign currency by transferring sterling bank deposits, and since these deposits are transferred to the E.E.A. at the Bank of England, the result is a fall in sterling bank deposits by £50 million and also a fall in the cash base and the cash ratio of the banking system as the cheques drawn on the primary banks are settled at the Bank of England.

(iv)   Unless other financial changes occur (e.g. the government may choose to reduce its borrowing from the non-government sector as a result of the inflow of £50 million from the E.E.A. to the Bank of England), a balance of payments 'deficit' has a contractionary effect on the domestic banking system as well as directly reducing the volume of sterling bank deposits and, therefore, the stock of money.

(b) *Balance of payments 'surplus'* For simplicity, let us assume that the balance of payments surplus arises from U.K. residents' purchases from overseas totalling £50 million, and overseas residents are buying £100 million goods, services, and assets from the U.K. The £50 million surplus will reveal itself as an excess of £50 million of foreign currencies being offered on the foreign exchange market in relation to the sterling being offered by U.K. residents. The relative shortage of sterling, without intervention, would result in a rise or appreciation in the value of the pound sterling. In order to avoid such an occurrence the E.E.A. will proceed to sell sufficient sterling (£50 million) to prevent the exchange rate changing, and will absorb the foreign currency being offered by overseas residents. As a consequence of the E.E.A. action we can draw the following conclusions.

(i)   The E.E.A. obtains foreign currency from the market and E.E.A holdings of such funds will rise by £50 million; Official Reserves will rise by £50 millions of foreign currency.

(ii) The E.E.A. requires £50 million sterling for sale on the foreign exchange market and these funds will be obtained by the E.E.A. selling £50 million Treasury bills back to the Bank of England.

(iii) Overseas residents will deposit the sterling received from the E.E.A within the U.K. banking system prior to making payment for the goods, services, and assets bought. Such receipts will increase the Bankers' balances at the Bank of England (the transfer of funds between the E.E.A. and the non-government sector being a cash transfer) as well as increasing the volume of bank deposits by £50 million. Not only will the cash base of the banking system rise, but so too will the cash ratio.

(iv) Assuming that there are no other financial changes taking place (e.g. the government may choose to increase its borrowing from the non-government sector as a result of the outflow of £50 million from the Bank of England to the E.E.A.), the balance of payments surplus will be an expansionary stimulus to the domestic banking system as well as directly increasing the volume of bank deposits and, therefore, the stock of money.

Briefly, our analysis of changes in the balances of payments under a system of fixed exchange rates suggest that initially

(a) a balance of payments deficit will tend to reduce the domestic money stock by roughly the amount of the deficit;

and

(b) a balance of payments surplus will tend to raise the domestic money stock by roughly the amount of the surplus.

At the beginning of this section we stated that after June 1972 the U.K. abandoned the tight control over the exchange rate which had been a feature of the previous twenty-eight years. In its place the exchange rate for the pound sterling was allowed to be determined by market forces of supply and demand. Under these circumstances we need to consider the effects on the money stock of changes in U.K. residents' spending abroad and overseas residents' spending in the U.K. If one can assume that the monetary authorities are allowing the exchange rate to be established entirely by market forces, and the E.E.A. is not intervening in foreign currency markets, then the changes in the domestic money stock resulting from official (E.E.A.)

transactions cannot, by definition, occur. This does not mean that the money stock is entirely unconnected with the behaviour of non-residents: the definition of sterling M_3 excludes U.K. residents' foreign currency deposits and non-residents' *sterling* deposits. If as a result of trade or capital movements, therefore, non-residents accumulate additional sterling bank deposits which were held previously by U.K. residents, the effect on the money stock statistics is to reduce the size of sterling M_3 and vice versa.

Our discussion of fixed and floating exchange rates leads us to the conclusion that under a system of fixed exchange rates the balance of payments will affect the money stock (unless offset by Bank intervention), and that the influence is both direct (caused by the movements in deposits as a direct result of the buying or selling of sterling) and indirect (associated with the secondary effects on bank deposits through changes in the cash base and cash ratio of the banking system). With floating exchange rates, any change in the money stock is brought about by changes in the composition of assets held by non-residents and the banking system.

6.4.2 DOMESTIC CREDIT EXPANSION

6.4.2.1 *Definition and calculation*

In 1969 the government stated in a Letter of Intent to the I.M.F. that it intended to adopt targets in respect of 'domestic credit expansion', and in September 1969 the Bank of England published an article which outlined its approach to the concept of domestic credit expansion (D.C.E.)[11] One of the main ideas underlying D.C.E. is embodied in Section 6.4.1 of this chapter, i.e. the recognition that changes in the balance of payments position may affect the size of the money stock. D.C.E. 'may be viewed as the total arrived at after adjusting the increase in the money supply to take account of any change in money balances directly caused by an external surplus or deficit'.[12] The external deficit or suplus was defined for the purposes of D.C.E. as the current account of the balance of payments plus short-term and long-term private capital flows, plus official lending overseas. In other words, the Bank was attempting to find a monetary indicator which would show the changes in the money supply caused by *domestic* pressures leading to a change in the credit component of the money supply. One might emphasize here the term 'credit' as used in the concept of D.C.E. Credit, or lending, is an item which appears on the assets side of banking institutions' balance sheets,

[11]Domestic Credit Expansion', supplement to the Bank of England *Quarterly Bulletin*, vol. 9, No. 3 (September 1969).
[12]Ibid.

whereas the money supply (largely composed of bank deposits) consists of items derived from the liabilities of the banks. Thus the calculation of D.C.E. is conceptually related to the assets side of the balance sheet rather than the more aggregative figure of bank deposits.

The two major borrowers are the public sector and the private sector, and examination of these two major borrowers (i.e. recipients of *credit*) represents a starting point. Earlier in this chapter (in Section 6.2.2) we saw the significance of government borrowing *vis-à-vis* the money supply. Government sector borrowing from the non-bank sector results in no change in the total of bank deposits or bank assets, whereas government borrowing which is not financed by funds from the non-bank sector is provided ultimately by the banking system in its residual financing role (see p. 133). This latter form of lending does result in a rise in both bank deposits and bank assets. Private sector borrowing from the banks in the form of advances also leads (as we saw in Section 6.2.1) to an increase in bank deposits as well as bank assets. Accordingly, the first calculation of D.C.E. is based on this approach and it can be presented thus:

Public sector borrowing requirement[13]

less sales of public sector debt to the non-bank private sector

plus bank lending to the private sector.

Two points of clarification are required.

(a) Part of the public sector's borrowing requirement may be financed by the overseas sector in the sense that a balance of payments 'deficit', (for example in a situation in which the goverment is stabilizing the exchange rate) will result in a flow of sterling to the government via the E.E.A. Such a flow of funds may reduce the need for the government to borrow domestically. Thus the item 'public sector borrowing requirement' *includes* the hidden financing of the public sector's deficit via the balance of payments position. Without the financing from the 'overseas sector', the government would have had to increase its borrowing from the domestic sector, possibly causing a rise in the money stock.

(b) In the 1969 calculation of D.C.E., bank lending to the private sector did not include lending to U.K. residents in foreign currency for investment abroad. The grounds for this exclusion were that such lending had virtually no effect *within* the U.K. whereas the D.C.E. calculation was intended to provide an indicator of domestic monetary changes. However, bank lending to overseas residents in sterling was included on the

---

[13] A similar – though broader – concept than 'government borrowing'. For a full explanation see Chapter 9, Sections 9.4 and 9.5.

grounds that such lending was likely to have a full impact
domestically.

We can now illustrate the calculation of changes in D.C.E. for the
period 1976–7 (*Table 6.1*). The contrast between changes in D.C.E.
and M_3 is brought out very clearly in the *Table 6.2*. If one accepts that
D.C.E. has significance as a monetary indicator, then it is clear that
observation of changes in M_3 considerably *understates* the extent of
monetary expansion within the U.K. during the period covered by
the table. Table 6.2 provides further illustration of the possible
differences in the money stock and changes in D.C.E.

TABLE 6.1
Change in D.C.E. – financial year 1976–7
(£ m.)

	Public sector borrowing requirement	+8,738
less	Sales of public sector debt to the non-bank	
	private sector	−7,459
plus	Bank sterling lending to the private sector	+3,414
		+4,738
	Adjustments:	
plus	Bank lending in sterling to overseas residents	+ 213
	Domestic Credit Expansion (changes in)	+4,951

Source: Bank of England *Quarterly Bulletin*, vol. 18, No. 1 (March 1978).

TABLE 6.2
(£ m.)

Financial years	(1) Changes in sterling M_3	(2) Changes in D.C.E.	(3) (2) − (1)
1971–2	+2,781	+2,370	− 411
1972–3	+5,263	+6,945	+1,682
1973–4	+6,125	+7,831	+1,706
1974–5	+2,738	+6,382	+3,644
1975–6	+2,453	+5,069	+2,616

Source: Bank of England *Quarterly Bulletin*, vol. 18, No. 1 (March 1978).

6.4.2.2 Uses of the D.C.E. calculation

We have discussed D.C.E. fairly thoroughly in this chapter because
the emergence and use of the concept by the authorities illustrated the

problem of choosing a staisfactory measure of monetary changes within an open economy. Although the D.C.E. series is still published by the Bank of England, it is probably accurate to say that D.C.E. no longer commands the same attention as formerly, or signifies greatly in official pronouncements, and that much more attention is paid to the basic money stock series, M_1 and M_3. There are at least two reasons for this relative decline in significance: one of them is probably the abandonment of fixed exchange rates three years after D.C.E. was introduced, and the other is that D.C.E. as a concept generated considerable criticism from economists. It is our intention in this section to present some of the objections which were put forward.

(a) D.C.E. may be interpreted simply as an adjustment to the basic money stock data. An important adjustment to the money stock data is the inclusion of changes in the overseas financing of the public sector. The connecting link between D.C.E., public sector borrowing requirement, and the money stock, is purely an arithmetic or accounting relationship. The links exist by virture of the definitions used and therefore cannot be taken to indicate causality or an economic relationship of importance. Interestingly, the published series in the Bank of England *Quarterly Bulletin* is no longer headed '*Influences* [our italics] on money stock and domestic credit expansion' but simply 'Public sector borrowing requirement, domestic credit expansion, and money stock'.

(b) In our earlier discussion of D.C.E. we drew attention to the explicit use of the term 'credit'. This credit component is, however, a limited concept since it includes only sterling lending by the U.K. banking sector to the private sector, and sterling lending overseas. The U.K. banking sector was in 1969 – and today still is – a somewhat arbitrary and limited classification of institutions which are involved in the provision of credit. A lending institution which happens not to be included in the Bank of England's definition of U.K. banking sector would not be included therefore in the total. The credit-creating activities of important non-bank financial intermediaries such as building societies and finance companies are not included in this 'credit aggregate': to suggest or imply that such financial firms are irrelevant or unimportant clearly is an untenable position. For example, trade credit, as we saw in Chapter 1, is a very important medium of exchange in the U.K. yet this very large volume of credit does not figure in the D.C.E. calculation.

(c) It may well have been the case that the construction and use of

D.C.E. either as an economic indicator or target was based largely on the ease of calculation and the relatively speedy availability of the data compared with other economic variables. If this was the case, then much more thorough research and evidence was required to justify the use of D.C.E. in this way and in particular its forecasting reliability as an indicator.

6.5 The stock of money

Most of this chapter has been concerned with identifying the major factors which exercise an influence on changes in the money stock (M_3) or alternative monetary indicators. Our descriptive analysis has yielded the following general propositions.

(a) The stock of money may change as a result of the business activities of the primary banks. Their capacity to lend may vary in response to the availability of liquid assets, in particular the cash base. Furthermore, their inclination to expand deposits through advances to customers may be dependent on the general state of the economy, which is something over which they have little control and which is likely to change markedly within fairly short periods of time.

(b) The banking system's capacity to change the stock of money in the economy may be influenced by other factors over which they have little influence. We drew attention to the various leakages from the banking system and particularly to the behaviour of the non-bank public – their preferences for holding cash and government securities.

(c) The flow of funds between the government sector and the non-government sector appeared to be of crucial importance in connection with the capacity of the banking system to vary its volume of business and deposit liabilities. Again, the banks have limited influence over these flows.

(d) Finally we examined how the balance of payments was likely to have a significant influence on the money stock.

We can now incorporate these various elements into an illustrative calculation of the money stock which is less aggregative than the examples used at the end of Chapter 2. Examining the various items in Table 6.3 and those on p. 140, one can see that the four points indentified at the beginning of this section are in fact incorporated: bank lending, public sector spending and receipts, sales of public sector securities to the non-bank public, and the balance of payments influence.

We must point out, however, that an important omission in this section is any reference to the *deliberate* manipulation of the stock of money by the monetary authorities (Bank of England and the

TABLE 6.3
Changes in sterling M_3 – financial year 1976–7
(£ m.)

Public sector borrowing requirement	+8,770
Purchases of public sector debt by private	
sector (other than banks)	−7,463
Sterling lending to the private sector	+3,414
Bank lending in sterling to overseas	+ 213
External and foreign currency finance:	
Public sector	−1,097
Overseas sterling deposits	− 175
Banks' foreign currency deposits (net)	− 58
Banks' non-deposit liabilities	− 776
Change in sterling M_3	+2,828

Source: Bank of England *Quarterly Bulletin*, vol. 17, No. 4 (December 1977).

Treasury) and the means by which such manipulation might take place. The omission was intentional so that we could identify basic elements affecting the money stock, abstracted from the complexities of U.K. institutional arrangements and conventions. It is the purpose of the next section and almost the whole of Chapter 7 to include these important qualifications to the basic analysis already developed.

6.6 Regulating the stock of money

6.6.1 CONTROVERSY

In recent years this topic has become highly controversial. We shall explain briefly the basic reasons for the controversy since Chapter 15 will examine this area of debate much more closely with its implications for monetary policy.

One aspect of the problem has been touched upon already in Chapter 2 and this relates to the actual definition of money and the appropriate series of financial statistics to match the chosen definition. For our purposes we can polarize the problem by suggesting either (a) that money can be identified uniquely on the basis of its means of payment function, or (b) that money is not only a means of payment in the economy but that it is also a financial asset for which there is a range of substitute assets. This area of economic analysis is somewhat complicated and for illustrative purposes we shall simplify the problem. If one asks the man in the street how much money he has, he is likely to reply with a catalogue of various types of assets: cash, funds in the National Savings Bank and the Trustee

Savings Bank, funds entrusted with a building society, and possibly deposits with a primary bank. From the individual's point of view, the inclusion of these various assets under the heading of money is legitimate since *to the individual* all these various assets are very liquid and represent almost instant spending power. Nevertheless, the economist's view might well be that these financial assets are not *really* spending power even though the individual feels that they are and acts accordingly (see Chapter 2, Section 2.4.2). The existence of a number of financial assets which possess, in varying degrees, some of the properties of money does mean that it is difficult to identify a single asset or group of assets which can be identified unambiguously as money.

The monetary authorities are not concerned primarily with establishing the definitive classification and definition of money assets in the economy, but rather to identify those financial assets which are most closely related to changes in aggregate expenditure within the economy, whatever their precise definition. If it is possible to identify such financial aggregates, then arguably it is these assets which the authorities should attempt to control. Unfortunately the problem does not rest there since one has then to decide whether the control of such financial aggregates will provide tight and reliable control over the economic aggregates with which one is primarily concerned: incomes, employment, the balance of payments, inflation. Merely to identify a relationship between two variables, A and B, does not imply that the relationship is stable or useful as an instrument of economic policy.

Finally, many economist have raised the very practical problem of whether control of the money stock (or an alternative monetary aggregate) is actually possible. Our analysis of the influences on the money stock in this chapter has revealed that there are many factors which will bear on the changes in the money stock. One fundamental problem is whether control or regulation really is feasible in an economy which has an elaborate financial system. Clearly it is vital to resolve this question since the *technical inability* to control the money stock (however defined) means that any theoretical justification for such activity instantly becomes redundant. This is discussed further in Chapter 7.

6.6.2 THE BASIS FOR CONTROL

So far in this chapter we have used simplified examples of banks' operations, but none the less the analysis has been sufficient to allow us to draw a conclusion relating to the problem of control. There are three elements: these are, first, that the volume of cash within and accessible to the banking system is relevant to the volume of deposits supportable by the system; secondly, that the banking system can not generate *cash* but is dependent on the central bank as the ultimate source; and thirdly, that the banks maintain (voluntarily or by instruction from the central bank) a minimum cash ratio. Given these three factors, one can conclude that the supply of cash to the banking system is the ultimate determinant of the volume of bank deposits, regardless of institutional and conventional factors. If the central bank wishes to control the volume of bank deposits (the bulk of the stock of money in the monetary system) all that is required is tight control of the supply of cash; and since the central bank is the source of supply, it would seem that there is little or nothing contentious about this proposition.[14] Indeed, there is nothing particularly remarkable about it at all since it follows from the structure and rules of the system. Deposits can be levered up or down on the fulcrum of the cash ratio with the quantity of cash acting as a lever. *The essential fact is that the lever and the fulcrum could be virtually anything, so long as the central bank (a) is capable of imposing on the banking system a ratio to be maintained, and (b) that it controls the supply to the banking system of the reserve asset(s) which the banking system is required to hold to fulfil the ratio requirement.* Much of the controversy in the literature on this matter confuses the validity of these propositions with the reality of a particular institutional framework and its idiosyncracies which sometimes appear to contradict or negate the basic conditions we have laid down.

6.7 Summary

i. By the use of a series of simplified bank balance sheets we showed how credit and deposit creation could take place. An essential feature which underpinned the whole process was the acceptability of bank deposits as a medium of exchange, i.e. money.

ii. In our *simple* model of deposit creation we suggested that the upper limit to such activity was provided by the size of the safe cash ratio and the volume of cash in the banking system. If either or both of these changed, then so would the upper limit to the volume of bank deposits.

iii. We established additional factors which influenced the process of deposit-creation by the bank (or banks); in particular, the existence of leakages of cash from the banking system into the non-bank sector, i.e. the fact that firms and individuals have a *demand to hold cash*. Further limitations could be identified as the demand for credit itself (if firms or individuals do not wish to

[14]We would point out that in reality neither the cash base nor a cash ratio are used for this purpose and that a cash ratio has been used in this chapter for illustrative purposes.

borrow there is little the banks can do about it), as well as the preparedness of the banks to provide credit to their customers.

iv. Section 6.3 emphasized the importance of the flow of funds between the government and the non-government sector and its effect on changes in bank deposits and the money stock of the community. We also highlighted the relevance of *how* the government may finance a budget deficit and its consequences for changes in the stock of money.

v. In an open economy, such as the U.K., the flows of funds associated with the changes in the balance of payments could affect the domestic money stock. A balance of payments 'deficit' may tend to diminish the money stock and a balance of payments 'surplus' may tend to add to the money stock.

vi. As a result of the potential distorting effects of the balance of payments on the domestic money stock, a new calculation was introduced in 1969 – domestic credit expansion – which was, in effect, an adjusted money stock calculation which eliminated the effects of the balance of payments.

vii. At the end of the chapter we outlined some of the problems associated with regulating the stock of money in the community, and considered whether or not a firm basis for control might exist.

7

The government sector and the financial system

7.1 Introduction

The position of the government in relation to the financial system is an ambivalent one. This is because the government has to perform two roles which are not necessarily compatible with each other. On the one hand, the government has the acknowledged responsibility for providing adequate supervision and control of the financial system consistent with overall economic policy; on the other hand, the government through its agent, the Bank of England, is a participant and user of the financial markets in a similar way to banks, other financial intermediaries and private-sector firms.[1] Putting the problem at its simplest, the government may decide to adopt a particular financial or monetary policy, e.g. raising interest rates, which is directed at financial markets, but since the government participates in such markets through the raising of funds, the monetary change adopted for reasons of general economic policy might also impinge on the government in an uncongenial way since its own borrowing costs will have risen. We shall be referring to this aspect of government involvement in this chapter.

The agent for the government in monetary matters is the Bank of England, and it is appropriate that we should now extend the brief study of the Bank's work contained in Chapter 4.

7.2 The Bank of England

7.2.1 FUNCTIONS

The Bank of England employs over 7,000 people in its various sections. Well in excess of 3,000 of these people work in the main banking departments and closer examination of this latter group reveals that about one-third are employed in the key department – the Chief Cashier's department. The work of the Chief Cashier's department provides us with a structure by means of which we can examine the functions of the Bank.

[1] We are not considering here the possibility or likelihood that a government may have objectives or interests which have a political *party* base.

The Chief Cashier's department can be divided into four main areas of activity: banking services, note issue, issuing house services, and market management. We shall examine each of these and use the classifications as a framework for examining the major functions.

Banking services. The Bank of England provides banking services restricted to the Government, the U.K. primary banks, discount houses, acceptance houses, a number of overseas banks, a few private customers together with Bank employees, and overseas central banks. In the Banking Department balance sheet these accounts are covered by the items: Public deposits, Special Deposits and Bankers' Deposits, and other accounts.

The Drawing Office handles the various customers' accounts, and the Bill Office is largely concerned with the Bank's clearing arrangements with the London Clearing Banks. The other important banking service is operated by the Dealing and Accounts Office which manages the E.E.A. and orders of customers (including those of the central banks) for buying and selling of foreign currencies and gold.

Note Issue. The Issue Office is responsible for the various requirements associated with the issue of banknotes. These include the arrangements for withdrawal of soiled notes and the issue of new ones to the various banks having accounts with the Bank – the Drawing Office making adjustments to these various accounts as appropriate. The Issue Office deals with the problem of estimating the community's needs for banknotes – volume as well as denomination.

Issue of Securities. The Chief Cashier's Department, through its Loans Office, arranges the issue of government stocks (gilt-edged) and Treasury bills, as well as the issue of bills, stocks, and bonds of the G.L.C. and a few other local authorities. The terms and timing of a government stock issue is decided by the Governors of the Bank and H.M. Treasury on the advice of the Government Broker and the Chief Cashier. Similarly, the weekly Treasury bill tender and issue is supervised by the Loans Office and the Chief Cashier's Office. The Loans Office also arranges the printing of bills and their redemption upon maturity.

Market management. The Chief Cashier's Department's responsibilities in the financial markets are primarily concerned with the day-to-day operations in (a) the gilt-edged market, i.e. the market for government bonds, (b) the money market, and (c) the foreign exchange market. These three operations by the Bank are of crucial importance to the Bank's role as the Treasury's agent for monetary management. Because of this, we shall examine more thoroughly the activities of the gilt-edged market and money market. The foreign exchange market dealings by the Bank have been given a preliminary examination in Chapter 6, and developed later in Chapter 11.

(a) *The gilt-edged market.* Official dealings in the gilt-edged market are largely those of the Issue Department of the Bank of England but include also those by the National Debt Commissioners. One can see from *Table 7.1* (p. 157) that the size of the Issue Department's holdings is substantial – over £6,000 million of securities. This large quantity of stocks arises from the Issue Department's role as underwriter to the government when a new issue of stock is made. Such issues are usually very large, as for example during the period January 1976 to January 1977 when the Bank issued almost £9,000 million new stock and the smallest single issue (apart from a small amount of short-dated bonds) was £400 million. If the stock is not fully subscribed, and this is usually the case, it is the practice of the Issue Department to take up the remaining stock and over the following months gradually to sell such stock to the market through the agency of the Government Broker, who is a member of a firm of London stockbrokers.

Although the tactics in the gilt-edged market have changed since 1971 with the introduction of *Competition and Credit Control*, it is unlikely that the basic objectives or strategy set out by the Bank of England[2] have altered significantly. Daily operation in the gilt-edged market through the Government Broker allows the Bank to achieve two objectives. One objective is that the Bank attempts to meet the needs of the large purchasers of gilt-edged, e.g. insurance companies and pension funds who may wish to switch from one stock to another. The Bank is unlikely to be co-operative, however, if the institutions wished to unload stock on the Bank without taking up other, longer-dated stock. By providing the required stock and taking in the other, the Bank helps to maintain the marketability of and therefore the demand for government securities. The other objective is to pursue an *active policy* in the market by means of the choice of stock prices at which the Bank is prepared to deal. If market conditions are suitable, the Bank will hope to adjust and sustain its market dealings so that the desired level and structure of interest rates is achieved[3] as far as possible on the stocks of varying maturity.

Government bonds, once issued, may be bought through the Stock Exchange and offer the buyer a wide range of yields and maturity

[2] See 'Official Transactions in the Gilt-Edged Market', Bank of England *Quarterly Bulletin*, vol. 6, No. 2 (June 1966).
[3] The rate of interest (i.e. yield) on government bonds varies inversely with their price. See Section 10.2 below which provides a numerical illustration.

dates from which to choose. By convention the maturity classification
of government bonds is short-dated (up to five years to maturity),
medium-dated (five to fifteen years to maturity), long-dated (over
fifteen years to maturity), and undated (no maturity date).

In addition to buying existing stock from the market, it is possible
to buy new securities either as they are issued or indirectly from the
Issue Department of the Bank of England as such 'tap stocks' are sold
via the Government Broker. In all, there are over seventy stocks
currently being bought and sold through the Stock Market. The
Bank's stated intention in its dealings in the gilt-edged market is not
only to sell as much stock as possible (see below) but also to influence
the behaviour of prices and yields. The Bank is able to do this because
of its close involvement in the daily operations of the market through
the Government Broker. As the Bank put it, 'the prices he [the
Government Broker] bids in response to an offer are therefore seen as
the expression of the Bank's current policy, and are closely watched
by the jobbers for any sign of a change of emphasis in the policy, such
as might lead the market to expect new movements in prices'.[4]

In our earlier discussion of the Bank of England, we noted the
considerable size of the Issue Department's holding of gilt-edged
securities and this, together with the dominance of gilt-edged
business in the Stock Exchange,[5] does mean that the authorities may,
if they wish, exercise considerable influence over the price and
therefore the yields on their securities. This must be so since the Bank
could, in the last resort, buy in unlimited quantities of gilt-edged by
printing the necessary money to purchase the securities (which would
push down yields) and, conversely, it could print and sell unlimited
quantities of gilt-edged at whatever market price necessary (which
would push up yields). Although the Bank of England would be
highly unlikely ever to approach such situations, nevertheless the
market is aware of the considerable power which lies within the Bank
and, therefore, the instrument does not have to be used in order to be
effective. Other interest rates and yields determined in financial
markets are closely influenced by the rates prevailing in the gilt-edged
market, for example British Savings bonds and interest rates on
holdings in the New Departments of the Trustee Savings Banks.
Indeed, any financial assets which represent possible substitutes for
gilt-edged securities will be influenced by variations in the yields on
the gilt-edged securities, especially as sales of gilt-edged securities
represent a very large proportion of the turnover in financial markets.

[4]'Official Transactions in the Gilt-Edged Market', Bank of England *Quarterly Bulletin*
(June 1966).
[5]In the four years 1974–7, gilt-edged securities have averaged around 70 per cent of
total Stock Market turnover.

For example, the yields on 20-year company loan stock and debentures are very closely related to the yields on 20-year gilt-edged. Although the Bank operates in order to influence yields, an overwhelming aim of operations in the gilt-edged market is, however, the encouragement of the widest possible variety of investors to increase their holdings of stock – the longer-dated the better. The Bank is not concerned with the financing of the government's day-to-day needs through the gilt-edged market since this problem is resolved by the issue of bills and the residual financing by the banking system (see Section 6.3.2). Rather, it has the longer-term aim of ensuring that the maximum amount of government borrowing is achieved through the issue of stock to the non-bank public (domestic and overseas) since this reduces the dependence on the banking system to provide the residual finance via the take-up of Treasury bills. Additional Treasury bills add to the liquidity of the banking system and, in principle, its capacity for additional credit creation. Put simply, the less successful the Bank is in selling stock to the non-bank sectors to finance the government's borrowing requirements, the greater is the reliance on the banks, and this in turn tends to swell the money stock. The Bank's stated tactics to achieve 'market conditions that will maximize, both now and in the future, the desire of investors at home and abroad to hold British government debt' are:

(i)   to issue new stocks that are tailored to the current demands of large investors;
(ii) to ensure that dealings do not become seriously inhibited by the absence of buyers to match sellers;
(iii) to ensure that the market does not become too volatile due to a preponderance of buyers unable to satisfy their demands for stock;
(iv) to spread the impact of the issue and redemption of large blocks of securities and, in particular, to minimize the disturbances in the market which large issues and redemptions may give rise to;
(v)   to slow down and moderate violent movements in prices unless there is likely to be a particular advantage in a rapid change, such as when Bank rate (Minimum Lending Rate) is changed. This last tactic has been modified and will be considered below in Section 7.4.1.1.

Towards the end of the 1960s and particularly since 1971 the Bank's commitment to these tactics was, and is, much less certain. As a result of the adoption of money supply targets, for example, the Bank will not take up automatically an excess supply of government securities in the market.

Although the Bank has a number of objectives connected with the gilt-edged market, there are also problems associated with the Bank's operations in the market, and it is to these that we now turn our attention.

1. The authorities have been faced with a dual problem of a substantial annual borrowing requirement in the post-war period (with the exception of only three years) and at the same time the need to meet large redemptions of earlier issues of bills and bonds. During the 1960s and 1970s the annual redemptions have averaged well over £1,000 million per year. The authorities have thus been faced with the need to raise substantial sums through bond sales rather than Treasury bills in order to avoid expanding the reserve assets base of the banking system. Managing such an operation has, on many occasions, presented the Bank with dificulties since the Bank obviously cannot force sales of bonds on unwilling investors.

2. The Bank maintains the view that the sale of gilt-edged is easier and successful only on a rising market, i.e. when prices of stock are rising. One reason for this is that such a rise provides actual and potential purchasers with the prospect of capital gains. Rising gilt-edged prices has as its corollary declining yields (interest rates) on such stock. However, the long-term trend of gilt-edged prices has not been rising but falling. For example, a long-dated bond was issued in 1967 (6½ per cent Funding loan 1985–7) which would be redeemed at the latest in 1987. If £1,000 worth of this stock had been purchased in 1967 and then sold, say, ten years later in the Stock Market the seller would have obtained only £790 for the stock. Those holders of gilt-edged who do not intend, or because of unforseen circumstances are unable, to hold such securities to maturity, are thus subject to considerable capital uncertainty.

3. Before 1969 the authorities' view of the gilt-edged market was that it was highly volatile and subject ot extrapolative expectations, i.e. if prices of stock began to fall, the conviction would rapidly gain ground in the market that the fall would continue. Rational behaviour by investors holding such views would be to sell their stock holdings. Clearly such action would be in the nature of a self-fulfilling prophecy since the act of selling would produce the anticipated fall in price; expectations would be realized and justify the action taken. Other investors would observe the decline in prices and in turn begin to sell some of their gilt-edged holdings. To prevent any collapse of confidence in the gilt-edged market the Bank chose in the 1960s to intervene in the Stock Market and instructed the Government Broker to buy up stock to support the price. Unfortunately, such action would result in two undesirable situations:

(i) Bond purchases by the Bank would add to the cash base of the banking system (see Chapter 6).

(ii) Bond purchases by the Bank would be inconsistent with a policy of pressing bond sales in order to finance the borrowing requirement and to offset redemptions.

The Bank believed, however, that such a tactic of support would result in the long run in greater confidence in gilt-edged securities as an investment and ultimately in larger net sales than would have been the case if the market had been left to itself. Such a view is contentious and has been, in fact, questioned by a number of economists[6] who have argued that the gilt-edged market is basically stable.

Even if it could have been argued that the Bank's support operations did, on balance, aid the long-run objectives in the gilt-edged market, there is none the less the serious problem that support operations 'at the whim of the market' could result in the authorities' loss of control over the cash base of the banks. If the authorities were prepared to support the market (i.e. preventing bond prices falling and therefore interest rates rising) when large investors were moving out of gilt-edged into, say, more liquid assets, the authorities were in effect pegging interest rates or only allowing them to change slowly at the same time as pouring out cash in exchange for stock. The authorities were faced with a problem of policy choice:

(i)   regulation of interest rates;

(ii) long run maximization of bond sales;

(iii) regulation of the money stock.

Up to the end of the 1960s the authorities probably took the view that a desirable combination would be (i) plus (ii) but with considerable emphasis on the long-run objective of maximizing sales of gilt-edged securities. The basis for this choice by the authorities may well have been the strong Keynesian tradition within the U.K. together with the influence of the Radcliffe Report. (For further discussion see Chapter 15.) The main point which we wish to emphasize, however, is that if the authorities did choose to influence interest rates – partly with their debt management objective in view – then the corollary of such a decision would be the loss of control of the money supply. The authorities may choose to regulate the 'price of money' (interest rates) *or* the supply of money, but not both. As we have seen earlier, the support operations in the gilt-edged market would result in the authorities exercising some control over the price of bonds (interest rates) but

[6]One of the earliest expressions of doubt was put forward by N. Kaldor in his evidence to the Radcliffe Committee.

the consequence was that the cash base and the money stock would expand.

In the 1970s the Bank of England moved towards the adoption of monetary targets, i.e. policy choice (iii), in particular sterling M_3. Consistent with this change the Bank has had to adjust its tactics in the gilt-edged market and accept larger variations in interest rates than it had hitherto.

(b) *The money market.* The money market relationship we are concerned with here is that between the primary banks, discount houses, and the Bank of England. In Chapters 4 and 6 we made fairly detailed reference to certain aspects of this market's operation, e.g. the lender of last resort facility, the buffer role of the discount houses, and the significance of the cash nexus. Our purpose here is to integrate these several aspects to clarify the operations of the Bank at the short end of the market.

We have already pointed out that the government's receipts and payments are uneven from day to day throughout the year and it is the role of the Bank to ensure that the government has sufficient funds to meet its daily needs as well as making certain that surplus funds are not left idle. Idle funds result in government borrowing being in excess of the actual required level, and to avoid this, the working balances of the government departments are kept to the minimum each day.

In earlier sections in Chapters 4 and 6 we outlined the significance for the banking system of the net flow of funds between the government sector and the non-government sector. Net outflows result in the banks and discount houses having surplus cash, and net inflows to the government result in cash shortages in the banking system and the discount houses. In a day when government disbursements exceed receipts, the cash surplus thus created would be offset by Bank sales of Treasury bills to the discount houses through its representative, the Special Buyer (a member of one of the discount houses). The bills sold to the market are likely to have a maturity which will suit the discount houses, i.e. maturing on a day when the discount houses consider that they may be short of cash. On the other hand, on a day when government receipts are greater than disbursements, the resulting cash shortage in the banking system and discount houses might be relieved in the following ways:

(i)   The Bank buys bills from the banks (termed indirect assistance or 'back door' help) and the funds thus obtained by the banks can be used to alleviate the discount houses' shortfall if the banks had made calls on the discount houses.

(ii) The Bank may decide to aid the discount market by lending 'as last resort' on security of bills and at a rate of interest of the

Bank's choosing. So long as the rate is sufficiently high, the discount houses' costs will rise and their discounting rates on future business will be adjusted upwards. Since non-government sector lenders to the discount market will note the discount houses' dependence on relatively costly borrowing from the Bank, they too will be induced to raise their lending rates to the discount houses. In this way, the authorities will have engineered a rise in short-term interest rates. However, if the Bank does not desire a change in short rate, it will alleviate a cash shortage by indirect help or by loans (or re-discounting of bills) at rates which do not disturb the market.

In practice, the Bank prefers a situation in which the market is short of cash since this ensures the Bank's supervisory control over the market; cash shortages may be relieved penally or not, depending on the chosen policy of the Bank. A cash shortage can be brought about in the following way: the Bank estimates the government's disbursements and receipts during the coming week(s), together with future redemptions of bills. The resulting figure gives an indication of the net cash flow between the government and the non-government sector. However, the following week's Treasury bill tender announced by the Bank will be intentionally greater than the government's net financial needs. The exact calculation has to take into account many factors, such as bond redemptions and the flow of funds into the E.E.A. Since the discount houses abide by the convention of 'covering the tender', i.e. tendering for all the Treasury bills on offer (although the discount houses may not obtain all the bills since other tenderers may offer higher bids), the result is that there will be a net shortage of cash in the non-government sector. A simplified arithmetic illustration should clarify the point.

Expected net Exchequer deficit	−£ 50 m.
Maturing bills	−£100 m.
Cash outflow from the government sector	−£150 m.
Bills for which tenders are invited	+£155 m.
Overall cash shortage in the market	+£ 5 m.

It might seem that the Bank's intervention in the money market as described above is unnecessarily elaborate, but without such intervention the authorities' control over short-term interest rates would not be possible. If we refer to the two basic situations we have identified – cash shortage and cash surplus in the money market – we need to ask what would be the consequences if the Bank neither alleviated a cash shortage nor absorbed a cash surplus.

In the case of an unrelieved cash shortage we would find the discount houses keenly seeking funds to repay the banks who are calling in their short loans. Since the shortage is one of cash, ultimate relief can only be provided by obtaining cash. If the whole banking system is unable to provide cash loans to the discount houses, the result of the discount houses' quest for funds would be fast rising short-term interest rates. Conversely, in circumstances where there is a cash surplus, the discount houses would attempt to utilize such funds by buying bills and/or bonds from the market. The excess demand for bills/bonds would push up their prices, or – in other words – lower their yields (rates of interest). Only when interest rates had fallen sufficiently to induce the holding of the (*zero*-earning) additional cash in the system would interest rates cease to fall. We pointed out earlier that the variations in government disbursements and receipt varies from day to day and by substantial amounts, and therefore if the Bank chose neither to alleviate cash shortages nor absorb cash surpluses, the result would be considerable oscillations of short-term interest rates from day to day. Since such occurrences would have consequences for the movement of short-term funds across the foreign exchanges, as well as feeding through into other financial markets, the Bank chooses to undertake the smoothing operations we have just described: supplying cash or bills.

It should be noted, however, that although the Bank smooths the ebb and flow of funds, this does not prevent it from raising or lowering short-term interest rates as part of monetary policy. A deliberate and persistent shortage of cash in the market, alleviated by the Bank at increasingly penal rates of interest, would result in rising discount rates and other rates on a wide variety of short-term assets such as commercial bills, Treasury bills[7], certificates of deposit, and time deposit rates. As the rates on these assets rise, so will the rates of interest on other forms of lending, particularly on bank loans and overdrafts. On the other hand, the Bank may push rates to a lower level by, in effect, creating a cash surplus. One means by which this can occur is for the Bank to purchase Treasury bills from the market (thus putting out cash) in quantities which exceed the amounts required for a simple smoothing operation. In practice, the Bank also makes use of a 'nod and a wink' to the market in order to move interest rates in a desired direction. The close contact maintained by the Discount Office of the Bank of England with the discount maket and other major financial firms is often a strong enough link to produce

---

[7]Note that the policy of raising short-term interest rates has the disadvantage for the government of raising its own borrowing costs. Since government borrowing is substantial, a small rise in interest rates will make a considerable difference to the interest payments made by the government.

the required change. The appropriate response from the discount houses to the 'nod and a wink' would be to alter their bid price for the next issue of Treasury bills. If the market's response were inadequate, the Bank would be quite capable, as we have seen, of making a desired change in rates effective.

7.2.2 BANK OF ENGLAND BALANCE SHEETS

The Bank Charter Act of 1844 laid down that the issue of notes was to be kept separate from the Bank's banking business. Accordingly, the accounts of the Bank – the Bank Return – are broken down into those of the Issue Department and the Banking Department. This division is purely one of accounting since the Bank is organized as a single entity. *Table 7.1* gives details of both accounts.

TABLE 7.1
Bank of England balance sheets, 16 November 1977
(£ m.)

Issue Department			
Liabilities		*Assets*	
Notes in circulation	7,338	Government securities	6,490
Notes in Banking Dept.	12	Other securities	860
	7,350		7,350

Banking Department			
Liabilities		*Assets*	
Public deposits	20	Government securities	1,709
Special deposits	1,171	Advances and other	
Bankers deposits	292	accounts	236
Reserves and other		Premises, equipment, and	
accounts	613	other securities	154
Capital	15	Notes and coin	12
	2,111		2,111

Source: Bank of England *Quarterly Bulletin*, vol. 18, No. 1 (March 1978).

Many of the items in the two balance sheets will be familiar to the reader but we shall refer briefly to them below.

Issue Department
Liabilities:
Notes in circulation. This refers to the notes held by the public and in the tills of the banks.

Notes in the Banking Department. These are notes held by the Banking Department to meet the needs of the banks and indirectly the public. If the public required additional notes and the Banking Department experiences a drain of notes, it can obtain more from the Issue Department in return for securities

Assets:

Government securities. We have referred already to this item which consists of unsold government stock used by the Bank for its operations in the gilt-edged market.

Other securities. This item includes securities of other governments.

Banking Department

Liabilities:

Public deposits. These deposits are the government's various accounts, in particular the Exchequer and National Loans Fund accounts as well as those of other departments.

Special deposits. This item includes both Special Deposits (when called by the Bank) and Supplementary Deposits under the December 1973 scheme.

Bankers' deposits. Clearing banks, discount houses, and other banks hold deposits with the Bank which are used mainly for clearing purposes.

Reserves and other accounts. Apart from reserves, this item consists of the accounts of a small number of private customers as well as accounts held by overseas money institutions, e.g. central banks.

Capital. This is the original share capital of the Bank.

Assets:

Government securities. These consist of gilt-edged and Treasury bills as well as loans to the National Loans Fund (in effect an overdraft facility known as 'Ways and Means Advances').

Advances and other accounts. This item consists of loans to the discount houses, discounted bills for the Bank's customers, and advances to the Bank's own customers.

Premises, equipment, and other securities. Apart from the value of tangible assets, this item includes other securities held by the Bank by virtue of its commercial activities conjoined with the banks, for example the holdings in Finance for Industry Ltd.

7.3 The parallel money markets

In this and earlier chapters we referred to the operation of the money market and described the important relationship between the Bank of England, discount houses, and primary banks. It would be useful at this stage if we drew some of the various strands together and linked them with the development of other, relatively new markets in short-term funds.

Twenty years ago it would have been possible to refer to 'the money market' with little or no ambiguity. Such a reference would have conjured up the picture of the discount houses (Section 4.4.2.3 and also Section 7.2.1 of this chapter) involved in the utilization of a primary bank's surplus funds (via 'money at call') and transmission of such funds to other banks who were temporarily short of funds, and who were therefore calling in their loans to the discount houses. The discount houses were performing the function of smoothing the temporary surpluses and deficits due to inter-primary-bank indebtedness. In addition to this function, the discount houses were active at the short end of the market through the discounting of both Treasury bills and various qualities of commercial bill as well as short-dated bonds. The bulk of funds (in 1952 a total of £1,028 million) was derived from domestic sources and especially from the London Clearing Banks, and most of these funds were used to purchase public sector assets, either Treasury bills or bonds. The business activity of the discount market at that time contrasts strikingly with the activity of acceptance houses and overseas and other banks in the U.K., since total deposits of the latter group of firms was only £835 million. Futhermore, almost half their funds was placed either with the discount market or with other U.K. banks.

From around the middle of the 1950s, and especially in the latter part of the 1960s, the activities of the various other banks – the secondary banks – expanded substantially. In addition, two other factors became important: (i) the financial needs of the local authorities which after 1955 had to meet a greater proportion of their borrowing requirement from the market; and (ii) the growth in business activity of the finance houses (hire purchase companies) who were increasingly providing credit for firms and individuals whose needs were not met by the primary banking system. Until credit controls became more extensive, the unavailability of bank finance usually resulted in a simple switch to the hire purchase companies.

Clearly the need of local authorities for funds would have to be satisfied somehow, otherwise they would not be able to perform their functions; and the available evidence also suggests that the demand for funds by firms and individuals for equipment and consumer durables is influenced much more by the availability of funds than by their cost. Therefore the local authorities and hire purchase companies could and would demand funds very actively, with the result that interest rates on their borrowings would tend to be higher than rates prevailing in the traditional markets. Not surprisingly, the secondary banks took advantage of this demand by undertaking the provisions of funds of large amounts for varying terms – the sort of business for which they were well suited. Coincidentally, the easier movement of short-term funds internationally after the end of the 1950s meant that the secondary banks (remember that this category includes the overseas banks in the U.K.) could usefully attract foreign currency deposits (mainly Euro-dollars) which could be converted into sterling or, as we have seen in earlier chapters, on-lent as a foreign currency deposit. The introduction of dollar C.D.s and later sterling C.D.s at the end of the 1960s provided a further fillip to the growth of the secondary banking sector.

Such massive banking expansion could not take place, however, without the parallel development of a money-market arrangement whereby the operators in these markets for funds could alleviate their cash and liquidity position from day to day or, indeed, during the day.[8] For an individual bank, the main financial instruments which provide such flexibility are inter-bank deposits (sterling and foreign currency) and C.D.s (sterling and dollar). The illustrative bank balance sheets used in Chapter 4 have shown the banks hold C.D.s as a liability and an asset, i.e. banks issue C.D.s as well as buying C.D.s. The variability of term on such assets, as well as their high degree of marketability, has meant that these assets have become much more a means of inter-bank borrowing and lending than financial instruments to attract funds into the banking system. We have also seen that the primary banks hold substantial deposits – both sterling and foreign currency – from other U.K. banks, and the borrowing and lending of these balances between the participant banks are a further source of financial flexibility, though mainly for the secondary banks. Since 1971 and the inception of *Competition and Credit Control,* there has been a very considerable growth in the use of sterling C.D.s and also inter-bank deposits. The substantial ebbs and flows of funds, occurring daily, are largely between the various banks rather than between the banks and the government sector, and the use of sterling C.D.s and inter-bank deposits as a means of offsetting such flows would seem to be the natural development. The accommodating role of the discount market is of importance primarily when the banks are, as a group, experiencing movements of funds between the government and the non-government sector.

It is likely that the rapid expansion of the secondary banking sector and the associated money-market development presented the authorities, and in particular the Bank of England, with food for thought about the future operation of monetary policy and

---

[8] The reader will recall that the development of the primary banks was associated with the discount houses and the Bank of England as lender of last resort.

management. We can identify a number of reasons for this.

(a) Controlling short-term interest rates through the discount market by means of the supply of Treasury bills and the use of the Bank rate[9] has been, and is, desired by the authorities. Prior to the development of the parallel money markets, the authorities were able to exercise such control since the Bank had direct and dominant influence over the discount market's operations. The development of the parallel markets (having no direct connection with the Bank of England as the discount market has through the Bank's acting as lender of last resort) meant that the Bank could not exercise such tight control over the interest rates operating in these markets. Other rates, such as primary bank deposit rates, were closely related to the Bank rate and the Treasury bill rate and, therefore, the Bank could regulate such interest rates.

(b) The growing concentration in the U.K. of Euro-dollar and other foreign currency business coincided, as we have seen, with the development of outlets for such funds, not only abroad but also within the U.K. Such funds flowing into the U.K. and converted into sterling could be used to purchase short-term government assets, e.g. Treasury bills, or competing assets in the secondary markets, such as short loans to local authorities. If the rates of interest in the parallel markets were more competitive than the more stable Treasury bill rate, the consequences would be (i) that the inflow of funds would tend to expand the domestic money supply[10], and (ii) that the very competitive rates of interest in the parallel markets acting as an attraction for foreign funds would provide the authorities with greater flexibility in the management of the short rates under their direct control, i.e. Bank rate, the Treasury bill rate, primary bank rates, since the authorities would not have to use their own short rate as the primary source of attraction for foreign funds. In this way, for example, a deliberate policy of reducing Bank rate in order to induce a reduction in linked rates such as building society rates (and therefore the mortgage rate) has been possible to some extent and without undue influence on the inflow of short-term funds and the balance of payments position.[11]

(c) In our earlier description of the secondary markets (Chapter 4)

[9]Bank rate was replaced by Minimum Lending Rate (M.L.R.) in October 1972.
[10]If the overseas investors place their funds in government assets, the rise in the money stock will not take place.
[11]This is probably less relevant with the introduction of *Competition and Credit Control* (see Section 7.4.2).

we pointed out that claims in the parallel markets were unsecured. Although participants protected themselves as far as possible through careful lending policies, the risks associated with these markets should perhaps have been considered more carefully both by the participants and by the Bank of England as the markets developed rather than action being taken by them only after the serious failures in the 1970s.

7.4 Control of the banking system

The government, as we have seen so far in this chapter, is an important participant in financial markets on its own account. The government is a large borrower and spender, as is the public sector generally, but it also assumes the responsibility for exercising control and supervision of the financial system and especially the banks. There are two simple reasons why the government attempts to exercise such control: one is that the fulfilment of the government's overall economic objectives may be assisted by regulating, for example, the stock of money in the community, interest rates, or the supply of credit, and the banks feature largely in influencing these various financial elements in the economy. The other reason is that the major banks are private sector firms with profit-making objectives, whose liabilities are the main medium of exchange in the community. From the point of view of the authorities it may be undesirable for such firms to pursue their profit objectives regardless of the overall needs of the economy. Large-scale expansion of credit and the money stock by the banks may well be highly profitable and possible, by virtue of their reserve position, but such activity could be highly inflationary.

In this section our attention is turned to the means by which control has been exercised by the authorities, and the problems connected with such control. Earlier chapters have not neglected this topic completely, but they have tended to emphasize the theoretical aspects of the problem. Chapter 5 examined the mandatory assets structure of the banks following the introduction of *Competition and Credit Control* and in Chapter 6 we explored the problems underlying the control of the money stock.

Between 1945 and 1951, the immediate post-war period, it would be no exaggeration to suggest that the authorities viewed monetary policy-instruments as rather limited in their effectiveness. The problems of physical shortages and the volume of highly liquid financial assets accumulated during the war (high incomes during the war period, with few goods and services to be bought, led to high savings) probably meant that attempts to regulate the economy by monetary means would have failed. The Labour government lost office in 1951, however, to be replaced by a Conservative one, and with this change came a different approach to economic policy which included the revival of monetary methods of control – in particular the manipulation of Bank rate and associated interest rates. Suffice to say that it became evident fairly soon that the existing monetary techniques of regulation were not sufficiently effective and in 1957 a Committee was set up by the Chancellor of the Exchequer to inquire into the working of the monetary and credit system in the U.K. This Committee – commonly known as the Radcliffe Committee after its chairman – produced a report in August 1959. This report, together with the minutes and memoranda of evidence, provided a considerable volume of information about the workings of the financial system in the U.K. as well as some of the views of monetary authorities (the Bank of England and the Treasury) as to how the system might be regulated. Of special interest was the Radcliffe Committee's view that control of the banking system was exercisable via the liquidity ratio and the supply of Treasury bills, and not through regulating the supply of cash (see Chapter 6, Section 6.6.2). Another view expressed was that the stock of money *per se* was not in itself of prime importance nor should it be the prime target of the authorities but rather that the authorities should concentrate on the liquidity of the whole system.[12]

Although the general tenor of the Radcliffe Report cast some doubt as to the strength of monetary methods of control – at least in the way they were being used at the time – monetary and fiscal instruments of control continued to be used to regulate the economy. During the 1960s, however, the use of market methods of monetary regulation (e.g. open market operations, shifts in interest rates) to influence the major part of the banking system (the primary banks) became of even more questionable value. There were a number of reasons for this, some of which have been uncovered earlier in the book.

(i)   The support operations in the gilt-edged market were proving to be an awkward commitment for the authorities. The gilt-edged market and the foreign exchange market were, and are, influenced by each other, so that a deterioration in the balance of payments tended to produce a weakness in the gilt-edged market. If the authorities intervened in the gilt-edged market to support prices, they would be tending to *add to* the liquidity of the banking system. But a deterioration in the balance of payments position was usually followed by economic policies designed to *curtail* credit and spending and therefore support operations in the gilt-edged market would be somewhat counter-productive

[12]The role of money in economic policy is considered in Chapter 15.

and inconsistent with overall economic policy. Such support operations would involve the Bank of England's buying gilt-edged and thus tending to expand the liquidity and lending potential of the banking system. Futhermore, the authorities did not control the supply of all the eligible liquid assets which could count towards the banks' liquidity ratio. We have seen earlier that the banks were able to substitute other liquid assets (money at call, commercial bills) as the supply of Treasury bills contracted.

(ii)   The rapid growth of the secondary banking sector meant that unsatisfied demand for credit from the primary banks could be met by the secondary banks, this sector not being subject to the liquidity ratio requirements. Squeezing the primary banks simply pushed some customers into the secondary sector. Indeed, the setting up of secondary banking subsidiaries by the primary banks is indicative of the slippage that was occurring.

The response of the authorities to the inadequacy of market methods of control was to introduce, and increasingly rely upon, non-market methods of regulation. The call for Special Deposits (see Chapter 5, Section 5.2.2.1) was varied on fifteen occasions between June 1960 and the end of 1966. Other methods of regulation used by the authorities were 'moral suasion' and direct controls. Moral suasion by the Bank of England was frequently directed at the *nature* of banking business (qualitative directives) rather than the overall *level* of business (quantitative directives) to which, say, the call for Special Deposits would be aimed. The Governor of the Bank of England on a number of occasions requested the banks to refrain from certain types of lending in favour of others. For example, in November 1967 the Bank issued a notice revealing new measures for credit restriction which stated that although finance for exports should be free of restriction, non-priority lending should be limited – or, as the Bank put it, 'the recent upward trend in lending to persons should be halted without delay.' A year later the Bank issued a further notice which suggested amongst other things that 'many customers of the banks whose borrowing is not of the highest priority for credit control purposes can therefore expect to be asked to effect as soon as possible a substantial repayment of borrowing outstanding.'

A direct control introduced in the 1960s was the use of the lending ceiling, i.e. a direct control on *credit* rather than, say, bank deposits. The November 1967 notice to which we have referred contained such a measure. The banks were asked to prevent lending rising above the level prevailing at the time. This lending ceiling was reinforced by a further statement by the Bank in November 1968 which gave the banks four months' notice to reduce their lending to 98 per cent of the mid-November 1967 level. At the end of May 1969 the Bank curtly announced that the banks had not complied with the earlier request for the attainment of the lower lending ceiling and that therefore the Bank intended to halve the rate of interest payable on Special Deposits for as long as the banks exceeded the lending ceiling. This penal arrangement came into affect from 2 June and would have cost the Clearing Banks about £150,000 per week as a result of the lost interest.

It is hardly surprising that the Clearing Banks found the use of both moral suasion and direct controls particularly irksome. Moral suasion caused the banks to discriminate between customers in a manner unrelated to their ordinary business relations: a customer who happened to be an exporter being eligible for funds, but an equally good customer who, say, imported manufactured consumer goods being deprived of necessary funds.[13] The firm application of market methods of control would have yielded a rise in interest rates which would have provided, albeit slowly, the allocative mechanism rather than the banks' having to discriminate against one customer in favour of another. In addition, the banks claimed that the authorities' monetary measures – particularly prior to 1964 – tended to restrict mainly the Clearing Banks, whereas other financial intermediaries (secondary banks, building societies, insurance companies, etc.) were relatively untouched. Thus it was argued that the non-market methods of control were discriminatory, limited in their application, and somewhat clumsy as instruments, producing distortions and inequities within the financial system. It is probable that both the authorities and the banking system felt the need for an alternative approach to monetary management, and after wide-ranging discussions between the Bank and financial intermediaries, the arrangements embodied in the document *Competition and Credit Control* became operative on 16 September 1971. Amplifications and amendments to these arrangements have been published since that date.

7.4.1 COMPETITION AND CREDIT CONTROL

Our approach to these changes may be divided conveniently into the two parts: the competition and the credit control aspects of the new arrangements.

---

[13]This is not in itself sufficient reason for abandoning such controls since the community's needs may be such that they far outweigh the disadvantages to the banks and their customers.

7.4.1.1 Competition

The proposals included a number of reforms which were intended to stimulate competition in the financial system and also to remove some of the discriminatory aspects of the previous methods of regulation.

(i)   The new reserve ratio arrangements[14] were to apply across the whole of the banking system and not merely to the London Clearing Banks.

(ii)   The Special Deposits (and after 1973 the Supplementary Special Deposits) scheme would be applied to all banks and the larger finance houses.

(iii) The collective agreement between the London and Scottish Clearing Banks on interest rates would be abandoned. The banks would be expected to compete with each other in both the attraction of deposits and also the making of loans.

(iv) The discount houses agreed to abandon their collectively-agreed price for the weekly Treasury bill issue, but they would continue to apply for a quantity of bills sufficient to cover the tender.[15]

(v)   The larger finance houses were expected to adhere to a slightly lower reserve ratio than the banks (10 per cent rather than 12½ per cent) but the reserve asset requirements would be the same as for the banks. Some of the finance houses chose to apply for bank status (under the Protection of Depositors Act – see Chapter 4, Section 4.7) and these finance houses would observe therefore the same reserve requirements as the other banks.

(vi) The Bank ceased to support the gilt-edged market but would sell gilt-edged when the market could absorb stock satisfactorily. If the market was weak, the authorities intended simply to withdraw rather than give support until it strengthened again, when gilt-edged sales would be resumed. Such a change of tactics in the gilt-edged market did not preclude intervention, but such intervention would be in accordance with the authorities' own requirements rather than in response to particular market changes. It should be realized that this change of tactics in the gilt-edged market is consistent with the objective of greater competitiveness since it allowed market forces to determine

---

[14] The details of the reserve requirements have been presented in Section 5.2.2.2 and the reader should refer to this section.

[15] The *Competition and Credit Control* arrangements which currently apply to the discount houses may be found in the Bank of England *Quarterly Bulletin*, vol. 13, No. 3 (November 1973), p. 306.

prices, and therefore yields, on government stock and close substitutes. For the authorities to have maintained their 1960s approach to the gilt-edged market would have been inconsistent with the other aspect of policy: flexibility of interest rates through greater competitiveness amongst banking and other financial intermediaries.   ,

7.4.1.2 Credit Control

(i)   The quantitative lending controls were abolished and the liquidity and cash ratio requirements as devices for regulating credit were to be replaced by the reserve asset ratio (this will be considered further).

(ii)   The authorities declared their intention of relying more on interest rate changes as a means of regulating both the direction (allocation) and volume of credit available.

(iii)   Special Deposits would continue to be used as a means of regulation, but the Bank indicated that in the future it would consider using Special Deposits in a more flexible way. The Bank stated that a call for Special Deposits might be related either to domestic or overseas sterling deposits and that the percentage rate of call might be different for domestic and overseas sterling deposits. One reason for such differentiation was that some banks, e.g. the secondary banks, were and are much more dependent on foreign business and that such business is based on finer margins. A uniform call for Special Deposits, it was argued, could upset their foreign business very substantially. A further reason was that the Bank might wish to influence the net inflow of funds to the U.K. either by means of a different application in respect of the type of deposits, or a different rate of call.

The introduction of *Competition and Credit Control* triggered off a considerable amount of comment and criticism from the City as well as from within academic circles. Furthermore, events since the new scheme was introduced seem to cast some doubt on the underlying approach as a basis for monetary management. We shall look now at some of the comments which have been made and attempt an evaluation of the new scheme.

7.4.2 COMPETITION AND CREDIT CONTROL AND ITS AFTERMATH

It will be remembered that one of the intentions of *Competition and Credit Control* was to increase competitiveness by eliminating the discrimination against the London and Scottish Clearing Banks which had existed under the old methods of control. Arguably the new arrangements simply replaced one form of discrimination with another, since the reserve assets ratio might be congenial to one type of bank but not to another. Furthermore, the imposition of *any* reserve asset ratio (other than perhaps a cash ratio) is a potential distortion within the banking system unless the reserve ratio is used to differentiate between banks and is reviewed over time as banking and financial practices change. It is certainly the case that in September 1971 the finance houses, for example, were clearly holding a mix of assets which was unsuitable since their reserve asset ratio in October 1971 was 1·7 per cent, whereas the finance houses ratio was to be 10 per cent. Similarly, the group of banks classified as 'other U.K. banks' had a reserve ratio of 9·9 per cent in October 1971 and thus had to build up their reserve assets (by approximately an extra £25 million) in order to comply with the new arrangements.

A further distortion stems from the nature of assets selected by the Bank to be eligible as part of the reserve asset ratio. One basic question which has been asked concerns the rationale for the assets selected: in particular, the exclusion of bills eligible for re-discount at the Bank of England (in excess of 2 per cent of eligible liabilities) and also refinanceable export credit seems curious since these assets are just as liquid as the other reserve assets.

One view of the new reserve ratio scheme was that it was to form the basis of a return to market methods of regulation and, in particular, the traditional use associated with open market operations in the bond market – bond sales generating a contraction of bank deposits by a multiple derived from the reserve asset ratio. It is unlikely that this was ever the intention since even a casual examination of the reserve assets reveals that the prescribed ratio fails to satisfy the criteria laid down in Chapter 6: namely that the reserve assets should be capable of tight control by the Bank of England and that the banking system should be unable to generate reserve assets. For example, the banking system could expand deposits and reserve assets by purchases from the non-bank public of some of the public sector assets eligible for inclusion in the calculation of the reserve asset ratio. It is more likely that the authorities took the view that they could exercise some control over the banking system by inducing the non-bank public to move into public sector debt by increasing the attractiveness of such debt through higher interest rates; and at the same time depress the growth of bank advances as a further consequence of higher interest rates.

The original proposals – and subsequent amendments – are unclear as to the underlying theoretical position adopted by the Bank. After 1971, the speeches made both by the Governor and by the Chief Cashier of the Bank of England did not clarify the position sufficiently. An important question was whether the authorities' chosen monetary target was to be the money stock (which definition?), sterling deposits of an original maturity of two years and under (the main eligible liability under the reserve ratio scheme), or the level and structure of interst rates. As we saw earlier (Section 7.2.1) it is not possible to regulate both interest rates *and* the money stock. In 1978, a lecture delivered by the Governor of the Bank of England did make clear that the Bank had moved away from interest rates as a target in favour of sterling M_3.

It is possible to draw some conclusions about the effect of *Competition and Credit Control* in the years after 1971 although it is not an easy matter to make firm judgments about either aspect of the competition or credit control policy. Nevertheless, we shall attempt to draw some inferences from the events of the last few years.

After the reconstruction of their balance sheets, the London Clearing Banks found that their reserve asset ratio was well in excess of the minimum 12½ per cent and this gave considerable scope for increased lending: between October 1971 and the end of 1974, London Clearing Bank sterling advances rose by almost £8,000 million. Other banks with comfortable reserve ratios in October 1971 increased their lending faster than the London Clearing Banks but the size of their operations was very much smaller than that of the London Clearing Banks. The authorities, however, viewed the massive expansion in lending and the money stock with some anxiety and, as a result, during 1972 they were allowing interest rates to rise – a policy consistent with the ethos of *Competition and Credit Control*. The interest rates quoted in *Table 7.2* indicate the effect of this approach.

TABLE 7.2

Selected U.K. interest rates, 1972–1974 (incl.)

	Bank rate/ M.L.R.	Treasury bill rate	Local authority (3 months)	War Loans 3½%
28 January 1972	5	4·35	4·69	8·14
30 June 1972	6	5·64	7·56	9·48
29 December 1972	9	8·31	8·75	9·81
29 June 1973	7·5	6·96	8·12	10·33
28 December 1973	13	12·42	16·06	12·26
28 June 1974	11·75	11·24	13·38	15·37
27 December 1974	11·5	10·99	13·25	17·45

Source: Bank of England *Statistical Abstract*, No. 1.

By the end of 1973, interest rates in the U.K. had reached historically high (nominal) levels, and yet it is clear that the authorities' use of this instrument as a means of curtailing bank credit was ineffectual. It should be pointed out, however, that although nominal interest rates were relatively high by the end of 1973 (and were to rise even higher in 1974 and 1975), the real rate of interest was not. This was because the rate of inflation between 1970 and 1975 was not only rising but was expected to rise still further. In line with such expectations, potential lenders would have been unhappy to observe nominal interest rates failing to rise sufficiently as inflation increased. We can use a simple arithmetic illustration. By deducting the inflation rate from the nominal interest rates we obtain a rough idea of the real rate which lenders obtain. For example if a loan of £100 is made for one year at a rate of interest of 10 per cent, and the rate of inflation during that year is 5 per cent, at the end of the year the £100 loan has lost 5 per cent of its value during the year (i.e. the lender can only buy £95 worth of goods at the end of the year compared with his real spending power at the beginning of the year). Furthermore, the interest he receives at the end of the year also has depreciated in value compared with the nominal return negotiated at the beginning of the year. The lender has only £104·50[16] of spending power and not £110. Thus, in inflationary conditions, and when inflation is expected to continue or to rise, the nominal interest rate is likely to rise in order that the real return to lenders is not whittled away by the inflationary process. Borrowers, on the other hand, may benefit considerably from inflation if the real value of their borrowing is reduced, i.e. at the end of the term of the loan they repay a nominal amount (principal plus interest) which may be substantially less in real terms than the original sum borrowed. Thus an inflationary situation might act as a stimulus to certain kinds of borrowers. It is an interesting speculation as to the increase in nominal interest rates which would have been required during the 1970s effectively to damp down the growth in advances and the stock of money.

Evidence that *Competition and Credit Control* was not working satisfactorily can be deduced from the introduction in 1973 of a powerful *non-market* method of bank regulation. This was the Supplementary Deposit Scheme. The scheme, announced on 17 December 1973, established a specific rate of growth for interest-bearing eligible liabilities for the period November 1973 to May 1974. The rate of growth chosen by the Bank was 8 per cent and the deposits base selected was calculated as the average for each bank and finance house on the make-up days of the last three months of 1973. If a bank or finance house moderated its growth of interest-bearing eligible liabilities (I.B.E.L.s) to that required, then there would be no penalty. Growth in excess of 8 per cent, however, would result in a sliding scale of supplementary deposits required by

[16] i.e. £110 − $^{5}/_{100}$ · 110.

TABLE 7.3

IBEL growth	*Supplementary deposit call*
8 per cent	nil
9 per cent	5 per cent of excess deposits
10–11 per cent	25 per cent of excess deposits
over 11 per cent	50 per cent of excess deposits

the Bank of England. It is clear from the figures in *Table 7.3* that the Supplementary Deposit scheme would make excess growth of I.B.E.L.s rather costly to the banks and finance houses which were obliged to make such supplementary deposits. These deposits do not bear interest, whereas the banks of course would be paying interest to their own depositors. The scheme was extended for a further six months at the end of April 1974 and the permitted growth of I.B.E.L.s was 1½ per cent per month. Since the scheme's inception it has been temporarily suspended and re-activated at various times, and the detailed operation has been altered as well.

This scheme is of interest for at least two reasons. It is a flexible scheme (the permitted growth may be varied, the excess growth percentages may be altered, the size of the supplementary deposit could be changed) and one which has a potentially strong influence on the growth of bank deposits. Any bank or finance house near to the penal growth limit would be likely to adjust its deposit interest rate downwards to depress the inflow of funds. It is notable also that the supplementary deposit scheme is a non-market method of control dealing directly with bank liabilities in a rather blunt way. The introduction of this scheme implied that market methods of regulating the banking system – an implicit feature of the ethos of *Competition and Credit Control* – were deemed to be functioning ineffectively by December 1973[17]. A much stronger and swifter instrument was required.

Although the Supplementary Deposit scheme undoubtedly provided a powerful weapon for the authorities, it does detract from the objective of encouraging competitiveness and the removal of distortions. When operational, the scheme imposes an arbitrary limit to the growth of interest-bearing deposits for banks and finance houses but not for *all* financial intermediaries. In other words, the financial intermediaries not covered by the *Competition and Credit Control* arrangements, e.g. building societies, would be able to offer attractive interest rates to depositors/investors and thus draw funds from the banking system and the finance houses. The scheme thus provides a

[17]This was admitted by the Bank in its Annual Report for the year ended February 1974.

penalty to one part of the financial system and thereby a boost to the remainder.

At the end of the first fifteen months of the operation of *Competition and Credit Control*, the Bank expressed the view that the 'creation of conditions conducive to greater competition between the banks has been attained'.[18] There were certainly signs that the banking system was competing more vigorously than before, and particularly through the medium of price, i.e. the banks and discount houses abandoned their cartel agreements on interest rates. Although such agreements were put aside, it is difficult to measure the effect of competitiveness by observing the prices (interest rates) prevailing. The fact that the major banks' business operations are very similar means that they are subject to the same market pressures and therefore their responses will often coincide.

A significant consequence of the introduction of *Competition and Credit Control* was the closer links which developed between the primary and secondary banking systems. We have seen already that the primary banks had moved directly into the secondary banking field as well as through their own subsidiaries. The uniform application of *Competition and Credit Control* to all banks and finance companies meant that the primary banks could operate directly in the secondary markets and the associated money markets on a much larger scale. After the changes in 1971 it is very noticeable that the primary banks' holdings of sterling C.D.s particularly, but also inter-bank deposits, increased very considerably.

Undeniably, the introduction of *Competition and Credit Control* provided a fillip to greater competition, but there were other factors which were contributing to greater competitiveness in the British financial system. In particular, the growth of the Euro-currency market resulted not only in an extension of banking activities but also in the setting up and the growth of overseas banks in the U.K. Such banks were active in the market but were becoming increasingly interested in extending their business activities in sterling, i.e. competing with British banks within the U.K. Our earlier discussion of secondary banking referred to the successful development of term lending to meet U.K. residents' needs, particularly companies, and this exemplifies the opportunities open to foreign banks with offices in the U.K. It is likely, furthermore, that operating in the Euro-dollar market gave appropriate experience to many banks which could have been the foundation for operations in the other parallel markets which began to develop in the 1960s.

Although *Competition and Credit Control* was explicitly intended to stimulate competition in the banking system, it is evident from the

[18]Bank of England Report, p. 5, year ended 28 February 1973.

intervention of the authorities since 1971 that they were not prepared to accept the full implication associated with the competitive ethos. We have considered already the rescue operation provided by the Bank after the fringe banking collapse so there is no need to consider this further.

A further illustration of the Bank's reluctance to see the full consequences of competition is linked to the behaviour of interest rates and the money stock M_3. During 1972 and the early part of 1973 banks were attempting to satisfy their reserve requirements by bidding for funds in the parallel markets which would then be put out at call to the discount houses (money at call is an eligible reserve asset). As a result of this vigorous bidding, the rates of interest on deposits rose, but the rates of interest on bank lending tended to lag behind. (Changes in bank base rates, and therefore lending rates, have as their proximate cause an *administrative* decision of the banks, i.e. they are not immediately market determined). The result of this situation was a process called round-tripping, or the merry-go-round, whereby it was profitable for some of the banks' customers to borrow (or fully utilize their advances facilities) at, say, base rate plus $1\frac{1}{2}$ per cent, and re-deposit the same funds with another bank, either as a time-deposit or more likely as a sterling C.D. The consequence of this round-tripping for banks' balance sheets was a simultaneous rise in advances and deposits. Thus M_3 rose entirely as a consequence of the arbitrage opportunities. The authorities clearly did not like this process and introduced measures in the Budget of 1973 to reduce the attractiveness of sterling C.D.s by removing the capital gains exemption and also by introducing a new tax deposit account offering competitive interest rates to companies who wished to make deposits against future corporation tax liability. But it was the introduction of the Supplementary Deposit scheme in December 1973 which effectively clamped down on round-tripping since the scheme, it will be recalled, could penalize the attracting of deposits by the banks. At the same time as the introduction of the new scheme, the banks agreed to adjust their base rates more swiftly as market conditions changed.

The greater flexibility of interest rates after 1971 and their independence from the officially determined rate, i.e. Bank rate, resulted in the old Bank rate being replaced in October 1972 by the Minimum Lending Rate. The immediate cause of this change was that the Treasury bill rate rose above Bank rate in September 1972 and this meant that Bank rate could not be a penal borrowing rate for the discount houses. The flexibility of short-term interest rates, including the Treasury bill rate, was one of the consequences of the greater competitiveness. Bank rate, however, was an administered interest rate and therefore 'sticky'. The Minimum Lending Rate

(M.L.R.) which was introduced could not be less than the prevailing Treasury bill rate because of the nature of its calculation. The M.L.R. was calculated as the average Treasury bill discount rate *plus* ½ per cent and then rounded to the nearest ¼ per cent above. The M.L.R. calculation resulted in its being a market-determined rate, except on those occasions when the authorities chose to suspend the method of calculation and fix the M.L.R. administratively. In May 1978 the Bank of England abandoned the M.L.R. mechanism whilst retaining the term M.L.R. and returned to the old Bank rate procedure whereby the discount rate became, once again, an administratively determined interest rate. One of the reasons for this reversion was that the authorities wished to exercise, whenever possible, tighter control of the key rates of interest in the economy – notwithstanding the avowed money supply targets.

The *Competition and Credit Control* document alluded to the possible discrimination which might be needed to protect savings banks and building societies against the loss of deposits stemming from the greater competitive opportunities of the banks. Because of the effect on the cost of mortgages and its political implications, in September 1973 the Bank asked the banks to observe a limit of 9½ per cent on deposits under £10,000. When interest rates began to fall in the early part of 1975, the 9½ per cent ceiling became redundant and it was withdrawn on the 8 February 1975. Apart from the evident discrimination against the small saver (those who had time deposits with the banks which were less than £10,000), this application of an interest rate ceiling was clearly a distortion and a deliberate attempt to prevent the effect of competition extending to certain financial intermediaries. It may well be argued convincingly that such discrimination is justified but our point here is that it is a distortion and one which is not consistent with the objectives of the new approach of the Bank of England.

An important disadvantage associated with the various qualifications and amendments to *Competition and Credit Control* introduced since 1971 is that the accompanying distortions tend to stimulate methods of avoiding their effects and this, in turn, induces further responses by the authorities to close the loopholes. Unfortunately, it is often the case that when one loophole is closed, another is found and used. One example of potential avoidance is in connection with the severe Supplementary Deposit scheme. The effects of the scheme might be evaded by the banks if they chose, say, to compete for interest-bearing deposits which had a term of greater than two years. If such deposits were obtained they would not qualify for inclusion as eligible liabilities, and would not be included therefore in the calculation of the rate of growth of such liabilities.

The introduction of *Competition and Credit Control* in 1971 was, as the Bank has admitted, an attempt to move away from direct restrictive controls in the monetary sphere as well as a move towards a system in which market forces could play a predominant role. As we have seen in this chapter, the inflationary environment of the 1970s was one factor which inhibited the fulfilment of the Bank's objectives. It is an interesting if debatable question as to how far the Bank is prepared to trade-off the 'competition objective' with the 'credit control objective'. It would be reasonable to suggest, however, that the more important target is credit/monetary control and this would not be sacrificed for the objective of greater competition. The introduction of the Supplementary Deposit scheme in 1973 made this clear.

7.5 Summary

i.   We examined the work of the Bank of England and concentrated our attention on the management of the gilt-edged market. Part of such activity could be designated as 'passive' in the sense that there is routine activity undertaken by the Chief Cashier's department. However, a more 'active' policy may be undertaken with the intention, for example, of altering the level and structure of interest rates in the economy.

ii.   Over the years the Bank of England's objectives in the gilt-edged market have changed, and this has been related mainly to the policy choice: should the authorities aim to control the money stock or interest rates – acknowledging that it is not possible to control both simultaneously?

iii. In the money market the Bank of England is able to exercise influence over short-term interest rates through the Treasury bill issue and the operation of the discount market, as well as through changes in the Minimum Lending Rate.

iv.   With the rapid growth of the secondary banking sector, we suggested that a money market arrangement – similar to that provided by the discount market for the primary banks – would be necessary to smooth the ebbs and flows of funds between the various banks. Such 'parallel markets' have in fact developed and deal largely in certificates of deposit and inter-bank deposits.

v.   We suggested that control of the banking system, including the secondary banks, was becoming a growing problem for the Bank of England. In the 1960s the Bank had to rely increasingly on non-market methods of control; methods which were not popular with the primary banks.

vi.   In 1971, following discussion with the financial institutions, the Bank devised *Competition and Credit Control*. This scheme introduced a new reserve ratio (replacing the liquidity ratio) which applied to all the banks, and it was hoped that other features of the scheme would stimulate competition in the financial area as well as allowing the Bank of England to exercise control over the financial sector by market, rather than non-market, methods of control.

vii. Events since 1971, we suggested, have indicated that the new scheme has not been entirely successful from the point of view of credit control and the Bank has had to move back to the use of non-market methods of regulation.

8
Other financial systems

Our study of the main elements of the financial system would be incomplete without an examination – albeit brief – of the way other countries' financial systems are structured and operate. We shall see that some of the differences between systems are less fundamental than first appearances would suggest. Perhaps one should not be surprised that there are similarities, since many of the basic ideas which we have examined in earlier chapters are applicable to most 'free market economies', whatever the institutional differences or idiosyncracies. In this chapter we propose to look at the financial framework of two countries: the United States of America and Germany. The approach we shall adopt will be similar to that which we have used in studying the elements of the U.K. system.

8.1 The American system

In understanding the American system it is essential to be aware of political aspects of the U.S.A.'s development. One important factor is that the U.S.A. is not a unitary state such as the U.K. but a federal state. This means that political powers and decision-making are split between the Federal government and the governments of the individual states. Some states are very jealous of their rights and powers under the Constitution and are suspicious or averse to Federal authority. A second factor, and one which is linked to the first, is mistrust of the concentration and centralization of economic and political power. The struggle for independence from the British Crown no doubt provided the springboard for these and other attitudes which became embodied in the Constitution of the U.S.A. as well as its other institutions, not least the financial ones.

8.11 THE MAJOR FINANCIAL INTERMEDIARIES

In *Table 8.1* we have identified several important financial intermediaries in the U.S.A. and the volume of assets held by these firms.

Since Section 8.1.2 deals specifically with the commercial or primary banks, we shall omit this group of banks from the following discussion of the various intermediaries identified in Table 8.1.

TABLE 8.1
Assets of selected U.S. financial intermediaries
($ billion)

Commercial banks	1,041
Mutual savings banks	142
Savings and loan associations	427
Life insurance companies	334
Credit unions	50

Source: Federal Reserve Bulletin, vol. 64, No. 1 (January 1978).

Mutual savings banks. As their name suggests, these banks are owned by their depositors and one of their prime functions is to afford a safe and reliable outlet for individual savings. They do not therefore provide demand deposit facilities but rather the provision of time deposit accounts which usually are repayable at short notice. As with any other bank, the mutual savings banks hold a general reserve and as an additional protection to depositors they are limited in both the range and proportions of assets which they can hold. The major asset in their balance sheet is real estate mortgages followed by corporate bonds and U.S. government securities. As an additional security for depositors, a large part of the mortgages are insured under Federal schemes, and in addition deposit accounts have insurance cover against default. Although this latter form of insurance cover is not total, it is highly likely that such cover does add to the security of this kind of bank which has most of its assets in a relatively illiquid form, i.e. mortgages.

Savings and loan associations. These associations are primarily in the business of providing conventional mortgage finance for residential property. Some associations are mutual whereby the depositors are the owners, and these associations are Federally chartered; other associations issue equity and are not mutually owned. The bulk of their assets are mortgage loans whereas their other assets consist largely of U.S. government bonds. The deposits which they attract are time deposits of the kind which U.K. building societies offer. As with the mutual savings banks, the accounts of the savings and loan associations are subject to a limited insurance cover through a Federal agency.

Credit unions. Credit unions provide their depositors with time deposit facilities and, as their name suggests, most of their assets arise from the provision of consumer loans. In addition to the credit co-operatives there are consumer finance companies which also provide funds for consumers.

In Chapter 4 we examined most of the major financial intermediaries established in the U.K. and this included insurance companies and pension funds. We shall simply refer the reader to this chapter, therefore, and not discuss these intermediaries in their U.S. setting.

8.1.2 U.S. COMMERCIAL BANKING

In Chapter 4 we suggested that there was some problem in defining the various kinds of financial intermediary. In particular, we saw that the banks which were predominantly the operators of the payments mechanism had attracted a variety of names. Our own preference was to ascribe to these banks the term 'primary banks'. The commonly used expression in the U.S.A. for this group of banks is 'commercial banks'[1] although the problem of definition is one acknowledged by American writers. We shall adopt, therefore, the U.S. convention in this chapter.

The development of commercial banking in the U.S.A. illustrates rather well our opening comments of this chapter. The establishment of a bank may be brought about through the conferring of a Federal charter or a state charter – there is no single method, nor is there a unified method of bank supervision. Furthermore, there was and is a strong aversion to branch banking in the form which is so familiar in the U.K.; the U.S. has over 14,000 commercial banks compared with the relatively small number in the U.K.

8.1.2.1 Classification and structure of U.S. commercial banking

The Federal structure of the U.S.A. has resulted in a diversity within the primary banking structure. We propose, therefore, to identify in this section the main types of bank and banking organization.

National banks. These banks are incorporated by a Federal charter and are subject to Federal regulations. About one-third of all banks are national banks and they comprise the largest banks in the U.S.A. As a group, the national banks account for around 60 per cent of banking business. It is an obligation of national bank status that such banks are members of the Federal Reserve System (see Section 8.1.3.2) and

---

[1]The long-standing use of the term 'commercial bank' derives from the early role of these banks in providing working capital for commerce.

for the protection of depositors all national banks have to insure each account with the Federal Deposit Insurance Corporation.[2]

State banks. As their name suggests, these banks are established and gain their charter under state law and regulation. Such banks comprise approximately two-thirds of all banks in the U.S.A. but their importance is indicated by their relatively small share of total banking business – approximately 40 per cent. Membership of the Federal Reserve System is optional for state banks, although around 10 per cent have chosen to join the System. Virtually all state banks have obtained insurance cover for accounts – through the Federal Deposits Insurance Corporation – even though such cover is not mandatory for those state banks which are not members of the Federal Reserve System.

The different methods of bank incorporation and supervision as well as inter-state variations in banking law have been key factors producing distinct banking relationships and structures. We shall proceed to examine the more important manifestations.

Unit banking and branch banking. Perhaps the most distinctive feature of U.S. commercial banking – certainly to a British eye – is the large number of single-office banks. The U.K. primary banking system is dominated by the four major banks together with their thousands of branch offices, whereas the U.S. commercial banking sector consists of around 9,000 single-office banks out of a total of over 14,000. There are powerful historical reasons for the significance of single office or unit banking (significant in terms of their number if not their share of banking sector assets) but important contemporary factors are the state laws which inhibit or prohibit branch banking development. An important example of such restrictions is the prohibition on a bank establishing branches outside the state in which it has been set up. Some states prevent banks having branches in more than one town, or prevent banks having more than one branch.

Group and chain banking. Partly as a result of the restrictions on branch banking, two devices have been used to gain the benefits of multi-office banking without contravening an embargo on branch banking. Group banking may be established through the setting up of a holding company which has control of a number of different banks. Although the use of the holding company effectively unites the banks under it, the various banks nevertheless retain their separate legal identity. Not all states permit this form of multi-office banking but

[2]In 1976 the F.D.I.C., in the event of bank failure, would refund up to $40,000 of each insured account.

even so this form of banking organization is of considerable importance, comprising around two-fifths of commercial bank business. In the case of chain banking, the method used is to acquire control of a number of banks by the purchase of the equity, and by the appropriate appointment of directorships the various banks can be brought effectively under common control. The difference between group and chain banking is that in the latter case a holding company is not set up.

Correspondent banking. Largely as a consequence of the very large number of single-office banks and the limitation on inter-state banking, there is a need for a banking relationship which allows banks and their customers to overcome the dislocations caused by the lack of national branch banking in particular. The device used is the inter-bank deposit. In the U.K., by contrast, the small number of banks and the large number of branches allows cheque clearing to take place either within the same bank or simply through the London clearing system in conjunction with the Bank of England Banking Department. In the U.S.A., however, a small bank is likely to hold

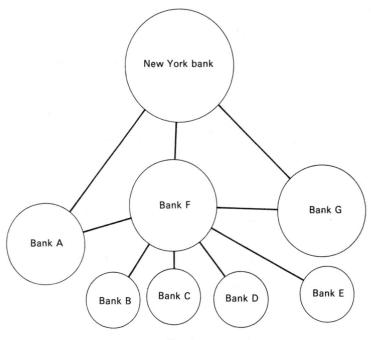

FIG 8.1

deposits with other, larger banks and, very likely, one of the larger banks will have offices in a nearby city, and another of the larger banks used by the smaller could be a New York bank. The diagram above (*Fig. 8.1*) might help to clarify the system of correspondent relationships. The smaller banks – A, B, C, D, and E – have a correspondent relationship with the much larger bank F, and bank F has a similar relationship with a large bank in New York. Bank A is a slightly larger bank than banks B, C, D and E and finds it convenient to have deposits not only with bank F but also with a New York bank. Similarly, bank F chooses to hold deposits with another large bank, bank G. What then are the benefits of correspondent bank relationships? For the individual bank the system allows cheque clearings to take place across state boundaries as well as within a state. But the correspondent relationship also provides a flexible system by which banks can make better use of surplus funds, since they can increase their deposits with a correspondent bank. Taking the system as a whole, it does provide a means of smoothing the shortages and surpluses of funds between the various banks. This is comparable with the function provided by the discount houses in the U.K., i.e. repaying call money to one bank and borrowing from another. Finally, the inter-bank deposit arrangement enables a bank to provide better services to its customers, e.g. the purchase of securities from the New York Stock Exchange through a correspondent bank in New York.

8.1.2.2 *U.S. commercial bank balance sheets*

In this section we are not concerned with the wide range of services provided by U.S. commercial banks – services similar to those provided by such banks in the U.K. Rather, our intention is to identify the main items on the collective balance sheet and comment on them. *Table 8.2* represents a condensed version of such a balance sheet for 30 June 1977.

Liabilities
- (a) *Demand deposits*. This type of deposit represents about 34 per cent of total liabilities and consists largely of the cheque accounts of individuals and firms (75 per cent). Other demand deposits are held by the U.S. government as well as state and local governments. One item to which we have referred already is the inter-bank deposits which are part of the correspondent banking arrangement.
- (b) *Time deposits*. These deposits account for 30 per cent of total liabilities and vary according to term to maturity, depending upon the customer's needs. This item also includes certificates

TABLE 8.2

U.S. Commercial banks balance sheet: selected items
($ billion)

Liabilities		Assets	
Deposits:		Cash assets:	139·1
Demand deposits	337·4	Bank cash	12·7
Time deposits	308·8	Deposits with the	
Savings deposits	215·8	Federal Reserve;	
Other liabilities	130·5	balances with	
		other banks	126·4
		Securities:	
		U.S. Treasury	101·6
		State and local	
		governments	154·1
		Loans:	
		Commercial and	
		industrial	192·7
		Real estate	161·3
		Individuals	127·7
		of which instal-	
		ment loans	101·4
		Other loans and	
		assets	116·0

Source: Federal Reserve Bulletin, vol. 64, No. 1 (January 1978).

of deposits (C.D.s) which have become increasingly important in the U.S. as in the U.K. The major holders or time deposits are individuals and firms, followed by state and local governments.

(c) *Savings deposits.* The American statistics distinguish between savings and time deposits, whereas in U.K. statistics they are combined. Savings deposit owners have passbooks and their accounts earn interest, as do time deposits. Although notice of withdrawal is a technical requirement, this is usually waived with the customary interest penalty. This type of deposit is held largely by individuals and represents 22 per cent of total deposits.

(d) *Other liabilities.* These other liabilities account for around 20 per cent of total liabilities and include borrowing from the Federal Reserve and borrowed federal funds. (These items will be considered in Section 8.1.3.2). The other borrowing under this general heading includes obtaining funds through the issue of promissory notes and other commercial paper.

Assets

   (a) *Bank cash.* This consists of notes and coin in bank offices which is required to meet the needs of customers. In addition, it constitutes part of the banks' reserve ratio.

   (b) *Deposits with the Federal Reserve.* These deposits also form part of the banks' reserves and are similar to the U.K. banks' balances at the Bank of England. We shall discuss this item in Section 8.1.3.2.

   (c) *Balances with other banks.* These balances are largely the correspondent inter-bank deposits.

   (d) *Securities.* This group of assets consists principally of government securities, both Federal and state (about 80 per cent) and, as with U.K. banks, these securities are of relatively short maturity.

   (e) *Loans.* Although the self-liquidating loan is provided by U.S. commercial banks, a relatively high proportion of lending is in the form of term loans to industry. This is in contrast to the traditional overdraft lending by U.K. banks although, as we have noted in earlier chapters, the U.K. primary banks are more involved in term lending than formerly. Almost one-third of total lending by U.S. commercial banks is mortgage finance, whereas in the U.K. the banks prefer to provide bridging finance rather than outright mortgage facilities. Consumer credit is provided by the U.S. commercial banks directly to their customers – around 25 per cent of total loans are in this form. Indirect provision is made through the making of loans to specialist firms in the field of consumer credit. Although loan finance as a proportion of total assets is not very much greater than that provided by U.K. primary banks, the nature of their lending is noticeably different. Generally, there is a greater willingness to indulge in longer-term lending, e.g. mortgages, term loans to firms, as well as the provision of consumer credit.

8.1.3 U.S. CENTRAL BANKING AND BANK SUPERVISION

The federal political structure of the U.S.A. is clearly matched by the organization of central banking. At first sight the arrangement seems complex and cumbersome by contrast with the simplicity of a single central banking entity such as the Bank of England. We shall discover, however, that there are many points of similarity between central banking in the U.S.A. and in the U.K. Indeed, the U.S. system in general has certain features which might well be of value within the British framework.[3]

[3] For example, the deposit insurance scheme has been in operation in the U.S. since the 1930s, whereas such arrangements have only recently received attention in the U.K. (Section 4.7).

8.1.3.1 Structure of central banking

For central banking purposes, the U.S. is divided into twelve (unequal) Federal Reserve districts, each of which has a separately incorporated Federal Reserve bank named after the city in which it operates. There are also a number of Federal Reserve bank branches, for example the Federal Reserve Bank of New York has a branch at Buffalo. Each Federal Reserve bank is owned by the banks in the district who have chosen to join the Federal Reserve System. Although the member banks have subscribed capital to their respective Federal Reserve bank (3 per cent of each bank's paid-up capital and surplus), a Federal Reserve bank is not *controlled* by its owners. Each Reserve bank has nine directors of whom only three are appointed by member banks. Three other directors are representative of local business and other interests in the district, and the remainder are selected by the Board of Governors of the whole system. One of the reasons for this arrangement was to avoid the control of the central bank system by bankers since there clearly could be a conflict of interest. Although only about 38 per cent of banks are members of the Federal Reserve system, these banks are the major banks in the U.S. handling about four-fifths of deposits.

Overall control of the Federal Reserve system is provided by the Board of Governors based in Washington, D.C. The Board consists of seven members appointed by the President of the U.S.A. for a term of fourteen years, with the Chairman of the Board having a term of four years. The Board has extensive powers which we normally associate with a central bank: the authority to determine banks' reserve requirements and central bank discount rates, control of the note issue, power to undertake open market operations. The Board of Governors also exercises authority and supervision over the component Federal Reserve banks.

A very important committee of the Reserve system is the Federal Open Market Committee. As its name suggests, this committee has control of all open market sales and purchases by the Reserve banks. To ensure central control and co-ordination of such an important function, the membership of the committee consists of all seven members of the Board of Governors plus five representatives of the twelve Reserve banks. The Federal Reserve Bank of New York is the largest of the Reserve banks and is also at the centre of the financial system, surrounded by the various financial markets, both national and international. Accordingly the New York Reserve Bank acts as agent for the Reserve system and has a permanent place on the Federal Open Market Committee.

8.1.3.2 Central banking operations

The Federal Reserve banks individually and as a system provide member banks (and some non-member banks) with the facility for clearing cheques and other transfers. The means for this provision is the mandatory requirement for member banks to hold deposits with a Reserve bank as part of the legal reserve requirements. This, together with the links between the various Reserve banks, allows inter-bank indebtedness to be settled by the simple means of a transfer of deposits at or between Federal Reserve banks, in just the same way that bankers' balances at the Bank of England are used. In other words, the Federal Reserve system, as part of the system of correspondent banking, operates as banker to member banks in the same way that the Bank of England acts as banker.

The lender of last resort function is also a feature of the Federal Reserve system. A member bank which experiences a loss of reserves (either in the form of bank cash or deposits with its Federal Reserve bank) may apply for a loan and such borrowing would not normally be refused. However, the philosophy underlining the provision and use of Federal Reserve loans is somewhat different from that prevailing in the U.K. It will be recalled that the discount houses in the U.K. have access to Bank of England help without stint. Furthermore, the Bank of England accepts that its lender of last resort function is an essential part of the smoothing operations in the money market. The Federal Reserve system had taken the view for many years – a view which seems to have changed – that borrowing from the Federal Reserve is a privilege and not a right. Such assistance was to be in the nature of a safety valve – a temporary means for alleviating unexpected shortages of reserves or where a bank was in serious difficulties. Sustained borrowing would result in disapproval from Federal Reserve officials and if a member bank persisted in its use of loans from the Federal Reserve, or if it was suspected that a bank's operations were imprudent, then the borrowing privilege could be revoked and the bank's affairs would be subject to Federal Reserve examination. In 1965 the Federal Reserve established a committee to enquire into the discount mechanism (Federal Reserve lending arrangements) on the basis that the safety valve principle was outdated and that the helping hand approach was more appropriate. In accordance with this development, the Federal Reserve has relaxed its policy somewhat and now provides three types of assistance to member banks: short-term adjustment, seasonal assistance, and emergency credit. Short-term adjustment is intended to assist banks which experience temporary and unexpected changes in their balance sheets; the seasonal assistance is largely taken up by the small banks, particularly those connected with agriculture, and must be arranged in advance of need; the emergency credit, as the name suggests, is for exceptional circumstances which require longer term assistance. Nevertheless, the lender of last resort role of the Federal Reserve is interpreted more severely than that of the Bank of England.

Not only does the Federal Reserve act as banker to the member banks, but it acts also as banker to the federal government, and this includes the limited power to lend direct to the federal government. In addition, the Federal Reserve acts as an adviser to the government on general economic matters as well as dealing with such things as the sale and redemption of government securities and foreign exchange market operations. In these matters the Federal Reserve's operations match closely those of the Bank of England.

As with the Bank of England, the most important function of the Federal Reserve is to monitor the monetary situation within the U.S.A. and to implement appropriate policies, i.e. to formulate and execute monetary policy. We shall provide a brief account of the main methods by which the Federal Reserve operates monetary policy, and we expect that much of this material will be familiar since it relates to the contents of Chapters 6 and 7.

The Federal Reserve has at its disposal a substantial quantity of federal government securities which amount to 80 per cent of the assets of the Federal Reserve banks. Open market operations are authorized by the Federal Open Market Committee and are carried out by the Federal Reserve Bank of New York. Intervention might be authorized because the Federal Reserve wishes to alter the reserves of member and non-member bank; security sales would tend to depress banks' reserves, and bond purchases would tend to expand reserves.[4] Such action would thus affect the volume of commercial bank deposits and the money stock.

Alternatively, the open market sale or purchase may be of a reversible kind. The arrangement with a stock market dealer may be that the stock sold to a dealer would be re-purchased after a period of several days, or that the dealer himself may agree to re-purchase stock bought by the Federal Reserve. These agreements with dealers are a useful device which can be used to offset temporary but substantial flows of funds between the Federal Reserve and the public. Without such agreements the effect could be substantial changes in prices (and therefore yields also) of government securities.[5] Thus the former kind

---

[4] The reader should consult Section 6.2.2 if uncertain about the effect of open market operations.
[5] A similar practice was adopted up to 1971 by the Bank of England, not only to achieve an orderly gilt-edged market but also add to the limited financial capacity of gilt-edged jobbers. The Bank was sometimes referred to as the 'jobber of last resort'.

of open market operation is intended to affect bank credit and the money stock, whereas the latter is essentially a smoothing operation.

So far in our discussion of U.S. central bank practice we have emphasized (i) that the Federal Reserve is a much less open-handed lender of last resort than the Bank of England, and (ii) that one form of smoothing operation is undertaken through open market operations in the bond market. Yet our examination of the functions of the Bank of England in Chapter 4 revealed that the daily ebb and flow of funds between the government and the non-government sector were substantial. Such movement of funds required off-setting measures to avoid large and undesirable variations in the cash base of the banking system, and short-term interest rates. It would be reasonable, therefore, to presume that a similar problem exists within the U.S. system and to consider how this problem is tackled. The device is interesting and consists simply of the U.S. Treasury having accounts (called tax and loan accounts) with around 12,000 commercial banks. Since the purpose of the device is to minimize disturbance of the reserve assets of the banks, the mechanism is essentially one of recycling deposits transferred to the federal government by, say, taxpayers back to the taxpayers' banks. By this means the Treasury also ensures that its deposits with the Federal Reserve banks are kept to a minimum. When the Treasury requires the funds which are on deposit with the commercial banks, it gives notice to the banks of the intention to withdraw and then takes payment by adjusting the banks' accounts at the Federal Reserve. The banks accordingly reduce the Treasury's deposit in their own accounts by the amount deducted at the Federal Reserve. The funds thus withdrawn by the Treasury are spent by the government and passed quickly through the Reserve banks in order to ensure the minimum disturbance to a member bank's reserves – bank reserves would fall on withdrawal and then revert to the original level after the funds have been spent.

Potentially a very powerful means by which the Federal Reserve may influence the commercial banks is by adjustments of the legal reserve requirements which the member banks have to maintain. The only legal reserve assets are bank cash and deposits with the Federal Reserve (the Federal Reserve does not designate a *range* of assets as in the U.K. system). Traditionally the size of the over-all reserve ratio depended on two factors: the composition of total deposits (demand and time deposits attract different ratios), and the location of the bank. The preference of the Board of Governors of the Federal Reserve has been for a reserve ratio arrangement which relates the size of the ratio to the volume of deposits, and since 1972 the Federal Reserve has been able to use the existing legislation in such a way as to bring about the desired change.

The required reserve in relation to demand deposits is based on a sliding scale with the reserve requirement rising as the volume of demand deposits becomes larger. For time deposits, the reserve required is not only lower than that for demand deposits but also varies with the maturity of the deposit. It is clear that with this kind of arrangement there can be no single reserve ratio for all banks, even though the rules apply uniformly. Although the power to vary reserve ratios rests with the Board of Governors and could have, in principle, a powerful effect on bank credit and the money supply – for example, lowering the ratios would stimulate the expansion of bank credit – such changes are not popular with member banks. This is because any rise in ratios would place member banks in a less competitive position *vis à vis* those state banks which operate under more lax banking regulations and are permitted to operate with lower ratios. Membership of the Federal Reserve system has been declining and the manipulation of mandatory reserve ratios for member banks would no doubt make membership of the system less attractive.

In Chapter 7 we explained that from 1972 to May 1978 the Bank of England abandoned its use of Bank rate – an *administratively* determined discount rate which was charged on 'last resort' borrowing – to replace it with the Minimum Lending Rate which was calculated on the basis of the Treasury bill rate – a *market* rate. In the U.S.A. the equivalent rate is known as the discount rate and it is very similar to the U.K. Bank rate. Since U.S. short-term interest rates are market-determined, there is the possibility that the discount rate may be less than current short rates, and under such circumstances it is profitable for member banks to borrow from the Federal Reserve. Rather than change the discount rate very frequently, the Federal Reserve tries, as we have recounted, to deter borrowing from the Reserve banks and encourages early repayment of past borrowings. This is not to suggest that variations in the discount rate do not occur in order to influence short-term interest rates. It is likely, therefore, that changes in the discount rate have an important influence on short-term interest rates through changing market expectations. Indeed, this was one of the factors influencing the use of Bank rate by the Bank of England.

As a result of the relatively tight approach to Federal Reserve lending, member banks make use of the federal funds market as a means of maintaining their reserve ratios. Banks whose reserve ratios are falling will attempt to borrow deposits at the Federal Reserve from member banks whose reserves are rising.

Finally, the familiar instruments of selective credit controls and moral suasion which have been used frequently by the Bank of England are also part of the armoury of the Federal Reserve.

8.1.4 BANKING SUPERVISION

The history of U.S. commercial banking is littered with the debris of bank failures. It is not surprising, therefore, that particularly at federal level the extent of formal banking supervision is considerable – certainly in comparison with the U.K.

Membership of the Federal Reserve system brings with it certain benefits; for example, borrowing from one's Reserve bank; but it also carries certain obligations.[6] In particular, member banks are required to maintain legal reserve ratios which may well be higher than those imposed under state charters. They are also subject to the scrutiny of their respective Reserve Banks.

Within each Federal Reserve District the Reserve Bank will aim to ensure that the member banks are solvent as well as being effective banking institutions. Each Reserve bank may conduct 'field examinations' of member banks to evaluate banks' assets and liabilities as well as their capital and liquidity positions. The capabilities of the management of these banks is also the subject of Reserve Bank scrutiny. The Reserve Banks have the authority to examine and supervise all national banks; a responsibility shared with the office of the Comptroller of the Currency. Furthermore, the Comptroller of the Currency has the authority to issue bank charters to new national banks only so long as he is satisfied as to the need for the bank and the financial probity and competence of its founders. The Federal Deposits Insurance Corporation also requires similar reassurances before insurance provision is made and clearly the risk or threat of no such insurance is a powerful sanction and inducement to sound banking practice. Banks which have received state charters are subject to state banking regulations and it is no doubt regretted by the Federal authorities that the standards imposed vary from state to state, with some states requiring lower standards than that which would be acceptable at the federal level.

8.2 Banking in the Federal Republic of Germany

At the end of the 1939-45 war, the Allies occupying Germany made considerable efforts to fragment the banking system – both the central banking arrangements and commercial banking. This policy was based probably on the assumption that one of the causes of the Second World War was the process of concentration in the industrial, financial, and political spheres. The strong historical as well as economic pressures towards concentration were not, however, eliminated and by the late 1950s much more rational arrangements

[6]Since membership is very much lower than, say, in the mid-1950s, it would seem that for many banks the obligations of membership outweigh the direct benefits.

had been established. The Federal Republic of Germany once again had a unified central bank – the Deutsche Bundesbank – and the three 'big banks' which had been split up in 1946 and 1947 were effectively united by 1958 and were operating throughout the whole of the Republic.

8.2.1 THE MAJOR FINANCIAL INTERMEDIARIES

Table 8.3 lists the major financial intermediaries operating in the Republic as well as the volume of their deposits.

TABLE 8.3
West German banks and other financial intermediaries: number and total liabilities
(November 1977)

	Number	Volume of business (DM million)	% of total liabilities
Big banks	6	179,520	9·7
Regional and other commercial banks	112	184,133	9·9
Foreign banks	51	32,995	1·9
Private banks	104	30,145	1·6
Savings banks	622	387,706	21·0
Central giro institutions	12	289,641	15·7
Credit co-operatives	2,352	171,578	9·3
Central institutions of credit co-operatives	11	72,939	4·0
Mortgage banks:			
public	26	227,937	12·4
private	14		
Building and loan associations	30	98,497	5·3
Other banking firms	173	170,225	9·2
	3,586	1,845,316	100·0

Source: Deutsche Bank *Monthly Report*, February 1978.

Commercial banks. There are around 300 commercial banks in the Republic with about 5,000 branches, and as a group they hold about a quarter of total deposits. In comparison with the U.K. structure the West German commercial banks are much less dominant in relation to the other banking institutions. Even within the commercial bank group, the six big banks hold only about 40 per cent of the group's deposits. These big banks are the Deutsche Bundesbank, Dresdner Bank, and Commerzbank (plus their West Berlin affiliates), and they operate branches throughout the Republic. In competition with the big six banks are the regionally based banks, and it is clear that the banks in the latter group have been successful since they now account for almost the same volume of business as the big banks. The private banks have declined in number in recent years and their share of banking business has also dropped slightly. Despite mergers, these banks face considerable competition from the other commercial banks and they rely on the provision of specialized and distinctive services for their customers in order to survive. Although they provide the usual range of banking services, they may be compared with the merchant banks and other small specialist banks which operate in the U.K. The foreign banks in West Germany hold a fairly small share of commercial banking business and, although their number has grown quite fast in recent years, it is likely that they find the competition very severe. It will be recalled that foreign banks in London found a range of business opportunities which they could exploit because of the fairly restricted banking activities of the primary banks: in West Germany this is not the case since banking specialization has not taken the form which developed in the U.K.

There is considerable diversity of business among the commercial banks, so we shall identify only the main points. The source of funds for the commercial banks is a mixture of sight (demand) deposits, time and savings deposits from the public, and of this only about 10 per cent are sight deposits – a surprisingly low proportion compared with the U.K. where it is about 40 per cent. This low proportion of sight deposits probably helps to explain the high proportion of long-term lending (exceeding four years) undertaken by the commercial banks. Although the commercial banks provide less long-term lending than other banking firms, nevertheless it is still high – well over one-third of all lending takes this form. The West German commercial banks are very important suppliers of short, medium, and long-term finance to West German industry in addition to the fact that they provide the sort of investment and new-issue advice associated with the secondary banks in the U.K. rather than the primary banks. The influence of West German banks in industry is extended further by the practice of bank customers who are shareholders in industry appointing their bank as proxy in matters requiring shareholders' decisions.

The remaining assets of the commercial banks are liquid assets in the form of reserves with the central bank together with commercial and Treasury bills. Only a very small proportion of their total assets are public sector debt since the West German national debt and public sector borrowing are relatively small.

Savings banks and central giro institutions. An interesting and remarkable feature of West German banking is the collective dominance of the savings banks. As a group they hold nearly as large a volume of deposits as the commercial banks put together. These savings banks are owned almost exclusively by local authorities and, with around 16,000 branches, they provide a wide range of banking services. Well over half their deposits are savings deposits and about 12 per cent are sight deposits – an indication of their competitive banking services. Furthermore, they hold well over 50 per cent of all savings deposits in the banking system. The traditional use of funds by the savings banks has been in the provision of mortgage finance and loans to local authorities and nationalized industries. Although they are not permitted to hold shares or indulge in risky business activities, they have moved into very active competition with the commercial banks in the field of industrial credit.

Linked with the savings banks are the twelve *Girozentralen* which provide the savings banks with a giro system and clearing arrangements. The savings banks hold part of their cash reserve with the *Girozentralen* (a mandatory arrangement) as well as purchasing bonds issued by these institutions. The *Girozentralen* not only obtain funds from the savings banks but also from the general public and public authorities. The funds so obtained are used for normal banking purposes, e.g. lending, discounting of bills, as well as providing funds to member banks (a kind of internal inter-bank lending), and operating in the money market.

Credit co-operatives and central institutions for co-operatives. The credit co-operatives are to be found in urban and rural areas and most of them are in fact agricultural co-operatives. These banks have a relatively small share of total banking business but none the less are numerous (over 2,000) and have nearly 20,000 branches. This suggests – as is indeed the case – that these banks are predominantly for the small saver, with the bulk of their deposits being savings deposits. Most of their business is in the provision of medium and long-term finance to tradesmen and farmers as well as providing the usual range of bank functions for their customers.

As with the savings banks, these credit co-operatives require a clearing arrangement and for this purpose there are twelve central institutions which hold their members' reserves and provide a clearing facility. Above these central institutions is the Deutsche Genossenschaftskasse (established by the Federal government) which acts as banker to the twelve central institutions, lending and borrowing as the need arises. In addition to this inter-bank role, the Deutsche Genossenschaftskasse also operates in the money market itself.

Mortgage banks. A very high proportion of the funds obtained by the forty mortgage banks is in the form of time deposits with a maturity over four years, or funds obtained through the issue of mortgage bonds on the capital market. Most of the mortgage banks are private sector firms and provide mortgage finance on various types of property. The publicly owned banks, as part of their obligations, have to provide finance for public sector housing schemes.

The banking sector is the most important source of mortgage finance – about 60 per cent of external finance – but there are also building and loan associations which operate rather like the U.K. building societies. They attract most of their funds in the form of savings deposits and, apart from reserves, they use the funds almost entirely for mortgage finance. In recent years these associations have become relatively less important as sources of external finance for house purchase, providing only about 20 per cent, and this is partly due to the greater competition from the other banks who have wished to increase this form of business.

Other banking firms. This group of banks includes the instalment credit firms and certain specialist banks, together with the postal giro and postal savings banks.

Our brief survey of the main financial firms operating in the Republic reveals a number of interesting characteristics which contrast with the situation in the U.K.

The banking system in West Germany is a dominant force in the channelling of personal savings and is highly successful in obtaining both time deposits and savings deposits. This situation is, of course, consistent with the very low level of sight deposits as a proportion of total deposits. The corollary of such a substantial flow of long-term savings is that non-bank financial intermediaries are relatively less important, particularly in the area of industrial finance.

West German banking is highly competitive in the sense that most of the banks (apart from the specialist banks) undertake universal banking, i.e. the whole range of banking services. The division between the banking role and, say, the function of providing capital funds for industry is a familiar, if increasingly less clear one in the U.K., but the dividing line is very difficult to discern in the context of West German banking. Indeed, the influence of the banks on the industrial sector is one which is highly characteristic of West Germany.

8.2.2 WEST GERMAN CENTRAL BANKING

In 1957 West Germany established a unified central bank based in Frankfurt am Main, the financial centre of the Republic. Prior to its establishment there had been controversy as to whether the system should be centralized or decentralized. In a sense, the result was a compromise in that although a unitary bank was established – the Deutsche Bundesdank – the previous *Land*[7] central banks became the offices of the central bank and the eleven presidents of the Landeszentralbanken were to be part of the organization of the central bank.

The organization and operation of the central bank is based on the Central Bank Council, which is the policy-making body and is composed of the President and Vice-President of the Deutsche Bundesbank, the presidents of the *Land* central banks, and members of the Directorate. The Directorate comprises the President and Vice-President of the Bundesbank and eight other well-qualified individuals appointed for eight years by the President of the Republic. The Directorate is responsible for implementing the decisions of the Council. The various *Land* central banks have not only a President and Vice-President but also a Board of Management, as well as an advisory board representing banking interests, industry, commerce, and agriculture. The power of appointment to the many posts is deliberately diffused, so that the Federal Government and Parliament, the Central Bank Council, the President of the central banks, as well as the *Länder* governments have a mixture of rights of consultation and appointment. The complex system which arises from this is one which is intended to protect the central banking system from political interference. Furthermore, and very crucially, the Deutsche Bundesbank is independent of instructions from the Federal Government, although it is obliged to support overall economic policy. This legal provision created probably the most autonomous central bank in Europe.

8.2.2.1 *Bundesbank operations*

The Bundesbank, in common with other central banks, provides the now familiar range of central bank services both to the banking system and to the government (local and federal) as well as to other public authorities. In respect of the banking system, the central bank not only acts as the bankers' bank but, in contrast to the Federal Reserve bank of the U.S.A., the Deutsche Bundesbank is statutorily obliged to act as lender of last resort. As for the handling of the government accounts, this is subject to a flexible arrangement. The

[7] A *Land* is a province or municipality.

Federal Government accounts are held with the central bank but the deposits of the *Länder* may be placed with state or other banking firms only with the permisssion of the Bundesbank. This latter arrangement provides the central bank with the opportunity to tighten or relax monetary conditions by altering the balance of public authority deposits held by the central bank and other parts of the banking system.

The prime role, however, of the Deutsche Bundesbank is the same as that for both the Bank of England and the Federal Reserve: the formulation and implementation of monetary policy. We shall now consider the main instruments at the disposal of the Bundesbank which enable it to perform this important function.

Reserve requirement of the banks. The calculation of reserve requirements for the various banks is more elaborate than that for the U.K. banks, and somewhat similar to the amended arrangements in the U.S.A. The most important determinants of the size of the reserves to be deposited with the Bundesbank are the total deposit liabilities of a bank and the type of deposits. The larger the bank, i.e. the greater the volume of deposit liabilities, the higher are the reserve requirements. As of March 1978, all three types of deposit (sight, time, and savings) were divided into three size categories – DM 10 million and under, DM 10 million–DM 100 million, more than DM 100 million – for the purpose of calculating the required reserves for a particular bank. The reserve requirements also depend upon the maturity of the various deposits, the required reserves falling with the increase in term of deposits. Thus there are higher reserve requirements for sight deposits, lower requirements for time deposits, and lowest of all for savings deposits. The ownership of the bank deposits is also relevant to the reserve requirements: foreign-owned liabilities may be subject to higher reserve requirements than domestically-owned deposits if the Bundesbank wishes to influence the inflow of funds to West Germany.

In December 1977 the average reserve ratios for all banks were:

Residents		
	Sight	10·9%
	Time	8·3%
	Savings	5·3%
	Total	7·3%
	(average)	
Non-residents		
	Total (average)	10·4%

Source: Deutsche Bundesbank *Monthly Report*, February 1978.

In contrast to both the U.S. and the U.K. situations, the Bundesbank is prepared to use the various reserve requirements as instruments of monetary management. Clearly the raising of reserve ratios will tighten monetary conditions and a lowering will relax them since such variations will affect banks' liquidity. Furthermore, the Bundesbank may impose a minimum reserve ratio on the increase in certain deposit liabilities – this is rather similar in effect to the Bank of England's Supplementary Deposit scheme. The main target for this incremental ratio device has been the inflow of foreign funds.

For many years West Germany has maintained a balance of payments position which has been the envy and the embarrassment of many countries, not least the U.K. One of the features of the very favourable balance of payments has been the substantial inflow of funds to West Germany (the strength of the Deutschemark in foreign exchange markets makes deposits in the Republic secure from capital losses through changes in exchange rates). From the point of view of the Bundesbank, such inflows of foreign funds, although adding to official reserves, are nevertheless a potential source of inflationary pressure if they add to the West German money stock. During the years 1966–76 the average rate of inflation in the U.K. was 9·9 per cent per annum, whereas in West Germany it was 4·3 per cent per annum, the largest rises taking place in the 1970s. Understandably the West German government and the Bundesbank wish to ensure that the rate of inflation in West Germany is maintained at a low level. The Bundesbank is prepared, therefore, to take action which will offset any inflationary consequences of large inflows of funds. For example, as from 1 January 1978, the Bundesbank raised the minimum reserves on banks' external liabilities in order to check the growth of liquidity in the banking system. The central bank not only raised the reserve ratio on the *level* of foreign deposits but an additional reserve ratio was imposed on the *growth* of these deposit liabilities, based on the levels in the last quarter of 1977. As a result of these changes, the minimum reserves on the level and growth of sight liabilities amounts to 100 per cent, on time liabilities 95 per cent, and on savings deposits 90 per cent.[8] It is clear from the size of these ratios that this instrument will be a powerful deterrent to the growth of these deposits. It will be much less profitable for banks to attract and hold such deposits from outside West Germany.

Rediscounting and rediscount quotas. The Bundesbank discount rate is the rate of interest at which it will discount eligible paper; the central bank lays down the criteria for eligibility, e.g. good-quality commercial bills. The rediscounting facility provided by the central

[8]Deutsche Bundesbank *Monthly Report*, February 1978.

bank to other banks is, of course, one of the ways in which reserve shortages may be alleviated by the Bundesbank acting as lender of last resort. Changes in the discount rate are likely to influence the banks with respect to their own rates and as the discount rate is altered so other rates are likely to move in sympathy. Between 1948 and 1977, the discount rate has been varied about twice a year by the Bundesbank. The discounting facility provided by the central bank differs from that in the U.K. (although it is somewhat similar to the U.S. Federal Reserve's arrangement) in that the discounting capacity of the various banks is limited by a quota. If banks have used their quota (or do not wish to exhaust their quota for reasons of flexibility), they may use another form of finance from the Bundesbank in the form of an advance on securities provided by the borrowing bank. The advances rate, or 'lombard rate' as it is known, varies between ½ per cent and 1½ per cent above the discount rate. Thus, for example, on 16 December 1977 the discount rate was 3 per cent and the lombard rate was 3½ per cent. For those banks who fail to maintain their minimum reserve requirements, there is a further facility offered by the Bundesbank but at a rate which is somewhat penal, being 3 per cent above the lombard rate.

Any bank which requires funds to sustain the required level of reserves may attempt to obtain such funds not from the Bundesbank but from the money market. The main participants in the money market are the larger financial institutions[9] including the big banks, regional banks, and the central institutions of the savings and co-operative banks. The other participant is the Bundesbank itself. The market's operations are divided between inter-bank loans and the purchase and sale of various short-term assets, e.g. Treasury bills, Treasury bonds, eligible commercial bills. Inter-bank loans may be offered on a day-by-day basis (repayable the following day), loans with a day's notice, and other loans ranging from one to six months. These inter-bank loans are made by transfers of deposits at the Bundesbank. The market's operations in the various kinds of short-term assets is largely dominated by the eligibility criteria laid down by the Bundesbank in respect of its rediscounting facility. Furthermore, the central bank's open market operations also influence the money market, in particular the structure of rates on various assets.

Open market operations. Open market operations have not been a feature of German central bank operations until relatively recently. The Reichsbank, which was the German central bank before the Second

---

[9] We saw earlier that the various central institutions for the savings and co-operative banks provide a kind of internal inter-bank facility for their affiliates.

World War, was not permitted to undertake open market operations until 1933, and it was not until 1955 that the West German central bank organization re-assumed the authority to undertake such market operations (this was before the setting up of the Deutsche Bundesbank). The Bundesbank is authorized to use a range of assets for open market operations, but in practice the central bank deals mainly in Treasury bills and mobilization paper.[10] Open market operations are used by the Bundesbank for two purposes: to impinge on the banking system's lending capacity, and as a smoothing device – which is, in effect, using open market operations as a form of indirect lender-of-last-resort assistance to the banking system. It may be recalled that the U.S. Federal Reserve uses the device of open market operations as a means of offsetting the ebb and flow of funds from the government to the non-government sector. The Bundesbank operates in a similar way. There is, however, a distinguishing characteristic in the Bundesbank's technique, which is that it publishes the selling rates (prices) of the various assets and is prepared to sell any amount which the market will absorb. The Bundesbank is capable of influencing market yields not only by altering its selling rates, but also by altering the difference between its selling rates and buying rates (the latter not being published). In the same way as the Bank of England and the U.S. Federal Reserve, the Bundesbank may move with market sentiment in respect of its open market rates or guide market rates by firmer operation in the market.

8.3 The European Economic Community and monetary union

Any discussion of comparative financial systems, however brief, would be incomplete in the European context without reference to the European Economic Community. This section provides such a survey with particular reference to the question of monetary union.

The primary objective of the E.E.C. – namely, the liberalization of trade between member countries – had been achieved by July 1977. With this accomplishment there has been increasing attention focused on a much broader and more intractable problem, that of economic and monetary union. A number of recommendations of the E.E.C. Commission relating to closer contacts between the central banks and finance ministers have been implemented, yet it is probably the case at the time of writing (May 1978) the E.E.C. members are very far from achieving monetary union. (See Section

[10] At the end of the Second World War the currency reform of 1948 resulted in the issue of equalization claims to banks and other financial institutions to compensate for losses caused by the currency reform. The Bundesbank holds almost DM 9,000 million of such claims, and is permitted to convert such claims into Treasury bills and Treasury bonds for the purpose of open market operations. Hence the use of the term 'mobilization paper'.

13.3 for information on further developments.) The instability of exchange rates in the late 1960s and 1970s, the floating of various currencies, the increases in the price of oil, and the rapid increase in inflation rates have contributed towards a greater concern by member states for their own internal welfare, rather than for the future development of the Community. It is arguable, however, that any further significant developments within the E.E.C. framework – particularly of a political nature – will be limited unless there is a move towards a higher degree of economic integration than that based merely on the elimination of trade barriers.[11]

8.3.1 MEANING AND IMPLICATIONS OF MONETARY UNION

An important document in the debate over monetary union is the Report to the Council and Commission on the Realization by Stages of Economic and Monetary Union in the Community. The report was the work of a number of experts presided over by the Prime Minister of Luxembourg, Pierre Werner, and it was presented to the Council of the E.E.C. in 1970. The Werner Report, as it is called, suggested that economic and monetary union could be achieved by 1980 through a series of stages. Without going into the details of the various stages, we can identify the meaning of monetary union as conceived by the Werner Group.

(i)   The total and irreversible convertibility of currencies.

(ii)   The elimination of margins of fluctuation in rates of exchange (i.e. reversion to completely fixed exchange rates).

(iii)   Total liberation of capital movements.

(iv)   The eventual introduction of a common currency.

(v)   The setting up of an E.E.C. central bank system which would manage the common currency and banking systems.

(vi)   Principal decisions on economic policy would be taken at Community level.

It would be useful to consider the main implications of these proposals, and by so doing we may understand why the E.E.C. has moved very little along the road to monetary union.

Fundamentally, the adoption of the Werner proposals would provide the individual states with two sorts of problem to consider: whether each state would be prepared to relinquish a wide area of economic policy-making to a central E.E.C. body, and whether the possible disadvantages associated with monetary union, particularly for the economically weak members, could be adequately offset by new or extended E.E.C. arrangements. We shall now illustrate more fully these two kinds of problem.

[11]We are not recommending such a move, but are presenting what is probably a generally accepted view.

The ability of an individual country to regulate its own exchange rate – either to let it float or to undertake occasional changes from a relatively fixed parity – has been seen for a long time as a policy instrument which provides a means of managing a country's balance of payments. In particular, a country which experiences chronic balance of payments disequilibrium resulting in loss of official reserves may well wish to float the exchange rate (thus 'eliminating' the balance of payments problem entirely),[12] or it may wish to devalue its currency, as the U.K. did in 1949 and in 1967. In the case of devaluation, it would be the expectation and hope that the ultimate consequences would be increasing growth of exports and a slowing down in the growth of imports. Furthermore, if the new exchange rate was deemed to be more realistic by the international financial community, the hoped-for consequence would be a stabilization of capital flows between that country and the other financial centres. On the other hand, if a government was committed by E.E.C. agreement to absolutely fixed exchange rates and it had a balance of payments deficit because, say, its country's inflation rate was higher than that of its competitors, *then that deficit would not be capable of correction by exchange rate adjustment.* The only available means would be domestic deflation to reduce spending and thereby reduce the demand for imports.[13] One result of such measures would be rising unemployment.

An E.E.C. central banking system would result in member countries losing independent control of both their own domestic money stock and the volume of credit within their own national boundaries. The implications of setting up a single central bank are, however, more far-reaching than loss of control of the money stock. As we have seen in Chapter 6, an important influence on the money stock is the extent to which governments finance their spending either through sales of bonds to the non-bank public or by reliance on the residual financing role of the banking system. It should be clear that if the control of the money supply is exercised by an E.E.C. central bank, then member states would not be able to rely on the residual financing role of their own banking systems to meet their fiscal deficits. It would be less easy, therefore, for member states to pursue independent fiscal policies. Monetary union and a single central bank controlled by the E.E.C. would mean some loss of freedom for individual governments to plan and implement their respective budgets.

Our final illustration concerning an E.E.C. central bank refers back to the problem of a member country's balance of payments. An

[12]See Section 12.1 for more detailed discussion of this.
[13]We do not imply that devaluation is an alternative to deflationary policies or that it prevents changes in real incomes.

economically weak member of the E.E.C. – one, for example, with higher than average rate of inflation, poor endowment of natural resources, intractable structural problems – is likely to experience balance of payments problems. These problems would reveal themselves in high levels of unemployment, lower than average growth rates, and the inability to attract capital (this latter kind of flow might have offset the current account deficit) since higher-growth regions will offer better and more secure rates of return. A common currency would impose restrictions on domestic policies intended to combat such problems, and the Community member would be dependent, therefore, on the available E.E.C. measures intended to offset that country's economic weaknesses, e.g. the use of the Regional Development Fund or some other special agency. The weaker members of the E.E.C. might well doubt the efficacy of such agencies since, taking the U.K. as an example, the problem of the depressed areas *within* the U.K. has proved over the last forty years to be an extremely difficult one to solve. Could the U.K. safely assume, for example, that the E.E.C. would be able to solve its own 'regional' problem where the region in this case would in fact be a member state?

8.3.2 E.E.C. FINANCIAL SYSTEMS AND MONETARY UNION

One of the factors affecting the ease with which E.E.C. monetary union might take place is the similarity or otherwise of the banking systems which operate in the member states. In this chapter we have examined the basic elements of the West German system which reveals not only certain similarities with the U.K. but also a number of differences.

(i)   Within the West German system the responsibility for banking supervision rests not with the Bundesbank but with a separate supervisory authority; the central bank, nevertheless, exercises considerable effective control over the banking system. Such control manifests itself in sets of rules or guidelines for the banks, in particular the various mandatory reserve ratios together with guidance on asset ratios. This is in contrast with the more informal arrangement which obtains in the U.K. Although both West Germany and the U.K. use the reserve ratio, the device operates more simply in West Germany since there is only one reserve asset, whereas in the U.K. the definition of reserve assets is more diverse. Furthermore, the legal aspects of bank incorporation in the U.K. is confused, as we saw in Chapter 4, and is in need of rationalisation. It is in this latter field that the E.E.C. has made some move towards harmonizing arrangements in the member countries.

(ii) The nature of commercial banking business in West Germany does contrast with other E.E.C. systems, including the U.K. As we have seen, the commercial banks in West Germany are heavily involved with industry in ways which seem far more direct than those of the primary banks in the U.K., e.g. the proxy voting arrangement with shareholders in industrial firms. Furthermore, the West German banks are much more uniform in the nature of their business – the various banks have moved into the provision of universal banking and are highly competitive. In the U.K. the differences between the primary banks and other banking sectors are still noticeable if somewhat more blurred than, say, ten years ago.

Although one may observe many differences in both banking structure and forms of banking business in the various E.E.C. member states, it is unlikely that this aspect of monetary union will produce the greatest difficulties. The spread of international banking operations in Europe and the commercial links which have developed between banking firms in different countries has produced already some degree of integration. It is more likely that the nature of central bank control will provide the major difficulty. The various central banks have in common a range of instruments at their disposal, for example the use of discount rates, open market operations, changing reserve requirements. An E.E.C. bank, however, may find certain difficulty in using such instrument on a Community-wide basis. If open market operations, for example, were to become a more vigorously used instrument, then one problem to arise could relate to the sort of financial assets which are suitable for such operations. The various member states have had rather different experiences since their respective financial markets have attained different degrees of development, and the kinds of assets used by central banks are not uniform.

The establishment of a single reserve ratio would be fairly easy to introduce, but there may well be difficulties in the implementation of this and the other instruments of control for quite some time. For one thing, it is likely that the financial markets of the E.E.C. will not be fully integrated and this could result in a situation where the E.E.C. central bank either may not wish to apply monetary instruments of control on a Community-wide basis, or it may not be capable of doing so. An analogy may help to make this point clearer: the Bank of England could use open market operations in any part of the U.K. (so long as a financial market existed, of course) and the highly integrated nature of the U.K. and its financial markets would result in the effect of such market operations being spread to all the other linked markets. If money and capital markets were highly compartmentalized, however, then the effect of open market operations would be limited, or it would spread much more slowly. Thus if E.E.C. money and capital markets were to remain compartmentalized, the E.E.C. central banks might need to act discriminately in the various financial markets of the member states to produce the desired effect. Conversely, as a consequence of compartmentalization, a uniform application of monetary control may be inappropriate. For these reasons, if no other, it is probable that any move towards monetary union within the E.E.C. would have to be made on the basis of a federal central banking system with the existing central banks becoming agents of the E.E.C. central bank. Even with this arrangement, however, there would still remain the problem of ensuring that monetary instruments of regulation were effective in the area of the E.E.C. for which they were intended.

8.4 Summary

i. Chapter 8 has provided a brief, comparative, study of two foreign financial systems: the U.S.A. and West Germany, and also a rudimentary examination of some of the financial and monetary aspects of the E.E.C.

ii. The various financial firms and institutions in the U.S.A. are similar in function, if not in name, to many such firms in the U.K. However, we have emphasized a number of fundamental differences between the American and U.K. systems and these differences stemmed partly from the federal political structure of the U.S.A. Control and supervision of financial intermediaries is divided between the individual states and the federal authorities.

iii. The American commercial banks' balance sheets are similar to their U.K. counterparts, with a few exceptions: the relatively low proportion of demand deposits held by the American banks; the different composition of loans provided by U.S. banks, e.g. a higher proportion of mortgage finance.

iv. U.S. central banking also exhibited federal characteristics – the U.S. central bank (the Federal Reserve) being essentially a federation of twelve component central banks operating within their respective Federal Reserve districts.

v. The operations of the U.S. Federal Reserve system as a central bank, are very similar to the operations of the Bank of England and other central banks: for example in the use of the familiar range of instruments such as the discount rate, open market operations, and reserve ratios.

vi. Similarly to the U.S. financial system, the West German structure is related to Germany's political history. It is highly likely, for example, that the size and importance of the regional commercial banks derive, in part, from the fragmented nature of Germany prior to unification as well as from its contemporary federal structure.

vii. The commercial banks are dominant providers of funds for West German industry – short-term as well as long-term – and, in contrast to the U.K., they are the most important providers of mortgage finance.

viii. West German central banking is federal in nature, notwithstanding the existence of a single central bank, the Deutsche Bundesbank. Of special importance is the Bundesbank's legal independence of instructions from the federal government. This situation is similar to that in the U.S.A., but is in sharp contrast to the U.K. where the Bank of England is entirely under the authority of the U.K. central government. Although there are a number of institutional differences, the main instruments of monetary policy exercised by the Bundesbank are very similar to those of the U.S. Federal Reserve and the Bank of England.

ix. Section 8.3 provided a brief description of the movement towards monetary union in the E.E.C. and some of the implications for member countries. In particular, we emphasized that monetary union would have serious economic (and probably political) implications since the various details of such a union, e.g. a common currency, would have as their corollary reduced fiscal and budgetary independence of the member countries.

x. Other problems which we identified were related to the technical problems which might face an E.E.C. central bank (if one were set up) attempting to implement E.E.C. monetary policies. It may be necessary for such policies to discriminate between member countries, and such action may prove difficult since member countries have different capital and money markets dealing in financial assets which are not homogeneous across the Community.

9
The government accounts

9.1 The definition of public expenditure

We have made reference in earlier chapters to the division of the economy into various sectors, one of which is the public sector. The principal feature of this part of the economy is that ownership and control are in the hands of government in one form or another. Therefore the public sector consists of central government, local authorities, and public corporations (the latter including the nationalized industries together with other bodies such as the Regional Water Authorities, the National Enterprise Board, and the Bank of England). However a problem arises when we want to quantify public expenditure because it may be defined to include *all* expenditure under the control of the public sector, or only that expenditure which has to be financed by taxation or borrowing. A good example here is the current expenditure of the nationalized industries; in most cases revenue from sales covers this expenditure, and so such spending would be excluded from any definition of public expenditure which is only concerned with that expenditure financed by taxation or borrowing.

The definition of public expenditure that was used for many years was as follows:

The current and capital expenditure of central government and local authorities, other than expenditure charged to the operating account of trading bodies, together with the capital expenditure of nationalized industries, and other public corporations and including debt interest and net lending.

This definition was designed to give an approximate measure of that public spending which has to be financed by means other than sales, charges, etc., and so it excluded the current expenditure of public corporations and other trading departments. The capital expenditure of the nationalized industries and other public corporations was included as much of this expenditure is traditionally financed by loans and capital grants from central government. But the above definition of public expenditure has now been amended, since it exaggerates the extent to which the activities of the public sector require to be financed by taxation or borrowing. Indeed, only part of the capital expenditure of the nationalized industries is financed by central government, the remainder coming from internal surpluses or from external sources such as domestic borrowing or borrowing from abroad. Accordingly the definition of public expenditure[1] (since 1976) no longer includes all the capital expenditure of the nationalized industries, but only that portion financed by grants, loans, or public dividend capital from central government. Thus the new definition is more precisely concerned with that public expenditure financed by taxation or borrowing.

9.2 The growth in public expenditure and its importance in the economy

In this section we will examine the extent to which public expenditure has grown in the U.K. economy since the mid-1950s, and we will look at some of the problems connected with trying to assess the importance of this growth for the economy as a whole. An immediate difficulty arises because of the existence of two separate definitions of public expenditure, each of which has been used in official statistics. Therefore *Table 9.1* provides details of the growth in public expenditure under both definitions.

Part A of Table 9.1 shows the rapid growth of public expenditure in money terms over the period 1955–75, with the early 1970s showing a particularly marked increase. But, even though there was almost an eightfold increase in public expenditure over the two decades, merely to measure the growth in money terms may not give an accurate indication of the changing importance of the public sector in the U.K. economy during an inflationary period. Instead, it might be more appropriate to measure the ratio of public expenditure to the value of goods and services (or Gross Domestic Product) available in the economy as a whole. There has been a large increase in this ratio over the period 1955–75 from approximately 42 per cent to 59 per cent, with the rise in the earlier part of the 1970s being particularly significant. Indeed the more recent definition of public expenditure utilized in Part B of Table 9.1 confirms that there was a rapid increase in the ratio in the early to middle 1970s. It is the growing importance of public expenditure measured in these terms which has caused much controversy and debate in the U.K.

[1]The definition of public expenditure used in the 1978 White Paper (Cmnd. 7049) is: the current and capital expenditure of central government and local authorities, excluding expenditure charged to the operating account of trading bodies; government finance in the form of grants, loans or public dividend capital provided towards the cost of capital investment by the nationalized industries and some other public corporations; the capital expenditure of the remaining public corporations; the contingency reserve; and debt interest.

TABLE 9.1
The growth in public expenditure
Part A – former definition of public expenditure

Year	Public expenditure (£m., current prices)	Public expenditure as a percentage of G.D.P.[a]	Goods and services[b] public expenditure as a percentage of G.D.P.
1955	7,048	42	27
1960	9,398	41½	26
1965	14,142	45	28
1970	21,880	50½	31
1973	32,109	51½	30½
1974	41,801	57½	33
1975	54,039	59	35

Part B – new definition of public expenditure (Cmnd. 7049)

Year	Public expenditure (£m., current prices)	Public expenditure as a percentage of G.D.P.[c]	General government expenditure[d] on goods and services as a percentage of G.D.P.
1972–3		39	22½
1973–4		41	24
1974–5		45½	26
1975–6	49,569	46	27
1976–7	54,950	44½	26

[a]G.D.P. at factor cost.
[b]With the former definition this also includes the capital expenditure of all public corporations.
[c]G.D.P. at market prices.
[d]Central and local government expenditure.

Source: Part A – various issues of *Economic Trends* and *National Income and Expenditure*.
        Part B – *The Government's Expenditure Plans* (the White Paper) 1978–9 to 1981–2 (Cmnd. 7049–1) and *Financial Statistics*.

But, as is often the case, the issue is not as clear-cut as the statistics might at first indicate. In fact the ratio of public expenditure to G.D.P. does not give a true indication of the extent to which the government sector absorbs resources in the economy, if this is how the ratio is interpreted. In order to appreciate this argument it is necessary to divide public expenditure into two broad economic categories, namely *Goods and services* expenditure and *Transfer payments and loans*. With the definition of public expenditure used in Part A of Table 9.1, *Goods and services* expenditure consists of: (1) current expenditure on goods and services by central government and local authorities; and (2) expenditure on fixed assets by central government, local authorities, and public corporations. With the current definition of public expenditure (Table 9.1, Part B), the capital expenditure of the nationalized industries is omitted to give *General government expenditure* on goods and services. However in both cases this category represents a real use of resources by the public sector since physical resources are absorbed from the economy and used in the production of goods and services such as roads, education, and defence. These resources are no longer available for the production of goods and services in the private sector of the economy, although such resource-using expenditure will still benefit the community. Nevertheless the fundamental difference here is that the individual no longer decides how much of the goods and services he buys; instead, allocation is made on the basis of government decision.

Transfer payments and loans includes such items as subsidies to the private sector, social security payments, and debt interest. This category differs from *Goods and services* expenditure in that the commodities bought with such transfer payments form part of personal consumption and investment, i.e. such items merely involve a transfer of money income from some members of society (through taxation) to others (through transfers) and do not involve the absorption of resources by the public sector itself, except in administration. Individuals still decide the amount of goods and services they purchase with such transfer payments through their willingness to pay. Thus the major effect of transfer payments and loans is on the distribution of income, i.e. the people who pay the most in taxes do not generally receive the most in transfer payments.

As an example of the significant difference between transfer payments and resource-using expenditure, compare two situations. Imagine an economy in which all incomes, in whatever form, are taxed at 50 per cent and the revenue is immediately returned to the taxpayers as transfer payments. If the transfer payments received by each individual are identical to the taxation paid, then such a policy will have very little effect on the economy; individuals still decide how much of any particular goods they want to buy, and in this case they still have the same funds with which to buy the goods. But public expenditure will account for 50 per cent of the national income. If the transfer payments received by *each* individual are not equal to the amount of taxation paid, then the distribution of income will be affected since some individuals will now have more to spend than before and others will have less. However, the decision as to which items to consume, and in what quantities, will still be taken by the individual.

Contrast this situation with one in which the government taxes all income at 50 per cent but then uses the revenue to produce goods and services for the benefit of the community. The decision as to the amount of these goods available for individual consumption is now taken by the state and not by the individual.[2] As before, public expenditure accounts for 50 per cent of national income, but this type of expenditure has a more profound effect on the economy.

So, if the intention is to establish the extent to which the public sector absorbs resources in the economy, a better measure might be the proportion of resource-using expenditure to G.D.P. From Table 9.1 it can be seen not only that resource-using expenditure represents a smaller proportion of G.D.P. but also that over the period 1955-75 (Part A) the proportion of national resources absorbed by public expenditure on goods and services did not grow as quickly as the relevant ratio for total public expenditure. Of course the reason for this is that transfer payments and loans was the fastest growing category. These conclusions are supported when we examine, in Part B of Table 9.1, the growth in resource-using expenditure during the 1970s under the new definition of public expenditure. In fact *General government expenditure* on goods and services as a proportion of G.D.P. rose by 3½ percentage points between the financial years 1972-3 and 1976-7, whereas the comparable figures for *Public expenditure* reveal an increase of 5½ percentage points. Although the statistics still represent a substantial increase in the proportion of national resources absorbed by government expenditure on goods and services, the crude figures for total public expenditure can be seen to give a misleading picture. Nevertheless, the growth in transfer payments and loans should not be ignored since, at the very least, this category of expenditure affects the distribution of income.

The lesson to be learned from this discussion is that various categories of public expenditure exist, each of which have different implications for the economy. Figures which merely show the growth in total public expenditure, either on an annual basis or as a ratio of national resources, ignore many important issues. It should also be recognized that international comparisons of public expenditure are complicated by differences in the definition of public expenditure. For instance, many countries exclude from their budget figures that part of social security benefits which is financed by contributions, whereas

---

[2]Of course the individual does have some influence on the decision via the voting mechanism.

the U.K. does not. Also local authorities and public corporations in other countries often borrow directly from the private sector, so the relevant expenditure is not included in public expenditure. Accordingly, international comparisons of public expenditure must be made with care and interpreted with caution.

9.3 Public expenditure by economic category, spending authority, and programme

To date we have focused attention on the two principal economic categories of public expenditure, that is *Goods and services expenditure* and *Transfer payments and loans*. Included in the first of these two categories are consumption and investment expenditure, whereas the latter consists of subsidies, grants, debt interest, and net lending. However public expenditure can also be analysed by *spending authority* (i.e. central government, local authorities, and some public corporations) and by *programme* (defence, education, etc.). In order to give a comprehensive picture, the Public Expenditure White Paper provides details of expenditure plans under all three headings. This annual document gives information on the government's plans for the financial year ahead, together with those for future years, considered against the background of the forecast for the resources available in the economy as a whole. The reader is recommended to consult the current document on the government's expenditure plans, whilst in the subsequent discussion we seek to provide some observations of a more general nature.

The breakdown of public expenditure by *spending authority* reveals that the largest spender is central government, followed in turn by local authorities and certain public corporations. Our discussion of the definition of public expenditure in Section 9.1 explained that the capital expenditure of the nationalized industries is only included to the extent that it is financed by central government, but even then the lending is counted as central government expenditure. The public corporations considered here as a separate spending authority are mainly the water authorities and new town and housing corporations, and so represent by far the smallest of the three spending units. Other complications exist with the division into spending authorities since, for example, a considerable proportion of local authority expenditure is financed from central government grants. To avoid double-counting, the consolidation of the public sector accounts excludes such grants from the expenditure totals for central government.

The breakdown of public expenditure by *programme* reveals fifteen major categories of expenditure. *Table 9.3* (p. 218) gives details of

central government expenditure by programme,[3] but the relative
importance of some individual programmes is different for total *public*
expenditure. An examination of total public expenditure during the
1970s reveals that Social security has been the largest individual
programme; followed by Education and libraries, sciences, and arts;
Health and personal social services; and Defence. This pattern differs
markedly from that before the Second World War when defence was
by far the most important single programme. Again there is the
problem of overlap, since more than one of the spending authorities
may have expenditures on any particular programme, e.g. both
central and local government spend directly on education as central
government is responsible for university expenditure and local
authorities for most other education expenditure.

The Public Expenditure White Paper covering the next financial
year and subsequent years is usually issued and debated in
Parliament several months before the Budget, which itself is
announced around April. Prior to the White Paper covering 1977–8
and subsequent years, the practice had been to issue expenditure
plans for a five-year period, with firm programme decisions being
taken for one year ahead. However the practice now appears to be
that the government indicates its expenditure plans for only the next
three financial years, with the plans for the year ahead constituting
the only firm decisions.[4] The Budget traditionally sets out how central
government intends to raise the revenue to meet its expenditure, but it
may also be used to announce some supplementary expenditure
decisions. The annual Budget has nowadays also become the occasion
when the Chancellor of the Exchequer reviews the progress of the
economy and economic policies. Additional Budgets are sometimes
used to announce further taxation changes if this is thought to be
necessary before the next annual Budget.

Irrespective of whether public expenditure is analysed by economic
category, spending authority, or programme, its growth has to be
considered against the prospects of the resources that will be available
in the economy as a whole. Then it can be decided whether public
expenditure should grow at a faster or slower rate than resources
generally, leading to an increase or decrease in the ratio of public
expenditure to G.D.P. Indeed the government's expenditure plans
are considered against the forecasts prepared by the Treasury for the
growth in the economy over the ensuing years, and decisions are

[3] The fifteen programmes for total public expenditure are identical in name except that
government lending to the nationalized industries replaces the Rate Support Grant as
the fifteenth programme.
[4] This observation is made on the basis of two White Papers covering a three-year
planning horizon – the government may revert to its former practice in the future.

made on the basis of such predictions. In the past the Treasury forecasts have often proved to be optimistic, and so an over-estimation of the future resources available may partly account for the growth in the ratio of public expenditure to G.D.P. exhibited in Table 9.1.

9.4 The public sector accounts

In this section we intend to focus attention on the construction of the public sector accounts and on some of the constituent components. This represents a valuable exercise in itself, but from our point of view it is particularly useful since it illustrates how important aggregates like the public sector borrowing requirement are derived, as well as the sort of influences which bring about changes in such aggregates. Our examination of how the public sector accounts are constructed requires us to select one particular financial year as an example, although the reader is warned that the relative importance of some of the components may vary according to the year selected. The figures presented here are thus to be regarded as being mainly illustrative, and it is recommended that current details should be collected from the sources indicated in *Table 9.2*.

Table 9.2 provides details of the public sector accounts for the financial year 1977–8, with the first section giving information on the components of the General government (i.e. central government and local authorities) current account for the year in question. It can be seen that the major items of receipts are taxes on income and expenditure, together with the National Insurance contributions of employees and employers. Additionally there are four economic categories of expenditure in the current account, that is consumption, current grants, debt interest, and subsidies. The difference between total receipts and expenditure in the General government current account gives the current surplus, which can be regarded as the balancing item.

The current surplus and taxes on capital (see Section 9.6) together constitute capital receipts in the General government capital account, whereas capital expenditure consists mainly of investment (gross domestic fixed capital formation) and capital grants and other transfers. This time the balancing item is the General government financial deficit, which is carried forward to the public sector financial account.

The addition of the financial deficits of the public corporations and General government gives the public sector financial deficit (P.S.F.D.). This item provides information on the financial position of the public sector as a whole and is utilized in the flow-of-funds accounts which we discussed in Chapter 1. There we argued that the

TABLE 9.2
The public sector accounts 1977-78
(£ m.)

General government – current account

Receipts		Expenditure	
Gross trading surplus and rent	2,226	Final consumption	29,178
Interest, dividends, etc.	2,890	Subsidies	3,307
Taxes on income	20,595	Current grants	17,200
Taxes on expenditure	21,188	Debt interest	6,694
National Insurance contributions, etc.	9,702		
Imputed charge for consumption of non-trading capital	1,008		
Total receipts	57,609	Total current expenditure	57,263
		Current surplus	346

General government – capital account

Receipts		Expenditure	
Current surplus	346	Gross domestic fixed capital formation	4,562
Taxes on capital	919	Increase in book value of stocks and work in progress	79
		Grants and other transfers	1,742
Total	1,265	Total	6,383
General government financial deficit	5,118		

Public sector financial account

Financial deficit of general government	5,125[a]
Financial deficit of public corporations	715
Public sector financial deficit	5,840
Net lending to private sector and overseas:	
General government	−756
Public corporations	303
	−453
Other financial transactions and receipts:	
Identified	−406

Unidentified	272
	-134
Public sector borrowing requirement	5,521

Note: public sector financial deficit + net lending to private sector and overseas – other financial transactions and receipts = public sector borrowing requirement.

[a]The financial deficit in the financial account is inconsistent with the figure given in the capital account due to later revisions.

Source: *Financial Statistics*, July 1978.

financial surpluses and deficits of the four major sectors cancel each other out in the aggregate, but individual surpluses and deficits give rise to changes in sector holdings of financial assets and liabilities. In this case a positive P.S.F.D. will need to be financed by the generation of financial claims against the public sector, and this entails borrowing from the other three sectors. However several other items not included in the P.S.F.D. need to be taken into account before we can calculate the full extent to which the public sector needs to borrow from other sectors. Thus any net lending to the private sector[5] and overseas has to be added to the financial deficit in the calculation of the public sector borrowing requirement (P.S.B.R.), because these loans add to the amount that has to be financed through borrowing. Also 'other financial transactions and receipts' have to be deducted from the P.S.F.D. to calculate the P.S.B.R. because these receipts reduce the amount that has to be financed by borrowing.

The existence of a large P.S.F.D. and P.S.B.R. in the financial year we have chosen is part of the trend that has been established throughout the period from the early 1970s. The size of the P.S.B.R. during these years was as follows:

Year	P.S.B.R
1973–4	4,447
1974–5	7,957
1975–6	10,630
1976–7	8,583
1977–8	5,521

Source: Financial Statistics, July 1978

Two major factors account for the size of the P.S.B.R. in these years.

[5]The private sector is divided into the personal and company sectors in the flow-of-funds accounts presented in Chapter 1.

First, the economy was suffering from an economic recession and so the government was intentionally operating a budget deficit to give a stimulus to aggregate demand (this type of policy is explained in Chapter 14). Accordingly a large P.S.B.R. was the inevitable result of such actions. Secondly, some items of government expenditure tend to rise automatically during periods of recession and rising unemployment, e.g. some social security payments, whereas the buoyancy of tax yield tends to be reduced. This will add to the P.S.B.R. in that the current surplus will be reduced by increased expenditure relative to taxation receipts.

We have focused attention in this section on the derivation of the P.S.B.R. since, as earlier chapters have indicated, its size has implications both for the money supply and interest rates. Therefore monetary policy aimed at either the money supply or interest rates has to take account of the expected size of the P.S.B.R. But forecasting the size of the P.S.B.R. is no simple matter, given that it is essentially the difference between two very large flows, some elements of which are demand-determined (e.g. unemployment benefits) and so not subject to the close control of government. However the implications of the magnitude of the P.S.B.R. for the conduct of monetary policy will be discussed further in Chapter 16. Finally it should be noted that the central government borrowing requirement is the largest component of the P.S.B.R. and is of concern since it adds to the size of the national debt (see Chapter 10).

We have already suggested earlier in this chapter that international comparisons of public expenditure can be misleading in that the U.K. definition of public expenditure tends to be broader than that used in many other countries. At the same time, international comparisons of the financial position of the respective public sectors can also be misleading since the U.K. position is often expressed in terms of the P.S.B.R., whereas the P.S.F.D. measure is closer to the practice of other industrialized nations. Indeed it has been suggested that the U.K. may have suffered in the past because international opinion in general has not always appreciated the more comprehensive nature of the traditional P.S.B.R. measure.

9.5 The central government accounts

Although our discussion of the public sector accounts in the previous section enabled us to focus attention upon the derivation of such aggregates as the public sector financial deficit (P.S.F.D.) and public sector borrowing requirement (P.S.B.R.), it is necessary that we examine the contribution of central government in more detail. This exercise is useful in that we can identify the major taxes levied by central government and the types of expenditure to which it is directed, while at the same time we can ascertain how the central government borrowing requirement is derived. As before, we will take one particular financial year as an example, but the reader is again recommended to collect current information from the sources indicated in the tables.

Central government transations are classified under two headings, the Consolidated Fund and the National Loans Fund. The Consolidated Fund is the central government's cash account and includes revenue and expenditure items, whereas the National Loans Fund deals with changes in financial assets and liabilities, i.e. with all transactions relating to the national debt and most transactions connected with central government lending. The Consolidated Fund account for 1977–8 is reproduced in *Table 9.3* and shows under the revenue column the major receipts from taxation collected by the Inland Revenue and Customs and Excise Departments. The remaining items of revenue include vehicle excise duties levied by central government but collected by local authorities, miscellaneous receipts such as broadcast licence fees, and a National Insurance surcharge on employers. The reader can see from Table 9.3 that income tax is by far the most important single tax in revenue terms; however taxation will be discussed in more detail in Sections 9.6 and 9.7 The expenditure column of the Consolidated Fund is divided into Supply Services and Standing Services, this distinction being largely one of procedure, with the former having to be approved by parliamentary vote. Supply Service expenditure is by far the most significant in money terms and is directed into fifteen major programmes, although the relative importance of central government expenditure on each of these programmes is not quite the same as that for total public expenditure. This, as was explained in Section 9.3, is because more than one of the three spending authorities may make expenditures on each of the fifteen listed programmes.

The Consolidated Fund surplus is simply the difference between expenditure and revenue, a negative entry indicating that central government has spent in excess of taxation receipts. During periods of recession a frequent policy of governments is to stimulate the economy – or at least to prevent economic activity declining even further – by means of a budget deficit (see Chapter 14). The existence of a Consolidated Fund deficit during 1977–8 suggests that this was the response of the government of the time to the prevailing economic recession.

The surplus or deficit from the Consolidated Fund is transferred to the National Loans Fund where it either reduces or increases the extent to which central government has to borrow. In the year in question the Consolidated Fund deficit is recorded as a payment in the

TABLE 9.3

Central government: Consolidated Fund revenue and expenditure, 1977-1978
(£ m.)

REVENUE		EXPENDITURE	
TAXATION		*SUPPLY SERVICES*	
Inland Revenue:		Defence	6,754
Income tax	17,420	Overseas aid/services	1,065
Surtax[a]	30	Agriculture, fisheries,	
Corporation tax	3,346	food, and forestry	653
Capital gains tax	340	Trade, industry, and	
Development land tax	7	employment	2,683
Estate duty[a]	87	Roads and transport	1,261
Capital transfer tax	312	Housing	2,498
Stamp duties	375	Other environmental	
		services	234
	21,917	Law, order, and	
Customs and Excise:		protective services	1,182
Value added tax	4,226	Education and libraries,	
Oil	2,465	science and arts	1,645
Tobacco	2,056	Health and personal	
Spirits, beer, wine,		social services	6,015
cider	2,062	Social security	5,227
Betting and gaming	320	Other public services	1,032
Car tax	286	Common services	1,023
Other excise duties	10	Northern Ireland	884
Protective duties,		Rate support grant,	
etc.	676	financial	
Agricultural levies	183	transactions	7,887
	12,284	Total Supply Services	40,043
Vehicle excise duties	1,072		
National Insurance		*STANDING SERVICES*	
surcharge	1,163	Payment to the	
		National Loans	
Total Taxation	36,436	Fund[b]	2,220
Miscellaneous receipts	2,337	Northern Ireland –	
		share of taxes, etc.	689
		Payments to the	
		E.E.C., etc.	977
		Contingencies fund	43
		Other services	17
		Total Standing Services	3,946
TOTAL	38,773	TOTAL	43,989
		Consolidated Fund surplus[c]	−5,216

[a] Surtax has now been replaced by higher rates of income tax, and estate duty by the capital transfer tax. However, some revenue is still being collected from previous years' assessments.

[b] Reimbursement to the National Loans Fund of interest and management charges on the national debt to the extent that they are not matched by interest received by the Fund on its own lending and by profits of the Issue Department of the Bank of England.

[c] A negative Consolidated Fund surplus is equivalent to a Consolidated Fund deficit.

Source: Financial Statement and Budget Report, 1978–9.

TABLE 9.4

Central government: National Loans Fund, 1977–1978
(£ m.)

RECEIPTS		PAYMENTS	
Interest, etc.:		*Service of the National Debt:*	
Interest on loans, profits of the Issue Department of the Bank of England	2,972	Interest	5,101
		Management and expenses	91
Service of the National Debt *less* balance met from Consolidated Fund	2,220		
Total	5,192	Total	5,192
Borrowing required[a]	6,160	Loans (net)[b]	
		To nationalized industries	−695
		To other public corporations	811
		To local and harbour authorities	1,034
		To private sector	−7
		Within central government	−199
		Total	944
		Consolidated Fund deficit[c]	5,216
	11,352		11,352

[a] The central government borrowing requirement also includes 'other funds and accounts', notably the surplus or deficit from the National Insurance Funds. In 1977–8 these other funds and accounts showed a surplus of £1,666 million, giving a central government borrowing requirement of £4,494 million.

[b] i.e. net of repayments on previous loans.

[c] This Consolidated Fund deficit is transferred from Table 9.3.

Source: Financial Statement and Budget Report, 1977–8.

National Loans Fund account reproduced as *Table 9.4*, Other payments include the interest and management expenses on the national debt and the net lending which is made mainly to the rest of the public sector. Some of the net lending entries in Table 9.4 are negative because in this particular year several of the bodies concerned repaid more of their previous loans than additional current borrowing. Interest on loans to these bodies, together with the profits of the Issue Department of the Bank of England, are classified as receipts in the National Loans Fund. However, central government makes a provision in the Consolidated Fund account for the difference between the costs of servicing the national debt and these receipts, the transfer being shown as the balance met from the Consolidated Fund. The balancing item in the accounts is the 'borrowing required', and is equivalent to net lending plus the Consolidated Fund deficit. To calculate the central government borrowing requirement, other funds and accounts not included in the National Loans Fund have also to be taken into consideration, notably the surplus or deficit from the National Insurance Funds. Thus with a borrowing requirement in the National Loans Fund of £6,160 million, and a surplus of £1,666 million in these other funds and accounts, the central government borrowing requirement in 1977–8 was £4,494 million.

9.6 Methods of taxation

Table 9.2 (p. 214) classifies central and local government receipts of taxation under the general headings of taxes on income, capital, and expenditure, whereas our more detailed breakdown of central government taxation receipts in Table 9.3 (p. 218) provides information on the yield of individual taxes. The major difference between total tax yields in these two tables are the rates on property levied by local government. However, this section intends to examine the various methods by which taxation can be raised (i.e. taxes on income, capital, and expenditure) and to classify the major U.K. taxes levied by these methods.

(a) *Taxes on income*. Taxes in this category are assessed on income from employment and other sources, and on the profits of businesses and corporations (profits are income to the firm). Therefore income tax and corporation tax are the two major U.K. taxes which come under this method of taxation. In both cases, certain allowances are deducted from gross income or profits before tax is levied, but the rate at which tax is charged is very different. The U.K. income tax rate varies according to taxable income (i.e. income after deduction of allowances) so that the higher the taxable income the higher the rate of tax. In fact the rate rises on successive bands of taxable income to a current maximum rate of 83 per cent on earned income. Corporation tax, on the other hand, is usually levied at a single uniform percentage of profits.[6]

(b) *Taxes on capital.* It is possible either to tax the value of capital on a regular basis, as with the proposed wealth tax,[7] or to tax the transfer of capital. To date the latter has been preferred in the U.K., with capital being taxed when transferred at death or during life (the capital transfer tax recently replacing estate duty), and certain types of capital transfer being taxed at sale through the capital gains tax. Stamp duties are also a form of taxation on the transfer of capital, but are officially described as taxes on expenditure because they are levied on the *purchase* of assets such as property, land, and shares. This last example illustrates the difficulty which sometimes arises when attempting to put individual taxes into the three categories.

(c) *Taxes on expenditure.* Taxes on income and capital are directed at individuals or firms and are assessed according to personal circumstances, whereas taxes on expenditure are levied on goods and services. This difference is the basis of the distinction between direct and indirect taxation; indirect taxes can be avoided to some extent by the consumer depriving himself of the goods upon which taxation is levied. Indeed this distinction is highlighted by the fact that taxes on income and expenditure come under the control of the Inland Revenue in the Consolidated Fund but the major taxes on expenditure, except stamp duties, are included under Customs and Excise. Rates levied by local government are not included in Table 9.3, although they are classified as a tax on expenditure when the purpose is to examine taxation in the public sector as a whole.

Value added tax (V.A.T.) has been the principal indirect tax raised in the U.K. since 1973 and is levied on a wide range of commodities. The other major taxes in the Consolidated Fund account are the excises on oil, tobacco, and alcohol. These taxes are specific (fixed in money terms) in contrast with V.A.T. which is levied on an *ad valorem* basis (a percentage of the price of the good). Because the tax per item is fixed in money terms, the excises have to be raised periodically if tax revenue is to keep pace with inflation.

The classification of taxes often includes National Insurance contributions from employees and employers because these payments are compulsory and are thus similar in character to other taxes. These contributions could be described as a tax on income because they are associated with employment and employee contributions are related to earnings.

[6]There is currently a reduced rate of corporation tax for small companies.
[7]See *The Wealth Tax* (H.M.S.O. August 1974).

9.7 Principles of taxation

In raising revenue through taxation, governments must take into account the effects of the structure of taxation they adopt on the operation of the economy. Accordingly there are certain criteria[8] which need to be considered, the most important being the following.

(a) *Equity*. The word 'equity' means 'fairness', and the tax mechanism is often used to try to achieve this since any system of expenditure and taxation is bound to affect the distribution of income and wealth in the community, especially in developed countries such as the U.K. with their high levels of government expenditure and taxation. Indeed, the question of the most appropriate distribution of income and wealth is one of the most contentious issues in modern society, and consequently different political parties tend to have divergent views on the most desirable distributions which ought to be established.

The first problem is what might be called *horizontal equity*, i.e. the construction of a taxation system which taxes equally people who are in *identical* economic positions. This objective requires the establishment of an appropriate tax base which can be used as a yardstick for measuring people's ability to pay taxes. But income, wealth, or expenditure may be insufficiently precise indicators on their own of relative economic positions. To use an extreme example, a gold hoarder and a beggar may each have zero income but few people would argue that they have the same taxable capacity. In this example it may not be considered equitable in the horizontal sense to tax only income in that ownership of wealth also confers control over economic resources. Therefore the achievement of horizontal equity may require taxation of income and wealth and expenditure if each of these methods of taxation is inappropriate on its own as a yardstick for measuring people's ability to pay taxes.

Even if the problem of horizontal equity and suitable tax base could be resolved, there would still be the question of *vertical equity*, i.e. the establishment of an equitable system of taxation for treating people in *different* economic positions. In this context we have to consider whether the tax system should be progressive, proportional, or regressive. Taking income as the tax base – even though this might be inappropriate as far as horizontal equity is concerned – we can define proportional taxation as the case when taxation takes the same proportion of income irrespective of the size of income; progressive taxation as the case when taxation takes a larger proportion of income as income increases; regressive taxation as the case when taxation

[8]Adam Smith's canons of taxation are a similar set of criteria.

takes a smaller proportion of income as income increases. To achieve vertical equity the government not only has to decide whether the tax system should be progressive, proportional, or regressive, but also to what extent the system should have these characteristics. Our description of the U.K. income tax in Section 9.6 indicates that it is broadly progressive, whereas the indirect tax framework is generally regressive with respect to income.

(b) *Incidence.* The term 'incidence' refers to the location of the ultimate resting point of the tax burden. With direct taxation the incidence is on the person who pays the tax, as with income tax, but with indirect taxation this may not be the case. For example the *formal* incidence of purchase tax (replaced by V.A.T. in 1973) was upon wholesalers, who paid the tax, whereas the *effective* incidence was mainly upon consumers, who paid higher retail prices as a result of the tax being passed on. This would represent forward shifting of the tax burden, but backward shifting might occur if wholesalers negotiated lower prices for the goods they bought from producers.

The incidence of an indirect tax can be upon producer or consumer, the burden of each party being determined by the conditions of demand and supply under which the good is produced. For example an increase in the tax on a commodity in inelastic demand, such as beer, will result in most of the tax being passed on to consumers as producers expect the volume of sales to be fairly insensitive to moderate price rises.

Incidence will therefore be an important consideration to take into account since indirect taxes may have their major impact on individuals other than those who actually pay the tax.

(c) *Incentives to work effort.* It is desirable that work effort in the economy should be encouraged if more goods and services are to be produced to satisfy wants. In this respect the government should take into account the effect of the level and types of taxes it adopts on the willingness to work within the community. However it is often claimed that the progressive nature of the U.K. income tax has a disincentive effect on work effort because of the high marginal rates of tax it imposes on extra earnings. If this claim is correct, the incentives criterion will be better satisfied by indirect taxes than by direct taxes such as income tax.

(d) *Resource allocation.* The taxation system may also influence the allocation of resources within the economy by disturbing the pattern of consumption and production. It is argued that taxation should not interfere with consumer preferences, but should just raise the revenue required. But when taxes fall upon certain items and not on others then consumer choice becomes distorted as some goods become relatively more expensive and therefore less of them is bought. As a result, the output levels of certain commodities will differ from that which would have prevailed in the absence of taxation, and so the allocation of resources in the economy will become distorted. In contrast, direct taxes such as income tax do not affect the choice between goods; the consumer simply has less to spend on all commodities. Furthermore, a general sales tax which imposes the same rate of tax on all goods is preferable in terms of resource allocation to a discriminatory tax such as purchase tax. In fact the present V.A.T. is more akin to a general sales tax than was purchase tax because V.A.T. taxes a wider range of commodities at a reduced number of rates.

(e) *Costs of collection/compliance.* The choice between different taxes needs to take account of the administrative costs both to the government and the taxpayer. The actual assessment and collection of tax may absorb resources, such as skilled labour, which could otherwise be used to produce goods and services. The present capital gains tax is a good example because of the complicated and therefore administratively expensive arrangements relating to the assessment of the tax. The government also needs to consider the hidden costs to the taxpayer which are associated with tax assessment and collection. Such costs of compliance are quite high under the income tax system because of the need for employers to provide staff and facilities for deducting tax from employees. V.A.T. has also been criticized on similar grounds because of the administrative expense for the taxpayer in the collection of the tax.

(f) *Buoyancy of yield.* An additional consideration is that the system of taxes should produce a sufficient yield to meet current expenditures and at the same time provide the opportunity for larger future yields if such requirements arise. The U.K. income tax meets this requirement well since incomes tend to rise along with prices over time and so generate increased revenue automatically. V.A.T. also produces a buoyant yield since it is levied at a fixed percentage of the price of goods and services.

Finally, it should be noted that the above criteria often conflict in the case of particular taxes. For example the U.K. income tax may be considered superior in terms of equity and resource allocation but indirect taxes may perform better in terms of incentives. Thus the U.K. government, along with others, relies upon a wide range of taxes for raising revenue.

9.8 The financing of the public sector borrowing requirement

We have examined in previous sections of this chapter how the central government and public sector borrowing requirements are derived in the government accounts. This section intends to explain briefly how the public sector borrowing requirement is financed, again using the same financial year as an illustration so that the reader can see how the details presented in the rest of the tables in this chapter are matched by the figures presented here. The central government borrowing requirement is invariably the major component of the public sector borrowing requirement, therefore the vast majority of debt is that of central government.

TABLE 9.5

The financing of the public sector borrowing requirement, 1977–1978
(£ m.)

PSBR	Take up of debt by the non-bank private sector		Borrowing in sterling from banks	External finance	
	Notes and coin	Other		Foreign currency borrowing from banks	Direct external finance
5521	1165	6555	2131	−50	−4280

Source: Financial Statistics, July 1978.

Table 9.5 provides information on how the public sector borrowing requirement in 1977–8 was financed through the take-up of debt by the non-bank private sector, borrowing in sterling from the banks, and external finance. The reader is reminded that current details can be obtained from the sources indicated in the table.

The non-bank private sector finances part of the public sector borrowing requirement by holding additional notes and coin issued by central government, and by holding other forms of debt such as British government securities, Treasury bills, and national savings. Borrowing in sterling from the banking sector includes additional bank holdings of British government securities, Treasury bills, and notes and coin, as well as any change in the banks' net indebtedness to the Bank of England Banking Department (see Section 4.4.2.2). Finally, external finance is provided either by foreign currency borrowing from the banks or by direct external finance. The latter consists primarily of the purchase by foreign residents of British government securities and Treasury bills, and also direct overseas official financing in the form of changes in the official reserves of foreign currency plus borrowing from (or repayment of loans to) overseas monetary authorities such as the I.M.F. Further discussion of central government debt (that is British government securities, Treasury bills, and national savings) will be given when we examine the types of national debt in Chapter 10.

9.9 Summary

i.   The crude ratio of public expenditure expressed as a percentage of G.D.P. does not give by itself an accurate measure of the effect of public spending on the national economy. We illustrated this point by drawing attention to the distinction between goods and services expenditure and transfer payments and loans, the former involving the absorption of resources by government. Furthermore, international comparisons of the ratio of public expenditure to G.D.P. should be treated with caution since individual countries tend to use different definitions of public expenditure.

ii.   The construction of the government accounts is a valuable exercise in that crucial aggregates such as the central government borrowing requirement (C.G.B.R.) and public sector borrowing requirement (P.S.B.R.) can be derived, and the various factors influencing their size can be identified. The finance of these borrowing requirements can result in changes in the money supply and interest rates which in turn may affect domestic economic activity.

iii. The existence of a C.G.B.R. and P.S.B.R. gives rise to the creation of financial claims which are crucial to the asset portfolios of almost every type of financial institution. Accordingly, changes in the government's borrowing position can have an important influence on the operation of the financial system.

iv   A positive C.G.B.R. adds to the size of the national debt (see Chapter 10) and therefore contributes to any potential difficulties which may be associated with the management of that debt.

v.   When raising revenue through taxation, governments have to consider the effects of that taxation on the operation of the economy. In this respect we established certain criteria, i.e. equity, efficiency in resource allocation, incidence, incentives, and costs of collection/compliance, which any system of taxation should satisfy.

10

The national debt

10.1 The origins and growth of the national debt

In the previous chapter (Section 9.5) we showed how the central government borrowing requirement was derived from the central government accounts, with a positive central government borrowing requirement indicating an excess of expenditure over taxation receipts. Any such deficit has to be financed by borrowing, as we explained in Section 9.8 of the previous chapter. The national debt is the consequence of accumulated central government deficits from the past, and so does not include the amassed borrowing of *all* the public sector. A positive central government borrowing requirement will therefore add to the debt whereas a budget surplus (or more precisely a negative C.G.B.R.) enables the debt to be reduced.

Apart from recent years, the national debt grew most quickly at those times in which war was being waged since it was then that taxation receipts were insufficient to meet the increased expenditures. Indeed the national debt is commonly assumed to have been inaugurated in 1694 when William III arranged a loan of £1 million through the newly-created Bank of England to finance a war against France. This pattern of war-time borrowing has continued over the years, indeed the debt increased elevenfold during the First World War to stand at £7,800 million by 1918. In the inter-war period the debt remained fairly stable but then rose to over £23,000 million by 1946[1]. During the late 1940s central government provided most of the finance for the substantial housing programmes of local authorities and also provided funds for the nationalisation of such industries as fuel and transport. Loans by central government to local authorities and public corporations have continued since then and are still important components of the central government borrowing requirement, as was indicated in Section 9.5. This recent pattern of borrowing represents a marked contrast to previous periods in that the post-war years have been associated with borrowing for the acquisition of capital assets. A *Treasury Broadsheet* on the national debt (November 1974) estimates that by March 1973, out of a total national debt of £37,000 million, nearly £23,000 million

[1]Most of this detail is taken from *Treasury Broadsheets* (New Series), No. 5 (November 1974).

was matched by assets such as houses, power stations and the national grid, telephone exchanges and the gas distribution system.

In the years since 1973 the debt has grown to over £63,000 million (1977) as a result of a series of large budget deficits. This debt is equivalent to around £1,100 per head of population and interest payments alone amounted to over £4,900 million in 1977. These crude statistics can give a false impression because it should be remembered that during inflationary periods nominal values are poor indicators on their own. If we measure the size of the national debt as a proportion of national income, and debt interest in a similar fashion, then a different picture emerges (see *Table 10.1*). The figures in the table give a more accurate impression of the impact of the national debt and debt interest than the crude details cited earlier. Over the last twenty years or so the debt has *decreased* when measured as a proportion of GDP, from around 1·6 (1955) to 0·5 (1977). Debt interest has remained a fairly constant proportion of G.D.P. over the same period, fluctuating around 4 per cent. This latter figure is probably explained by the fact that nominal interest rates on the debt have increased even though the size of the debt in real terms (i.e. as a proportion of G.D.P.) has fallen. The question of whether the debt represents some kind of burden will be dealt with later in Section 10.5, but our discussion so far casts doubt on the value of crude figures which merely show its growth in money terms over time.

TABLE 10.1
The growth of the national debt

Year	National debt £ m. at end of March (1)	Debt interest £ m. (2)	G.D.P. £ m. (factor cost) (3)	Col. 1 Col. 3	Col. 2 Col. 3
1955	27,761	708	16,873	1·65	0·04
1960	28,979	867	22,642	1·28	0·04
1965	30,461	973	31,227	0·98	0·03
1970	32,366	1,298	43,327	0·75	0·03
1973	36,526	2,192	63,581	0·57	0·035
1974	39,490	2,699	73,656	0·54	0·04
1975	44,495	3,323	92,929	0·48	0·04
1976	54,041	4,266	109,065	0·50	0·04
1977	63,604	4,959	122,453	0·52	0·04

Source: Bank of England *Quarterly Bulletin*, vol. 17, No. 4 (December 1977).
Financial Statistics, July 1977.
Economic Trends, April 1978.

10.2 Types of debt

Given the size of the national debt, it is important that a large and stable market for it exists so that the government can continue to finance any excess of expenditure over revenue by borrowing. This consideration will require the issue of different types of debt in order that the various tastes and preferences of the potential market may be met. Accordingly this section examines the types of debt that are issued by the U.K. central government.

A fundamental distinction is that between marketable and non-marketable debt. Marketable debt is that portion which can be bought and sold on organized markets before the final maturity date. Government stocks (gilt-edged) can be traded on the Stock Exchange and Treasury bills can be sold in the discount market at any time, and so the original buyer does not have to hold these assets for the rest of the period to final redemption. This feature adds to the liquidity of such assets as far as the market is concerned, and so adds to their attraction. However the price at which these assets can be sold will depend upon market conditions, especially the current rate of interest. Non-marketable debt must be held and redeemed by the original buyer, and therefore organized markets do not exist for the resale and purchase of these assets. Because of the comparative illiquidity of non-marketable debt, it is not attractive to the financial institutions but it is to the private individual for whom its particular characteristics are designed.

The relative importance of marketable and non-marketable debt can be seen from the figures for the sterling national debt[2] on 31 March 1977 (*Table 10.2*).

Marketable debt represents about 84 per cent of the total and within this category government stocks are the predominant form of debt. These gilt-edged securities are issued with various dates to final maturity and are classified as follows:

(a) Short-dated.
    The government pays back the borrowed sum to the holder of the security at some specified date within 5 years.
(b) Medium-dated.
    The government pays back the borrowed sum to the holder of the security at some specified date within 5–15 years.
(c) Long-dated.
    The government pays back the borrowed sum to the holder of the security at some specified date over 15 years.

---

[2] The *sterling* national debt excludes that part of the debt which is payable in foreign currency (£4,372 million at the end of March 1977). The figures in *Table 10.1* refer to the sterling national debt.

TABLE 10.2
Classification of the national debt by type, end March 1977

	£ m. nominal	% of total
Marketable debt:		
Government and government guaranteed stocks	42,503	66·8
Treasury bills	11,203	17·1
Non-marketable debt:		
National savings securities	5,285 ⎫	
Ways and means advances	1,162 ⎬	
Interest-free notes due to the I.M.F.	3,429 ⎬ 16·1	
Other	22 ⎭	
TOTAL DEBT	63,604	100·0

Source: Bank of England *Quarterly Bulletin*, vol. 17, No. 4 (December 1977).

(d) Undated.

The government is not obliged to pay back the borrowed sum at any future date, unless it so wishes, so there is no fixed redemption date.

The reader may be inquisitive as to why any individual or institution would want to hold an undated security if the government does not pay back the borrowed sum. The reason is that the government is obliged to pay interest on all stocks regardless of maturity, consequently there is a market for the sale and purchase of such securities.

As an example of an undated stock let us take 3½ per cent War Loan. When this security was issued a nominal amount of £100 would carry a coupon rate of interest of 3½ per cent per annum, i.e. each year £3.50 would be paid by the government to the holder of the nominal £100. If rates of interest were to rise to approximately 7 per cent on this type of security, then the market would not accept a price of £100, since this gives a yield of only 3½ per cent, whereas the market now requires 7 per cent. Indeed the market price would have to fall to £50 for the coupon rate of interest to give a yield of 7 per cent. Therefore with an undated government security there is a proportional inverse relationship between the market price of the security and the market rate of interest, as in the above example. Similarly, expectations about future movement in interest rates will give rise to fluctuations in demand for securities because of the potential for capital gains or losses. For example, 3½ per cent War Loan with a market price of £50 (current yield 7 per cent) would rise in price to £100 if interest rates on this type of security are expected to fall to 3½ per cent, and so a large capital gain could be made by buying now. Therefore market expectations about future interest rate movements in particular are an important source of fluctuation in the demand for government securities.

Before the First World War the government relied principally on undated stock as a source of borrowing, but with the subsequent increase in the scale of borrowing and the volatility in interest rates it became more difficult to employ this method, so dated stock became the major component of the national debt.

Holders of dated debt receive interest payments, but additionally there is a guaranteed sum paid on maturity which complicates the relationship between the price of gilt-edged and the current rate of interest. With undated securities there is a simple relationship between the annual amount receivable in interest and the purchase price, which can be described as the flat yield. With dated securities there is also a potential capital gain or loss because of the difference between the current market price and the redemption value received at maturity. The *gross redemption yield* is therefore calculated as the relevant rate of interest and is defined as the gross flat yield together with the apportionment of the capital gain or loss on dated securities held to redemption. Nevertheless there is still an inverse relationship between the price and yield for dated gilts, although the nearer the date to maturity the less the effect on market price of a given change in interest rates because of the certainty of a large fixed payment in a short period of time.

Our preceding discussion is directed essentially at gilt-edged securities for which there is a fixed coupon rate of interest. When interest rates are generally expected to rise in the near future the Government Broker can have great difficulty in selling bonds with fixed coupons as the investor would face a potential capital loss if interest rates did actually rise and security prices fall. Conversely the demand for fixed interest bonds is very buoyant when interest rates are generally expected to fall because of the potential for capital gains. The market for fixed interest stock can therefore fluctuate according to expected interest rate movements, and to try and alleviate this problem the government issued in 1977 stocks with variable interest rates. During this year two issues of variable rate stock totalling £800 million were made on which the interest rate payable was the daily average, over a six-month reference period, of the Treasury bill discount rate plus the addition of a fixed margin of ½ per cent. These two issues were fairly popular because the market for conventional fixed interest stocks was subdued at the time. However, the use of variable rate bonds in the future is at the moment uncertain because up to the time of writing (July 1978) no further issues have been made.

The remainder of the marketable debt consists of *Treasury bills*, accounting for around 17 per cent of the total sterling debt at the end of March 1977. This component is sometimes called the floating debt because such very short-term borrowing has to be continually re-financed whereas dated securities, although requiring to be re-financed at maturity, pose periodic rather than continual re-financing problems. Treasury bills are issued to the market by tender each week and they mature 91 days from original purchase. On Friday of each week a certain amount of Treasury bills is offered to the market, the amount available being announced the previous Friday, and if the amount applied for exceeds the amount offered then the allocation goes to the highest bidder. Section 7.4.2 indicated how the average rate of discount at the weekly Treasury bill tender was used to determine the Bank of England's Minimum Lending Rate until May 1978. M.L.R. is, of course, the minimum rate at which the Bank is willing to act as lender of last resort. The central government has issued Treasury bills even when it has not had a borrowing requirement for the year as a whole. This practice results from the fact that expenditure flows tend to be more regular than taxation receipts, the bunching of the latter at particular times in the year necessitates borrowing for short periods via Treasury bills.

Besides issuing Treasury bills by weekly tender, the government through the Bank of England also issues them on 'tap', i.e. government departments with temporary surpluses of funds purchase Treasury bills. This distinction between tap and tender bills will be discussed further when we examine the holders of the debt in the next section (10.3).

Table 10.1 (p. 228) indicates that the largest category of non-marketable debt is *National Savings securities*. This comprises national savings certificates, defence bonds, national development bonds, British savings bonds, premium savings bonds, national savings stamps and gift tokens, and the contractual savings schemes of the Department of National Savings such as the index-linked retirement certificates and Save-As-You-Earn scheme. *Way and Means advances* represent short-term lending by the Bank of England to the National Loans Fund, the liabilities of which are equivalent to the National Debt. *Interest-free notes due to the I.M.F.* are a consequence of the U.K. drawing on its gold and other tranches with the I.M.F., and the reader is recommended to turn to Section 12.2.2 for an explanation of these arrangements.

10.3 The holders of the national debt

The range of holders of the national debt indicates the success that the central government has in providing types of debt which appeal to both financial institutions and private individuals. The main holders (March 1977) are summarized in *Table 10.3*. (Readers are encouraged to consult the December issue of the Bank of England *Quarterly Bulletin* for current statistics on the size and distribution of the national debt.) In this section we will identify these holders and examine their motives for holding the debt.

Official holdings were the largest single category of holders in 1977 and were responsible for approximately 23 per cent of the debt. Because the national debt is the debt of the central government, and not that of the whole public sector, official holders include only the central government sector and those bodies which have a role in the management of the debt (i.e. the Bank of England). Local authorities and public corporations, the other components of the public sector, are considered to be part of the market. Official holdings may therefore be considered as borrowing by central government from itself and consequently is a form of double counting which inflates the size of the debt.

Approximately £5,700 million of the official holdings were held by the Issue Department of the Bank of England as backing for the note issue. This large holding of government securities facilitates the intervention of the Bank in the gilt-edged market for the purposes of debt management (see Section 10.4) with new issues of government securities often being taken up by the Issue Department at first and then fed into the market as conditions permit. The Banking Department of the Bank of England held about £1,500 million, also in marketable debt, as was explained in Section 7.2.2. Thus the Bank of England holds marketable debt, largely in the form of government stocks.

The other large official holders are the National Debt Commissioners, who are responsible for investing the National Insurance Funds and the Ordinary deposit accounts of the National and Trustee Savings Banks (but from 1976 onwards the National Debt Commissioners have been reducing their control over the funds of the T.S.B.s following the Page Committee's Report – see Section 4.6.2). Until recently all these funds were automatically invested in central government debt, but since 1973 the National Debt Commissioners have been granted wider investment powers which permit them to direct their balances into other investments, such as local authority debt. The rest of the official holdings are held by other government departments in the form of tap Treasury bills or by the Bank of England in exchange for Ways and Means advances.

TABLE 10.3

Estimated distribution of the sterling national debt, 31 March 1977
(Nominal values: £ m.)

	TOTAL	Treasury bills	Stocks				Non-marketable debt
			Total	Short-dated	Medium-dated	Long-dated/undated	
Official holdings	14,418	7,566	5,690	2,536	1,554	1,600	1,162
Banking sector:							
Banks	3,336	1,119	2,217	2,036	181	—	—
National Giro	15	5	10	8	2	—	—
Discount market	1,406	1,077	329	321	8	—	—
Total	4,757	2,201	2,556	2,365	191	—	—
Other financial institutions:							
Insurance companies	9,215	17	9,198	1,152	1,181	6,865	—
Building societies	2,293	3	2,290	1,898	384	8	
National Savings Bank, investment account	474	9	465	67	182	216	
Trustee Savings Banks, new departments	1,032	12	1,020	421	403	196	
Local authority superannuation funds	1,150	—	1,150	50	100	1,000	

Other public sector superannuation funds	1,255	5	1,250	50	100	1,100	—
Private sector superannuation funds	3,007	7	3,000	300	300	2,400	—
Investment trusts	261	5	256	79	82	95	—
Unit trusts	37	—	37	11	16	10	—
Other	174	169	5	5	—	—	—
Total	18,898	227	18,671	4,033	2,748	11,890	—
Overseas holders:							
International organizations	3,601	93	79	19	60	—	3,429
Central monetary institutions	1,719	711	1,008	607	170	231	—
Other	1,805	12	1,791	415	248	1,128	2
Total	7,125	816	2,878	1,041	478	1,359	3,431
Individuals and private trusts	12,480	—	7,620	2,838	1,504	3,278	4,860
Other holders[a]	5,860	393	5,022	2,817	159	2,046	445
Total debt	63,604	11,203	42,503	15,664	6,644	20,195	9,898

[a]Includes Public Trustee and various non-corporate bodies, industrial and commercial companies and other holders who cannot be classified.

Source: Bank of England *Quarterly Bulletin*, vol. 17, No. 4 (December 1977).

The *Banking sector* in 1977 held around 7 per cent of the debt
exclusively in the form of marketable debt. Like all other financial
institutions, the banks are concerned with the balance between
liquidity and yield as far as their asset structure is concerned. These
two qualities of liquidity and yield are usually inversely related, as we
pointed out in Chapter 3. However the banks are biased more
towards liquidity than some other financial institutions, primarily
because their liabilities are mostly short-term and subject to instant
withdrawal. Therefore Treasury bills and bonds are attractive
investments for the banking sector because of their easy marketability
and relatively attractive yields. Although the above is an important
motive for the banking sector's holdings of gilts and Treasury bills, a
crucial consideration is the fact that certain categories of the national
debt constitute eligible reserve assets under the *Competition and Credit
Control* arrangements. Treasury bills and all government stocks with
less than one year to final maturity are classified as reserve assets in
applying the 12½ per cent reserve assets rule. Furthermore, the
discount houses have to follow a reserve requirement rule (see Section
7.4.1) which ensures that they rely upon holdings of public sector
assets, particularly Treasury bills and bonds.

Other financial institutions held approximately 30 per cent of the total
debt in 1977 and like the banking sector they are concerned only with
the marketable portion. As most people have some form of connection
with building societies, insurance companies, etc., then almost
everyone in our society is at least indirectly involved in holding the
national debt. Again, like the banking sector, all financial institutions
are concerned with the balance between liquidity and yield but,
unlike banks, other financial institutions tend to have longer-term
liabilities and are more inclined towards yield rather than liquidity.
For example, superannuation funds deal in contractual savings which
are withdrawn at retirement, and therefore they need to ensure a
secure but reasonably profitable rate of return so that these future
obligations can be met. As the yield on long-dated gilts is the highest,
then such institutions tend to hold this type of marketable debt rather
than, say, Treasury bills. Investment and unit trusts usually do not
hold a great deal of government debt since they are primarily
concerned with high yields, but in recent years government stocks
have become relatively more attractive compared with equities. So,
even though these other financial institutions are a heterogeneous
group with different functions, their holdings of marketable debt can
be explained by the fact that government stocks are an attractive
investment for their purposes. Under the *Competition and Credit Control*
arrangements the larger finance houses (included under insurance

companies in Table 10.3) are required to maintain a similar ratio to the banking sector (see Section 7.4.1) and so this partly explains their holdings of some types of the debt.

Overseas holders had around 11 per cent of the total debt in March 1977, in the form of both marketable and non-marketable debt. This component is called the 'external debt' and changes in its magnitude can have implications for the balance of payments. International organizations hold mainly non-marketable debt in the form of interest-free notes due to the I.M.F., as we pointed out in Section 10.2. Central monetary institutions consist of central banks which prefer to keep their sterling balances in Treasury bills or stocks. These holdings can be fairly volatile because oil-exporting countries, for example, balance the advantages from any potentially higher interest rates in the U.K. against the possibility of depreciation of their sterling assets (see Section 11.1.2). 'Other' overseas holdings are estimated from various sources of information, and include individuals and institutions not included in the other two categories of overseas holders.

Individuals and private trusts held about 20 per cent of the debt in 1977, but the figures in Table 10.3 (p. 235) should be treated as merely estimates because of the large number of accounts which are not in the beneficiaries' names, which makes identification of the actual owners difficult. A significant proportion of the total holdings in this category is non-marketable debt designed to appeal to the individual because of the special characteristics it possesses. Government securities are also held by private funds and trusts because these investments traditionally give safe yields which may compare favourably with other financial assets. Another consideration is that stocks held for longer than one year receive generous tax treatment, compared with alternatives such as equities, since the former are exempt from capital gains tax.

Others (around 9 per cent in 1977), together with private funds and trusts, are calculated as residual items in the national debt estimates, i.e. all unidentified holdings of the debt are placed in this section, and so the statistics should be treated with caution. Included here are the holdings of Public Trustee and various non-corporate bodies, and those of industrial and commercial companies, but most of the holdings in this category would belong under one of the other major headings if the actual holders could be identified.

10.4 Debt management

The management of the national debt has implications for the money supply and the level and structure of interest rates in the economy. Since these are the variables which monetary policy attempts to influence, monetary policy is inextricably linked with debt management. This section establishes these linkages so that full consideration can be given to them when we discuss monetary policy in greater detail in Chapters 15 and 16.

Debt management problems arise when existing debt matures and is refinanced, and also when there is a positive central government borrowing requirement which adds to the size of the total national debt. Of course maturing debt can be financed out of taxation receipts if there is an excess of taxation receipts over expenditure (or more precisely if there is a negative central government borrowing requirement), but this has not been the case since the early 1970s. The Bank of England *Quarterly Bulletin* estimates that in the years 1977–81 the average amount of stock to be redeemed will be £2·7 billion per year, compared with an average of less than £1·5 billion over the period 1970–4, and new issues of securities will therefore have to accommodate these amounts *plus* any additional amounts that result from future central government borrowing requirements.

The major aims of debt management can be summarized as: (a) to influence the major monetary variables in line with current monetary policy; (b) to ensure a stable market for government debt; and (c) to minimize the cost of servicing the debt.

(a) Marketable debt in the form of Treasury bills and bonds are an integral part of the U.K. financial system. We have already pointed out in the previous section that government securities are of paramount importance to the asset portfolios of practically every financial institution. Furthermore, much of the work of the discount market is based on dealings in Treasury bills. Accordingly the amount and type of central government debt provided to financial markets will influence the level and structure of interest rates in the economy.

Earlier chapters (see Chapter 7) have established that the *level* of interest rates is influenced by the central bank's discount rate. Before *Competition and Credit Control* the level of interest rates tended to move in line with Bank rate, which was directly determined by the monetary authorities. Since *Competition and Credit Control*, Bank rate has been replaced by M.L.R. which was usually determined by a formula linking it to the average rate of discount at the Treasury bill tender, i.e. the discount rate was nominally determined by the market. In practice, the authorities were able to have some influence on M.L.R. through their control of the supply of Treasury bills and through the position of the Bank of England as lender of last resort.

But M.L.R. has been determined administratively since May 1978, and so the monetary authorities now hope to be able to exert closer control over interest rates in general.

The amounts of government stocks supplied to the market will also influence the *level* of interest rates because of the relationship between quantity, price, and yield (rate of interest) which we discussed in Section 10.2. Also the *relative* amounts of short, medium, and long-dated bonds issued will affect the *differential* yield on such assets, and ultimately the *structure* of interest rates generally will be disturbed because of the dominating influence of government securities on financial markets.

Our discussion of money supply creation in Chapter 6 indicated that the sale of government securities also has an impact on the various measures of the money supply. Firstly, purchases of public sector debt by the non-bank private sector reduce the monetary measures M_3 and D.C.E. because of the transfer of balances from banks to the Bank of England, which acts as the government's agent. Lending to the private sector by the banking sector is another element in the money supply and this will be affected by the size of the banks' reserve ratio in relation to the minimum requirement. Treasury bills and gilt-edged securities with one year or less to maturity are reserve assets, and so the availability of debt in this form may influence the money supply via changes in the reserve ratio and the consequential effects on bank lending (see Sections 6.3 and 7.4).

Now that we have established that sales of central government debt affect the major monetary variables in the economy, it is apparent that knowledge of who owns the debt and their motives for so doing is necessary for the conduct of monetary policy. Such knowledge is important, for example, when the objective is to stimulate the demand for public sector debt from the non-bank private sector with the intention of curtailing the growth in the money supply. Finally, it should be noted that the monetary authorities cannot succeed in controlling both interest rates and the money supply through their debt operations because intervening in the market to determine interest rates implies that the authorities automatically supply money to the financial system. This policy choice will be explained below.

(b) Because of the large size of the national debt, and the frequent need to add to it through a positive central government borrowing requirement, it is essential that the government should be able to maintain a stable and growing demand for the securities it produces. Indeed, throughout the sixties, this was the prime aim of debt management (see Section 7.2.1). The argument was that holders of debt would be discouraged if the market prices of bonds (and therefore their yields, or rates of interest) were subject to undue fluctuation. The policy of 'leaning into the wind' was adopted whereby the authorities intervened in the gilt-edged market to moderate fluctuations in market prices and therefore yields. This did not mean that market prices were stabilized at a particular level, only that fluctuations in rates were ironed out. The adoption of this policy meant that money supply control was relinquished since the authorities would always buy back any large amount of bonds that were sold, thereby automatically providing the market with money. In other words, control of the money supply was sacrificed in order that interest rates could be stabilized.

This objective of ensuring a stable market for the national debt is still supported by the methods which the Bank of England uses to operate the business of debt management. The monetary authorities intervene in the gilt-edged market through the Government Broker who follows the instructions of the Bank of England. The authorities do not wait until stocks reach final maturity before redeeming them because this would present large refinancing problems which would disturb the market. Instead, the Government Broker buys in stocks when they become available on the market any time within the year prior to final redemption. When replacing this debt the authorities will not try to sell large amounts of gilts immediately, unless there is a strong market demand, since such action would depress the market price and so upset the market. The new stocks would be taken up first by the Issue Department of the Bank of England, and then fed on to the market as conditions permit. This method of re-financing maturing debt and of financing new borrowing is known as the 'tap' issue of stocks. The stocks provided must satisfy the market in terms of yield and maturity, so the Bank of England normally has a supply of two or three tap stocks, of differing maturities, to sell whenever market conditions are ripe. As a rule, the government will attempt to replace maturing stocks and Treasury bills by long-term debt (a process known as 'funding') to reduce the frequency with which the debt has to be refinanced.

Although the methods of managing the debt remain the same, the policy of 'leaning in the wind' was abandoned under the *Competition and Credit Control* arrangements. Before this the Bank of England automatically bought bonds when their market prices were falling, but under the new scheme the Bank of England announced that it would no longer support a falling market as a normal practice, though it reserved the right to do so occasionally. This meant that the monetary authorities were prepared to accept more fluctuations in interest rates after 1971. This recent change in the operation of debt management reflects greater concern with the money supply rather than with interest rates as the prime target of monetary policy (see Chapters 15 and 16).

(c) The costs of servicing the national debt were shown to be a potential strain on the National Loans Fund in Table 9.4 (p. 219). The nominal size of the debt, and the coupon rates of interest paid on it, will determine the amounts of current taxation or additional borrowing that have to be raised to meet the total interest costs. Governments have always concerned themselves with minimizing these costs, but this objective nowadays has a subsidiary role compared with the other aims of debt management. It should be noted that during inflationary periods the costs of refinancing the debt and meeting the interest payments fall in *real* terms. This is a consequence of the debt being fixed in money terms (i.e. when the government borrows £100 it pays back £100 in x years time) and also of there being a fixed coupon rate of interest paid on that nominal debt over the years (e.g. the government pay £10 a year on this nominal amount, and this payment will remain fixed irrespective of the current rate of interest). Inflation will therefore reduce the real cost of managing the debt, so some commentators have argued that the government does not have any great incentive to eliminate inflation because of this.

It is relevant to note that, despite the big increase in the nominal size of the debt, it now represents a smaller proportion of G.D.P. than in previous years and interest payments on it have remained a fairly stable proportion of national income.

10.5 The burden of the debt

It is a popular claim that the national debt, either now or in the future, imposes some sort of burden on the community. There are several different arguments put forward in support of this claim and we will examine some of them in this section. However, almost every commentator who argues that the debt is a burden points out that interest payments, together with the principal on maturing debt, have ultimately to be met out of taxation receipts from future generations. Maturing debt can be refinanced but this will give rise to more interest payments thereafter. It is also claimed that the increasing size of the debt, especially in recent years, has made the situation worse. The latter point has already been discussed in some detail in Sections 10.1 and 10.4 where it was argued that a distinction should be made between nominal amounts and real amounts. Although the debt has increased in money terms, it represents a smaller percentage of G.D.P. and interest payments associated with it have not increased when measured in similar terms.

Any addition to the national debt is criticized because it is supposed to impose a tax burden on future generations merely to pay for profligacy in the present. This apparently leads to the passing on of the burden of the debt to our children and so should be condemned as immoral. Although this reasoning seems quite persuasive, it can easily be shown to be fallacious. Certainly future generations will face tax payments to meet interest payments on the debt, and also possibly to meet repayment of maturing debt, *but* these payments will be transferred to other people in the same generation who receive those interest payments. This process will simply involve transfer payments between members of the same generation and at worst[3] will affect the distribution of income. So, the real burden of the debt is incurred at the time when the borrowed funds are raised because it is then that people forego current consumption to lend to the government.

The conclusion of the preceding argument seems to be that the imposition of tax burdens on future generations is by itself insufficient ground for claiming that the national debt is a burden. Accordingly, we may say that the welfare of future generations depends not on whether they inherit tax payments or government securities but whether they inherit additions to the real stock of capital. This gives rise to the distinction between 'productive' and 'deadweight' debt. Deadweight debt relates to previous borrowing which has not been used to add to the existing stock of capital assets, and therefore does not assist the production of goods and services. A typical example of this would be old war debts. The debt may also be increased as a result of borrowed funds being channelled into capital assets, and this is the productive component of the debt. Such investment occurred when several industries were nationalized after the end of the Second World War and also when public corporations and local authorities borrowed from the National Loans Fund to finance capital formation. Section 10.1 has already established that a significant part of the debt comes under the title of productive debt, and therefore it cannot be dismissed as a burden on present or future generations because it facilitates the production of goods and services. Indeed it is analogous to company debt in that both types of debt involve a reduction in current consumption in order that capital goods can be produced which will supply more consumption goods in the future. However, we cannot claim that all expenditure on capital assets financed by borrowing is productive since the public sector, as well as the private sector, sometimes makes poor investment decisions. Nevertheless, this distinction between productive and deadweight debt is an important consideration in answering the question of whether or not

[3]This ignores the possibility that some of the interest payments may go abroad, thereby affecting the balance of payments.

the national debt represents some form of burden to the community.

A further argument for claiming that the debt is a burden on the community arises from the distinction between the external and internal debt. Internal debt is that debt which is held within the community, whereas the external debt is held abroad. An external loan enables a country to consume more than it is currently producing, but at the expense of consuming less than future production when the debt is repaid. Internal borrowing does not enable a nation to consume more than it produces, although it does allow it to divert consumption from the present to the future if internal borrowing finances capital expenditure, and its major effect is to bring about an internal transfer of purchasing power in the future when debt interest is paid.

The external debt is claimed to be a burden because of its effect on the balance of payments. The purchase of the U.K. national debt by overseas residents will assist initially the U.K. balance of payments on capital account because of foreign currency inflows. However, the resale of this debt to U.K. residents by foreigners or repayment to foreigners on maturity of the debt result in capital outflows. But the periodic interest payments to foreign holders of debt are recorded as outflows in the invisibles section of the balance of payments current account. Thus it necessarily follows that outflows of currency will exceed inflows, and therefore the outcome will be detrimental in aggregate for the balance of payments.[4] This is a burden in the sense that debt interest paid abroad represents a charge on the balance of payments which has to be met by increased exports, reduced imports, or other net capital inflows, if the external position is to remain unaltered. The size of the external debt is kept under close scrutiny because of this consideration, although in the case of the U.K. the proportion of the national debt held by overseas holders is not very large, as we illustrated in Table 10.3 (p. 235). It should be noted that even the external debt may not impose a burden on the community; if such borrowing is used for productive investment, then the goods and services produced may be sold abroad or may replace imports and so could offset the interest payments that arise in the balance of payments accounts.

10.6 Summary

i. The national debt is the accumulated debt of central government. Although the debt has grown in money terms over the years, it has shown a tendency to fall as a percentage of

[4] It should be noted that foreign holdings of *other* U.K. public sector debt also give rise to interest payments abroad, but that U.K. holdings of foreign government debt produce inflows of interest payments into the U.K.

G.D.P. and interest payments on it have remained a fairly constant proportion of G.D.P.

ii. The debt can be broadly divided into marketable and non-marketable types, with the former being the most important. Marketable debt consists of government stocks and Treasury bills, two crucial assets in the U.K. financial system.

iii. The holders of the national debt are attracted to these financial assets because of the varying degrees of liquidity and yield which they possess. Furthermore financial institutions which have to maintain reserve ratios will have a special interest in debt in the form of Treasury bills, and government stocks with one year or less to maturity, since these constitute eligible reserve assets.

iv. Because of the influence of changes in the national debt on the money supply and the level and structure of interest rates, debt management will be inextricably linked with the operation of monetary policy in the economy. Accordingly, we argue that one of the aims of debt management will be to influence the major monetary variables in line with current monetary policy. Additionally, debt management policies will also take account of the need to ensure a stable market for government borrowing, otherwise the option of running future central government borrowing requirements may be restricted. A third aim of debt management is to minimize the cost of servicing the debt, so that the government is not faced with excessive payments of interest in the future. We noted that these three aims of debt management often conflict, so it may become a matter of choice as to which has the greatest priority.

v. The argument that the creation of the debt imposes a taxation burden on future generations ignores the fact the future interest payments are paid back to the same generation. What matters for the economic well-being of future generations is the capital stock available for the production of goods and services, and this was the basis of our distinction between productive and deadweight debt. The national debt might represent a burden if held overseas because of the effects on the balance of payments, and this was the basis of our distinction between the external and internal debt.

I I
The balance of payments

11.1 The balance of payments accounts

The balance of payments account of any one country is essentially a record, over a period of time, of all economic transactions between domestic residents and residents of other countries. Residents include not only individuals but also governments and firms, even though the last may be foreign-owned subsidiaries. In the subsequent discussion we will use the U.K. balance of payments records for 1977 as an illustration, but the reader is again reminded that up-to-date statistics can be collected from the sources indicated in the tables.

11.1.1 THE STRUCTURE OF THE ACCOUNTS

The U.K. balance of payments account for 1977 is presented in *Table 11.1*. All currency flows are measured in sterling and, where payments are received or made in foreign currencies, they are converted into sterling at the appropriate exchange rate. The structure of the accounts is broadly similar for other countries, therefore most of the following discussion is applicable to them also.

The *current account* consists of all transactions involving goods and services and can be subdivided into the *visibles* and *invisibles* sections. The visible balance is simply the difference between the value of *exports* and *imports*, a positive or negative sign indicating a net inflow or outflow of currency respectively. An analysis of the type of imports reveals that over the years the U.K. has traditionally imported raw materials and foodstuffs, but since the 1950s the proportion of imports made up of manufactured and semi-manufactured goods has increased significantly. Consequently an increasing proportion of U.K. imports now comes from industrial nations, particularly the E.E.C. countries. A similar analysis of exports shows that the U.K. traditionally exports manufactured and semi-manufactured goods, and that the proportion of U.K. exports destined for the E.E.C. has increased since the 1950s also. The U.K. visible balance has regularly been in deficit, so the deficit in 1977 confirms previous experience. In fact there have been only three occasions since the end of the Second World War when there has been a surplus in this section of the accounts, 1971 being the last occasion. However the position is expected to improve in the late 1970s when increased North Sea oil

TABLE 11.1

The U.K. balance of payments account, 1977

(£m.)

(1) The current account

Exports	+32,176	
Imports	−33,788	
Visible balance		−1,612
Services and transfers (net):		
government	−1,878	
other	+3,250	
Interest, profits, dividends (net):		
public	−699	
private	+1,104	
Invisible balance		+1,777
Current balance		+165

(2) Investment and other capital flows

	Inward flow (+)	Outward flow (−)
Overseas investment in the U.K.:		
private sector	3,012	
public sector[a]	2,183	
Official long-term capital		283
U.K. private investment overseas		2,151
Exchange reserves in sterling		19
Overseas currency borrowing or lending (net) by U.K. banks to finance U.K. investment overseas and other transactions	320	
Export credit		398
Other external banking and money-market liabilities in sterling	1,471	

−2,851

Import credit	94	
Other short-term flows	128	
		+7,208

Balance of investment and other capital
flows = +4,357

(3) *Official financing*

Current balance	+165
Investment and other capital flows	+4,357
Balancing item	+2,839
Balance for official financing[a]	+7,361

Sources of official finance

Net transactions with overseas monetary authorities:		+1,113
I.M.F.		
Others	—	
Foreign currency borrowing by:		
H.M. Government	+871	
Public sector under the exchange cover scheme	+243	
Official reserves (additions to −)	−9,588	
Total official financing		−7,361

[a] Excludes foreign currency borrowing by the public sector under the exchange cover scheme, which is shown as a financing item.

Source: Bank of England *Quarterly Bulletin*, vol. 18, No. 2 (June 1978).

production should reduce oil imports and provide some oil exports. It is pertinent to note that exports and imports constitute a high proportion of G.D.P. and so the U.K. can be described as an 'open economy'. The U.K.'s dependence on world trade has important ramifications for the health of her economy in that fluctuations in world trade or in her own trading performance can have potentially serious effects on domestic income and expenditure flows, and therefore on output and employment levels (see Chapter 14).

The invisibles section of the current account records a variety of transactions between one country and another, although they can all be generally described as services. Earnings from and payments for *private services* include such activities as shipping, aviation, banking, insurance, and travel. In recent years the U.K. has done particularly well in the areas of travel (via tourism), banking, insurance, and other financial services. On the other hand the balance of *government services and transfers* is always a deficit item for the U.K. and other developed economies, mainly because of their expenditures on overseas aid, grants, and the like, to the less-developed countries of the world. *Interest, profits, and dividends* earned on U.K. private investments overseas or on overseas investments in the U.K. are typically a net surplus item, as was the case in 1977. This surplus indicates the benefits which the U.K. balance of payments now receives from previous long-term investments overseas and from interest and profits on current financial operations. Again, the public sector currently produces a net deficit as far as *interest, profits, and dividends* are concerned, and this deficit reflects the extent to which the public sector as a whole has to pay out interest on that part of its debt held abroad.

The U.K. invisibles balance is invariably in surplus, despite the deficits incurred by government. Indeed it is estimated[1] that the U.K. accounts for around 9 per cent of world invisibles receipts; more than any other country except the United States. But, despite the large surplus on the invisibles account, the *current balance* for the U.K. has often been in deficit.

The current account quantifies how well a particular country performs in the buying and selling of goods and services with the rest of the world, whereas *investment and other capital flows* records capital transactions. Before discussing individual items, it is useful to make some general comments about the types of flows in the capital account. First, there is the distinction between official and private transactions, the former being carried out by government or governmental agencies and the latter by the rest of the community. Secondly, most capital movements can be classified into those which

[1]See the *Economic Progress Report,* June 1977.

are long-term and therefore more permanent in nature, and those which are short-term and more easily reversible. Long-term transactions are usually carried out after consideration of the general prospects for profitability in other countries, whereas short-term transactions are determined more by interest rate differentials or by the prospect of capital gains or losses from potential exchange rate movements. Finally, a distinction is often made between direct investment and portfolio investment, even though the former is generally long-term and the latter short-term in nature. Direct investment includes capital expenditure abroad on factories, equipment, and the like but portfolio investment takes the form of stocks, shares, and other financial assets.

With these distinctions in mind we can now examine the types of flows included in the capital account, using the U.K. balance of payments records in 1977 as an illustration. Table 11.1 shows that long-term capital flows are carried out at an official and private level, as is indicated by the entries *overseas investment in the U.K., official long-term capital*, and *U.K. private investment overseas*. So when a U.K. firm builds a factory overseas there is a capital outflow $(-)$, but when interest, profits, and dividends arise from such investments there is an inflow of currency $(+)$ in the invisibles section of the current account. The entries *overseas currency borrowing or lending by U.K. banks to finance U.K. investment overseas, exchange reserves in sterling,* and *other external and money-market liabilities in sterling* are all short-term flows but the last two items come under the general heading of 'sterling balances' (see Section 11.1.2). These flows can be quite volatile because their holders are sensitive to comparative interest rate movements in other countries and to the prospect of capital gains or losses which arise from potential exchange rate movements. The two remaining items in the capital account, apart from *other short-term flows*, are *export* and *import* credit. When overseas residents delay payment for U.K. exports, then the value of those exports in a stated period of time will exceed the money payments received by the amount of export credit. Similarly, import credit arises when U.K. residents do not pay for the goods and services received from abroad during the period in question (i.e. credit is granted to U.K. importers). The *balance of investment and other capital flows* gives the net inflow $(+)$ or outflow $(-)$ of currency in the capital account.

Section 3 of Table 11.1 shows the summary balance of payments. The current balance and the balance of investment and other capital flows are included here along with the *balancing item*. This last entry arises because of errors and omissions in the recording of payments, and it is simply the difference between the total value of recorded transactions and the actual flow of money. If the balancing item is positive, as in 1977, then more foreign money has actually come into the country than the estimates of recorded transactions show. The sum of all the items in section 3 of the accounts gives the *balance for official financing*, which is the net inflow (+) or outflow (−) of money into or out of the country as a result of normal economic transactions. However, the balance of payments must balance, like any other set of accounts, and this is achieved through official financing.

A negative balance for official financing has to be financed either by a reduction in the official reserves of foreign currency or by borrowing from abroad; a positive balance allows a country to increase its official reserves, to lend abroad, or to repay previous loans. Consequently official (or accommodating) transactions are carried out for different reasons from the rest of the transactions recorded in the balance of payments accounts. The major sources of official finance are listed in Table 11.1. *Net transactions with overseas monetary authorities* include drawings on the available credit tranches and other I.M.F. facilities (see Section 12.2.2), plus *other borrowing* such as the stand-by credits made available by the Group of Ten (see Section 12.2.2). Central government itself may also borrow *foreign currency* in international financial markets, such as the Euro-currency market, or some of the various components of the public sector may be encouraged by the central government to borrow in the Euro-currency market under the *exchange cover scheme*.

Apart from foreign currency borrowing, the other source of official finance is the *official reserves*. These official reserves of gold and foreign currency will tend to increase automatically when, for example, exporters exchange foreign currency earnings for sterling, but decrease when importers purchase foreign exchange with sterling. Any official financing not carried out by variations in the official reserves is met either by borrowing or lending.

The foregoing discussion confirms that a balance of payments 'deficit' cannot exist; indeed, the accounts must balance through official financing. But countries can face a problem if they have a negative balance for official financing because the extent to which any one country can run down its reserves or borrow from abroad is limited in the long term. A requirement for official financing can arise under fixed and floating exchange rate systems, however, but explanation of how the official financing operations of the authorities vary under these different exchange rate systems will be given in Chapters 12 and 13.

Although the accounts must balance, it is still common practice to talk in terms of balance of payments 'deficits' and 'surpluses'. The usual interpretation, which we will adopt in future chapters, is that a deficit and surplus refers to a negative and positive balance for official financing respectively. However the question then arises as to whether the balance for official financing is the best indicator of a country's balance of payments position. The balance for official financing is an important guide since it incorporates all the elements in the balance of payments account. But by itself it can be misleading in that a country may, for example, be able to offset a current and long-term capital account deficit by pushing up domestic interest rates to attract short-term capital inflows. Such a situation would in fact confirm that a country was facing a balance of payments problem, with high domestic interest rates constraining economic activity and so giving rise to increased domestic unemployment. Alternatively, emphasis is often given to the current balance as an important indicator since this section of the account indicates the trading success of a nation. However it is possible that a current account deficit or surplus is more than offset by capital flows in the opposite direction, so that a current account surplus may not prevent a run-down in the official reserves and/or the need to borrow from abroad. This brief discussion suggests that any *one* particular indicator may not be considered appropriate in all cases and therefore we need to look at all aspects of a country's balance of payments account before we can attempt to assess its balance of payments position. Indeed it is often preferable to separate the account into two sections, the current and capital account, and to look at the sort of adjustment problems which countries face in each of these areas.

11.1.2 THE STERLING BALANCES

When we examined the capital account in the U.K.'s balance of payments records we noted that the sterling balances are a volatile source of capital movements. These balances have frequently posed serious problems both for the U.K.'s balance of payments policies and for the functioning of the international monetary system. Their influence merits separate treatment in this section.

The sterling balances can be defined as sterling bank deposits, money-market liabilities, British government stocks, and Treasury bills held by overseas residents. These balances do not consist of all external sterling claims since overseas holdings of equities, for example, are not included. The key characteristic associated with the liabilities defined as sterling balances is that they are short-term.

Table 11.2 presents the sterling balances as they stood at the end of 1977, but the reader is again reminded that current statistics should be collected from the indicated sources. The table shows that the sterling balances can be subdivided into that part held by overseas monetary institutions (official holdings) and private holdings. The size of the balances at one point in time is subject to wide variation,

TABLE 11.2

The sterling balances, 30 December 1977

(£ m.)

	Central monetary institutions (Official)	Others	Total
E.E.C.	174	1,309	1,483
Oil-exporting countries	1,360	747	2,107
Other countries	598	2,899	3,497
International organisations (other than the I.M.F.)	703	—	703
Total	2,835	4,955	7,790

Source: Bank of England *Quarterly Bulletin*, vol. 18, No. 1 (March 1978), Table 19.

with some holdings tending to fluctuate according to anticipated exchange rate movements. Thus when sterling is generally expected to depreciate, holders of sterling balances may liquidate these claims because of the anticipated capital losses which may accrue to them. Of course these holders also have to take into account any interest rate differential which may be obtained if their funds are held in sterling, indeed a rise in interest rates is one of the traditional weapons used by central banks to contain such speculative outflows.

A liquidation of the sterling balances affects the balance of payments via the capital account and so exerts pressure on the sterling exchange rate. By trading sterling for other currencies the holders of sterling balances cause a reduction in the exchange value of sterling or else a reduction in the official reserves, or both. The fall in official reserves may come about if the authorities use the Exchange Equalization Account to purchase pounds in the foreign exchange markets and thereby support the rate of exchange. However, the extent to which support for the exchange rate can be given is limited in the first instance by the size of the official reserves of foreign currency. Indeed the size and volatility of the sterling balances has often posed problems for the exchange rate policies of U.K. governments, especially as the official reserves have often been limited in comparison with the value of the sterling balances.[2]

[2] For example, official reserves at the end of December 1976 stood at $4,129 million (approximately £2,426 million), whereas the sterling balances amounted to £6,123 million.

The sterling balances originally came into existence as a consequence of Britain's dominant role in nineteenth-century international trade. Traders in others countries started to use sterling as a means of settling debts between themselves, as well as with the U.K., rather than use a less common means of exchange for which the trading value was uncertain. So sterling became an internationally acceptable means of exchange in a similar manner to an asset that becomes commonly acceptable as a means of exchange within the domestic economy. The monetary authorities of overseas countries also found it convenient to hold sterling balances because these balances provided a means of support for their own traders and a reserve for their international operations.

During the Second World War, Britain was able to purchase a great deal of her raw materials and imports by simply crediting the sterling accounts of overseas governments, especially the Commonwealth countries, and this meant that there was a substantial increase in the size of the sterling balances. Thus the acceptability of sterling as a reserve currency in international operations was advantageous to Britain because it meant that for a time she was able to finance her current account deficits by generating an increase in the sterling balances. The balances remained more or less stable in size after the war until the mid-1960s, although their ownership did change. During this period the dollar was the dominant key currency in international trade, and so at times in the 1960s, the United States was able to finance her payments imbalances by increasing the supply of dollars.

A country's currency will only remain internationally acceptable (i.e. its liabilities will be acceptable as a means of exchange) if its value *vis-à-vis* other currencies remains fairly stable. By the mid-1960s it had become increasingly obvious that the U.K.'s current account was showing signs of chronic imbalance, and this made the holders of sterling balances uneasy about the prospect of capital losses if sterling were devalued. Accordingly some of these holders switched their funds to other currencies, with the result that the overall balance of payments position deteriorated. So a run-down of sterling balances exacerbated the current account problem and led to pressure on the exchange rate which eventually resulted in the devaluation of sterling in 1967. By this time it was widely recognised that the sterling balances were a potentially disturbing force upon the U.K. balance of payments and exchange rate, therefore measures were introduced to try and nullify the effect of any future liquidation of these balances.

The first attempt to deal with the sterling balances problem on an international basis was made in 1966 under the so-called currency 'swap' arrangements. A group of central banks and the Bank for

International Settlements agreed to make available to the U.K. swap facilities (i.e. foreign exchange in return for sterling) to offset any reduction in the U.K. reserves caused by a fall in sterling balances, either private or official. After a devaluation in 1967 the countries in the overseas sterling area[3] still continued to diversify their reserves into other currencies, and so a new arrangement was needed to deal with this specific problem. Accordingly the Basle facility of 1968, again arranged through members of the Bank for International Settlements, provided the U.K. with credit facilities of $2,000 million to meet reductions in the official and private sterling balances of the overseas sterling area. Furthermore, the U.K. made individual agreements with sterling area countries whereby each undertook to hold a certain proportion of its reserves in sterling in return for a dollar guarantee on the bulk of their sterling reserves. However these arrangements were not extensively utilized, primarily because of an increase in confidence in sterling after a successful period for the U.K. balance of payments, and by the time the sterling guarantee arrangements terminated in 1974 only £130 millions had been paid in compensation.

The early 1970s saw an increase in the sterling balances, largely as a consequence of the substantial rise in the official holdings of the OPEC countries which followed a massive increase in the price of oil. Sterling was an attractive currency for the reserve holdings of these countries because London was one of the few financial centres capable of dealing with such large inflows. But the U.K. balance of payments had started to deteriorate by 1973 as a result of an increasing current account deficit (due mainly to more expensive oil imports) and a run-down of the official sterling balances. Consequently the sterling exchange rate fell rapidly and the official reserves declined as attempts were made to support the exchange rate. After a series of such crises, in which the run-down of the official sterling balances was a prime factor, there was a further attempt to deal with the sterling balances.

In early 1977 another Basle facility was concluded under which the Bank for International Settlements, with the support of the central banks of eleven countries, agreed to provide the U.K. with a $3,000 million facility in respect of any net decline in official sterling balances below the amount outstanding in December 1976. The agreement permitted the U.K. to draw on the facility over a two-year period, with provisions for an extension for a further year. The scheme was

[3] The overseas sterling area consisted mainly of Commonwealth or ex-Commonwealth countries which pegged their currencies to the pound and held their reserves in sterling. Since 1972 the number of countries pegging their currencies to the pound has diminished markedly, and they now hold only a proportion of their reserves in sterling.

supplemented by an offer of foreign currency bonds to official holders of sterling balances, with the intention of promoting an orderly further reduction in the international reserve role of sterling. However only about £400 million was taken up under the foreign currency bond scheme, and this was no doubt partly a reflection of a widely-held optimism in the future benefits of North Sea oil production on the U.K. balance of payments and exchange rate.

11.2 The adjustment problem

In Section 11.1.1 we explained that it is sometimes difficult to ascertain a country's balance of payments position without looking at several aspects of its balance of payments account. However some form of adjustment will inevitably be required if a country persistently faces the problem of finding official finance, given that the official reserves are finite and the extent to which a country can borrow abroad may be limited. Therefore adjustment may need to be carried out on the current or capital account, or on both. But adjustment problems may arise for any size of unit for which inflows and outflows are not identical, ranging from an individual to a region or even to a larger geographical area such as a country. Later in this chapter we will examine the nature of the adjustment problem according to the size of area under consideration, and we will see that there are some similarities in the problems faced by the regions of the same country and those of different countries.

When investigating the adjustment problem it is useful to make the distinction between automatic and discretionary adjustment. The basic difference is that automatic adjustment comes about by itself as a result of prevailing economic forces, whereas discretionary adjustment requires policy actions to rectify the disequilibrium. Thus automatic adjustment may come about if a fall in the demand for an area's goods and services leads to a fall in prices or incomes in that area. The result will be an improvement in the area's balance of payments since its exports are more competitive and yet lower incomes will give rise to reduced imports from other areas. Discretionary adjustment may come about if the government of the area under consideration reduces demand for the commodities imported from other areas (through increasing taxes or reducing government expenditure, for example), or if it reduces prices in the area relative to its competitors (perhaps by devaluing the value of the area's currency, assuming it has its own currency).

It should be pointed out here that the distinction between automatic and discretionary adjustment is easier to make in theory than in practice. For example an area may suddenly face a reduction in the demand for its goods and services which brings about partial automatic adjustment as a consequence of reduced prices and incomes in that area. The government may attempt to assist the adjustment process by reducing the demand for the area's imports, but it is then difficult to establish the extent to which any observed reduction in imports is a result of this discretionary adjustment or of the automatic adjustment.

11.2.1 DETERMINANTS OF THE CURRENT ACCOUNT BALANCE

When the adjustment problems facing any size of geographical area are analysed, it is possible to identify those general factors which influence the current and capital account. In this section we intend to concentrate attention on the determinants of the current account, and for the sake of convenience we will direct our discussion at this stage to the adjustment problems facing countries. Also we will treat visibles and invisibles as synonymous since, apart from some governmental services and transfers, there is no economic distinction between selling motor cars (visibles) and selling insurance (invisibles).

The factors which influence a country's current account include the prices of exports and imports, the level of demand at home and abroad, the respective quality of products traded in competitive markets, and the length of the delivery period. Of these probably the most significant, and certainly the most easily influenced by government policy, are prices and the level of demand. A relevant observation in the latter case is that the level of imports into the domestic economy is directly related to the level of domestic demand since the consumption of most goods, including imports, tends to increase as economic activity rises. By similar reasoning, the level of imports into other countries (e.g. U.K. exports) will be related to the level of demand in these countries, and therefore U.K. exports are a function of overseas demand. From the policy viewpoint the national government cannot directly influence foreign demand, but it is able to use fiscal, monetary, and incomes policies to manipulate the level of domestic demand.

When discussing the impact of prices on the current balance, it is first necessary to recognize that value consists of quantity multiplied by price. Accordingly the effect of a change in the price of exports or imports on their respective values is dependent upon what happens to quantity. In international markets one of the major influences on the relative prices of traded goods and services is exchange rate movements. Now conventional economic theory states that the quantity sold of any good or service tends to vary according to price, other things being equal. Therefore a rise in the domestic price of imports, perhaps because of a decline in the exchange rate, should lead to a fall in the quantity demanded. The relationship between price, quantity, and value is, of course, known as elasticity. The elasticity of demand for imports is calculated as the percentage change in quantity demanded divided by the percentage change in price. If this value is greater than 1 (i.e. elastic), then the rise in price will bring about a greater percentage fall in the quantity sold and so the value of imports will decline. If the elasticity of demand for imports is less than 1 (i.e. inelastic), then an increase in the price of imports will bring about an increase in the value of imports.

To take an example, let us assume that the U.K.'s total imports amount to 72 units of a particular good priced at £50 per unit, giving rise to an import bill of £3,600. Suppose now that the price of each unit of the good rises to £60 because of a 10 per cent decline in the exchange value of sterling. The application of the concept of elasticity can be illustrated by taking three examples of what might happen to the quantity sold in response to this rise in the domestic price. In case A in *Table 11.3* the quantity sold falls to 60 units, giving an identical import bill of £3,600. When measuring elasticity, it is essential to recognize that the calculation of the percentage change in quantity and price depends on whether we work from the initial values to the final values, or vice versa.[4] In practice, it is necessary to calculate the change in quantity (12 units in case A) and the change in price (£10 in case A) and divide each by the *average* quantity (66 units in case A) and the *average* price (£55 in case A). The percentage change in quantity is then 12/66 and the percentage change in price is 10/55, giving an elasticity of demand for imports of 1. In cases B and C different assumptions about the change in quantity imported in response to the

TABLE 11.3

	Quantity	Price	Value of imports	Elasticity of demand for imports	
Initial situation	72	£50	£3,600		
Case A	60	£60	£3,600	$\dfrac{12/66}{10/55}$ =	1
Case B	58	£60	£3,480	$\dfrac{14/65}{10/55}$ =	77/65
Case C	62	£60	£3,720	$\dfrac{10/67}{10/55}$ =	55/67

[4] If we start from the initial situation, then the percentage change in quantity is 12/72 and the percentage change in price is 10/50, giving an elasticity of 5/6. Starting from case A and working back gives a percentage change in quantity of 12/60 and a percentage change in price of 10/60 – an elasticity of 6/5.

10 per cent rise in price give elasticities of greater and less than 1 respectively, indicating a decrease and an increase in the value of imports.

The calculation of elasticities allows us to evaluate the consequences of a depreciation of the domestic currency. What factors determine the elasticity of demand for imports? One consideration is whether or not there are close substitutes at home for the imported products and, assuming there are, if it is relatively easy for demand to be diverted to home-produced substitutes. If the imports consist of items which are difficult or impossible to produce in the domestic economy, such as essential raw materials and foodstuffs, then one would expect the demand for such imports to be inelastic. Furthermore, if substitutes do exist then can domestic industry immediately supply the extra goods and services to replace imports? It usually takes time for specific industries to increase their output of import substitutes and so the elasticity of demand for these goods and services may be low in the period immediately following a price change, but the elasticity may be higher when domestic industry has had more time to increase its output. It may also be the case that an increase in demand for the products of some domestic industries gives rise to an increase in price, thereby reducing the price advantage gained through the increase in the price of imports.

When there is a depreciation of the exchange rate, the foreign price of a country's exports should fall but the price charged in terms of the home currency will probably remain the same. The goods and services exported will become more price-competitive in foreign markets and so the quantity sold should increase. Any rise in the quantity sold will increase the value of exports measured in terms of the home currency since the domestic price is unchanged. Accordingly a depreciation of the exchange rate will increase the value of exports as long as the elasticity of demand is greater than zero. However, supply constraints may again exist in the domestic economy when certain industries have to increase their production in order to satisfy an increase in export demand. Consequently the value of exports will rise subject to the length of time it takes to increase domestic output in the export industries.

The above arguments suggest that the influence of a fall in the exchange value of the domestic currency on the current balance will depend upon the elasticity of demand for imports and exports measured in terms of the home currency, acknowledging that supply constraints may reduce the respective elasticities in the period under consideration. The latter qualification gives rise to what is known as the 'J curve' effect, i.e. the current account might at first deteriorate as a result of a fall in the exchange value of the domestic currency but then improve when domestic industry has had sufficient time to increase its output of import substitutes and exports.[5]

Our discussion of the factors affecting the current account also needs to take account of the influence of the terms of trade, which is the ratio of export prices to import prices. A change in the exchange value of the home currency will alter the terms of trade and subsequently influence the current account in the manner described earlier. However factors other than the exchange rate affect the terms of trade and therefore the current account. One example is the oil crisis of the 1970s during which oil-exporting countries experienced a rise in their export price index and oil-importing countries faced a rise in their import price index. Some countries therefore benefited from an improvement in their terms of trade whilst others suffered a deterioration, and this resulted in increased current account surpluses in oil-exporting nations and increased deficits elsewhere. (In the case of oil, demand proved to be inelastic and so the rise in price dramatically improved the current balance of oil exporters.)

11.2.2 ADJUSTMENT BETWEEN REGIONS

Adjustment to a payments imbalance between any size of geographical area can be analysed by considering the nature of adjustment on the current and capital accounts. Adjustment between regions seems to attract much less attention than adjustment between countries, mainly because capital account adjustment is much easier for regions of the same country.

If region A (e.g. Yorkshire) incurs a trading deficit with the rest of the U.K. as a result of a fall in the demand for its goods and services, then the first indication will be a fall in the monetary balances held by people in region A. However there is no immediate problem for inhabitants of region A because the branch banking network, which covers the country as a whole, is in a position to make extra loans to region A. So banks in region A will find that they have a higher ratio of loans to deposit liabilities, but branches in other regions will find that they have a lower ratio. Accordingly the existence of a branch banking network facilitates the immediate financing of trading imbalances between regions, although the branch banking network may not be willing to finance such deficits permanently.[6]

A payments imbalance will itself set in motion economic forces

---

[5] A graph of the current balance over time would presumably show a deterioration at first, followed by a marked improvement to a better current balance than initially, and then the absence of any further improvement. Hence the use of the letter 'J.'

[6] With a unit banking system, in which each area has its own reserves, there may be more immediate problems because payments imbalances will lead to pressure on the reserves of the banks in deficit areas.

which should bring about some adjustment on the current account. For example, a reduction in employment and incomes in region A as a result of a fall in the demand for its goods and services will constrain the demand for imports from other regions. If the payments balance persists, then region A can finance the current account deficit by either trying to borrow more from the branch banking system, selling financial assets to other regions, or raising new finance on the national capital and financial markets. This capital account adjustment is generally much easier for a region than for a country since capital inflows are more readily attracted by the existence of a common currency, common capital and financial markets, and the absence of restrictions on capital movements between regions. Financial assets of a similar type from separate regions are generally acceptable in the country as a whole since these assets are not subject to exchange rate movements, different conditions regarding sale and purchase, restrictions on transfer between regions, etc. As a result, the ease with which capital transactions can be conducted between regions ensures that the finance of current account deficits can take place without many of the problems which countries with separate currencies face. These observations suggest that regions with current account imbalances can finance their deficits without a great deal of difficulty and disruption.

Although the finance of current account deficits is much easier on a regional basis, it does not mean that such finance can take place indefinitely without there being some adjustment on the current account. Indeed, the branch banking network is unlikely to continue extending loans to the deficit region without there being some indication of action to reverse the monetary flows. But it is likely that some adjustment will take place automatically on the current account because employment and incomes in region A will fall as a result of a fall in demand for its goods and services, and this tendency will be reinforced by the unwillingness of the banks to continue extending loans. Since imports are related to income levels, it may be expected that the current account situation should improve by itself. Such automatic adjustment may be more effective at a regional level because the marginal propensity to import (i.e. the proportion of any additional income spent on imports) will tend to be higher the smaller the area under consideration due to the increased dependence on trade with other areas. Thus a given fall in incomes will tend to have a larger effect on the level of imports. Furthermore, automatic adjustment may be reinforced by relative price movements (e.g. unemployment may lead to lower wage costs in the depressed region) which reduce the price of region A's goods in national markets and so possibly improve the trading balance of region A, given the appropriate elasticities. But because region A does not have its own currency, it is not possible for a depreciation to bring a relative price change.

In summary, adjustment between regions of the same country is greatly assisted by the ease with which capital movements can take place. Capital inflows are smoothly carried out because of the existence of a common currency and common capital and financial markets, and because of the lack of restrictions on capital movements. Thus flow adjustment (current account) is greatly assisted by the ease of stock adjustment (capital account). Nevertheless, current account problems still exist, as is evident from the persistent regional disparities in income, wealth, and employment. In such situations automatic adjustment, via changes in demand and relative prices, may not be very effective in preventing sustained economic decline in particular regions, and therefore regional policies (i.e. discretionary adjustment) may be required.

11.2.3 ADJUSTMENT BETWEEN COUNTRIES

The extent to which capital movements can finance current account deficits between countries is constrained by the existence of separate currencies. The foreign holder of financial assets produced in *country* A now has to take into account such factors as potential exchange rate movements, the effect of country A's financial and monetary policies on their financial markets, changes in taxation in country A, and the existence of exchange controls. These considerations imply that capital movements between countries are not as smooth or as easily achieved as capital movements between regions. Futhermore, potential exchange rate movements may also lead to speculation in country A's financial assets with the result that these financial assets become less attractive because of uncertainty in their international value.[7] Thus the substitutability of financial assets between countries tends to be much lower compared with regions despite the existence of some common financial markets (e.g. the Euro-currency market). Indeed, countries have to keep a stock of internationally acceptable reserves to finance their trading imbalances because capital account adjustment is not smooth and immediate.

Some automatic adjustment should take place when a country's current account position deteriorates. Indeed our earlier discussion indicated that a fall in export demand, for instance, will reduce domestic national income and thereby decrease the value of imports (by an amount given by the marginal propensity to import). A contraction in the monetary measure M_3 brought about by a deterioration in the balance of payments (see Section 6.4 for an

[7]This happened with the sterling balances in the 1960s and 1970s – see Section 11.1.2.

explanation of this relationship) may constrain national income also. Additionally, price movements may encourage some automatic adjustment, given the appropriate elasticities, either through the reduction in demand causing the home country's products to be more price-competitive or through the reduced demand for home currency leading to a decline in its exchange value.

Despite the working of automatic adjustment forces, most governments adopt some form of discretionary adjustment (i.e. policy measures by the authorities) because of the constraints associated with the financing of trading imbalances. In particular, the domestic stock of internationally acceptable reserves is limited and the 'costs' of borrowing abroad may prohibitive.[8] So the domestic authorities may have insufficient time to wait for automatic adjustment, even if it would work eventually.

The two major types of adjustment policies are known as 'expenditure-reducing' and 'expenditure-switching'. The former policy is based on the observation that the level of imports is related to domestic national income. Fiscal and monetary policies designed to reduce domestic demand should improve the current account by reducing the value of imports. Exports should not be affected as much because they are related more to overseas demand. An expansion in demand could be used to increase the value of imports in a country experiencing a current account surplus, but countries having such surpluses usually attempt to avoid participating in the adjustment process. It is the deficit countries which have borne the main brunt of the adjustment burden. Expenditure-reducing policies include cuts in government expenditure, increases in taxation, and changes in monetary variables such as interest rates and the money supply (see Chapters 15 and 16 for further discussion). Besides undertaking expenditure-reducing policies, the government can implement policies to change the division of a given volume of expenditure between imports and exports. Expenditure-switching policies include such measures as import controls and devaluations (or managed depreciations) of the domestic currency. Of course a decision to devalue/depreciate the currency must be taken only under conditions in which the relative elasticities are of an appropriate value, otherwise it will be unsuccessful.

These two discretionary forms of adjustment are often used as complements rather than as alternatives. For example, the devaluation of sterling in 1967 (expenditure-switching policy) was supported by an expenditure-reducing policy in the form of an increase in Bank rate, cuts in government expenditure, and lending

[8] If borrowing is via the IMF, then the loans raised are often conditional upon certain types of domestic policy being carried out to improve the balance of payments.

ceilings applied to the commercial banks. A rationale for using such a combination of policies is that for a devaluation to be effective U.K. firms have to produce more goods to replace imports and to supply the extra export demand. At the time, government policies were aimed at restricting domestic demand to create the conditions in which industry could supply the extra requirements. The current balance worsened immediately after the devaluation but then showed a surplus for the years 1970–2, only to return to a deficit again in 1973. This fluctuation in the current balance after the 1967 devaluation illustrates the 'J curve' effect referred to in Section 11.2.1.

11.2.4 THE ADJUSTMENT PROBLEM: SOME GLOBAL CONSIDERATIONS

We have seen already that the nature of the adjustment problem tends to vary according to the size of area under consideration, as is indicated by our comparison of the problems faced by regions and countries. If we take a global perspective, we will find that adjustment at the national level has profound implications for the functioning of the world economy as a whole.

If there were only two countries engaged in world trade, then the deficit of one country would be equivalent to the surplus of the other since one country's exports are the imports of the other. By similar reasoning, when we consider trade between many nations we would expect deficits and surpluses to cancel out in the aggregate since it is still the case that one country's exports constitute imports elsewhere. The important point, therefore, is that adjustment between deficit and surplus countries should be carried out in such a way that international trade is encouraged rather than discouraged. Thus individual nations would find it easier to achieve high output and employment in their domestic economies.

Is there a danger, then, that the adjustment policies of trading nations might conflict and so be detrimental to trade, output, and employment on an international scale? If deficit countries adopt expenditure-reducing policies to contain domestic demand for imports, there will be a reduction in world trade unless surplus countries simultaneously undertake policies to expand their economies. Indeed an expansion of demand in surplus countries also would assist the overall adjustment process since imports would be stimulated into their economies and export demand would be encouraged in deficit countries. Our argument suggests that the adjustment process should be seen as applying to surplus as well as to deficit countries, otherwise the world economy could suffer from a deflationary bias if deficit countries undertake expenditure-reducing policies without offsetting policies being carried out elsewhere.

The argument that adjustment policies need to be co-ordinated to promote the development of world trade can be extended further: governments need to take cognizance of the fact that their domestic policies often influence the operation of the international economy. One positive response to this is for governments to acknowledge that a sustained world economic recession of the type experienced since around 1974 necessitates common action by the countries concerned to bring about a more speedy recovery. A country on its own may be reluctant to stimulate demand through the introduction of the appropriate fiscal and monetary policies because this may lead to increased imports into the domestic economy and associated balance of payments problems. However, agreed and co-ordinated action by all countries to expand their domestic economies should bring about the desired expansion in demand without imposing balance of payments problems on one particular country.[9] Indeed it is possible that countries' balance of payments positions will remain more or less the same – if that is desired – so long as governments collectively agree on an appropriate degree of expansion in their respective economies.

It seems sensible, therefore, to suggest that the interests of the world community as a whole would be furthered if all trading nations accept that their policies can have an effect on other parties. Co-ordinated and agreed action would appear to provide the best approach to international economic problems of which the adjustment process is a prime example. In this respect it would seem to be in the interests of trading nations as a whole to devise exchange rate systems and international institutions which facilitate adjustment to payments imbalances without discouraging trade and reducing output and employment. It is against this background of the need for co-ordinated adjustment policies that we will examine in Chapters 12 and 13 the operation of exchange rate systems and the associated roles and functions of international organizations. Then the advantages and disadvanatages of alternative adjustment arrangements can be evaluated.

11.3 Summary

i.   The balance of payments account must balance like any other set of accounts. For example, any net outflow of currency on the current and capital accounts will be offset by official financing in the form of a reduction in the official reserves or borrowing from abroad. However a nation will face problems if it persistently requires official financing since such sources of finance are limited in supply.

[9] It may be the case, however, that a general expansion of demand would stimulate inflation in the world economy. But the argument that policies need to be co-ordinated would still apply.

ii. The sterling balances pose a problem for the U.K. balance of payments as they consist of capital balances which are likely to be liquidated at short notice. Indeed the U.K. balance of payments has been vulnerable over the years to sudden run-downs in the sterling balances which have subsequently led to pressure on the sterling exchange rate and the need for appropriate policy measures.

iii. Balance of payments adjustment may come about automatically, as a result of existing economic forces, or governments may deem it desirable to intervene by undertaking policies to assist the adjustment process (discretionary adjustment).

iv. In terms of the current account, the major avenue through which automatic adjustment operates is via changes in the exchange value of the domestic currency, assuming floating exchange rates are in operation. The effect of a depreciation on the current account depends upon the elasticity of demand for imports in the domestic economy and the elasticity of demand for exports from the domestic economy. Additionally, the time period over which such elasticities are measured is of importance since supply constraints may restrict the extent to which the production of exports and import substitutes can be increased.

v. Current account adjustment also may come about through governments undertaking expenditure-reducing or expenditure-switching policies. In the former case the government attempts to reduce the demand for imports by operating restrictive fiscal, monetary, and incomes policies. In the latter case a typical policy response is for a government to depreciate the value of its country's currency, thereby giving domestic products a price advantage both at home and in international markets. But again the success of an exchange rate variation of the current account balance depends upon the elasticities of demand for imports and exports.

vi. The nature of the adjustment problem can be highlighted by comparing the problems faced by different sizes of geographical area. A region (e.g. Yorkshire) does not face immediate difficulties if it experiences a current account deficit because capital account adjustment is faciliated by the existence of common currencies. However countries with their own currencies have a more immediate need for discretionary adjustment in that their financial liabilities are not as readily acceptable as those of regions of the same country.

12

The Bretton Woods system

12.1 Exchange rate systems

In the previous chapter we identified the major variables which influence the current account of the balance of payments and examined how automatic and discretionary adjustments operate to rectify payments imbalances. Although we identified the exchange rate as one of these important variables, we did not examine how different exchange rate systems affect the adjustment process. This section is designed to explain briefly the operation of various exchange rate arrangements before we analyse in more depth in this and the next chapter how the type of exchange rate system influences the adjustment mechanism.

International trade is complicated by the existence of separate currencies, each used as mediums of exchange within their own national boundaries. Consequently an effective system of international trade requires the adoption of exchange rate arrangements which enable the currency of one country to be exchanged for currencies of other countries. But how is a rate of exchange between two currencies established? Since a rate of exchange measures the price of one currency in terms of another, its determination can be compared with the price of any other item. When market forces are allowed to operate, rates of exchange are determined by the *demand* and *supply* of currencies. The *demand* for the domestic currency in foreign exchange markets derives from exports of goods and services plus capital inflows, irrespective of whether payment is made in domestic or foreign currency. For example, if U.K. exports or capital inflows into the U.K. are paid for in sterling, then foreigners have to purchase pounds in foreign currency markets with their own currencies, thus giving rise to a demand for pounds. If U.K. exports or capital inflows into the U.K. are paid for in foreign currencies, then U.K. residents will sell these currencies in foreign exchange markets to purchase pounds, since only the latter can be spent in the domestic economy, and so the demand for pounds will rise. Conversely the *supply* of the domestic currency in foreign exchange markets derives from imports and capital outflows, irrespective of whether actual payment is made in domestic or foreign currency. For example, if U.K. imports and capital outflows from the U.K. are paid for in sterling, then foreigners receiving these sterling payments will exchange them for their own currencies in the foreign exchange markets, and so the supply of pounds in these markets will rise. If U.K. imports and capital outflows from the U.K. are paid for in foreign currency, then domestic residents have to obtain foreign currency with pounds, and so the supply of pounds will increase in foreign exchange markets.

When market forces alone are allowed to determine the exchange value of currencies, a free-floating exchange rate system is said to exist. But will a free-floating exchange rate system operate smoothly? If a country faces a current account deficit due to a sudden rise in the value of its imports, there will be an increased supply of the domestic currency in foreign exchange markets which should depreciate the exchange rate. But actual movements in the exchange rate will also depend upon capital transactions. Indeed, capital movements may offset the current account deficit if speculators think that the exchange rate will recover to its former level in the near future, as could be the case if the current account deficit is thought to be temporary. In this situation capital inflows should increase and capital outflows decrease because buying the domestic currency now would provide capital-account transactors with a potential capital gain. Alternatively speculators might think that the exchange value of the domestic currency will fall even further in the future, perhaps because they expect the current account deficit to become permanent, and so capital inflows will decrease and capital outflows decrease accordingly. In the latter case the exchange rate will depreciate even further due to net capital outflows at the existing rate of exchange. Therefore an exchange rate will be established at which capital account transactions offset the current account balance, but the demand and supply of currency may be equated (i.e. there should be no need for official financing) only at the expense of large fluctuations in exchange rates.

In practice, governments are usually reluctant to leave exchange rate determination completely to private market forces because of this danger that large fluctuations in exchange rates might ensue. If large fluctuations in exchange rates are to be expected under free-floating, such a system may be undesirable for international trade and payments since the uncertainty[1] caused by price fluctuations could inhibit world trade, output, and employment.

[1]Such uncertainty can be partially offset by dealings in the forward market. This market enables traders to agree a rate of exchange, now, at which foreign currency can be exchanged for domestic currency at an arranged future date, this rate being fixed regardless of what happens to the rate of exchange in the meantime. However there is a cost to the trader in terms of a premium, and this may be high when large exchange rate fluctuations are experienced.

It is also possible to have a rigidly fixed exchange rate system in which the exchange values of currencies are fixed in terms of some common unit such as gold. In fact a gold standard operated in the international economy prior to 1914 and for a period after the First World War. The essential feature of the gold standard was that each country's currency had a fixed value in terms of gold (i.e. gold was the numeraire), and therefore exchange rates were effectively fixed. Under a gold standard it is possible for gold to circulate domestically as the legal tender along with banknotes which can be exchanged on demand for gold. An alternative, which operated in the U.K. from 1925–31, is that the central bank is not prepared to convert banknotes into gold for domestic residents but is willing to convert such paper into gold for foreigners. In the latter case the Bank of England would have to hold a gold reserve to meet the demand of foreigners who wanted to convert sterling into gold. One notable feature of the gold standard was that it allowed automatic adjustment to take place via changes in expenditure and output. A country facing a payments imbalance would suffer an outflow of gold which would necessitate a reduction in the domestic money supply since gold was required to support the note issue. Interest rates would then rise as the central bank increased its discount rate to discourage borrowing and the demands for legal tender. The higher cost of borrowing would discourage spending on investment and other goods, therefore domestic output and employment would eventually fall. Accordingly adjustment to payments imbalances would come about since deficit countries would experience deflationary pressures which would constrain their demand for imports and make their exports more competitive due to lower wages and prices. Surplus countries would experience inflationary pressures from an inflow of gold which would increase their demand for imports and make their exports less competitive. However, the gold standard did not always work as smoothly or effectively as this description indicates since many countries were unwilling to follow the simple rules of the game. In particular, surplus countries often neutralized an inflow of gold by preventing it from adding to the domestic money supply. The adjustment mechanism did not work very effectively in such circumstances, as the history of the operation of the gold standard in the period after the First World War indicated.

So far we have briefly explained how a free-floating and rigidly fixed exchange rate system are supposed to operate. Between these two extremes there are various alternatives, two of which have operated since the ending of the gold standard in 1931. A system of managed floating enables exchange rates to be determined essentially by private market forces, but governments intervene in the foreign exchange markets to try and moderate any short-term fluctuations which may arise due to destablilizing capital flows or other factors. Such official intervention can in theory reduce the degree of exchange rate volatility, and so partially reduce the uncertainty in world trade that might result from a free float. A system of managed floating has existed in the international monetary system since 1973, and its operation will be discussed in Chapter 13. However, managed floating also was adopted in the 1930s when the gold standard was abandoned in the severe economic conditions of the time. The experience then was that floating did not appear to be very successful since individual countries depreciated their currencies so as to gain a competitive advantage over their trading rivals. Consequently a lack of co-operation in the international monetary system only served to intensify the economic problems of the 1930s.

Another alternative is an adjustable peg arrangement under which exchange rates are fixed at agreed values, but revaluations and devaluations of currencies can be undertaken under certain conditions. Such a system may provide fairly stable exchange rates for the development of world trade and yet still permit some degree of adjustment via the exchange rate. The remainder of this chapter will investigate this type of system as it operated in the international economy from the Second World War until 1973.

12.2 The adjustable peg system

At the Bretton Woods Conference in 1944 the Allies came together in an attempt to design an international monetary system that would operate in the post-war period. One of the main objectives of the negotiators was to devise a new system which would avoid a return to the economic conditions of the 1930s. Accordingly the Bretton Woods Conference resulted in the formation of the International Monetary Fund (I.M.F.) and its associated Articles of Agreement, which put into effect the agreed views of the negotiators. In the following discussion we will summarize the features of the Bretton Woods (or 'adjustable peg') system under the headings of adjustment, liquidity, and co-operation.

12.2.1 ADJUSTMENT

One characteristic of the Bretton Woods system was the arrangement for fixed but adjustable exchange rates. This was an attempt to retain some of the advantages of the gold standard since stable rates of exchange were thought to be beneficial to the conduct of trade and other international transactions, and yet adjustments in the exchange rate were deemed desirable for a country facing a permanent payments imbalance. The Articles of Agreement stipulated that gold was the official numeraire in terms of which each currency's exchange value was to be pegged, but it became common practice for countries to adopt a par value for their currencies expressed in terms of the dollar. Individual monetary authorities were then responsible for maintaining the exchange value of their currencies within a band 1 per cent either side of this agreed par value. From 1949 until 1967, for example, the U.K. agreed to maintain the exchange value of the pound within a band 1 per cent either side of the agreed central value of £1 = $2·8. If exchange rate pressure arose to force the market rate outside this limit, then the central bank concerned (the Bank of England) was obliged to intervene in the exchange markets. When the pound was approaching the rate £1 = $2·82, the Bank of England would sell pounds and buy dollars; if the rate approached £1 = $2·78, the Bank of England would sell dollars and buy pounds. Additionally, the exchange value of the dollar was pegged in terms of gold at the rate of $35 an ounce. The U.S.A. authorities were willing to buy and sell gold[2] to other central banks at this price, therefore currencies were convertible into gold via the dollar.

The dollar was therefore the key currency under the adjustable peg system. Domestic monetary authorities had to hold dollar reserves to support their exchange rates in foreign exchange markets and at the same time currencies were officially convertible into gold via the dollar.

Adjustment to a payments imbalance is restricted under a rigidly fixed exchange rate system since the authorities lose one of their policy tools, that is the ability to vary the exchange rate of their currency. However, the Bretton Woods arrangements allowed countries to change their par values if they experienced a 'fundamental disequilibrium' in their balance of payments. The criteria were never carefully defined, but the necessary I.M.F. approval was granted if the country concerned was judged to have a persistent need for accommodating (i.e. official) financing. If the proposed change in par values was less than 10 per cent, then prior approval of the I.M.F. was not required. It was envisaged, therefore, that long-term changes in the competitive position of a particular country could be rectified by a change in the par value of its currency.

12.2.2 LIQUIDITY

International liquidity can be defined as those assets which are internationally acceptable in the payment of debts. The supply of international liquidity is of concern since sufficient finance must be available to assist the development of trade, and yet excess liquidity should be avoided since it may stimulate inflation. Now the need for

[2]After the war the U.S.A. held approximately 60 per cent of the world reserves of gold.

liquidity derives both from the demands of individuals and private bodies to finance trade and investment flows, and from the operations of central banks. The finance of trade and capital flows can be carried out in various currencies when the latter are freely convertible into each other, although payment may be preferred in currencies which have a more stable exchange value. Central banks require reserves of international liquidity for two reasons: (a) to support the domestic exchange rate in foreign exchange markets; (b) to meet the possibility that in any given time-period payments to foreigners will exceed receipts.[3] Governments had the obligation to maintain the par values of their currencies under the adjustable peg system, and the arrangements described in Section 12.2.1 indicate that the dollar was used primarily in this capacity. The dollar also became a principal source of liquidity for private transactions (e.g. oil payments) because of the dollar's crucial position in the international monetary system, which made it a safe and acceptable medium of exchange.

Further arrangements were made by the I.M.F. under its General Account to organize an additional source of liquidity to meet the temporary needs of deficit countries. The facilities have survived the adjustable peg system and are still in operation today. Each member country[4] has a quota which reflects its economic size and importance as a trading nation. The size of the quota determines the extent to which a country can draw currencies from the pool held by the I.M.F. as well as each country's contribution to the pool. Each member originally contributed 75 per cent of its quota in domestic currency and the remaining 25 per cent in gold, although the latter proportion can now be contributed in foreign currencies. If a country requires foreign exchange (e.g. dollars) to support the par value of the domestic currency, then it purchases foreign exchange with its own currency. Such a drawing results in an increase in the Fund's holdings of the member's currency and a decrease in the I.M.F. holdings of the currencies that are borrowed. If the U.K., for example, purchases foreign currencies when the Fund's holdings of sterling are 75 per cent of the U.K. quota,[5] then drawings equivalent to 25 per cent of U.K. quota are available without restriction. This drawing is known as the gold tranche because it is equivalent to the contribution of gold from the member country. After this tranche has been drawn, the Fund's holdings of sterling will be 100 per cent of the U.K.'s quota.

Countries can purchase additional foreign currencies from the

[3]Both these requirements are met by official financing in the balance of payments accounts.

[4]There were originally 30 members, but by 1977 the number had increased to 130.

[5]If the Fund's holdings of sterling are less than 75 per cent of the U.K. quota, the U.K. can purchase, without restriction, foreign currencies up to the point where the Fund's holdings of sterling equal 100 per of the U.K. quota.

Fund, but only if they accept increasing restrictions upon their domestic policies. A country can draw by additional tranches, each equivalent to 25 per cent of its quota, until the Fund's holdings of that member's currency are 200 per cent of its quota. Thus four tranches are available after the gold tranche has been utilized, each known as a credit tranches. However, the I.M.F. requires increasingly detailed programmes of how the member concerned will rectify its payments imbalance before access to the higher credit tranches is granted. Often these programmes are expressed in terms of agreed monetary and financial targets to which the member country is expected to adhere. As a result, drawings are phased over a number of years and are granted in accordance with the successful attainment of the agreed programme. A country is required within 3–5 years to re-purchase its drawings through buying back its own currency with foreign currencies. But countries now have the option of making drawings under a stand-by arrangement whereby they negotiate access to the credit tranches but only use the facility if and when it is required.

With the increasing value of world trade, it became necessary to periodically adjust the quotas of member countries. Even so, the I.M.F. facility was often insufficient to meet the needs of countries requiring foreign currencies to support their rates of exchange. During the early 1960s a group of ten of the larger and richer members of the I.M.F. agreed to make available to the Fund additional resources which could then be used by any member of this Group of Ten. These arrangements, known as the General Agreements to Borrow (G.A.B.), have been utilized extensively by the U.K. over the years.

The I.M.F. also introduced supplementary facilities during the 1960s. The compensatory financing facility was designed to give temporary support to countries facing short-term fluctuations in export earnings, predominantly primary producing nations. The buffer stock financing facility was designed with the intention of making finance available for schemes to allow the holding of buffer stocks to prevent undue price fluctuation in certain products. In the 1970s a temporary oil facility was established through which oil exporters made finance available, via the Fund, to assist the balance of payments problems caused by the sudden rise in the price of oil.

All the above arrangements were made in order that members of the I.M.F. could finance any short-term balance of payments deficit without variations in their exchange rates. If there was a 'fundamental disequilibrium', then the appropriate action was a devaluation of the currency since temporary finance would delay rather than solve the basic problem.

12.2.3 CO-OPERATION

The economic recession of the inter-war period had been intensified by the adoption of 'beggar my neighbour' policies since many countries abandoned the rules of the gold standard and attempted to gain a competitive advantage over their trading partners by introducing tariffs and depreciating the value of their currencies. These sorts of policies were bound to be self-defeating, as we indicated in Section 11.2.4, since the volume of world trade contracted and therefore output and employment stagnated on an international scale. It was against this background that the negotiators at Bretton Woods accepted that more co-operation would be required after the end of the war.

A strong element of participation and co-operation is embodied in the institutional arrangements for the operation of the I.M.F. Each member of the Fund appoints a Governor to the Board of Governors, and this body is ultimately responsible for policy decisions. The large number of members involved means that a full meeting of this Board would be too cumbersome for the day-to-day administration of the I.M.F. and so it meets only once a year, mainly to ratify any new proposals. Most of the business is carried out under the control of an Executive Board of twenty Directors. The five largest members (France, Germany, Japan, the U.K. and the U.S.A.) appoint their own Directors, and the remaining Directors are elected by groups of other members. Although all members participate in the decision-making process, votes are allotted to members in proportion to the size of their quotas. Therefore a Governor or Executive Director exerts influence in accordance with the economic importance of the area he or she represents. Over the years, the I.M.F. has provided a forum for many important discussions affecting the international monetary system, and this process of debate and collective decision-making has encouraged co-operation in this area.

The Bretton Woods arrangements tried to ensure co-operation in the international monetary system not only through the institutional arrangements for the operation of the I.M.F. but also through the widespread acceptance of certain rules of conduct. International trade was to be encouraged by member countries maintaining par values for their currencies so that stable rates of exchange would prevail. General agreement to minimize trade and currency restrictions, although not possible at first, was also considered to be another essential step in this direction. Of course long-term adjustment must be carried out as countries' competitive positions change, but expenditure-reducing policies seem to be the only option for the authorities under a fixed exchange rate system. The danger, then, is that such a system may suffer from a deflationary bias as a result of the attempts of deficit countries to resolve their payments imbalances by reducing domestic demand. The Bretton Woods arrangements recognized these problems by encouraging long-term adjustment to be carried out through deficit countries devaluing when their balance of payments was in 'fundamental disequilibrium'. Indeed it was hoped that overall adjustment would take place successfully through the co-operation of member countries in accepting such rules of conduct.

12.2.4 OPERATION OF THE SYSTEM IN THE 1940S AND 1950S

Although the I.M.F. began operations almost immediately after the Second World War, the Bretton Woods system did not become fully operational until after 1959. The war caused such widespread damage and disruption to national economies and trading patterns that the system of pegged exchange rates could not be operated without recourse to exchange controls. The effective working of the adjustable peg system required deficit countries to have official reserves at their disposal for supporting their currency at the par value. Since many countries had depleted reserves and weak trading positions, they adopted extensive exchange controls in an attempt to regenerate their economies without being subjected to the full rigours of the adjustable peg system.

The late 1940s witnessed the general operation of a system of bilateral arrangements for trade and payments. In effect, country A fixed its exchange rate against that of country B by closely controlling the amount of country B's foreign exchange available to its residents for trade and other purposes. However, these bilateral arrangements were not universal in that the dollar and sterling areas were each characterized by a system of multilateral trade and payments based on the dollar and sterling respectively. In the sterling area, for example, all inter-country trade was conducted in sterling so that the receipts from any one country in the area could be used to make payments to any other.

The Bretton Woods arrangements were designed to foster a network of multilateral trade and payments in the world as a whole, since this was deemed desirable for the development of world trade. A general system of multilateral trade and payments became more tenable in the 1950s when the European Payments Union was formed to take over payment settlements between European countries (including their colonies and dependencies). The E.P.U. recorded surpluses and deficits of any one of its members with each of the others, and settlement was made via the E.P.U. on the net deficit or surplus of one country with the rest. Accordingly a system of mutilateral payments came into operation in the area covered by the E.P.U.; one country's deficit with another member of the E.P.U. was now identical to a deficit with any other in the area. So the non-communist world came to be dominated by two payments systems, the dollar area and the E.P.U., each involving multilateral payments arrangements.

The moves towards a common system of multilateral payments were concluded with the general acceptance of current account convertibility in December 1958. Individuals from any one country were now able to obtain any other currency for trade purposes simply by purchasing it via the foreign exchange markets. However, most countries still retained some degree of control over capital account transactions, mainly because the volatile nature of capital flows presented potential problems for the stability of their exchange rates.

12.2.5 THE STRAINS OF THE 1960S

Our previous discussion has explained that the Bretton Woods system did not become fully operational until after the general acceptance of current-account convertibility in 1958. However, most of the next decade was a testimony to the wisdom of the Bretton Woods arrangements since international trade grew at an unprecedented rate. As a consequence, almost every economy benefited from high output, employment, and growth. There can be little doubt that the new order in the international monetary system, characterized by its arrangements for adjustment, liquidity, and co-operation, was a major factor in these developments. As the 1960s progressed, however, it became evident that certain strains were developing in the Bretton Woods arrangements.

A major problem arose from the way in which the adjustable peg system was operated. Section 12.2.1 has already indicated that the intention of Bretton Woods was to erect a system of fixed but adjustable exchange rates within which countries experiencing a 'fundamental disequilibrium' in their balance of payments could devalue. However, a devaluation of the domestic currency came to be regarded almost as a sign of failure by countries facing permanent imbalance, and so was avoided for as long as possible. Consequently exchange rate adjustment to long-run changes in a country's competitive position was not carried out in the manner visualized by the founding fathers of the system. The U.K.'s position in the mid-1960s provides a good example since she tried to avoid a change in her par value for as long as possible but in the end was forced to devalue because of increasing capital outflows.

Adjustment also came to be regarded as a problem relevant to deficit and not to surplus countries. Thus the whole burden of adjustment was thrown onto certain weaker economies who were themselves reluctant to devalue and preferred to adopt expenditure-reducing policies. These developments gave rise to the claim that the system suffered from a deflationary bias since expenditure-reducing was the major policy weapon used. Nations such as Germany and Japan, increasingly recognized as chronic surplus countries, were reluctant to *revalue* their currencies to assist the overall adjustment process. The Bretton Woods conference had accepted that adjustment should be borne by surplus as well as deficit countries through including a 'scarce-currency clause' in the Articles of Agreement. If I.M.F. holdings of a particular currency were depleted to an extent that threatened its ability to provide that currency to other countries, then that currency could be declared 'scarce'. The I.M.F. was then authorized to ration that currency among its member countries, and the latter were allowed to discriminate against the exports of the country in question. Such a clause if invoked, would obviously encourage a country to reduce its surplus, but it was never called into effect.

Towards the end of the 1960s, however, the adjustable peg system came under increasing pressure from the growth in short-term capital movements. Increased capital mobility was a result of a number of factors. The growth in world trade led to the development of multinational corporations and banks whose increased scope of operation made them more concerned with the placement of funds in a wide range of currencies. Indeed, the development of the Euro-currency market meant that most large organizations became increasingly aware of the possibility of switching funds between currencies in order to make capital gains (or avoid capital losses) and to benefit from interest rate differentials. If a country was facing a payments deficit, then short-term capital outflows would tend to increase because of the potential capital gains accruing to holders if that country devalued its currency. A rate of exchange of £1 = $2·8, for example, would give $2,800 for every £1,000. If the pound was expected to devalue to £1 = $ 2·4 then the holder of sterling balances could sell his £1,000 now (at £1 = $2·8), buy back pounds at a future date (at £1 = $2·4), and hence make a sterling capital gain of £167. Such speculation was of a 'one-way' nature in terms of risk; the holder of these (sterling) balances would make a capital gain if the currency was devalued but would suffer no losses if the exchange rate remained unchanged. Thus there was every incentive for speculation[6] against

[6]Such 'speculation' may have been for basic commercial reasons since, for example, the widespread belief that sterling might be devalued encouraged U.K. traders buying overseas goods to purchase the required amount of foreign exchange immediately, while it was relatively cheap, whereas overseas traders making payments in sterling would delay buying pounds since sterling was expected to cost less in terms of foreign currency in the future.

the weaker currencies, as the U.K. for example, found to its cost prior to the 1967 devaluation. These increased capital flows led to mounting pressure on the adjustable peg since an increasing stock of reserve currencies was required to maintain par values in the face of larger capital movements.

Another major problem for the adjustable peg system was the liquidity arrangements discussed in Section 12.2.2. The system was a form of gold-exchange standard since all currencies were expressed in terms of the dollar and the latter was officially convertible into gold at the fixed price of $35 an ounce. Nevertheless the dollar was the principal reserve asset, and was likely to remain so for as long as the rest of the world accepted dollars and the monetary authorities of individual countries did not exert their option of exchanging dollars for gold. Indeed, during the 1950s there had been fears that there might be a liquidity shortage unless the U.S.A. took steps to increase the supply of dollars. But by the early 1960s opinions had changed markedly, partly as a result of the arguments put forward by Robert Triffin. He argued that the international monetary system, based largely on the dollar, contained certain inherent contradictions. The demand for reserve currencies was growing more quickly than the supply of gold, so a liquidity shortage could only be avoided if the supply of dollars was increased. But an increase in the supply of dollars implied a persistent U.S.A. balance of payments deficit (e.g. exporters to the U.S.A. accept payments in dollars or payments overseas by U.S.A. residents are made in dollars), and this would undermine confidence in the dollar as a reserve currency because dollar claims were growing in relation to U.S.A. gold reserves. The effect of a loss in confidence would be a desire to convert dollars into gold at the official price, and accordingly the system would collapse since the most widely held reserve asset would cease to be accepted as such. The world would face either a liquidity shortage which constrained the development of trade, or else there would be a collapse of the system as confidence in the dollar waned.

Triffin's theoretical analysis gained more credence when the U.S.A. balance of payments appeared to move into overall deficit. Although America's current account was always in surplus during the 1960s, her net capital outflows, particularly private investments overseas, more than offset the current account surplus in most years. As a result, the U.S.A. suffered a net outflow of gold in every year but one during the 1960s as pressure of the kind described by Triffin built up.

A potential solution to the liquidity dilemma was the introduction of some other form of reserve asset. The I.M.F. set about the problem by devising the *Special Drawing Right* (S.D.R.) as a means of settlement among its members. This new form of liquidity, unlike gold, was essentially a book-keeping transaction which created additional reserve assets for member countries. It was introduced in 1970 following an amendment to the Articles of Agreement of the I.M.F. and the formation of a Special Drawing Account. The nature and purpose of the S.D.R. can be described as follows.

(a) Participating countries are allotted S.D.R.s in proportion to their quotas, these allocations being known as their 'net cumulative allocations.' The amounts issued were for a basic period of three years, the total allotment being $9·5 billion.

(b) Any participating country is able to use its allocation of S.D.R.s when it faces a balance of payments or reserve problem. Such a country activates its S.D.R.s through the Special Drawing Account, and the Fund designates other participants to whom the S.D.R.s may be transferred in exchange for foreign currency.

(c) Creditor countries are expected to accept a transfer of S.D.R.s in exchange for currency up to a limit set at three times their net cumulative allocation.

(d) Participating countries using the S.D.R. facility are subject to the limitation that over a five-year period a country's average holding will not be less than 30 per cent of the average of its net cumulative allocation over the same period. A country has to re-purchase S.D.R. holdings (known as 'reconstitution') to the extent that they fall below this average 30 per cent level. In effect, this meant that a country could use about 70 per cent of its allocation more or less permanently without the type of restrictions applicable to credit tranches (see p. 272).

(e) The S.D.R. was originally defined in terms of gold at a value of $^1/_{35}$ of an ounce (equivalent to $1 at the prevailing official price), hence its former title of 'paper gold.' In 1974 the value of the S.D.R. was linked to a basket of sixteen national currencies, so the link with gold was severed.

(f) An incentive for creditors to hold the S.D.R. was given by the fact that its value was linked to gold at the time of the issue and it carried an interest payment (originally 1½ per cent) which was met by a similar charge on debtor countries.

In theory, the S.D.R. possesses several major advantages over gold as a reserve asset. The supply of S.D.R.s can be controlled in line with the demand for reserve assets, and the costs of provisions are very low since it is merely a book-keeping transaction. However the first allocation proved to be the last (to date), and the increased payments deficits of the U.S.A. during the early 1970s provided the international monetary system with extra liquidity in the form of dollars.

12.2.6 BREAKDOWN IN THE 1970S

The eventual collapse of the adjustable peg system came about as a result of an intensification of the pressures that had developed during the 1960s. Exchange rates had only been adjusted as a last resort by deficit and surplus countries, and so were not used speedily enough to prevent prolonged payments imbalances and exchange rate crises. However, the weaknesses of the adjustment mechanism became critical when the United States, the linch-pin of the system, suffered continual balance of payments problems. It appeared difficult for the dollar to be devalued since the exchange value of all other currencies were tied to it and the dollar itself was tied to gold. Furthermore, confidence in the exchange value of the dollar was essential since it provided the bulk of the reserve assets in the system: any devaluation of the dollar would give rise to fears that it might be devalued again, hence there would be a reluctance to hold dollars as a reserve currency. It was feared that a severe liquidity crisis might ensue and that the world economy would then be plunged into economic recession.

Confidence in the dollar as a safe reserve asset declined markedly from around 1970 onwards when the U.S.A. encountered larger balance of payments deficits. The U.S.A. wanted surplus countries like Germany and Japan to revalue since it was difficult for payments imbalances to be resolved through a devaluation of the dollar. In contrast, surplus countries argued that the U.S.A. should solve her balance of payments problems by introducing expenditure-reducing policies at home, as had other countries. The U.S.A. had never needed to undertake such policies previously, since acceptance of the dollar's role as a key reserve asset had meant that she could meet any payments deficit simply by increasing the supply of dollars. Thus there was fundamental disagreement on what steps should be taken to resolve the problem, and co-operation between members of the international monetary system reached a low ebb.

The American administration adopted a policy of 'benign neglect' in the early 1970s in accordance with its view that surplus countries should revalue. This policy meant that the U.S.A. did not take any special steps to control her deficit but instead allowed the balance of payments to deteriorate. But the increased mobility of international capital flows was bound to bring added pressure on the system of fixed exchange rates under such conditions. Other countries, especially those in surplus, were facing an inflow of dollars in exchange for their currencies because of the potential capital gains that would accrue to speculators if the dollar was devalued. These speculative pressures encourage countries to utilize the option of converting their official holdings of dollars into gold at the fixed price of $35 and ounce. The U.S. Treasury began to experience a depletion of its gold stock, so in August 1971 it announced that official convertibility of dollars into gold was temporarily suspended.[7] An essential link in the Bretton Woods arrangements, that of official convertibility into gold via the dollar, had thus been broken.

In response to these events, the monetary authorities of countries other than the U.S.A. decided that they would no longer intervene to stabilize their exchange rates against the dollar since this would have meant their accumulating large quantities of dollars for which (a) the exchange value was uncertain, and (b) the option of convertibility into gold at a fixed price had been terminated. Accordingly individual currencies were allowed to float since there was no other option, although the governments concerned ensured that it was a 'managed' rather than a free float. Then in December 1971 the Smithsonian Conference was convened in an attempt to reach agreement, on a multilateral basis, for some new arrangement to perpetuate the adjustable peg system. Several steps were taken in this respect.

(a) There was a revaluation of most major currencies against the dollar, notably a 13½ per cent increase in the value of the Deutschmark and a 17 per cent increase in the value of the yen.

(b) The band of fluctuation either side of the new parities was widened from 1 per cent to 2¼ per cent, thus allowing for a larger margin of exchange rate fluctuation before official intervention was required.

(c) The official price of gold was increased to $38 an ounce, but this move had little significance since the dollar was no longer officially convertible into gold.

Although the conference brought about the first international agreement on a multilateral adjustment in exchange rates, it did not prevent the collapse of the adjustable peg system. Indeed, once the dollar had been devalued it became more likely that the same might happen again in the near future. Consequently lack of confidence in the dollar, combined with the high mobility of capital flows, led to severe pressure on the new parity structure. The U.K. floated sterling in June 1972, largely because of her own balance of payments difficulties, and most other major economies had followed suit by March 1973.

12.3 The World Bank (The International Bank for Reconstruction and Development)[8]

(i) *Origin and purpose.*

(a) The World Bank, like the I.M.F. was designed at Bretton

[7]The temporary suspension turned out to be permanent.
[8]Much of the detail is taken from the publication 'Recent Developments in the International Monetary System.' issued by the Bank Education Service.

Woods and began operations in 1946. The two institutions have adjoining offices in Washington.

(b) One of the initial purposes of the World Bank was to aid post-war reconstruction through the provision of finance since private capital markets were not expected to be able to cope with the scale of the problem. In practice, the U.S.A. Marshall-Aid programme provided most of the necessary finance and the World Bank came to be responsible for assisting economic development in mainly the poorer countries.

(ii) *Source of funds.*

(a) Member countries have to make capital subscriptions which reflect their I.M.F. quotas. However only 10 per cent (originally 20 per cent) of this subscription is paid into the Bank, the remaining 90 per cent acting as a guarantee for the Bank's lending.

(b) Any net income from its operations as a borrower and lender goes into its funds.

(c) The major source of funds is through borrowing. The World Bank issues bonds on the world's capital markets, such as the New York market.

(iii) *Nature of its operations.*

(a) It lends on a commercial basis since the intention is to supplement private finance, not to compete with it. Consequently the Bank satisfies itself that the borrower can meet the interest and capital repayments before it makes the loan. Also the Bank makes a general appraisal of the merits and priority of each proposal as it tries to allocate its total resources effectively.

(b) It lends to governments and governmental agencies, although private organizations can borrow if the national government guarantees the loan.

(c) The length of the loan is dependent upon the character of the project and the debt position of the borrower, but twenty years is a typical period.

(d) Lending is normally limited to the financing of the foreign exchange costs of the imported goods and services to be used in the project.

(e) The Bank also provides its members with technical assistance and advice on projects since the less-developed countries often lack the required technical expertise.

(f) Many of the less-developed countries have found it very difficult to meet the service charges on their loans from the World Bank. To accommodate this, the World Bank was expanded into the Bank Group after the creation of the International Finance

Corporation (1956) and the International Development Association
(1960). The latter has extended loans for up to 50 years, with no
interest payable and capital repayments deferred for the first 10 years
in some cases.

(iv) *Recipients of loans.*

(a) Loans go mainly to the Asian, African, and South and Central
American countries with low levels of G.N.P. per head (usually much
less than $1,000 per annum). The Bank's total lending has increased
from $250 million in 1947 on one project to $3,400 million on 148
projects in 1973.

(b) Loans made during the 1950s were mainly for the development
of infrastructure, such as transport and electric power schemes.
Loans have more recently been extended to finance education and
other socially-orientated projects.

12.4 Summary

i. Various exchange rate arrangements can be adopted, ranging
from free-floating at one extreme to a rigidly fixed system at the
other. The extent to which the exchange rate can contribute to
the adjustment mechanism, either in an automatic or
discretionary manner, is influenced by the type of exchange rate
system in operation.

ii. The adjustable peg system was characterized by its
arrangements for adjustment, liquidity, and co-operation. With
adjustment, the essential feature was the fixed but adjustable
exchange rate structure in which the dollar held a central
position. All currencies came to be expressed in terms of the
dollar, and the dollar was officially convertible into gold at a
fixed price. Consequently world trade was encouraged since all
currencies were exchangeable for each other and for gold at
stable rates of exchange.

iii. The liquidity arrangements came to be based on both the I.M.F.
quota scheme and the supply of dollars. However there was an
intrinsic weakness in such a system, as was pointed out by
Triffin. He argued that the system was bound to collapse, either
because a liquidity shortage would ensue if the supply of dollars
failed to keep pace with the growing world demand, or because
the persistent balance of payments deficits of the U.S.A. (which
provided dollars to the world) would reduce confidence in the
dollar and so lead to the conversion of official dollar balances
into gold.

iv. Co-operation in the international monetary system was
enhanced by the institutional arrangements made at Bretton

Woods. Through the creation of institutions such as the I.M.F. and the World Bank, a forum was provided for discussion and decision-making on an international scale. At the same time rules of conduct were established for the behaviour of member nations.

v. The causes of the breakdown of the adjustable peg system are related to its three major features described above. The adjustment mechanism in the 1960s was characterized by the reluctance of all countries to adjust their exchange rates, especially those countries in surplus. Accordingly, adjustment via the exchange rate was not able to compensate adequately for long-term changes in competitive conditions. The deterioration in the United States' balance of payments in the early 1970s caused particular concern since the dollar was the linch-pin of the international monetary system. When the United States authorities failed to undertake domestic policies to remedy the external situation, some countries started to exercise their option of converting their dollar balances into gold. These moves brought about the suspension of the official convertibility of the dollar into gold and the eventual adoption of floating exchange rates.

13
Managed floating

13.1 The general operation of the system, 1973–1978

13.1.1 HISTORICAL BACKGROUND

Chapter 12 has already examined the reasons why the adjustable peg system collapsed. In summary, an exchange rate system needs to be sufficiently flexible to cope with long-run changes in countries' competitive positions. But the adjustable peg system did not adequately specify if and when countries in surplus or deficit were to undertake exchange rate adjustment. Such a shortcoming is illustrated by the imprecise meaning of the term 'fundamental disequilibrium,' the required condition for a devaluation by a deficit country. This deficiency proved fatal when the dollar faced a prolonged confidence crisis in the early 1970s. It was extremely difficult for the U.S.A. to devalue since all currencies were expressed in terms of the dollar, and yet surplus countries were not very keen to revalue their currencies. However, speculative pressure, stimulated by the increasing size and mobility of capital flows, eventually brought about the suspension of official dollar convertibility into gold and the subsequent abandonment by individual monetary authorities of their obligation to maintain fixed exchange rates.

The adoption of floating exchange rates was thus a consequence of the collapse of the adjustable peg, rather than the result of a collectively planned decision. Once the system of fixed exchange rates had been abandoned there was no alternative but for currencies to float. However the system of floating exchange rates was thought at the time to be a temporary feature of the international monetary system: it was hoped that a new framework would be found for a return to some kind of adjustable peg in which the burden of adjustment was clearly defined, both for deficit and surplus countries, and in which reserve assets were not based primarily on one currency. Accordingly, many negotiations took place within the I.M.F. (especially through the so-called Committee of Twenty) in an attempt to find some generally acceptable basis for a return to such a system. But these extensive discussions failed to provide a common area of agreement, mainly because of divergent national interests and unfavourable economic developments such as inflation, recession, and the Oil Crisis.

The first few years of floating proved to be fairly successful, especially in the light of the prevailing economic conditions. Consequently floating came to be accepted as a permanent feature of the international monetary system, even though the Bretton Woods Conference had disapproved of such arrangements. Therefore at the Jamaica Conference of the I.M.F. in January 1976 a Second Amendment to the Articles of Agreement (the First Amendment being the introduction of S.D.R.s) was made by which the system of floating exchange rates was legalized. In fact the rules were changed so that now an 85 per cent affirmative vote is required before the I.M.F. can sanction a return to an adjustable peg arrangement.

A floating exchange rate should, in theory, 'solve' the balance of payments problem automatically. In practice, however, the elasticity of demand for imports and exports may not be of an appropriate value or else it may take considerable time before such automatic forces become effective. Under such circumstances speculative capital movements cannot be relied upon to offset any temporary deficit on the current account because capital flows may prove to be volatile in an uncertain world. Accordingly *managed* floating was generally adopted when the adjustable peg was abandoned. Under managed floating, the domestic monetary authorities intervene in the foreign exchange markets to neutralize any short-term fluctuations in the exchange rate. But it can be difficult to ascertain whether exchange rate pressure is temporary or permanent in nature, consequently the decision when and to what degree the central monetary authority should intervene is largely a matter of judgement. If a country's exchange rate is generally thought to be overvalued, however, then the central bank concerned would face heavy losses of foreign currency if it attempted to maintain the exchange rate at its current value. Large reserves of foreign currencies would then be required to buy the domestic currency in support operations, but the growth and mobility of capital flows has made most countries accept that such a defence is impractical.

With floating, a potential complication arises because of the difficulty in establishing whether the domestic currency's exchange value is increasing or decreasing. The home currency may appreciate in terms of one currency and yet depreciate in terms of another. To take an example, sterling appreciated against the dollar in early 1975 but depreciated against most of the E.E.C. currencies. If we want an overall measure of the value of the domestic currency then some weighted average of changes in its exchange value against all other currencies is required. The weights should indicate the relative importance of each of these currencies, perhaps in terms of the volume of trade which the respective countries conduct with the domestic economy. Sterling and the other major currencies use the 'effective exchange rate' as a general measure of the exchange value of the domestic currency, and it is calculated on such a basis. However, it is still common to see exchange rates expressed in terms of the dollar, partly because this had long been the accepted practice under the adjustable peg, and also because of the U.S.A.'s continuing dominance in the world economy.

To facilitate comparison with the adjustable peg, the major features of managed floating can be described under the headings of adjustment, liquidity, and co-operation.

13.1.2 ADJUSTMENT

Under floating, the exchange rate can operate as a form of automatic adjustment to payments imbalances, although such adjustment may not be full or immediate. Floating exchange rates have the added advantage that responsibility for the burden of adjustment does not have to be assigned to particular countries: with floating, the exchange rate mechanism itself should lead to an appreciation of strong currencies and a depreciation of weak currencies. In contrast, the operation of the adjustable peg was characterised by disputes as to whether the burden of adjustment should be borne by deficit or surplus countries.

Discretionary adjustment via the exchange rate is not possible under managed floating. The existence of large and mobile capital flows makes it extremely difficult for national governments to overcome market pressure and maintain an exchange rate which is not compatible with general market sentiment. Nevertheless some form of discretionary adjustment is still required, especially for deficit countries, since there is not guarantee that the exchange rate will adjust in such a manner as to ensure an equilibrium in the balance of payments. This conclusion is borne out by the record of managed floating since 1973, which is surveyed in more detail in Sections 13.2 and 13.4. At this stage, however, it is sufficient to note that some countries have had persistent balance of payments surpluses (e.g. Germany) whereas others have had regular deficits (e.g. Italy and the U.K.), despite appreciations and depreciations of the respective currencies. Under these circumstances, deficit countries have still utilized expenditure-reducing policies in an attempt to limit imports, and surplus countries have often been encouraged to expand their economies.

An additional consideration is that the adjustment process prior to floating was influenced by the one-way nature of speculative flows. Since countries were obliged to maintain par values, it was possible for speculation to be carried out against the stronger and weaker currencies in the knowledge that the currencies concerned might be revalued or devalued respectively, but there was no danger of the strong currencies being devalued or the weak currency being revalued. With managed floating there is a risk that speculators will suffer capital losses since the monetary authority is no longer attempting to defend a rigid par value, and so the exchange rate can move in either direction in response to market pressures. This reasoning suggests that capital flows are potentially more stabilizing under floating. However, both the weaker and stronger currencies have experienced bouts of speculative pressure, thus indicating that capital flows have not been stabilizing under managed floating.

The competence of the adjustment mechanism under managed floating was given a thorough testing by the Oil Crisis. From late 1973 onwards, the increase in the price of oil gave rise to massive surpluses in the oil-exporting countries. These surpluses were of the order of $57,000 million in 1974, $35,200 million in 1975, and $35,800 million in 1976.[1] At first glance the size of the surpluses, and the corresponding deficits in oil-importing countries, would appear to pose an overwhelming problem for any type of exchange rate system. Indeed some commentators have argued that the adjustable peg system could not have coped with the scale of the problem, whereas the system of managed floating apparently has.

Although the members of O.P.E.C. (Organization of Petroleum Exporting Countries) have experienced hugh surpluses, practically all payments to them have been made in the currencies of the major oil-importing countries, predominantly the dollar. In fact this method is the traditional means of payment for oil, since the currencies of the O.P.E.C. countries are of minor importance in the international monetary system. So any automatic adjustment can only come about through the distribution of oil deficits between the oil-importing countries; oil exporters have had to use their surpluses to accumulate assets (i.e. capital account transactions) from such countries. In practice, therefore, floating exchange rates could enable the currencies of countries with large overall payments imbalances to depreciate against other currencies.[2] However it is difficult to establish whether the mechanism has worked in this manner because the fluctuations that have taken place in exchange rates since 1973 have also been affected by other factors, such as the different rates of domestic inflation.

The preceding discussion indicates that the O.P.E.C. surpluses have been available for financing the deficits of other countries.

[1] See the Bank of England *Quarterly Bulletin* for current details.
[2] Note that not all oil-importing countries have suffered overall deficits – increased payments for oil may merely have reduced a country's surplus.

However the O.P.E.C. surpluses are not necessarily invested in those places where large oil deficits have to be financed, and so there may be what is known as a recycling problem. Additionally, there is a danger the O.P.E.C. members will switch their resources from one currency to another and so bring about severe exchange rate pressure on particular currencies. In fact the U.K. in 1976 experienced a large outflow of short-term sterling deposits, held predominantly by O.P.E.C. members, which resulted in a large depreciation of sterling. However the recycling problem has been greatly assisted by the rapid development of the Euro-currency market since 1973. A large proportion of the oil surpluses has been deposited in the Euro-currency market and then on-lent to the monetary authorities of deficit countries, thus enabling them to finance their deficits. Consequently the 'market' itself has been able to manage the recycling problem, and it seems likely that flexibility in the market has been encouraged by the adoption of market-determined exchange rates.

The oil surpluses have also been recycled via the I.M.F. notably through the Oil Facility. Oil-exporting countries placed some of their surpluses in a special I.M.F. account and member countries were then allowed to borrow if their balance of payments accounts had been adversely affected by the rise in oil prices. Approximately S.D.R. 2,500 million was recycled in this manner in 1974, and S.D.R. 3,900 million in 1975, before the facility finally was ended. It can be seen from the sums involved that most of the recycling was carried out by the market rather than through the I.M.F.

The system of managed floating coped much better with the Oil Crisis than was first expected. Indeed the overall distribution of oil deficits was probably assisted by the flexibility in exchange rates, and the recycling of oil revenues has been accomplished fairly satisfactorily through the growth in the Euro-currency market. Accordingly most commentators agree that the system of floating exchange rates has responded more quickly and effectively to such a large disturbance than would have been the case with the adjustable peg system.

13.1.3 LIQUIDITY

The abandonment of a fixed exchange rate in favour of floating means that there is potentially less need for government intervention in foreign exchange markets, and therefore a reduced need for international liquidity to meet this purpose. Governments, however, have still intervened in foreign exchange market to influence their respective rates of exchange, although a greater variety of currencies has been used now that exchange rates are no longer pegged exclusively to the dollar. On the other hand, the growth in the Euro-currency market has provided an enlarged source of borrowing for monetary authorities who wish either to support their exchange rates or to meet the needs of official financing. Therefore more concern has been expressed in recent years over whether there is a danger of an over-supply of liquidity which could stimulate world inflationary pressures. For example, governments may be able to ignore the effects of domestic inflation on the balance of payments if excess liquidity provides an ample source of borrowed funds.

Some nations have continued to use the I.M.F. facilities, despite the success of the Euro-currency market in providing large-scale finance. Indeed in December 1976 the U.K. negotiated a standby facility of S.D.R. 3,360 million ($3,900 million), the maximum amount available under the British credit tranches. Other I.M.F. facilities have also been utilized extensively, especially by the less-developed countries. All these countries have been willing to borrow from the I.M.F. – even though there are conditional policy restrictions – because the Euro-currency markets have become more concerned with the credit-worthiness of their customers. In fact there have been several instances where the banks in the Euro-currency market have been willing to extend credit only if the country in question has already obtained I.M.F. credit and its associated conditionality.

What, then, has happened to the dollar and gold, the two key reserve assets under the adjustable peg? The prolonged speculative pressure against the dollar in the final stages of the adjustable peg system indicated there was an over-supply of this currency. But the Oil Crisis led to renewed demand for dollars, since most payments to oil-exporting countries were made in this form. The dollar, therefore, has continued to be used as a reserve currency; and the recycling of dollars through the Euro-currency market has made such funds available to borrowing countries. However, periodic exchange rate pressures on the dollar have cast some doubt on its desirability as a reserve currency.

The role of gold has always been a controversial issue in the international monetary system, but with the advent of floating its importance as a source of international liquidity has been reduced in several ways. When currencies were allowed to float, gold was no longer the ultimate numeraire in which exchange values were expressed, indeed discussions at the time accepted that the S.D.R. (based on the value of sixteen national currencies since 1974) would be the numeraire in any future return to an adjustable system. Moves towards the demonetization of gold went further when, under the Second Amendment to the Articles of Agreement at Jamaica in 1976, it was agreed that the I.M.F. should dispose of one-third of its gold holdings. One-half of this was to be sold by auction, and the profits above the official price of $42·2 an ounce were then to be used to promote aid to the less-developed countries, whereas the other half was to be sold back to members at the prevailing official price. The notion of an official gold price at which inter-central bank transactions were to be conducted was also abandoned. Finally, countries were no longer required to pay a quarter of their I.M.F. quotas (or quota increases) in gold; in future they were allowed to use foreign currencies or S.D.R.s, assuming further allocations of the latter were to be made.

13.1.4 CO-OPERATION

The replacement of the adjustable peg by floating implies that fewer rules of conduct are necessary for co-ordinating the system of exchange rates. Countries no longer have to decide the rate of exchange at which currencies should be pegged, or the responsibility for ensuring that par values are maintained at agreed values. Indeed, advocates of floating have frequently argued that the need for fewer rules, and reduced formal co-operation, confers in important advantage on the present system over its predecessor.

It must be remembered, however, that the Bretton Woods arrangements and the associated rules of conduct were designed with the intention of avoiding the conflicts of national interest which had been associated with the previous period of floating. At that time, the adoption of floating exchange rates was also thought to be advantageous since the constraints of the gold standard could be abandoned. Nevertheless the pursuit of policies based on national self-interest led to competitive depreciations and the introduction of tariffs and other trade restrictions; trade, output, and employment suffered as a consequence on an international scale. The present system of managed floating does contain the possibility of direct conflict if official intervention is carried out at cross-purposes. Thus the central bank of country A might buy currency B in order to keep the domestic exchange rate at a competitive level, whereas country B might simultaneously try to keep the value of its currency down by buying currency A. In this manner a lack of co-operation, fostered by a system of floating exchange rates, can lead to conflict and mutually frustrating policies.

In summary, co-operation is still necessary if trade, output, and employment are to develop to their full potential. This need for co-operation is especially pressing during a period of economic recession, since nations are then more concerned with gaining a competitive advantage over their rivals so that domestic employment levels can be maintained. Accordingly, the danger with floating exchange rates is that the less formal arrangements for co-operation may foster insufficient international co-ordination of policies for the alleviation of the sustained economic recession which has prevailed during the current period of managed floating.

13.2 U.K. experience

The supporters of floating exchange rates maintain that one of its major advantages is that it enables the exchange rate to act as a means of automatic adjustment. However, the effectiveness of the exchange rate in this role does, as we have seen in Sections 11.2.1 and 13.1.1, depend upon the elasticity of demand for imports and exports, and upon the stability of capital account transactions. We will now examine the record of the U.K. balance of payments under floating to ascertain whether movements in the exchange rate have provided an effective adjustment mechanism in this case.

When evaluating whether the U.K. balance of payments record under floating reveals any relevant information as to the effectiveness of the exchange rate as an adjustment mechanism, it must be remembered that other variables also exert an influence on the balance of payments. For example, a depreciating exchange rate may not improve the current balance if the country concerned is continually suffering a deterioration in her competitive position due to high domestic inflation, low productivity, or other factors which more than offset the price advantage gained by depreciation. However we can make some tentative suggestions, based on the data presented in *Table 13.1*, of the effectiveness for the U.K. of a floating exchange rate as an adjustment mechanism during the period since 1972.

The U.K. current balance over the years 1967–77 is presented in Table 13.1, the years up to 1972 being a period when the adjustable peg system was in operation. We can see here the 'J curve' effect referred to in Section 11.2.1, with the devaluation of 1967 not apparently exerting its desired effect on the current balance until 1969 and afterwards. The pound was floated against other major currencies in June 1972, but the calculation of the Effective Exchange Rate for sterling is based on exchange values determined at the Smithsonian Conference in December 1971. Over the period of floating, sterling has depreciated by approximately 34 per cent (from 99·0 in June 1972 to 65·2 in December 1977), but the figures for the current account balance reveal a deficit in every year except 1977. Furthermore, the marked improvement in the current balance during 1977 was probably due as much to the increased production of North Sea oil, which reduced the domestic demand for oil imports, as to the

TABLE 13.1

The U.K. balance of payments and the Effective Exchange Rate

Year	Current balance[a]	Balance for[b] official financing	Effective Exchange[c] Rate, year end
1967	−300	−671	
1968	−287	−1,410	
1969	+440	+687	
1970	+710	+1,287	
1971	+1,074	+3,146	100·0
1972	+126	−1,265	90·2
1973	−883	−771	83·0
1974	−3,515	−1,646	82·6
1975	−1,617	−1,465	72·6
1976	−859	−3,628	61·1
1977	+165	+7,361	65·2

Sources:

[a] and [b] *Economic Trends*, June 1978.

[c] As revised and presented in the March 1977 issue of the Bank of England *Quarterly Bulletin* and in subsequent issues.

effects of the depreciating pound on export and import volume. Therefore the evidence presented here, although limited in value because of the sort of qualifications made earlier, does at least suggest that altering the exchange rate has not been very speedy or effective in improving the U.K. current account balance.

Supporters of flexible exchange rates do not believe, however, that the operation of this system will reduce current account deficits to zero. Instead, they argue that capital account transactions will be undertaken in such a manner as to establish an exchange rate at which current account deficits and surpluses are offset by capital movements in the opposite direction, thereby bringing about an overall balance of payments. But Table 13.1 reveals that substantial official financing has been carried out by the U.K. authorities since 1972, as was the case prior to floating, and so suggests that private capital flows have not been stabilizing. Again, however, one could argue that these conclusions are contentious; less intervention by the U.K. authorities in foreign exchange markets may have enabled an exchange rate to be established at which an overall balance of payments would have taken place without official intervention.

In conclusion, we can say that the system of managed floating as it has operated to date does not seem to have been very successful in adjusting the U.K. balance of payments. One reason for this may be that official intervention has prevented an exchange rate being established at which a balance of payments equilibrium would have occured. The U.K. government has perhaps been reluctant to leave exchange rate determination completely to private market forces because of the belief that capital flows are basically unstable, and that overall balance of payments equilibrium would only be produced, without intervention, at the expense of wildly fluctuating exchange rates.

The question now arises of whether movements in the exchange rate under managed floating have been smooth and continuous, or whether destabilizing capital flows have brought marked fluctuations in exchange rates and subsequent uncertainty to international trade. There is, however, a complication in examining the stability of foreign exchange markets, and it is that domestic monetary authorities have intervened under managed floating and so movements in exchange rates may partly reflect their success or failure. With this in mind we present data in Fig. 13.1 on the stability of the exchange rate between sterling and the dollar during 1976. It can be seen that the weekly sterling exchange rate depreciated from $2·02 at the start of the year to around $1·70 at the end. But the depreciation was by no means smooth. The graph indicates that movements in the exchange rate were volatile, and the downward trend was dominated by two periods of rapid depreciation. Movements in the exchange rate during these two periods were strongly influenced by heavy speculative flows which the U.K. authorities tried to moderate by purchasing sterling with their foreign exchange reserves.

Movements in the weekly sterling exchange rate against the dollar during 1976 do not give a fair impression of the general stability of exchange rates under managed floating. Indeed 1976 was an unstable year for sterling during which the U.K. authorities took steps to prevent further exchange rate pressure from the run-down of the sterling balances (see Section 11.1.2), and during which a loan was negotiated from the I.M.F. (see Section 13.1.3). However the data in Fig. 13.1 does indicate that movements in the exchange rate have often been erratic, and uncertainty in world trade will tend to increase under such circumstances.

Another feature of the system of managed floating which has affected the U.K. is that a depreciation in the exchange rate stimulates inflation in the domestic economy, especially when the demand for imports is inelastic, since import prices increase as a result of the depreciation. In fact it has been estimated that a 4 per cent fall in the value of sterling puts approximately 1 per cent on the Retail Price Index. Therefore floating exchange rates may add to the inflationary pressures encountered by a weak economy, and so

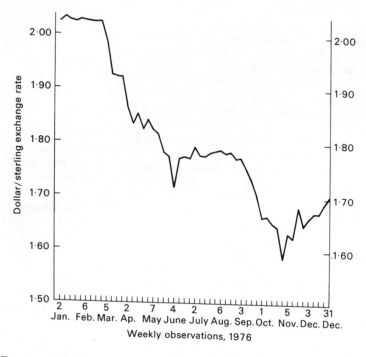

FIG 13.1. *Movements in the dollar/sterling exchange rate, on a weekly basis for 1976.*

attempts to control inflation through incomes policies and the like may be frustrated.

13.3 Monetary union and the snake

Whereas the previous section examined the effect of floating on the U.K. we are concerned here with its implications for the aspirations of the E.E.C. toward monetary union. In fact the widespread adoption of floating exchange rates imposed a set-back to the plans for economic and monetary union within the E.E.C.

Monetary union has long been seen as a way of bringing about greater economic and political unity within the Community, as we explained in Section 8.3. The Werner Report of October 1970 mapped out a stage-by-stage plan to achieve Economic and Monetary Union (E.M.U.) by 1980, although it concentrated more on monetary union and assumed that economic union would automatically follow. The stages outlined in the Werner Plan are as follows:[3]

(i) a progressive narrowing of the margins within which the exchange rates of member currencies would be permitted to fluctuate *vis-à-vis* each other, with some arrangement for financing of countries in deficit by the countries in surplus;

(ii) a pooling of foreign exchange reserves;

(iii) eventually the elimination of exchange rate margins, with the establishment of a common currency recognized as being perhaps the best way of embodying this; and

(iv) the establishment of a single central bank.

The Report's recommendations were approved in principle by the E.E.C. in 1971 and, as a prelude to the first stage, central banks were invited to restrict fluctuations in their currencies around the existing par values. Under the then prevailing adjustable peg arrangements, any one currency could fluctuate within a band (or 'tunnel') 1 per cent either side of the dollar par value, so if one E.E.C. currency moved from its floor to its ceiling and another moved from its ceiling to its floor there would be a 4 per cent relative fluctuation in the values of the two currencies. The avoidance of such fluctuations was considered desirable not only as a first stage in monetary union but also for the smooth operation of the Common Agricultural Policy, since food prices are calculated according to the exchange value of member currencies.

However the widening of the margin of fluctuation either side of par to 2¼ per cent at the Smithsonian Conference in December 1971 posed a threat to E.E.C. plans for limiting exchange rate fluctuations amongst member currencies. If one E.E.C. currency rose from its floor to its ceiling against the dollar, whilst another fell from its ceiling to its floor, there would be a 9 per cent change in the relative values of the two currencies. Accordingly the 'snake in the tunnel' scheme was devised as a way of restricting E.E.C. exchange rate fluctuations. The basic idea (see *Figure 13.2*) was that members agreed to maintain no more than a 2¼ per cent band around *all* their respective currencies so as to set a limit to the degree to which exchange values could fluctuate (the 'snake'). At the same time, all E.E.C. currencies would move together as a bloc within the 4½ per cent Smithsonian band of fluctuation against the dollar (the 'tunnel').

Obviously the snake arrangements require intervention by domestic monetary authorities when currencies look likely to break out of the 2¼ per cent band. Therefore the E.E.C. central banks made arrangements to sell the stronger currencies when they threatened to break through the snake ceiling and to buy the weaker currencies

[3]See the *Midland Bank Review*, winter 1977.

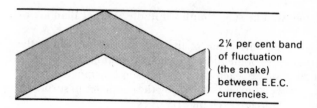

2¼ per cent band of fluctuation (the snake) between E.E.C. currencies.

4½ per cent band of fluctuation (the tunnel) against the dollar.

FIG 13.2. *The snake in the tunnel.*

when they seemed likely to fall through the snake floor. Furthermore, a settlement arrangement was made whereby the creditor countries could exchange on a monthly basis their accumulations of the weaker currencies (which they had been buying in the E.E.C. exchange markets) for some other form of reserve asset. The six original members of the E.E.C. commenced operating the 'snake in the tunnel' scheme in 1972 and the U.K. along with Eire and Denmark also participated in May 1972 while negotiating entry to the Community. But sterling was soon withdrawn from the scheme when the pound was floated in June 1972.

The advent of generalized floating in early 1973 meant that there was no longer any requirement to keep the snake in the tunnel. The snake was now allowed to float against the other major currencies, but a maximum spread of 2¼ per cent was still retained for the currencies in the snake. Also in 1973, the European Monetary Co-operation Fund (E.M.C.F.) was established as a body to operate the snake arrangements, its major responsibilities being to record the currency transactions between the central banks of the participating countries and to administer the short-term financing settlements. However the successful operation of the snake was hindered by the adverse circumstances of the time: exchange rates were no longer pegged against the dollar; there had been a massive increase in oil prices which resulted in larger payments imbalances and severe exchange rate pressures; domestic rates of inflation were showing a tendency to diverge markedly; and the world economy was moving into recession. Under such pressures it proved very difficult for monetary authorities to intervene in foreign exchange markets to ensure stable rates of exchange between all E.E.C. currencies. Indeed, Italy left the snake in February 1973; France left in January 1974, rejoined, and then left again in March 1976; and the U.K. and Eire have remained outside the scheme since 1972. The E.E.C. seemed to have moved further away from the aims of the first stage of the Werner recommendations now that most exchange rates in the Community were floating against each other.

Although the Werner Plan has failed, the concept of E.M.U. has not been abandoned. Indeed it is still argued that determined efforts should be made towards monetary union so that eventually a common currency can be issued by a European central bank. Such a development would aid economic and political union and, like the existence of a common currency between regions of the same country (see Section 11.2.2), would facilitate capital account adjustment between member countries. However it is now recognized that progress in this direction requires a great deal more co-operation in other fields, such as monetary and budgetary policy, than was originally acknowledged. The Marjolin Report (1975) identified such weaknesses in the previous conception of E.M.U. and suggested that co-operation on a much wider basis was required before E.M.U. is tenable. The Tindemans Report (1976) recommended a gradual approach towards E.M.U. and suggested that the countries able to proceed in the direction of monetary union should do so, and others should follow suit later when conditions became more favourable. Neither of these reports, however, have made the previous mistake of trying to set targets or deadlines for the eventual achievement of E.M.U. At the Bremen summit conference in July 1978 a new impetus was given towards monetary union by the agreement of Heads of the nine Common Market governments to press ahead with a detailed study for a new European monetary scheme. The main points of the plan, intended to promote closer economic and monetary integration in the E.E.C., are as follows.

(i)   The scheme would aim to limit fluctuations of all E.E.C. currencies against each other. The exact margins of currency fluctuations permitted have yet to be decided, but the intention is that the exchange rate margins would be at least as strict as those observed currently by participants in the snake (i.e. 2¼ per cent against other currencies). Countries not party to the snake agreement would be allowed wider margins for a temporary period.

(ii)   Exchange rate stabilization would be achieved by the setting up of a substantial E.E.C. joint fund for intervention purposes. It is envisaged that countries would deposit gold and foreign currencies equal perhaps to 20 per cent of their combined reserves (currently around $50,000 million), and in addition they would deposit their own national currencies up to a similar value. These foreign currencies would be the main means of intervention on the foreign exchange markets.

(iii)   While a substantial part of the proposed central fund would be set aside for direct exchange market intervention, it would also be authorized to issue medium-term credits in a similar

way to the I.M.F. But these credits would be made available
only if borrowers met certain conditions, as is the case with
most drawings from the I.M.F.

(iv)   E.E.C. Finance Ministers agreed to launch a detailed study
of the new currency proposals with the intention of setting up
the system by 1 January 1979.

At the time of writing (July 1978) it is uncertain whether the proposed
scheme will be introduced since certain problems remain to be
resolved before it can operate successfully.[4] It might be extremely
difficult to maintain fixed exchange rates between all E.E.C.
currencies unless some means is found of strengthening the position of
the weaker economies. Furthermore, the aim of maintaining fixed
exchange rates between E.E.C. currencies might require the
subordination of domestic policies to this purpose (see Section 8.3).
The weaker economies in particular might be reluctant, therefore, to
join the proposed European Monetary System.

13.4 Fixed versus floating exchange rates

The previous chapter and the present one have examined in detail
the operation of both a fixed and floating exchange rate system. This
section attempts to identify the major strengths and weaknesses of
these two systems. It should be recognized that floating exchange
rates have usually been adopted (e.g. in the 1930s and in 1973) when
adverse conditions have caused a breakdown in the prevailing system
of fixed exchange rates. Therefore the comparison of the two systems
in practice should take account of the unfavourable circumstances in
which floating has been introduced.

The case for floating (against fixed) exchange rates.

(a) *Simplicity.* There is no need for countries to decide what
constitutes the appropriate exchange rate or for their general
agreement on whether deficit or surplus countries are responsible for
the adjustment burden. It is simply demand and supply pressures
which determine the appropriate exchange rate for each currency.

(b) *Continuous adjustment.* If a country is suffering balance of
payments difficulties because of a long-run decline in its competitive
position, then a floating exchange rate allows a gradual depreciation
of the home currency to come about, thus providing a continuous
stimulus to exports and a continuous discouragement to imports. In
contrast, the adjustable peg system was characterized by long periods
of crisis in deficit countries such as the U.K. with exchange rate
adjustment occurring infrequently and belatedly, e.g. the devaluations of 1949 and 1967. Accordingly the operation of the adjustable
peg required deficit countries to carry out expenditure-reducing

[4] See Postscript p. 365.

policies between exchange rate adjustments, whereas floating permits automatic adjustment to take place via the exchange rate.

(c) *Independence of domestic policies*. Under the adjustable peg system, deficit countries had to direct fiscal and monetary policies at the external situation since expenditure-reducing was the only way in which the balance of payments could be improved without devaluation. In the U.K. for example, booms often had to be cut short by restrictive domestic policies as an increased demand for imports led to a deterioration in the balance of payments. Consequently internal policies were often dictated by the external situation. But if exchange rate variations are successful in bringing about automatic adjustment, then governments may have greater independence in the use of domestic policies.

(d) *Insulation from external inflation*. With fixed exchange rates, inflation abroad is transmitted directly into higher import prices. Of course the effect on the domestic price level will be influenced by the importance of imports in the home economy and by the ability of domestic industry to provide substitutes for the higher-priced imports. Floating, on the other hand, insulates a country with stable prices from world inflation since its currency would be continually appreciating, thereby offsetting the rise in import prices.

(e) *Reduced need for official reserves*. With floating, there should in theory be no need for official intervention in foreign exchange markets, and therefore no need to accumulate large stocks of official reserves. But in practice, government intervention is required to neutralize short-term disturbances in the exchange markets. Nevertheless, as long as floating exchange rates are not too volatile, there should be a reduced need for official reserves.

The case for fixed (against floating) exchange rates.

(a) *The effectiveness of current account adjustment under floating*. A floating exchange rate may not be very effective in eliminating a country's current account deficit (or reducing a current account surplus) if the elasticities of demand for imports and exports are of an inappropriate value. Therefore continuous current account adjustment via a floating exchange rate may not always be successful.

(b) *Uncertainty*. Capital flows are basically unstable, and so an overall balance of payments equilibrium can only be maintained, even with considerable official intervention in foreign exchange markets, at the expense of marked fluctuations in exchange rates. This argument is based upon the apparent instability of short-term capital flows during the period of floating. Indeed one commentator has argued that:

By its very nature, the foreign exchange market is a nervous, high risk, ultra-sensitive mechanism, primarily geared to short-term developments. Of the tens of billions of dollars in daily transactions cleared through the market, only a fraction derive from such fundamental factors as foreign trade and long-term investment. On a day-to-day basis, the market is instead dominated by short term capital movements in search of quick profits or a hedge against exchange risks.[5]

If there are considerable fluctuations in exchange rates under floating, world trade may be inhibited since traders will become reluctant to enter into commitments because the price paid on delivery may vary to such an extent that the transaction is no longer profitable to one of the parties.[6] In contrast, exchange rate fluctuations cannot by definition be a source of uncertainty in world trade under a fixed exchange rate system.

(c) *Effects on domestic inflation.* If exchange rate fluctuations are fairly large under floating, then economies with depreciating currencies should encounter rising import prices. These rising import prices will tend to feed back into domestic prices, especially if imports are a large proportion of G.D.P. and the elasticity of demand for imports is low. Indeed, Section 13.2 has already indicated that his has been the experience of the U.K. With fixed exchange rates, an inflationary impulse from the exchange rate can only arise when there is a devaluation of the domestic currency. Furthermore, supporters of fixed exchange rates argue that under their system countries have to take action to control domestic inflation or else they will lose reserves under their commitment to support the exchange rate at the prevailing parity. But with floating, it is argued, no such discipline exists. The domestic authorities can simply allow internal inflation to push down the rate of exchange.

(d) *Independence of domestic policies.* The extent to which floating exchange rates enable governments to have greater independence in their domestic policies may be exaggerated. Although the domestic authorities do not have the immediate problem of defending a fixed exchange rate under the present system, the external situation has still had an overriding influence on most countries' domestic policies, as U.K. experience has indicated.

(e) *Need for official reserves.* Because governments have extensively intervened in foreign exchange markets, the operation of floating exchange rates has, like the adjustable peg system before it, required the availability of official reserves. The major reason for this is that exchange markets appear to be fairly volatile, and therefore

---

[5] Charles A. Coombs *The Arena of International Finance* (John Wiley, 1976).
[6] Note that exchange risks can be covered by dealings in the forward exchange markets, but such transactions can be expensive.

governments have required large reserves of foreign currencies to moderate unwanted fluctuations in the exchange values of their currencies. Therefore, managed floating does not have the advantage of making redundant the holding of official reserves.

Any judgement on the preferability of fixed or floating exchange rates must take into account these considerations and recognize that it is a matter of balancing advantages against disadvantages. However, it must be acknowledged also that the conditions of the time have an important part to play in determining the feasibility of any particular type of exchange rate system. Under stable conditions some form of fixed exchange rate system may work effectively, but floating may be the only option when the world economy is in a state of instability. Thus floating has often been adopted as a last resort when a system of fixed exchange rates has collapsed, as was the case in 1973.

13.5 Prospects for the future

Major reforms of the international monetary system are rarely undertaken unless the existing system proves to be inoperable. One of the reasons for this is that it is unusual for governments to be willing to abandon existing arrangements in any sphere until they are convinced that a better alternative exists. Furthermore, a return to some kind of fixed exchange rate system requires general agreement on an appropriate structure of exchange rates and associated rules of conduct, and such agreement is unlikely to occur as long as the existing system appears to be working adequately. This latter point is supported by the practical consideration that, since the Jamaica Conference of 1976, an 85 per cent affirmative vote is required before the I.M.F. can sanction the replacement of floating with some kind of fixed exchange rate system. Nevertheless a tentative discussion of future prospects is useful since any particular system has its merits and demerits. Accordingly we examine these prospects from the point of view of adjustment, liquidity, and co-operation.

(a) *Adjustment*. The fact that floating and fixed exchange rates both have advantages and disadvantages, as we have seen in Section 13.4, implies that there is room for dispute as to which provides the 'best' system. Indeed many people prefer to have rules of conduct of the Bretton Woods type as a basis for national policies. But a return to the adjustable peg system in its old form now seems very unlikely, since the permanent payments imbalances arising from the increase in oil prices and sustained economic recession in the world economy do not provide the ideal conditions for the operation of this form of fixed exchange rate system. However, other alternatives to the existing system, apart from the adjustable peg, have been put forward.

One suggestion is for a 'crawling peg' (or 'sliding parities') system whereby exchange rates are fixed but are more frequently adjusted than under the Bretton Woods arrangements. Thus gradual adjustment can take place by stages and wider margins of fluctuation around par can provide the system with additional flexibility. Although this type of system has worked fairly effectively in Chile and Brazil in the past, its general operation presupposes that speculative capital movements would not be destabilising in the presence of wider margins around par.

(b) *Liquidity*. The steps taken at the Jamaica Conference seem to have reduced even further the role of gold as a reserve asset in the international monetary system. Indeed our earlier discussion (Section 13.1.3) has already explained that the Second Amendment to the Articles of Agreement of the I.M.F. led to the abandonment of gold as the ultimate numeraire in which exchange values are expressed, and declared the objective of making the S.D.R. the principal reserve asset. This reduced influence of gold was considered beneficial because it is expensive to produce and its supply is difficult to control. Thus a future return to some form of fixed exchange rate system may involve the adoption of the S.D.R. as the major reserve asset.

The present system of managed floating requires multi-currency intervention by the authorities now that a country's exchange rate is free to fluctuate against that of any other country. Therefore the supply of one reserve currency, that of the dollar, is no longer as important given that a variety of currencies is required for official intervention. These changes, together with the growth in the Euro-currency market, imply that the financing of balance of payments deficits is made easier by the present arrangements. But future problems may arise if the easy availability of finance encourages domestic authorities to ignore the effects of domestic inflationary pressures on the balance of payments and by such laxity contribute to worldwide inflation.

(c) *Co-operation*. Some degree of international co-operation is required under managed floating, otherwise there is a danger that the pursuit of national policies may conflict and bring about economic and political disharmony. To date, the period of floating has been associated with economic recession, and therefore co-ordinated inter-country policies may be required if world output and employment are to be fully expanded. Indeed, it has frequently been suggested that surplus countries in particular should stimulate their economies since they can afford to increase domestic output without suffering a current account deficit.

The current account surpluses in the O.P.E.C. countries have, of course, given rise to deficits elsewhere, but especially in the less-developed countries. Rising aspirations in the Third World, together with greater awareness of their problems, imply that co-operation on an international scale is required to alleviate their problems. Some steps have already been taken in this direction, in particular the growth in the lending of the World Bank and other development organizations as well as the redistribution of the profits from the official I.M.F. gold sales to the less-developed countries. One further suggestion, known as the 'Link,' is that any future issue of S.D.R.s should be linked to the objective of transferring real resources to the poorer areas of the world. But one objection to this scheme is that the Link might undermine the monetary integrity of the S.D.R., primarily because excessive production for the unlimited needs of development finance might reduce confidence in the S.D.R. as a reserve asset and so make countries reluctant to use it as such.

13.6 The European Investment Bank

In this chapter we have examined the impact of floating exchange rates on the hopes for economic and monetary union within the E.E.C. At the same time we explained the role of one E.E.C. institution, the European Monetary Co-operation Fund, in helping to moderate exchange rate fluctuations between the currencies of the members of the snake scheme. Here we intend to explain the operations of another E.E.C. institution, the European Investment Bank, which will probably have an important part to play in any future progress towards economic and monetary union within the E.E.C.

(i) *Origin and purpose.*

(a) The European Investment Bank (E.I.B.) is an E.E.C. institution set up under the Treaty of Rome in 1958 as a source of project finance primarily within the Community. The Board of Governors consists of the E.E.C. Finance Ministers (including the U.K. Chancellor of the Exchequer), who appoint a Board of Directors to carry out the day-to-day management.

(b) The terms under which the E.I.B. was formed prescribe that the purpose of finance provided shall be to support: projects aiding development of less advanced regions of the Community; modernization and conversion projects in essentially declining areas; projects, usually large, which are of interest to several member countries or the Community as a whole.

(ii) *Source of funds.*

(a) Its main source of funds is bonds and loans raised on a commercial basis on the capital markets in the E.E.C. and on other international markets also.

(b) In addition, it has capital subscribed by member states of the E.E.C. The Bank's Statute stipulates that its lending cannot exceed 250 per cent of its subscribed capital.

(iii) *Nature of its operations.*

(a) It operates on a non-profit making basis and so its interest charges are close to the average rates it has to pay in the E.E.C. and international capital markets. These relatively low interest rates make it an attractive source of finance to borrowers, and the fact that it is a non-profit making organization means that it can involve itself in socially-orientated projects which may have long pay-off periods.

(b) Loans are intended to supplement finance obtained from other sources, and so the E.I.B. only lends up to 40 per cent of the cost of fixed investments of a project with a minimum size of around £1 million. The term of the loan is approximately 7–12 years for industrial projects but can go up to 20 years for infrastructure investments (these are investments in areas such as energy, transport, and communications which are beneficial to economic expansion in general).

(c) It is also intended to help finance small ventures and the E.I.B. grants 'global loans' to intermediary financial institutions, such as the I.C.F.C.[7] in the U.K., which on-lend the funds for suitable projects after prior approval from the E.I.B. Finance for major projects is provided by loans negotiated directly with the Bank.

(d) Adequate security for loans is required since the E.I.B. itself borrows at commercial rates. Thus the Bank prefers a guarantee from industrial or financial groups associated with the project, a public authority, or from the government in whose territory the project is being undertaken.

(e) E.I.B. loans are usually made in the form of a 'cocktail' of several currencies, depending upon the currencies which the Bank has available at the time of the loan. Loan repayments are due in the currencies in which they are made.

(f) Repayments can be delayed for up to four years until the project yields a return but thereafter they are normally due in six-monthly instalments.

(g) The European Unit of Account (E.U.A.) is the unit used in the E.I.B. accounts and is defined in terms of a basket of member currencies. The value of the E.U.A. is based on fixed quantities of

[7] The I.C.F.C. is now part of the Finance for Industry group.

E.E.C. members' currencies, and so its value varies according to the fluctuations in the exchange values of E.E.C. currencies and their respective weighting in the calculation of the E.U.A. It is interesting to note that most supporters of economic and monetary union within the E.E.C. suggest that the value of any future common currency should be calculated in a similar manner to the E.U.A.

(iv) *Recipients of loans.*
(a) At the end of December 1976, the E.I.B. had outstanding loans of £3,636 million. Around 87 per cent went to projects located within the E.E.C. with about three-quarters of this directed into regional development. Italy was the largest single beneficiary, but the U.K. was the second largest. Indeed the U.K. has received some very substantial loans, which include four, totalling £47·8 million, granted to the British Gas Corporation for parts of a pipeline system to bring natural gas from the Frigg field in the North Sea.
(b) The E.I.B. also lends outside the E.E.C. to the less-developed countries and, although this represents a small proportion of the total lending, it is growing in importance.

13.7 Summary

i. Under managed floating, exchange rates are free to move according to market forces but governments intervene in an attempt to stabilize any short-term fluctuations. The characteristic features of an international monetary system based on floating are:
(a) *adjustment* can now come about automatically via the exchange rate although the success of this mechanism depends upon the elasticity of demand for imports and exports as far as the current account is concerned, and on the stability of capital flows for an overall balance of payments.
(b) *liquidity* is based less on the dollar or other key reserve assets and more on variety of currencies, since multi-currency intervention is required in exchange markets;
(c) *co-operation* seems to be less of an immediate necessity with market-determined exchange rates, but co-ordination of national policies still seems desirable if conflict and economic stagnation are to be avoided in the long run.

ii. U.K. experience of managed floating seems to suggest that the exchange rate is not very effective in eliminating current account deficits, perhaps because of the inelastic demand for imports and Britain's consistently high domestic inflation rate compared with her trading competitors. Furthermore, the volatility of capital flows has meant that foreign exchange markets have frequently been subject to heavy speculative pressures which have brought about undesirable fluctuations in exchange rates.

iii. The general adoption of floating has also posed problems for the objective of economic and monetary union within the E.E.C. It had been hoped that the removal of exchange rate fluctuations between E.E.C. currencies would constitute the first stage toward monetary union, but the widespread acceptance of floating has made this aim more difficult to achieve.

iv. Both fixed and floating exchange rates have advantages and disadvantages, although the history of managed floating to date does cast doubt on some of the stronger claims originally made in favour of floating. However, floating has occurred previously, as in 1973, because of a breakdown in fixed exchange rates rather than as a result of a collective decision based on an assessment of its relative advantages. The success of floating should be judged in the light of the fact that it has usually operated under unfavourable circumstances and thus the concerted adoption of floating exchange rates in more stable circumstances might well yield different results and evaluation.

14
A simple macroeconomic model

14.1 Introduction

In the remainder of the book we intend to examine macroeconomic theory and policy in order that the reader can appreciate how government decisions in the area of fiscal and monetary policy affect the economy in general and the banking and financial system in particular. But before we can understand the operation of macroeconomic management it is first necessary to construct a simple model within which some of the more fundamental macroeconomic relationships can be identified and explained.

The purpose of any model is to identify and summarize the more important features of the problem under investigation. Economic models are particularly useful since millions of daily transactions are carried out in the real world and so some means must be found of expressing the essential characteristics of the problem at hand. A macroeconomic model by its very nature must be highly simplified since its purpose is to simulate what is happening in the economy as a whole. It is only on the basis of such a model that the government, which considers one of its basic functions to be the management of the economy, can predict what the effect will be of a change in one of its policies. However the danger with relying upon such a model is that the necessity to summarize and simplify the more relevant economic relationships can lead to the omission or misrepresentation of some important features. This potential weakness has to be borne in mind when macroeconomic models are used as a basis for policy prescription.

The rest of this chapter will be concerned with developing one particular model, known as the income–expenditure model,[1] which has frequently been used as a basis for explaining the operation of fiscal policy. Our basic model is developed from the circular flow relationship that was established in Chapter 1, and so the reader is recommended to refer to that chapter as a background for the present

[1] The model we are going to examine is one version of the income–expenditure model: other more complicated versions are often used in macroeconomics texts.

discussion. Readers who find the discussion too brief may wish to consult one of the many basic economics textbooks which cover this area.[2]

14.2 The basic model

Our basic model is developed from the circular flow approach which we adopted in Chapter 1. In Figure 1.1 we divided the economy into two sectors, households and firms, and we assumed that all the households' income earned in the current week was used to purchase the output of firms. Accordingly total expenditure (E) in the period under consideration was composed entirely of consumers' expenditure (C), and total income (Y) in the community was identical to this expenditure. The assumptions can be expressed as follows:

Income (Y) = Expenditure (E) = Consumers' expenditure (C). However, we did point out in Chapter 1 that the above summary is an over-simplified representation of the real world, not least because it ignores the existence of the government and external sectors. We have explained elsewhere in this book that the government sector gives rise to taxation and expenditure flows (see Chapter 9) and that the external sector gives rise to export and import flows (see Chapter 11). At the same time we have to take account of the fact that some of the households' income will be channelled into saving, and that additional spending on the output of firms will arise from investment. How, then, can the circular flow be extended to include all these other flows?

If we analyse all the uses to which income is put, then it is immediately obvious that for the economy as a whole consumers' expenditure on goods produced in the domestic circular flow is only one element. Some income will be taken in direct taxation, such as income tax, and so will not be available for other uses. The amount of income left over after deduction of this taxation is known as disposable income. This disposable income is not all directed into consumption on goods and services produced by firms in the domestic economy because some portion will be saved and some part will be used to purchase goods and services produced by firms in other countries (i.e. imports). Therefore we can classify the various uses of income as in *Figure 14.1*. We can refer to taxation, saving, and imports as *leakages* from the domestic circular flow as such flows are not immediately used to purchase goods and services produced in the domestic economy. However these flows may be ultimately recycled into the domestic circular flow because governments invariably spend

[2]See, for example, R. G. Lipsey, *Positive Economics* 4th ed. (Weidenfeld and Nicolson, 1975).

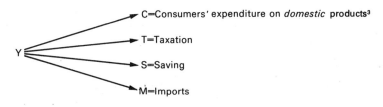

FIG 14.1

what they raise in taxation, expenditure on investment goods is frequently financed out of current saving, and other countries often spend on domestically-produced goods and services at the same time as we purchase their products. But the point is that there is no *automatic* mechanism to ensure that taxation, saving, and import flows are immediately returned to the domestic circular flow.

If we examine all the categories of total expenditure in the economy, then consumption of domestic products is only one component. Aggregate expenditure also consists of government spending, exports, and investment, all of which contribute to the demand for domestically- produced goods and services. Therefore we may classify the various types or expenditure as in *Figure 14.2*. We can refer to government expenditure, investment, and exports as *injections* into the circular flow because they add to consumers' expenditure on domestic products. This total expenditure is often referred to as *aggregate demand,* i.e. the total demand for goods and services in the economy which arises from consumption on domestic products, government expenditure, investment, and exports.

FIG 14.1

Now that we have identified the types of leakages and injections associated with the circular flow, we can begin to explain the assumptions that the basic model makes about the determinants of these various flows.

[3] In Chapter 1 we used C to refer to *total* consumption, i.e. consumption on domestically-produced goods and services plus imports.

(a) *Consumers' domestic expenditure* (C) is assumed to be related to income levels (Y). This consumption relationship in its simplest form is often expressed as:

$$C = a + bY \text{ where}$$

　　a = some constant consumption irrespective of income levels; and

　　b = some fraction of additional income (known as the marginal propensity to consume) which would be less than 1 but greater than 0 for the community as a whole.

Many detailed studies have been carried out on the nature of the consumption relationship and all seem to agree that, for the community as a whole, consumption is related in some way to income.

(b) *Taxation* (T) in the circular flow has been interpreted as income taxation and is the difference between gross and disposable income. Other forms of taxation may be introduced as well, but for the sake of simplicity we will confine our discussion to income taxation. It is taken for granted that such taxation is related to income levels because the amount taken in income tax varies directly with incomes.

(c) *Saving* (S) in the economy is assumed to be related to income levels also, in a similar manner to consumption. The proportion of any additional income that is saved (the marginal propensity to save) will tend to vary according to the tastes and preferences of the individual, and one might expect the proportion that is saved to increase as income increases. For the community as a whole, however, total saving will tend to vary directly with the level of income.

(d) *Imports* (M) will absorb a certain fraction of any additional income received by the community, the relevant proportion being known as the marginal propensity to import. The actual proportion will depend upon many factors, but whatever the fraction the basic model assumes that import spending is directly related to income. Again, this seems a justifiable assumption to make because the experience of the U.K. and other countries confirms that imports rise when incomes rise.

(e) *Government expenditure* (G) is determined by political decision, as we noted in Chapter 9. Accordingly, the model assumes that government spending is determined by factors outside the circular flow. In other words, the level of government expenditure is assumed to be exogenous, i.e. given from outside the model.

(f) *Investment expenditure* (I) also is assumed to be exogenous in our model, with factors such as business confidence and the expectations of entrepreneurs being considered more important determinants of the level of investment than the current level of income. However this may be an over-simplified assumption because the current level of economic activity will certainly influence business expectations and confidence. It is recognized, also, that investment may be influenced by interest rates, with fluctuations in the latter having a direct effect on the cost of borrowed funds and therefore on the profitability of potential investments. This relationship should be borne in mind when we examine monetary policy in the next two chapters.

(g) *Exports* (X) from the domestic economy are related to income levels in the rest of the world, along with other factors such as the exchange rate (see Section 11.2.1). The value of exports is assumed to be determined by factors outside the domestic circular flow and so is assumed to be exogenous in our model.

In summary, our basic model assumes that leakages from the circular flow (T.S.M.) are determined within the model by income levels, and so can be described as endogenous. Injections of expenditure (G.I.X.) are exogenous, however, because they are given from outside the model.

Now that we have classified the various sources of income and types of expenditure, as well as identifying the assumptions that the model makes about the nature of these flows, the next matter to discuss is the relationship between total income (Y) and aggregate expenditure (E). In Figure 1.1 the reader will notice that income equals expenditure in the period under consideration. In fact income and expenditure also will be identical when we take into account all the various leakages and injections connected with the circular flow, because income and expenditure are simply two different ways of measuring the value of the same set of economic transactions. Expenditure by one party will be equivalent to income for another, and so total income must be equal to aggregate expenditure in the domestic circular flow. Indeed the National Income Accounts measure the value of goods and services produced in the economy (Gross Domestic Product), by both an income and expenditure method. The use of these two methods of estimating Gross Domestic Product (G.D.P.) provides a cross-check on the accuracy of the recorded information. Income must equal expenditure when all the sources of income and types of expenditure are classified and measured.

We are now in a position to express our discussion in terms of a set of definitions:

$$Y \equiv C + T + S + M$$
$$E \equiv C + G + I + X$$
$$Y \equiv E$$
$$\text{therefore } C + T + S + M \equiv C + G + I + X$$
$$\text{or } T + S + M \equiv G + I + X$$
$$\text{and } (G-T) + (I-S) + (X-M) \equiv 0$$

The Appendix has explained how the last expression can be used as a basis for illustrating the flow-of-funds accounts, with each of the bracketed expressions representing the various sectors in the economy. But here the reader should notice that total injections (G + I + X) must equal total leakages (T + S + M). How, then, are these flows brought into balance in the model which we are investigating? It is at this point that the assumptions made about the nature of injections and leakages are relevant. For instance, imagine that there are increased injections into the circular flow in the form of investment, or government expenditure, or imports. Income will start to rise as a result of this additional spending, but leakages will rise also because taxation, saving, and imports are all related to the level of national income. In other words, extra spending automatically generates additional leakages from the circular flow. Accordingly, income and expenditure will increase as a result of additional injections of spending until once again total injections equal total leakages, but at a *higher* level of income and expenditure. On the other hand reduced injections will have a contractionary effect on income levels in the domestic circular flow. Leakages of saving, taxation, and imports will fall as income declines until once again total leakages equal total injections. In this case, however, the economy will operate at a *lower* level of income and expenditure.

So, it is variations in income levels which equate total injections and leakages, even though these flows are the results of the decisions of millions of different economic agents. This equality comes about in our basic model through leakages being directly related to income levels. The important question, however, is at what *level* of national income (and therefore national prosperity) will injections equal leakages and income equal expenditure? The answer to this question is of concern to government because it has responsibility for managing the economy in the interests of the community.

14.3 The multiplier

In the previous section we indicated the *direction* of changes in national income and aggregate demand when there were increased or reduced injections into the circular flow. The other crucial feature of the process is the *magnitude* of change in national income: if injections increase by £100 million, for example, does national income rise by the same amount?

We will investigate the magnitude of change in national income by first of all considering changes in government expenditure, one of the three categories of injections. Suppose the government spends an additional £100 million on the construction of a new motorway. This £100 million will be received by workers, contractors, suppliers, etc., who are engaged on building the motorway and so the first round effect will be an equivalent increase in national income of £100 million (remember, income must equal expenditure).

Let us suppose that the proportion of any additional income absorbed as leakages is 0·6. Therefore £60 million of the additional income will be channelled into taxation, saving, and imports with the remaining £40 million being spent on consumer goods and services produced in the domestic economy. This extra consumers' expenditure will give rise to additional income of £40 million in those domestic industries producing the required goods and services. The second-round effect of the increased government expenditure will be a further increase in national income of £40 million.

Again some proportion (60 per cent) of this additional income will leak from the circular flow while the remainder is passed on as extra consumers' expenditure on domestic goods and services. This time £24 million (£40 million × 0·6) will be absorbed in leakages and £16 million will be received as additional income in the circular flow. The third round effect of the increase in government expenditure will be a further increase of £16 million in national income.

The process will continue, and with each stage the amount of income passed on to others in the circular flow will be reduced by leakages of taxation, saving, and imports. The following increases in national income will take place after the initial increase in government expenditure of £100 million:

£100 million, £40 million, £16 million, £6·4 million, £2·56 million, etc.

A simple formula exists for calculating the sum of such a series:

Total increase in income $= \dfrac{\text{Initial expenditure}}{1 - \text{proportion of income spent on domestic products}}$

$= \dfrac{\text{£100 million}}{1 - 0\cdot4}$

$= \dfrac{\text{£100 million}}{0\cdot6}$

$= $ £167 million (approximately).

This amount represents the total increase in national income following from the initial injection of government expenditure. Indeed the total increase in national income (£167 million) divided by the initial injection of expenditure (£100 million) is known as the *multiplier*. When leakages absorb 60 per cent of any additional income, therefore, the value of the multiplier is 1·67.[4] This value is simply the reciprocal of the proportion of income taken in leakages, i.e. 1/0·6 = 1·67.

We are now in a position to see the significance of government expenditure and taxation flows in the determination of national income levels. An increase or decrease in government spending will stimulate or contract national income by an amount given by the value of the multiplier. A similar effect takes place when the government changes the rate at which taxation is levied because such changes alter the proportion of additional income which is absorbed by leakages. For instance, a cut in the basic rate of income tax would reduce the proportion of income taken in leakages and so would increase the value of the multiplier. Government spending and taxation will therefore have a magnified effect on total income and expenditure flows, thereby providing the fiscal authorities with a very useful tool for managing the economy.

We could examine the workings of the multiplier by considering changes in other injections into the circular flow. An increase in exports would be particularly beneficial in that the balance of payments would improve and at the same time national income will rise by an amount greater than the initial increase in exports. If we retain the assumption that leakages constitute 60 per cent of additional income, then a multiplier of 1·67 would apply to the increase in exports. The multiplier process would apply to additional investment expenditures also, but with both exports and investment expenditures the government has little direct control over the size of these flows. Certainly the government may exert an indirect influence on these injections (e.g. investment may be encouraged by lower interest rates), but the degree of control is not as powerful or certain as that which it exercises over government expenditure. Of course changes in national income also can be brought about by variations in the proportion of national income that is taken in imports and saving. Again, however, the authorities cannot control these leakages directly whereas they can vary tax rates through their own budgetary powers. Accordingly, variations in government spending and taxation might provide the best avenue for policies

[4] It has been estimated that the value of the multiplier in the U.K. economy during 1976 was 1·45 (see A. R. Prest and D. J. Coppock, *The U.K. Economy*, 6th ed. Weidenfeld and Nicolson, 1976).

aimed at controlling the level of national income. This is not to say that other injections and leakages are less significant, only that they are less easy for governments to control.

14.4 Fiscal policy

Since the government has responsibility for managing the economy, it is particularly interested in the level of national income generated by the circular flow process. More precisely, the government has certain economic objectives that it would wish to achieve and all are affected in some way by national income levels. The reader is referred to Chapter 16 for a more thorough discussion of the compatibility of these economic objectives. At this point, however, it is useful if we explain briefly what the principal economic objectives are and how their attainment is influenced by the level of national income.

Full employment. National income is a measure of the money value of goods and services produced in the economy during a certain period of time. The money value of goods and services is derived from two components, quantity and price. If an increase in national income is the result of an increase in the quantity of goods and services produced, then we would expect the level of employment to rise as more people are employed in the production of additional output. The employment objective may be attained, therefore, by increasing the quantity of goods and services produced. One obvious policy for the achievement of this objective is for government to stimulate aggregate demand by some means or other. The preferred method may be through variations in government expenditure and taxation since these flows are under the direct control of the authorities.

Stable prices. Rapid inflation is regarded as undesirable for many reasons, not least because of the danger it poses for the stability of the economic and political system (see Chapter 16 for further discussion). Accordingly one of the objectives of government may be to achieve stable prices, or more realistically to reduce the rate at which prices are rising. But when governments expand aggregate demand in an attempt to secure the employment objective, there is a danger that the extra spending will increase prices rather than output. In theory it is conceivable for any increase in aggregate demand to raise output and employment levels so long as full employment of the labour force has not been reached. After full employment is reached, extra spending will only serve to add to the rate of inflation. In practice, however, bottlenecks in production are likely to develop well before this physical limit is reached because of equipment and labour shortages in specific industries. In such circumstances the achievement of the prices objective may necessitate a reduction in aggregate demand through cuts in government expenditure and increased taxes.

Balance of payments equilibrium. For most countries the achievement of a balance of payments equilibrium is desirable because the authorities can then apply their economic policies solely for domestic purposes. We have argued earlier that the value of imports is related to the level of national income in the domestic economy and that the value of exports is related to aggregate demand abroad. Therefore an expansion of aggregate demand in the domestic economy which is not matched by comparable increases in other economies will result in a deterioration in the balance of payments. Conversely, a contraction in domestic national income relative to that in other countries may improve the balance of payments.

A high rate of growth. The rate of growth is a measure of the increase in output over a period of time. But booms and slumps in economic activity occur periodically so that the relevant time-period over which to measure economic growth is a number of years, e.g. the average rate of growth of output over 10 years. Over such periods high growth rates, and rapid improvements in living standards, are dependent upon an increase in productive capacity rather than on temporary changes in the level of demand. However investment is required to augment productive capacity, and the maintenance of a high and stable level of aggregate demand may provide the appropriate environment for high investment expenditures.

Our brief discussion of economic objectives and their relationship to the level of national income suggests that control over aggregate demand is necessary if the government is to achieve all or some of these objectives. U.K. governments have relied traditionally upon fiscal policy, i.e. variations in government expenditure and taxation, as the primary weapon to achieve its objectives. The income–expenditure model has often been used as a framework for justifying this role for fiscal policy because government expenditure and taxation directly and fairly reliably influence national income levels. Fiscal policy can be used in three different ways:

(a) *A budget deficit.* This is the situation when government expenditure exceeds taxation receipts, as we have seen to be the case in the U.K. during recent years (see Chapter 9). A budget deficit is the traditional response of the government to the problems posed by a slump in economic activity. Keynes first suggested in the 1930s that the government should take action through its own budget to stimulate aggregate demand and then wait for the multiplier effect on national income, output, and employment.

(b) *A budget surplus.* This course of action involves setting taxation receipts to exceed government expenditure. It is the traditional response of governments to the problems posed by an over-expansion of aggregate demand in the economy and inflation. Under these circumstances a budget surplus may be used to tackle such problems.

(c) *A balanced budget.* This fiscal position is achieved when government expenditure equals taxation receipts. It may be the appropriate course of action to take when the government is broadly satisfied with the state of the economy, although this is very rarely the case. It is interesting to note that the balanced budget was the traditional maxim of governments before they became responsible for managing the economy, the argument being that the government should plan to spend no more than it receives, except in wartime.

The preceding discussion suggests that the operation of fiscal policy should pose few difficulties. But the typical situation facing the government has been what to do when the economy suffers from more than one problem simultaneously, e.g. unemployment *and* inflation. The co-existence of these two problems means that a choice must be made between a budget deficit and a budget surplus depending on the government's preference: higher employment or stable prices. The response of most governments has been to manipulate the economy in order to secure some trade-off between the conflicting economic objectives. This question of trade-offs, and the 'fine-tuning' of the economy in order to achieve these objectives, will be examined further in Chapter 16.

Two other considerations relevant to the conduct of fiscal policy also should be mentioned. Firstly, when governments plan for a budget deficit or surplus they tend to rely more upon changes in taxation rather than in their expenditures. Part of the explanation for this is that government spending tends to be planned over a number of years (e.g. hospitals, schools, and other capital expenditure takes several years to complete; governments are reluctant to dismiss teachers, policemen, and other employees for short-term economic reasons), consequently such expenditure tends to be fairly inflexible, especially downwards, in the short run. In contrast, tax rates are relatively easy to alter and so are the major instruments through which fiscal policy is carried out when changing economic conditions require action. Secondly, when governments spend in excess of taxation receipts the budget deficit incurred will be reduced as income levels rise and taxation receipts subsequently increase. Thus part of the expense of an increase in government expenditure will be met by additional taxation receipts as national income and expenditure rise to higher levels than previously.

Now that we have outlined the basic operations of fiscal policy, it is desirable to conclude by pointing out some of the limitations of this approach to economic management.

(a) The achievement of a predetermined budgetary target (deficit or surplus) may prove difficult. When the government makes fiscal decisions it has to estimate the levels of taxation and expenditure that are required to achieved the desired level of economic activity in the time-period in question, typically a financial year. However, this forecasting exercise is subject to error because other income and expenditure flows as well as taxation and government spending affect the level of economic activity. Even though fiscal decisions have calculable effects on national income levels once the value of the multiplier is known, these other income and expenditure flows are outside the direct control of the authorities. Therefore economic activity may diverge from the expected level, and these forecasting errors in turn will lead to a change in the actual budget surplus/deficit because most items of taxation and some types of government spending vary with national income levels.

(b) The supporters of fiscal policy as the principal macroeconomic policy defend their position by arguing that changes in government expenditure have a *direct* effect on economic activity. The argument is that government spending and taxation unambiguously influence total income and expenditure. But this approach tends to neglect the monetary effects of budgetary decisions. Earlier chapters (see Chapter 10 especially) have indicated how the financing of budget deficits has implications for the size of the money supply and the level of interest rates, and it is to the relationship between these monetary variables and economic activity that we will turn in Chapter 15. However, *our* basic model may be criticized in advance of this discussion in so far as it ignores the monetary effects of fiscal decisions.

(c) The achievement of multiple economic objectives is especially difficult if the government relies exclusively upon one type of policy which operates essentially through the channel of aggregate demand. Accordingly, additional policies may be required to complement fiscal policy if the government is to have a better chance of achieving its various objectives.

14.5 Summary

i. In our basic model we established that: (a) total expenditure (or aggregate demand) derives from consumers' expenditure on domestically-produced goods and services (C), government expenditure (G), investment (I), and exports (X); (b) national income (Y) consists of consumers' expenditure on domestically-produced goods and services (C), taxation (T), saving (S), and imports (M); (c) aggregate demand is equivalent to national income. From these relationships it was established that total leakages (T+S+M) must equal total injections (G+I+X).

ii. Since leakages are assumed to be related to income, and injections are assumed exogenous, then variations in income equate total income and expenditure flows in the circular flow model. The important question, however, is at what *level* of national income does income equal expenditure?

iii. Governments have a direct influence over the process of national income determination through their control over public expenditure (G) and taxation (T) flows. The management of the economy through fiscal policy is assisted by the multiplier which magnifies any injection of expenditures or leakages of income into or out of the circular flow.

iv. Fiscal policy provides government with a potentially powerful method of managing the economy in order to achieve its macroeconomic objectives. However government expenditure and taxation flows also exert an influence on monetary variables – and therefore affect economic activity – since the size and financing of the public sector borrowing requirement are crucial elements in the determination of the money supply and interest rates.

15
Money and economic activity

The last two chapters of the book are primarily concerned with the problems and policies of macroeconomic management, with special emphasis being given to the role of monetary policy. Before we can look at the appropriate policies for macroeconomic management, we must first investigate the theoretical relationship between money and economic activity. Such a discussion is essential since it enables us to judge the degree to which the successful conduct of monetary policy can influence economic activity and thereby achieve economic objectives.

For quite a long time the prevailing view among economists had been that money does not affect the relative prices of commodities, but that it does determine the overall price level. These ideas, embodied in the so-called Quantity Theory of money, dominated economic thinking until the 1930s. Since then we have witnessed the development first of all of the 'Keynesian' view of the importance of money, followed by the 'monetarist' view which is at odds with the former and is closely associated with the original Quantity Theory. It is the aim of this chapter to examine these theoretical issues, especially the Keynesian versus monetarist debate, since theoretical controversy has had a profound influence on the attitude of most governments towards monetary policy as an approach to macroeconomic management.

15.1 The Quantity Theory

The Quantity Theory reflected the view of economists prior to the 1930s that the quantity of money in existence does not have an effect on the real sector of the economy (that is on output and employment levels), but does determine the general price level. The Quantity Theory is based on the following relationship, which is known as the equation of exchange:

$$MV = PT$$

where M = the quantity of money in the economy;

V = the velocity of circulation, or the average number of times a unit of money is used in a stated period;

P=the general price level, expressed as an index;

T=the total number of transactions in the stated time-period. As expressed here, the relationship between MV and PT constitutes a truism, or identity, as can be illustrated by an example. Consider a simple economy consisting of one fisherman and one farmer. During a particular week the fisherman sells the farmer two fish at £4 per fish, and during the same week the farmer sells the fisherman eight loaves at £1 per loaf. So the total number of transactions will be ten, and the average price of each transaction is £16/10=£1·60. Suppose the money stock consists of only eight £1 notes, then what will be the velocity of circulation of the money stock during the week under consideration? Of course some pound notes may be used more frequently than others, and some may not be used at all, but the velocity of circulation measures the *average* number of times a unit of currency is used. Since the value of transactions is £16 and the quantity of money is £8, the velocity of circulation is 2. We can express the above information as follows:

$$M=\pounds 8, \quad P=\pounds 1·60,$$
$$V=2, \quad T=10.$$
$$\text{i.e.} \quad MV=PT=\pounds 16.$$

In fact MV *must* equal PT since both simply measure the same set of economic transactions in two different ways: indeed we can only observe P,T, and M, so V cannot be calculated independently of the rest of the variables in the equation, as can be seen in our example. Now if V and T are fixed, or are uninfluenced by M (i.e. V and T are independent of M), then the equation of exchange can be expressed as the Quantity Theory which states that an increase/decrease in M will lead directly to an increase/decrease in P.

But why should T and V be fixed, or independent of M? Before the sustained economic recession of the inter-war years it was thought that the economy automatically moved towards full employment, even though periodic booms and slumps were experienced at the time. Thus the total number of transactions (T) in the economy can be taken to be fixed if full employment is the norm, or alternatively the assumption that the quantity of money has no effect on the real sector of the economy implies that T is independent of M. Consequently there should be a definite relationship between the quantity of money and the price level if the velocity of circulation can also be shown to be independent of M.

Supporters of the Quantity Theory argued that V will be influenced by the customs and payments practices prevailing at the time, and that these change only slowly over time. If, for example, workers are paid weekly, then a smaller amount of money will be required compared with a monthly system of payment; a worker will require to hold money balances to meet his purchases only for a maximum of one week at any particular point in time. But with monthly payment, money balances will be held to meet expenditures up to one month in the future. So although the quantity of money required will be larger in the case of monthly payment, the velocity of circulation will be lower than for weekly payment (assuming total spending is the same). Therefore it was supposed that payments practices, and other institutional arrangements which change only slowly over time, have more influence on the velocity of circulation than any temporary changes in M. But can we conclude from this that V is independent of M? An increase in the quantity of money given the payments practices will mean that, other things remaining unchanged, a typical unit of currency will now be used less often and so the velocity of circulation should fall. In other words, V may be affected by M. Of course another possibility is that the increase in the quantity of money will lead instead to a rise in prices rather than a change in the velocity of circulation, but the Quantity Theory does not explain why this should be the case.

15.2 The Keynesian and monetarist views of the demand for money

The Quantity Theory fell into disrepute during the adverse conditions of the inter-war period when there no longer appeared to be a direct link between the money supply and the price level. During these years J. M. Keynes developed new theories to account for the sustained economic recession of the time – the central elements of this theory were discussed in Chapter 14 – and at the same time he examined the importance of money by analysing the underlying reasons why there is a demand to hold money.

The traditional Keynesian approach divides the demand for money into three elements: the transactions, precautionary, and speculative demands. The *transactions demand* is related to the function money performs as a medium of exchange in that a certain quantity of money balances is required by economic transactors simply to purchase the goods and services they expect to buy during the period in question. For example, a man may earn £100 per week and out of this he may plan to spend £70, and thus his transactions demand would be £70 in this particular week. What factors influence the size of the transactions demand? In most cases a man earning £300 per week would be expected to spend more than the man earning £100 per week, and so the transactions demand should be larger for the former. Furthermore, during inflation money incomes will normally rise together with prices and so more money will be required simply to purchase the same collection of goods and services. For both these reasons, therefore, one would expect the transactions demand to be a function of money incomes.

In our example the man earning £100 per week plans to spend only £70, therefore he can save the remainder and purchase a range of financial assets such as building society shares or national savings certificaties and thereby earn a rate of return. However, such savings cannot immediately be turned into cash since there is inconvenience, cost and even uncertainty of value with some financial assets. Accordingly the man in our example may prefer to keep an additional fraction of his income as money balances in excess of his transactions demand, just in case something unexpected happens which necessitates immediate expenditure. For example, the man may travel to work each day by car and so carry an extra £20 with him just in case his vehicle breaks down and needs to be repaired at once. This *precautionary demand* for money will also be related to money incomes since: (a) the higher your regular income then normally the more expensive are the items you own, e.g. the Rolls-Royce is usually more expensive to repair than the Mini; (b) if money incomes rise due to inflation then the same items cost more to replace or repair.

If the level of money incomes in the economy is known, it might be possible to estimate the transactions and precautionary demand for money. The extent to which the money supply exceeds this combined transactions and precautionary demand determines the amount of money left over to satisfy the *speculative demand*. If the transactions and precautionary demands are estimated at £80 million during a certain time period, and the money supply is fixed at £100 million, then the speculative demand is £20 million. These speculative balances are available for the purchase of types of wealth such as financial assets, since wealth held as money, although it has the advantage of being perfectly liquid, earns no rate of return. A crucial Keynesian assumption is that if holders of speculative money balances decide to hold their wealth in some other form, they are likely to purchase financial assets since these are taken to be closer substitutes for money than other types of assets. The idea of substitution has been examined earlier in Section 2.4.2, but the reader is reminded by an example. Butter and margarine are close substitutes, and so any increase in the price of butter would be expected to lead to an increased demand for margarine as consumers substitute the latter for the relatively more expensive butter. In a similar way, the Keynesians argue that changes in rates of interest (price) bring about substitution between various financial assets, including money. Thus speculative balances are likely first of all to be spent on financial assets which are close substitutes for money, rather than on real assets such as land, buildings, and the like.

But will speculative balances always be used to purchase financial assets, or will economic transactors prefer in some cases to hold wealth in a perfectly liquid form? To answer this question it is first necessary to examine the relationship between the price of a financial asset and its yield. If we take an undated bond as an example of a financial asset, Section 10.2 has already explained that the price of the bond and its yield have an inverse relationship. In the case of dated bonds and other financial assets there will still be an inverse relationship between the market price and yield, but it will not be proportional. Now the holder of speculative balances not only has to consider the yield on close substitutes such as bonds, but he also has to take into account any prospective capital gains or losses which may accrue when buying the bond. If holders of speculative balances are of the general opinion that the price of bonds will fall in the near future (i.e. their yield will rise), then they will not purchase these assets at the moment because they will suffer a capital loss if their expectations are borne out by experience. Instead they will prefer to remain liquid, and this will give rise to a large speculative demand for money in preference to other forms of financial wealth. Thus the speculative demand for money will be strongly influenced by the expectations of the market as to the future course of financial asset prices.

What, then, are the implications of an increase in the money supply according to the Keynesian view of the demand for money? Since there is no reason to expect money incomes to be directly affected by the money supply, we can assume that the transactions and precautionary demands remain unchanged. The extra money balances are therefore available as a direct form of wealth holding, or else they can be used to purchase financial assets for which they are a close substitute. An increased demand for financial assets will lead to a rise in their price, and thus a fall in their yields. Consequently the first effect of an increase in the money supply is expected to be a decrease in interest rates. Of course market expectations may constrain the movements in interest rates since any increase in the money supply could simply be absorbed into speculative balances if the general opinion is that the price of financial assets will fall in the near future. Under these circumstances the rate of interest will not fall any further. But, apart from this possibility, an increase in the money supply should lead to a fall in interest rates, other things being equal.

An alternative view is closely associated with the work of Milton Friedman from the middle 1950s onwards. Over this period an influential school of thought called monetarism has developed around his ideas and has come to challenge the Keynesian orthodoxy as the dominant academic influence over monetary policy. Friedman set about re-defining the Quantity Theory in such a manner that it can be expressed as a demand for money relationship.[1] He argues that money is just one form in which wealth can be held, other forms including bonds, equities, *and* physical goods such as houses, property, and even consumer durables. The actual proportion in which each individual holds his wealth depends upon the relative yields he receives on the whole range of assets, and upon his individual tastes and preferences. The yields concerned may be of the direct money kind, as is the case with equities and bonds, but may be implicit in the form of services or benefits received, as with owner-occupied houses. The individual receives an implicit yield on money because of its convenience value as a means of payment. Thus the demand for money is seen to depend upon the relative yield or attraction of money and a wide range of other assets.

Since the demand for money is related to a number of variables, according to Friedman and the monetarists, then it may be difficult to measure the precise effect of a change in one of these variables on the demand for money. However, the basic argument of the monetarists is that money is a unique asset which is not a close substitute for any particular range of assets, but instead is a substitute for all assets both real and financial. This fundamental point is illustrated by the nature of Friedman's re-definition of the Quantity Theory as a demand for money function related to the yields on a wide range of alternative assets. Thus the substitutability of money for other assets is the crucial area of difference between the Keynesians and monetarists: whereas the former argue that money is a close substitute for financial assets, the latter claim that money is a substitute for all assets.

What, then, are the implications of an increase in the money supply according to the monetarists? The increased supply of money will encourage economic transactors to substitute other forms of wealth for money as the convenience yield on excess money balances will be exceeded by the potential yields on the wide range of alternative assets. Increased demand for these assets, both real and financial, will lead to a rise in their price. Therefore an increase in the money supply should eventually bring about a rise in the price level, as is predicted by the crude Quantity Theory, and this will probably be followed by an increase in money incomes as wages adjust upwards to compensate for the higher prices.

The Keynesian and monetarist views seem to lead to very different conclusions as far as monetary policy is concerned. But it is first necessary to consult the available empirical evidence on the relevant theoretical issues before we turn to their recommendations for the

[1]See M. Friedman, 'The Quantity Theory of Money – a Restatement,' *Studies in the Quantity Theory of Money* (1956).

conduct of monetary policy. The essential difference between the two views is that the Keynesians believe that money is a close substitute for financial assets, whereas the monetarists argue that money is not a particularly close substitute for any specific range of assets. The Keynesian would therefore expect there to be a close relationship between the demand for money and the yield (rate of interest) on close money substitutes, but the monetarist would expect no particularly significant relationship because of his belief that money is a substitute for all assets alike. The empirical evidence does suggest that there is a definite relationship between the demand for money and the interest rate on near-money substitutes, *but* it is not as strong as the Keynesian theory suggests. Therefore the extreme versions of both theories do not seem to be supported by the empirical evidence on the demand for money, although it should be pointed out that the measurement of the demand for money is complicated by various definitional and conceptual problems. For example, what definition of money is taken and which financial asset (or assets) is it best to use in the investigations? For these and other reasons, the empirical evidence on the demand for money does not provide conclusive evidence in support of the extreme versions of the two theories.

15.3 The role of monetary policy

Our preceding discussion has concentrated upon the two major views of the importance of money, and this section intends to clarify their implications for the direction and significance of monetary policy. Indeed we will see that the outcome of the Keynesian view is that monetary policy should be directed at interest rates, rather than the money supply, but that in any case monetary policy should be subsidiary to fiscal policy. On the other hand, the monetarist recommends that control of the money supply should be the major concern of the monetary authorities and that such a policy is of paramount importance for the conduct of macroeconomic policy.

We have already established the Keynesian view that an increase in the money supply will lead to the purchase of financial assets. Further, these purchases are expected to lead to an increase in the price of financial assets and a fall in their yields (i.e. interest rates) However this process now needs to be spelled out a little more clearly if we are to gain insight into the effectiveness of the increase in money supply on the level of interest rates. It is first necessary to recognize that some financial assets are closer substitutes for money than other financial assets, and so are the more likely to be immediately affected by a change in the money supply. Therefore any adjustment which comes about as a result of an increase in the money supply will probably take place first of all through purchases of short-term highly liquid financial assets such as Treasury bills. As a consequence, the prices of these assets start to rise, i.e. their yield falls, and economic transactors are assumed to compare the yield on Treasury bills with close substitutes such as short-dated bonds. Accordingly there will be a substitution of short-dated bonds for the relatively less attractive Treasury bills, and so the price of these bonds will rise and the yield on them will fall. In this way the Keynesian sees the original increase in the money supply spreading through the whole financial market until eventually the less liquid financial assets such as equities are affected. At each stage, yields will fall as economic transactors adjust to the 'disturbance' through the purchase of close substitutes.

The overall effect of the above process should be a fall in interest rates throughout the whole spectrum of financial assets. But precisely because the effect is dispersed through the whole market the Keynesian argues that, unless there is a massive increase in the money supply, the impact on interest rates in general may be relatively small. Furthermore, the process may be unpredictable as far as individual interest rates are concerned because the movement in the prices of financial assets is subject to the expectations of the market.

How will the change in interest rates affect economic activity? The Keynesian answers this question in terms of the income – expenditure model of Chapter 14. To summarize, the level of economic activity is determined by the level of injections and withdrawals into the circular flow of income. Keynesians assume that investment expenditures are the more likely to be influenced by changes in interest rates since raising money to purchase capital goods – perhaps through the issue of equities or through borrowing from the banks – is more attractive when interest rates are lower. It thus becomes a matter of the sensitivity of investment to changes in interest rates, i.e. what is the interest-elasticity of investment?

In the early post-war years it was believed that investment expenditures were not very responsive to changes in interest rates, and most of the empirical evidence at the time tended to support this view. The Keynesian concludes, therefore, that an increase in the money supply would not have a marked effect on economic activity since: (a) the money supply only influences economic activity indirectly via interest rates, and the latter may not be significantly affected anyway because all parts of the financial market bear the burden of adjustment; and (b) investment expenditures may not be very sensitive to changes in interest rates. So, the Keynesian argues that monetary policy will be more effective if the authorities aim to control interest rates directly, rather than indirectly through the money supply. Furthermore, monetary policy is not as crucial as

328   BANKING AND FINANCE

fiscal policy because the latter has a *direct* impact on economic activity via government expenditure and taxation, whereas monetary policy only affects economic activity *indirectly* via the tenuous link between interest rates and investment. Indeed, some Keynesians went so far as to to say that money is unimportant since it only exerts an influence on economic activity via interest rates, and then without much success.

The assumption that money is a substitute for all assets, both real and financial, leads the monetarists to conclude that an increase in the money supply brings about directly an increase in prices as a consequence of increased purchases of all types of assets. Also Friedman and his associates have undertaken many detailed empirical studies to investigate whether changes in the money supply are a cause of fluctuations in national incomes and prices. Their results show that, in different time-periods and in different countries, changes in the money stock precede changes in money incomes and prices. On the basis of his theoretical and empirical analysis Friedman concludes that rapid fluctuations in the money supply are the cause of economic instability.[2]

Unfortunately empirical evidence rarely leads to the resolution of economic debates, primarily because the economist cannot control his experiments in such a way as to isolate the effect of one variable (e.g. the money supply) on others (e.g. money incomes). Perhaps the most fundamental criticism of the empirical work of the monetarists is that evidence of correlation does not by itself prove causality. For example there is a very good correlation between the arrival of swallows and summer, but no one suggests that the presence of swallows causes summer. Similarly, the fact the increases in the money supply precede increases in money incomes does not prove causality. Professor Kaldor has pointed out[3] that an increase in the note issue precedes the Christmas spending spree, to facilitate the extra demand for transactions balances, but the absence of such an increase would not prevent the spending boom. Instead the given money stock might be used more intensively (i.e. a rise in V) as notes, coin, and bank deposits are exchanged more frequently. So, despite the detailed and extensive studies of the monetarists, there is still disagreement as to whether the money supply is the prime cause of fluctuations in money incomes and prices.

Although the monetarists claim that there is a direct link between the money supply and money incomes, they do point out that a variable and unpredictable lag exists. Indeed U.S.A. studies indicate that the lag may vary from between six months and two years. It is argued, therefore, that the money supply should not be manipulated

[2] M. Friedman, 'The Role of Monetary Policy,' *American Economic Review* (March 1968).
[3] N. Kaldor, 'The New Monetarism,' *Lloyds Bank Review* (July 1970).

on a short-term basis because the existence of such lags would make the effects of monetary policy uncertain. The best policy, according to the monetarists, is for the authorities to aim for a steady growth in the money supply in order that economic expansion can continue without undesirable fluctuations in money incomes and prices.

The Keynesian versus monetarist debate gives conflicting advice to governments on the role and importance of monetary policy. The Keynesians argue that the interest rate is the most important variable for the monetary authorities to control, but that monetary policy should be subsidiary to fiscal policy. In contrast the monetarists argue that a steady growth in the money supply is the best policy to follow, and that monetary policy directed to this purpose is of paramount importance. Certainly the Keynesian view provided the academic basis for the conduct of monetary policy in the period from the Second World War up to the late 1960s, with the influential Radcliffe Report (1959) supporting this general approach in the U.K. However the 1970s have witnessed a change in opinion towards the monetarist camp, as can be seen from the adoption of firm monetary targets in most advanced economies. But the conduct of macroeconomic policy will be discussed in more detail in Chapter 16.

15.4 Summary

i.   An appreciation of why governments follow certain types of economic policies requires an understanding of the theories which influence the decisions of the policy-maker. Thus the relationship between money and economic activity is of crucial importance to the direction and emphasis of monetary policy.

ii. The original Quantity Theory suggested that the major impact of the money supply is on the general price level, but this crude theory fell into disrepute during the inter-war years with the absence of any well-defined link between money and prices. Nevertheless the relationship between the money supply and prices has received continued attention, with the monetarists trying to provide theoretical and empirical support to the argument that changes in the money supply cause fluctuations in money incomes and prices.

iii. The Keynesian and monetarist views provide opposing theories of the importance of money upon which the authorities can base their policies. The Keynesians argue that money is a close substitute for financial assets, so they see an increase in the money supply resulting in an increase in the price of financial assets and a fall in the yield received. In contrast, the monetarists argue that money is a substitute for all assets, so they see an increase in the money supply resulting in an increase in prices in general, not just in the price of financial assets.

iv. These divergent views on the demand for money lead to very different policy conclusions. The Keynesian view implies that the money supply has its major effect on economic activity via the impact of interest rates on investment expenditures. The Keynesian then considers the implications in terms of the income – expenditure model of Chapter 14, with any increase in investment bringing about a magnified increase in national income through the workings of the multiplier. However the Keynesian sees the effect on economic activity as being unpredictable and indirect, and instead attaches more significance to fiscal policy.

The monetarist position is that control of the money supply is essential for the successful conduct of macroeconomic policy since they see a direct link between the money supply and prices. But they argue that the money supply should not be manipulated on a short-term basis because of the variable and unpredictable lag which exists before prices and money incomes are affected.

It is therefore a background of academic controversy which provides the theoretical framework for the conduct of macroeconomic policy in general, and for monetary policy in particular.

16
Macroeconomic management

16.1 Macroeconomic objectives

The major macroeconomic objectives are usually summarized as:
- (a) full employment of the labour force;
- (b) stable prices;
- (c) balance of payments equilibrium;
- (d) a satisfactory rate of growth.

However, this list may be far from complete since most governments have objectives in other areas, notably the distribution of income and wealth. Nevertheless it is very difficult to achieve even the major objectives listed above, either because some of them conflict in practice or else the policy-tools are insufficient in number or effectiveness to complete the task adequately. Thus the policy-maker is invariably in the position where he has certain aspirations in terms of macroeconomic objectives, but he has to decide which are to be given priority. Obviously such choices are political decisions, which will involve social and other considerations, but it is first necessary to establish the nature of the trade-offs between macroeconomic objectives so that the policy-maker is well aware of the sacrifices involved. Accordingly the economist would seem to have two crucial roles:
- (a) to identify and measure the trade-offs that exist between economic objectives so that the policy-maker is made aware of how much of one must be given up to get more of another, e.g. 2 per cent more inflation or ½ per cent less unemployment; and
- (b) to search for the most appropriate policy-tools which will enable the government to achieve its economic objectives more satisfactorily.

There would be no need for a choice between economic objectives if the latter were all uniformly related to one controllable variable. Chapter 14 explained that although the four macroeconomic objectives listed earlier are each related in some manner to the level of demand, the relationship is by no means uniform or in the same direction. Output and employment may be improved through using fiscal policy to expand aggregate demand, but at the same time there is an increased likelihood that inflation will be exacerbated by such an injection of spending. Furthermore, a higher level of demand will probably result in an increase in the value of imports, implying that the balance of payments objective may also conflict with the employment objective. So fiscal policy on its own cannot be relied upon to achieve all the macroeconomic objectives simultaneously since it operates essentially through the channel of aggregate demand. In fact it is generally the case that the achievement of more than one independent policy objective requires the adoption of a combination of policy-tools.

We will investigate the nature of the trade-offs between macroeconomic objectives in the U.K. economy from the 1950s onwards. In this period not only did the nature of the trade-offs change but at the same time the policy-makers came to attach more or less importance to particular objectives.

During most of the 1950s and 1960s U.K. governments as a whole concentrated predominantly upon the employment objective, with the balance of payments frequently exerting a constraint on the achievement of this goal. Indeed the problem was that fiscal and monetary policies designed to stimulate employment often resulted in a deterioration in the balance of payments under the then existing fixed exchange rate system. Specifically, an expansion of demand would result in a reduction in unemployment but would also lead to a balance of payments deficit as imports increased. One possible solution was that fiscal policy could be used exclusively for the management of the level of employment, and monetary policy could be directed at raising interest rates to attract capital inflows and thereby offset the increase in imports in the balance of payments accounts. Unfortunately such capital inflows tend to be very volatile in nature, as we have seen in earlier chapters, and this is one reason why this option did not provide a permanent or reliable solution. Instead more reliance was attached to expenditure-reducing policies (see Section 11.2.3) as a solution to the balance of payments problems, and this involved the use of both fiscal *and* monetary policies to bring the expansion of demand to a sudden end. Consequently the policy of expanding and then contracting demand, which came to be known as 'stop–go,' was a result of the direct conflict between the employment and balance of payments objectives since control over the level of aggregate demand was relied upon in order to achieve both goals.

The use of fiscal and monetary policies to influence the level of demand also has implications for the prices and growth objectives. An expansion of demand can give rise to inflationary pressures, and the frequent *expansion* and *contraction* of demand (stop–go) provides an inappropriate environment for investment spending and therefore economic growth. In fact the more immediate objectives for most of the 1950s and 1960s were employment and the balance of payments. Our discussion on page 331 suggests that: (a) a trade-off might need to be established between these two objectives; and (b) additional policy-tools need to be used to achieve a more desirable combination of objectives. In the case of (a), it could be concluded that equilibrium in the balance of payments might only have been accomplished with the existing policies by accepting higher levels of unemployment. In the latter case (b), the availability of additional policy-tools for the achievement of balance of payments equilibrium was limited. Indeed the adjustable peg system was operated in such a way that the exchange rate was rarely used as a means of adjustment, and import restrictions were not allowed under the Bretton Woods Agreement.

During the same period it was also established that there was a trade-off between unemployment and inflation, which came to be known as the Phillips curve. This trade-off was based on the original observations by Professor A. W. Phillips of the relationship between the rate of change of money wage rates and unemployment levels over long periods of time going back as far as 1861. *Figure 16.1* gives an example of a Phillips curve, with the horizontal axis measuring the level of unemployment. On the vertical axis is plotted the recorded rate of increase of money wage rates and it may be assumed the rate of inflation can be closely associated with these rates of wage change because the latter are usually the largest component of costs. To the extent that a growth in productivity allows a certain increase in

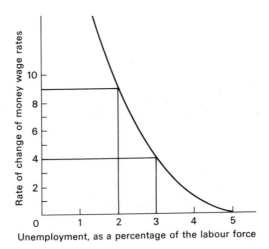

FIG 16.1. *A hypothetical Phillips curve.*

money wages to take place without price increases, then this productivity growth can be deducted from actual wage rises to calculate price increases. Thus with 2 per cent productivity growth, a 4 per cent rate of wage increase can be associated with an inflation rate of 2 per cent. When such adjustments are made the Phillips curve apparently gives the policy-maker a choice between employment and inflation – more of one can only be gained at the expense of the other. For example, our hypothetical Phillips curve shows that a 4 per cent per annum wage increase (equivalent to 2 per cent inflation with a 2 per cent productivity growth) is associated with a 3 per cent unemployment rate, and that a 9 per cent per annum wage increase (equivalent to 7 per cent inflation) is associated with a 2 per cent unemployment rate. In other words, a reduction in unemployment is associated with a certain increase in the rate of inflation. By the early 1960s, therefore, it had become accepted that fiscal and monetary policies could only be used to reduce unemployment at the expense of a deterioration in the balance of payments *and* a higher rate of inflation.

So far we have explained the existence of trade-offs between the employment and balance of payments objectives, and between employment and changes in prices. Furthermore, we have noted that in the U.K. during most of the 1950s and 1960s employment and the balance of payments were considered to be the most important macroeconomic objectives by both Labour and Conservative governments. But by the late 1960s world inflation had gathered pace to such an extent that most governments came to regard this as the major problem confronting them. Moreover, high inflation rates were and are of particular concern because of the danger that the monetary and financial systems might collapse as conventional money no longer becomes accepted as the medium of exchange. Past experience in Germany and other countries in the inter-war years suggests that hyperinflation can ultimately lead to the collapse of the economic and political system as well. Accordingly, the prices objective has become more important in most economies, and by the middle of 1970s it had replaced full employment as the principal objective of the U.K. government.

The traditional Keynesian approach has tended to regard unemployment and inflation as being inversely related, as is depicted by the shape of the Phillips curve. Indeed the implication of the Phillips curve relationship was taken to be that control of demand via fiscal and monetary policies allowed the government to operate the economy at full capacity, yielding high employment but rising prices; or at lower levels of demand, producing more stable prices but higher unemployment. But the coexistence during the 1970s of high unemployment *and* inflation seems to cast doubt on both the usefulness of the Phillips curve as a representation of a trade-off, and on the excess demand explanation of inflation.

Our commentary suggests that the nature of the trade-offs between economic objectives may change over time, and that the policy-maker needs to be advised of such changes when deciding upon the preferred combination of objectives. Another issue which needs to be considered is whether or not new policy-tools can be found to enable the authorities to achieve their objectives more effectively, and to this we will turn next.

Incomes policies were first adopted in the U.K. in the late 1940s but became a regular feature during the 1960s. The argument was that fiscal and monetary policies could be used to achieve the government's objectives as regards full employment and the balance of payments (although such policies were not very successful in that they gave rise to stop–go), and that incomes policies could be used to contain the inflationary consequences. Indeed, increasing concern over inflation has led to the operation of more or less continous incomes policies during the 1970s. Moreover, succeeding governments have tried to operate the economy at lower levels of demand and therefore at higher levels of unemployment – in order to reduce inflationary pressures. The search for new policies has led additionally to the widespread adoption of monetary targets in most economies, including the U.K., apparently giving some acceptance of the monetarist claim that inflation is a consequence of a rapid growth in the money supply. The conduct of monetary policy, and its changing emphasis over time, will be discussed further in Section 16.6

Since 1972 in the U.K. there has been available an additional means for the achievement of the balance of payments objective: the adoption of floating exchange rates. This enables easier adjustment to take place, although in practice the balance of payments has continued to pose problems for the U.K. economy. The urgency of such problems, however, is not usually as acute under floating, since the government is no longer obliged to defend a fixed exchange rate and to direct domestic policies to this purpose.

Our discussion so far is intended to highlight the point that macroeconomic objectives often conflict, and that the policy-maker has to choose the most desirable combination. Also the nature of the trade-offs may change over time, as may the choices of the policy-maker. The economist's role in all this is essentially to make the policy-maker aware of these trade-offs and to advise him of the suitability of alternative policy-tools for the achievement of objectives.

16.2 The framework of macroeconomic management

Our discussion in Section 16.1 broadly indicated how fiscal, monetary, and incomes policies might be used to achieve some combination of macroeconomic objectives. In this section we intend to explain how such policies involve the relationship between *objectives, targets* and *instruments*.

(a) *Objectives* have been defined already in Section 16.1, where it was stated that priorities are decided by the policy-maker in line with political, social, and other considerations. In the subsequent discussion we intend to concentrate upon employment, prices, and the balance of payments as the most relevant objectives. This approach seems to be consistent with U.K. post-war experience since policy-makers have tended to concentrate their attention upon the more short-term objectives rather than on economic growth.

(b) *Targets* (or intermediate variables) are the variables through which government actions have an influence on macroeconomic objectives. The relevant fiscal targets are the levels of government expenditure (G) and taxation (T), each of which the government tries to control via instruments. But both these target variables are also influenced by variables outside the direct control of the authorities. For example, government expenditure on unemployment benefits is related to the number of people out of work, state pensions are related to the number of people over retirement age; taxation receipts are influenced by the incomes of the community (via direct taxes) and by prices (via indirect taxes).

With monetary policy the target variables may consist of some measure of the money supply or interest rates. But again the monetary authorities do not control these variables directly, instead they are able to exert influence over their chosen targets via their control of instruments.

(c) *Instruments* (or techniques) enable the authorities to influence target variables. In the case of fiscal policy the major instruments are changes in tax rates and allowances, and variations in expenditure plans. Chapter 9 has already explained the role of the Budget and the Public Expenditure White Paper in this context. It is through changes in instruments that the fiscal authorities influence the levels of taxation and government expenditure, the two target variables. A variety of instruments are available for the conduct of monetary policy, such as reserve requirements, special deposits, open market operations, and the central bank discount rate. These instruments can be directed at the two monetary targets, the money supply and interest rates.

TABLE 16.1

Some of the major objectives, targets, and instruments

Objectives	Targets (or intermediate variables)	Instruments (or techniques)
1. Prices	Fiscal: taxation receipts(T)	tax rates
2. Employment	government expenditure(G)	expenditure plans
3. Balance of payments	Monetary: money supply (Ms) interest rates (r)	reserve requirements, open market operations, special deposits, the central bank discount rate, directives

Table 16.1 uses fiscal and monetary policies as illustrations of the difference between objectives, targets, and instruments. But it should be remembered that these two policies are not to be treated as mutually exclusive: the fiscal position often has important ramifications for the conduct monetary policy.

Our discussion of macroeconomic management emphasizes that the link between instruments and objectives is by no means direct or precise. Accordingly we can identify two necessary conditions which must be fulfilled before macroeconomic policies are likely to be successful.

(i) Macroeconomic objectives must be sensitive to changes in target variables.

(ii) The authorities must be able to control target variables via instruments.

For any type of policy to be successful *both* of these conditions need to be satisfied or else the policy instruments under consideration will fail to give an adequate degree of control over macroeconomic objectives. For example, it may be of little value that the authorities are able to control interest rates via monetary instruments if the relevant objectives are not very sensitive to changes in interest rates. These two conditions will be examined in the next two sections.

16.3 The sensitivity of economic objectives to changes in target variables

The relationship between target variables and economic objectives is subject to several qualifications. First, target variables may influence economic objectives either directly, as with the effect of indirect taxation on prices, or indirectly, through some other variable such as the level of demand. Secondly, the extent to which changes in target variables achieve economic objectives may differ according to the targets and objectives under investigation. It is these two issues which we will examine in this section in an attempt to evaluate the sensitivity of macroeconomic objectives to changes in target variables. Of course another important question for economic management concerns the speed with which target variables achieve their objectives, but this matter will be discussed later in Section 16.5

Let us begin by examining fiscal policy, the relevant target variables being listed in Table 16.1. The question to be posed is whether employment, prices, and the balance of payments (for the sake of convenience we again ignore economic growth and any other objectives) are directly and significantly related to changes in the levels of government expenditure and taxation. Now the employment objective may be directly related to government expenditure because the public sector is a very large employer. So any variation in government expenditure which involves a change in the number of public employees will obviously have a direct effect on overall employment. Furthermore, changes in government expenditure and taxation both have an indirect effect on the level of employment because of the changes in aggregate demand that result from budget deficits and surpluses. Indeed Chapter 14 established that such variations in injections and leakages have a multiplier effect on aggregate demand.

The prices objective may be directly associated with the conduct of fiscal policy since indirect taxes, such as V.A.T. influence the prices of the goods and services on which they are levied. Thus an increase in the standard rate of V.A.T. usually leads to a rise in prices. In this case, however, the link is between the instrument (a change in V.A.T. rate) and the objective, rather than between targets and objectives. But quite often changes in the level of taxation and government expenditure exert an indirect influence on prices, as well as on output and employment, through variations in aggregate demand.

Finally, one may identify an indirect relationship between fiscal targets and the balance of payments, again through the channel of aggregate demand. In this respect a stimulus to economic activity, either through a decrease in taxation or an increase in government expenditure, will be expected to lead to increased spending on goods and services of which some component will be manufactured overseas. In fact fiscal policy has frequently been used in the U.K. economy as an expenditure-reducing policy designed to improve the balance of payments through restricting domestic demand and hence imports.

The nature of the link between monetary targets and economic objectives is, as Chapter 15 explained, subject to differences of opinion. If we deal with the prices objective first, then the monetarists argue that the link between the money supply and inflation is both direct and important. Moreover, the monetarists claim that the most frequent cause of fluctuations in the price level is variations in the money supply. In contrast, the Keynesians argue that the money supply has only an indirect effect on inflation through the influence of interest rates on investment expenditure and therefore aggregate demand.

The Keynesian versus monetarist debate is also relevant to the question of whether monetary targets affect employment levels. It is the Keynesian view that changes in the money supply influence aggregate demand and therefore employment via interest rates. The Keynesian view suggests that the significance of the relationship depends upon the responsiveness of investment to changes in interest rates, which empirical evidence seems to suggest is quite low. So the Keynesian view is that monetary variables have an indirect effect on employment, and not a very significant effect at that. Although the monetarists argue that changes in the money supply have a direct effect on prices, they doubt whether the former can be used in such a manner as to have a permanently beneficial effect on real variables such as the level of employment. However, they do claim that tight control of the money supply can help prevent the fluctuations in economic activity which lead to high levels of unemployment.

Interest rates may have a fairly direct influence on the balance of payments through their impact on capital flows: a rise in domestic interest rates relative to the rest of the world should result in capital inflows, and a fall in interest rates should lead to capital outflows. However any improvement in the balance of payments due to short-term capital movements may be temporary because of the volatility of these flows.

It is more difficult to separate an incomes policy into targets and instruments, but it might be reasonable to say that the target is a desired overall rise in wages and salaries and that the instrument is either legislation (with compulsory incomes policies) or exhortation (with voluntary incomes policies). Such policies usually have prices as their major objective, the argument being that a slower growth in labour costs has a direct effect on the rate of inflation. Indeed U.K. governments have frequently introduced prices and incomes policies which have attempted to control price increases directly through legislation. Although the record of incomes policies in the U.K. suggests that they are fairly effective in limiting price increases during the operation of the policy, prices often rise quite rapidly afterwards when the community tries to make up for the slow growth in incomes. The balance of payments may improve as well if exports become more competitively priced as a result of a restraint on labour costs, and success here could also increase employment since the demand for domestic goods and services would rise.

We should now consider two other target variables which are related primarily to the balance of payments objectives. The exchange rate is a target variable which the authorities attempt to control by using their holdings of official reserves to intervene in foreign currency markets. The balance of payments then may be improved by a managed depreciation of the domestic currency, but the effectiveness of such a policy in improving the current account depends upon the elasticities of demand for exports and imports. Of course the extent to which the authorities are able to manage the exchange rate in this manner is very limited, as was pointed out in Chapter 13. Additionally, the exchange rate will tend to have a fairly direct effect on the prices objective since changes in import prices feed into the domestic price level, and indeed the effect can be quite significant if imports represent a large proportion of national income, as in the U.K. But the size and mobility of short-term flows may inhibit the authorities influence over a floating exchange rate.

Import controls are an alternative policy which may influence the balance of payments, as well as the other economic objectives. With this policy it is probably more accurate to refer to import controls as the instrument, which have as their target a reduction in the volume of imports. But, although restrictions on the volume of imports may have a significant effect on the balance of payments, it should be remembered that not every category of imports can be substantially reduced in this way, i.e. countries cannot produce for themselves all the goods they require. More important, the total impact on the balance of payments is complicated by the fact that other countries might impose similar restrictions in retaliation, thus reducing a country's exports. It is also worth noting that the successful imposition of import controls might have an effect on the employment objective; more goods produced at home to replace imports implies higher domestic employment, assuming of course that employment in export industries is not reduced owing to retaliatory measures by other countries.

16.4 The ability of the authorities to control target variables

The other necessary condition for the successful conduct of macroeconomic policy is that the authorities should be able to control the appropriate target variables with the available instruments. However, there are two considerations relevant to the satisfaction of this condition. First, the instruments (e.g. a change in tax rates) must be under the tight control of the authorities, and this may not be the case if there are significant technical or political constraints on the use of these instruments. Secondly, it is necessary that the instruments available should exert a satisfactory degree of influence over the designated target variables. The latter requirement may be achieved with a small number of instruments if these are particularly effective, otherwise a wide range of instruments might be necessary.

In the operation of fiscal policy there is a close relationship between a change in tax rates, allowances, or expenditure plans (instruments) and the levels of taxation and government expenditure (targets). However, one problem may be that there are certain political, social, or other constraints on the use of fiscal instruments for the purposes of demand management. Public expenditure plans may be subject to political disagreement as to the appropriate size of the public sector, and this could be particularly important if a minority government were to require the support of the other political parties. Proposed changes in taxation are also subject to wider considerations, especially the criteria of equity, efficiency, and incentives discussed in Chapter 9. Thus the ability of the authorities to control fiscal targets via instruments may be limited by such constraints and considerations.

When we consider the ability of the authorities to control monetary targets, we must realize that it is not possible to control both the money supply and interest rates; a choice must be made between one target or the other. This point can be illustrated by considering the technique of open market operations. The authorities may wish to control the money supply by selling/buying gilt-edged securities to/from the non-bank sector at whatever price (i.e. rate of interest) is necessary to achieve the target. Alternatively they may wish to control interest rates by selling/buying gilt-edged to achieve the desired price, thereby accepting the implications of such a policy on the money supply. In the first case the authorities' control of the money supply leaves the determination of interest rates to the market, and in the second case the authorities' control of interest rates relegates money supply determination to the market. Of course factors other than the instruments of the authorities influence monetary targets, and this may limit further their ability to control the chosen target. With a large public sector borrowing requirement, for example, the attainment of a low growth in M_3 may prove difficult.

Previous incomes policies have been fairly successful instruments in containing the growth in wages and salaries during the period of the policy, especially when legislation was used to make the prescribed limits on earnings compulsory. But past experience suggests that the degree of control is never complete, partly no doubt as a result of overtime payments and various kinds of allowances and bonuses by which the policy can be partially avoided. However, a significant constraint is associated with the adoption of the instrument itself; in particular the presence of opposition from trades unions, other political parties, or the general public may discourage a government from introducing an incomes policy.

In respect of exchange rate policy, the appropriate instrument – foreign currency reserves – may not be under the close control of the authorities, since the size of the official reserves is partly determined by previous movements in the exchange rate and by the associated intervention policies of the authorities. Thus in 1976 the U.K. official reserves were very low after severe exchange rate pressure on sterling, and restricted subsequently the degree to which the authorities could intervene in the foreign exchange market. The basic problem, however, is that intervention by the authorities is not likely to be successful as a means of *permanently* influencing the target variable, which in this case is the exchange rate. Our discussion of managed floating showed that it is a fruitless exercise to attempt to use official intervention to oppose the trend movement in the exchange rate, mainly because of the threat posed by the size and mobility of short-term capital flows.

16.5 Other complications

The conduct of macroeconomic policy is clearly no simple matter. Our analysis has suggested that the authorities cannot directly achieve their economic objectives; instead, they use their control of instruments to bring about changes in target variables in the expectation that these variables exert an influence over employment, prices, and the balance of payments. We have seen earlier that such actions are subject to two principal constraints: first, that the authorities may be able to exert only limited control over target variables via the available instruments; second, that the economic objectives may be only partially responsive to changes in target variables. In both cases there is the problem that many factors influence target variables and economic objectives, apart from government-controlled instruments. The question then arises as to how we know when changes in the level of employment, etc., are due to the effect of instruments or else due to other influences outside the direct control of government? Although this is an important question, it is the case that no matter what the cause of variations in employment, prices, and the balance of payments, the application of instruments needs to be capable of modification in the light of changing circumstances. But the broader problem then arises of the time taken before the instruments have their desired effect on economic objectives. It is this question of timing to which we will now turn our attention.

The whole process of economic management, involving the use of instruments to achieve objectives via some set of intermediate target variables, is subject to delay and uncertainty because of the existence of various lags. In the following discussion we will identify the major lags, with special reference to fiscal and monetary policy.

(a) *The recognition lag.* Effective economic management would require the authorities to take action as soon as a disturbance occurs which is judged to have an adverse impact on the desired combination of macroeconomic objectives. But in practice a certain period of time may elapse before the authorities are able to recognize that a problem exists. One reason for this is that suitable up-to-date information on employment, prices, etc., may not be immediately available, partly because it takes time for such data to be collated. Furthermore, the authorities will require sets of consistent data before they accept that action is required. For these and other reasons, there may be a recognition lag before the fiscal and monetary authorities consider activating their policy instruments to cope with what is perceived as a change in circumstances.

(b) *The administration lag.* Even when the authorities recognize that action is required, there may be a further lag before the available instruments are brought into action. In the conduct of fiscal policy the government has to receive Parliamentary approval before proposed changes in taxation or public expenditure can be made effective, and obviously the planning of a Budget and its acceptance by Parliament is a time-consuming process. The administration lag should not be as long for monetary policy since formal Parliamentary approval is not required. However delays may occur if the authorities have failed to make contingency plans to meet the change in circumstances, and consequently prolonged discussion may be necessary before a decision is made to use particular instruments in a certain way. But the monetary authorities in most advanced countries normally do make such contingency plans, and therefore the administration lag is unlikely to be excessive.

(c) *The operation lag.* More time may elapse before the activated policy instruments exert their full impact on employment, prices, and the other macroeconomic objectives. A lag exists between the change in instruments and their effect on intermediate target variables. With monetary policy, for example, the money supply may not decrease immediately following open market sales of public sector debt to the non-bank sector. Instead, the money supply might contract over a period of time as the banking sector adjusts stage by stage to successive sales of gilt-edged securities. In the conduct of fiscal policy, several months may pass – due to the delay in adjusting individuals' tax codes – before a change in personal taxation influences the tax paid by the community. Another lag, for example, is that between changes in instruments and the achievement of the employment and prices objectives. For instance, employment and prices may react slowly to variations in the money supply or interest rates. Indeed, the monetarists argue that frequent manipulation of the money supply is a mistaken policy because of the long and variable lag before prices are affected. Thus the monetarists recommend a steady growth in the money supply.

The overall conclusion to be drawn from this discussion is that the various lags can complicate the business of macroeconomic management, and may even make it counter-productive. One common criticism of the U.K. government during the 1950s and 1960s was that fiscal and monetary policy were conducted in such a way that these policies ultimately exerted their full influence at the wrong time. It was suggested that the authorities tried to manipulate aggregate demand – primarily through fiscal policy – in order to achieve their desired combination of economic objectives but, because of the lags mentioned earlier, such policies exerted their full effect much later when economic conditions had changed as a result of the fluctuations in the business cycle. To give an extreme example, fiscal policies designed to increase employment might take effect after a year, when, say, the economy had begun to move out of the recession. The stimulus to demand would be felt during a period of expansion and so would exacerbate any inflationary pressures which might be building up. Moreover, it was argued that contractionary policies introduced during boom periods to reduce the growth in imports and inflationary pressures had their full effect when the economy had begun to move into recession. Therefore the contraction in demand engineered by the government only succeeded in adding to the unemployment problem. The manipulation of aggregate demand by the government, and in particular the fairly frequent changes in policy instruments, became known as 'fine-tuning.' By the end of the 1960s many economists were critical of this policy of fine-tuning on the grounds that it added to the instability of the economy rather than reduced it.

16.6 Monetary instruments (or techniques)

In Chapters 9 and 10 we examined in detail how fiscal instruments can be used in the conduct of macroeconomic policy. Although the various monetary instruments have been discussed in different chapters, it is our intention in this section to draw the strands together by presenting the range of instruments available to the policy-maker for the conduct of monetary policy. We shall explain as well how these instruments might be used in the light of current opinion as to the appropriate use and emphasis for the conduct of monetary policy.

Section 16.4 has shown that the authorities need to make a choice between interest rates and the money supply as the appropriate target, given that it is impossible to control both variables simultaneously. However it may prove difficult to achieve the desired value of either of the targets. The reason for this is that several factors influence target variables: if sterling M_3 is the chosen target, the size of the public sector borrowing requirement (P.S.B.R.), sales of government debt to the non-bank public, and bank lending will influence the growth in this measure of the money supply; if interest rates are the preferred target, then supply and demand pressures in financial markets determine the level and structure of interest rates. Careful consideration is therefore required by governments as regards the choice of target variable and its appropriate value.

During the 1960s the official view on the role of monetary policy in the U.K. was largely determined by the influential Radcliffe Report of 1959. The view expressed there was basically Keynesian in nature: that is, monetary policy should be directed specifically at interest rates rather than the money supply. The Report recommended that

> The authorities thus have to regard the structure of interest rates rather than the supply of money as the centre-piece of the monetary mechanism. This does not mean that the supply of money is unimportant, but that its control is incidental to interest rate policy.[1]

Out discussion in Chapter 15 also argued that the extreme Keynesian view attaches subsidiary importance to monetary policy, given that investment expenditures do not appear to be sufficiently responsive to movements in interest rates. Consequently the U.K. government during the 1960s tended to assign primary responsibility to fiscal policy and relegated monetary policy, directed essentially at interest rates, to a secondary role.

By the 1970s, academic and official opinion had become more sceptical of the conventional Keynesian view on the choice and significance of monetary targets. Two major factors contributed to this change in opinion: first, the development of monetarism and the apparent empirical verification of some of its more important assumptions and predictions; and second, the emergence of inflation as the key economic problem facing Western economies for which the

[1]*Committee on the Working of the Monetary System: Report,* Cmnd. 827 (H.M.S.O. 1959), Para. 397.

monetarist prescription of control of the money supply was specifically designed. Indeed the introduction of *Competition and Credit Control* in 1971 signified the change in official opinion in the U.K. since, at the time, the new arrangements were seen as a move in the direction of the control of monetary aggregates. Additionally, the authorities suggested that interest rates would be used more freely in the future to influence such monetary aggregates as M_3. But attempts to expand the economy in subsequent years were associated with a rapid growth in the money supply, and it was not until 1976 that the U.K. first publicly adopted declared quantitative targets for this variable. However it should be pointed out that the U.K. authorities have not wholeheartedly accepted the monetarist philosophy, since this would entail almost sole reliance upon control of the money supply for the conduct of macroeconomic management. Instead the official view appears to be that publicly declared money supply targets will provide a background of financial stability for the conduct of other macroeconomic policies, notably fiscal and incomes policies. Furthermore, with the achievement of a lower rate of inflation still regarded as the primary economic objective, the knowledge that a firm money supply target is to be adopted is thought to be beneficial in that it gives a clear indication to those involved in wage bargaining and price-setting of the extent to which the authorities are prepared to see inflation validated by lax monetary and fiscal policies. At the time of writing the U.K. authorities, along with those in most other advanced economies, appear to have accepted that the money supply is the appropriate target to which monetary instruments should be directed.

Before we examine the range of instruments available to the authorities, it is useful to identify some of the problems connected with the adoption of quantitative money supply targets. Firstly, since there are several measures of the money supply, there is the question of which measure is the appropriate target variable. When the U.K. adopted publicly declared money supply targets in 1976, greater emphasis was placed upon the D.C.E. measure (see Section 6.4.2). However it has become common practice to express monetary targets in terms of the sterling M_3 measure, and probably this will remain as the central monetary target for as long as the balance of payments does not deteriorate markedly. So, for example, if a yearly inflation rate of 10 per cent is judged to be acceptable, then the monetary authorities will choose a target growth of sterling M_3 in line with this objective. A second consideration is that any system of quantitative money supply targets requires the authorities to forecast accurately on the basis of *current policies* the size of such elements as the P.S.B.R., sales of government debt to the public, and bank lending. Then, in the light of such forecasts, to activate the instruments in such a way as to achieve the desired growth in the money supply. But the size of the P.S.B.R. etc., are not easy to predict and so the authorities have to be prepared to vary their use of instruments in response to changing circumstances. A related issue is the frequency with which monetary targets are to be revised; annual targets have been adopted in the U.K. to date, but in the future it is possible that some system of rolling targets based on shorter periods may be preferred (the Federal Reserve currently operates quarterly targets in the U.S.A.). However various unforeseen circumstances can lead to marked fluctuations in any aggregate in the short-term, e.g. temporary market conditions may inhibit sales of public sector debt and so fail to prevent a sudden increase in the money supply in subsequent months. The adoption of rigid, short-term, monetary targets may therefore be avoided unless the government is willing to direct all its policy instruments at achieving the desired growth in the money supply.

Given this background to the selection of monetary targets, we can now turn to the instruments themselves. Our detailed discussion of monetary techniques in earlier chapters enables us to concentrate here upon how these instruments might be used to bring about desired changes in the money supply or interest rates.

(a) *Reserve requirements.* Chapters 6 and 7 have already examined how various reserve requirements imposed on the banking system by the central bank can restrict the extent to which lending, and therefore the money supply, can be expanded. Accordingly variations in the reserve requirement, such as an increase in the present minimum reserve asset ratio from 12½ per cent to 15 per cent, could be used to curtail the growth in bank lending. However the U.K. authorities, unlike some of their counterparts overseas, do not resort to overt variations in reserve requirements; instead, they prefer to use given ratios in conjunction with other instruments such as special deposits and open market operations. The definition of reserve assets and method of calculating the ratio adopted is important since the operation of these other instruments may be ineffective if the banking system can obtain easily the requisite reserve assets, thereby restoring the ratio to the required level. The present *Competition and Credit Control* arrangements define reserve assets in such a way that they consist largely of public sector assets. Where private sector assets are included their contribution to the ratio is restricted, e.g. commercial bills qualify to a maximum of 2 per cent of eligible liabilities. The present arrangements seem to meet the necessary condition that the reserve assets are under the control of the authorities, but in practice this may not be the case since the banking system could obtain reserve assets from other sectors (see Section 7.4). Furthermore, the existence of a large public sector borrowing requirement makes it difficult for the government to control the supply of public sector assets to the banking system and so the present reserve requirements may not provide an operational fulcrum for other monetary instruments. Indeed some commentators have suggested that a cash ratio might provide a better fulcrum since the authorities do appear to have closer control over currency plus deposits at the central bank (i.e. the cash base).

(b) *Open market operations.* The Bank of England, as agent for the government, may buy or sell Treasury bills or bonds in the market in order to influence either the money supply or interest rates. Section 6.6.2 explained how sales of government securities to the public, given the reserve requirements, can have a contractionary effect on bank deposits and therefore on the money supply. Conversely the authorities can buy or sell securities in sufficient quantities so as to bring about changes in the yield, or rate of interest, on such assets. In the former case the Bank of England has to be prepared to accept interest rates consistent with the money supply target, and in the second they have to be prepared to accept the money supply implications of achieving a certain set of interest rates. However, sales or purchases of government securities by the Bank of England are often used as an adjunct to debt management policies rather than as an instrument of monetary policy.

(c) *Special Deposits.* Our discussion in Section 5.2.2.1 explained that two types of Special Deposit exist, ordinary and supplementary Special Deposits. In both cases their intended use is broadly the same: to exert pressure on the reserve asset ratio of the institutions subject to the call for Special Deposits by asking them to lodge a certain percentage of their gross deposits with the Bank of England. Ordinary Special Deposits have been used in this way since 1960 and are expressed as a fixed percentage of gross deposits. Such deposits usually receive interest currently equivalent to Treasury bill rate. Supplementary Special Deposits, first introduced in 1973, were designed specifically to combat the rapid growth in bank liabilities and the money supply which followed the increased competition by banks in the wholesale money markets during 1972 and 1973. The essential feature of the scheme, when in operation, is that banks and finance houses have to place *non-interest*-bearing supplementary deposits with the Bank of England if their interest-bearing eligible liabilities (I.B.E.L.s) grow faster than a rate specified by the authorities. Chapter 7 described how the percentage of funds taken in supplementary Special Deposits varies progressively according to the extent to which the growth in I.B.E.L.s exceeds the stipulated rate. The scheme has been activated periodically to date and seems to have been successful in containing the growth in the money supply.

(d) *Directives*. The banks must allocate funds to the highest bidders if they are to maximize their profits. Those customers who are willing to pay the highest interest rates are usually able, therefore, to negotiate loans from the banks. But the authorities, operating in the 'national interest,' may deem it desirable to interfere with this process either through qualitative or quantitative directives issued by the Bank of England. Section 7.4 has explained that qualitative directives are used to encourage bank lending to certain types of customers, and not to others, because of the alleged benefits to the economy as a whole. In recent years, qualitative directives have been given which recommend banks to treat favourably those requests for loans from exporters, farmers, and manufacturers; but the banks have been discouraged from lending for property speculation or for the finance of personal consumption. Quantitative directives were used prior to *Competition and Credit Control* and took the form of lending ceilings. Again the market mechanism was being interfered with since presumably a sufficiently high rise in interest rates, brought about through monetary policy, would have curtailed bank lending in the desired manner. However, such large rises in interest rates may not be politically acceptable notably because of their impact on domestic investment and on household mortgage payments.

(e) *The central bank discount rate*. The central bank's discount rate has effect on the domestic banking system because it represents the rate at which the central bank is willing to lend to the banking system. During the 1960s, when interest rates were often the prime target, the authorities were able to exercise influence by changing Bank rate. Indeed most other interest rates were tied rigidly to this rate, and so the authorities relied upon Bank rate as the major monetary instrument.

From 1972 until May 1978 the discount rate of the Bank of England, known as Minimum Lending Rate, was in most instances determined by a formula linking it to Treasury bill rate. But on occasions the Bank suspended the formula and fixed M.L.R. at a rate it considered to be appropriate, as was the practice with the old Bank rate. The moves towards controlling the money supply have meant that the authorities have tried to use interest rates for achieving this target in the belief that higher interest rates will discourage bank lending and assist sales of gilt-edged, thereby containing the growth in sterling M_3. The recent change of M.L.R. to an administered rate may give the authorities a more direct influence over interest rates in their attempt to control the growth in the money supply.

16.7 Summary

i. Governments have certain objectives in such areas as employment, prices, the balance of payments, and growth, but these objectives may prove to be incompatible in practice. The policy-maker will have to take account of economic, social, and political considerations in deciding which combination of objectives is both feasible and desirable. The economist has two major functions in this respect: (a) to identify and measure the trade-offs that exist between economic objectives so that the policy-maker is made aware of how much of one must be given up to get more of another; and (b) to search for the most appropriate policy-tools which will enable the government to achieve its macroeconomic objectives more satisfactorily.

ii. Macroeconomic management is concerned with the relationship between instruments, targets, and objectives. The government has at its disposal instruments which can be directed at chosen target variables, and movements in these variables are expected in turn to help bring about the desired economic objectives. Successful macroeconomic management will require that: (a) macroeconomic objectives are *sensitive* to changes in target variables; and (b) the authorities are able to *control* target variables via instruments. The satisfaction of *both* these conditions is necessary for the effective operation of fiscal, monetary, and other macroeconomic policies.

iii. The conduct of macroeconomic management, involving the use of instruments to achieve objectives via target variables, is complicated by the existence of time-lags. In particular the existence of recognition, administration, and operation lags can seriously undermine the effectiveness of fiscal and monetary policies.

Appendix

For those readers who are familiar with the circular flow model outlined in the earlier section of Chapter 1, this Appendix is intended to provide a slightly more rigorous approach to that which has already been developed in Section 1.2 – Section 1.5.

Beginning with the diagram used earlier in *Figure 1.3,* we can see that this system has all the major flows of expenditure and income incorporated within it. Looking first at expenditure flows, we can identify *total* expenditures within the economy as the sum of *consumption spending* – the personal sector, *investment spending* – the industrial and commercial sector, *investment and current spending* by the government, local authorities, and the public corporations – the public sector, and the *net position with respect to imports and exports* ('net' since imports represent expenditure on output of another economy) – the overseas sector.

Having identified the main sectors we can now include them in the circular flow approach adopted in Figure 1.2 in Chapter 1, p. 5. All the sectors transact with another sector in some way, either in the form of production and sale of goods and services or borrowing and lending (the production of financial assets and liabilities) or indeed both types of transaction. *Figure A.1* and *Tables A.1 and A.2* illustrate these relationships. Beginning with the industrial and commercial sector (in Figure 1.2 we simply call this sector 'firms'), these firms are paying out in each period (a year) £13,500 million which is largely wages and salaries to employees. A further £4,000 million is spent by this sector on the importation of necessary inputs from abroad (raw materials, etc.), as well as the £2,500 million spent on investment, and finally the firms pay £1,500 million corporation tax. In terms of market prices the industrial and commercial sector produces £10,000 million of consumer goods and services, and £5,000 million capital goods of which half is used by the sector itself and the other is purchased by the public sector. We have assumed for simplicity that the public sector's current spending of £5,000 million flows entirely into the industrial and commercial sector in return for goods and services. The personal sector earns in return for contributing to current production (no pensions are received by individuals in our model) a gross income of £13,500 million and of this sum, £3,000 million is paid in income tax to the public sector. The personal sector's disposable income of £10,500 million is distributed between £10,000 million consumer purchases and £500 million savings. The public sector as we have already seen spends £7,500 million on current expenditure and capital goods. The receipts of this sector amount to only £6,000 million, comprising £3,000 million income tax, £1,500 million corporation tax, and £1,500 million in V.A.T. It is evident that the public sector is running a deficit of £1,500 million. We have assumed that exports amount to £3,000 million and that imports are £4,000 million; the external sector has a surplus of £1,000 million (this does of course represent an

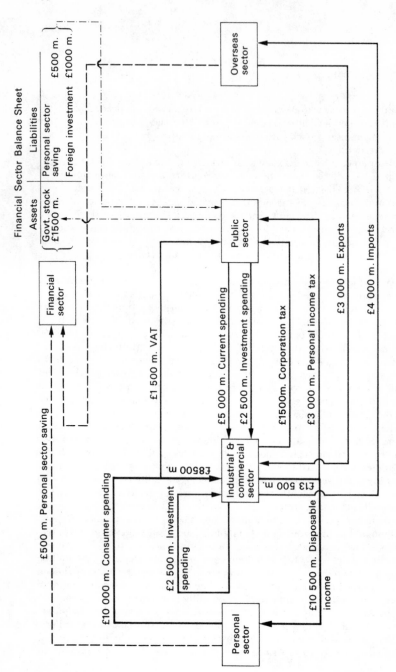

Fig A. I

TABLE A.I
Total expenditures at market prices
(£ m.)

Domestic			
Consumption	10,000	C	
Investment	5,000	I	
Government			
Current spending	5,000	G	$(C + I + G + X - M) = E$
Exports	3,000	X	
Imports	−4,000	M	
	——		
	19,000		

TABLE A.2
Income of the community
(£ m.)

Private consumption	10,000	C	
Private saving	500 ⎫	S	
Corporate saving	2,500 ⎭		$(C + S + T) = Y$
Income tax	3,000 ⎫		
Corporation tax	1,500 ⎬	T	
V.A.T.	1,500 ⎭		
	——		
	19,000		

unfavourable balance of payments for the country represented in the model). *Table A.1* provides a summary of total expenditure as outlined at the beginning of the Appendix.

Since spending also generates income for members of the community, we can also consider the income of the community as being disposed of in three ways: consumption, savings, and the payment of taxes. *Table A.2* provides the alternative presentation.

Table A.3 (p. 354) examines each of the sectors we identified at the beginning of the Appendix. It will be noticed that the personal sector has a surplus of receipts over expenditures of £500 million, the public sector has a deficit of £1,500 million, the external sector has a surplus amounting to £1,000 million, and the industrial and commercial sector is in balance. However the sums of the deficits and surpluses exactly offset one another so that all sectors together have neither a surplus nor a deficit. Nevertheless for an *individual* sector, as we have already seen in Section 1.3, this need not be the case since income can exceed expenditures and vice versa. Using the information and identities of Tables A.1 and A.2, we can express some of these ideas symbolically:

$$Y \equiv E \equiv C + I + G + X - M \equiv C + S + T \qquad (1)$$

TABLE A.3
(£ m.)

Personal Sector			Industrial and Commercial Sector	
Gross income	13,500		Consumer spending	8,500
Income tax	3,000		Government current spending	5,000
Disposable income	10,500		Government investment spending	2,500
Consumption	10,000		Private investment	2,500
			Exports	3,000
Surplus	500			
				21,500
			Factor payments	13,500
			Imports	4,000
			Corporation tax	1,500
			Investment	2,500
				21,500
			Surplus/deficit:	Nil

Public Sector			External Sector	
Income tax	3,000		Exports (foreign spending)	3,000
Corporation tax	1,500		Imports (foreign receipts)	4,000
V.A.T.	1,500			
	6,000		Surplus	1,000
Public sector current spending	5,000			
Investment	2,500			
	7,500			
Deficit	1,500			

Financial Sector

Liabilities		Assets	
Personal sector saving	500	Government stock	1,500
Foreign lending	1,000		
	1,500		1,500

and we can rearrange this to:
$$Y \equiv E \equiv C + I + G + X \equiv C + S + T + M \qquad (2)$$
and
$$Y - E \equiv (I + G + X) - (S + T + M) \equiv 0 \qquad (3)$$
or
$$(I - S) + (G - T) + (X - M) = 0 \qquad (4)$$

Since $Y \equiv E$ then $Y - E$ must be equal to zero and the propositions above follow from that identity. In the last statement (4) you will notice that the bracketed expressions approximate to our sectors, the industrial and commercial as well as the personal $(I - S)$,[1] the public sector $(G - T)$ and the external sector $(X - M)$, and that although they must all sum to zero it does not follow that each expression must be equal to zero. Thus investment spending by firms may be greater or less than the volume of saving, government spending may be greater or less than tax receipts, and exports may be greater or less than imports, but it must be the case that a deficit or surplus in one sector is exactly offset in one or more of the other sectors. For example, using the figures in Tables A.1 and A.2:

$$(\quad I \quad - \quad S \quad) + (\quad G \quad - \quad T \quad) +$$
$$(\pounds 5,000 \text{ m.} - \pounds 3,000 \text{ m.}) + (\pounds 5,000 \text{ m.}) - \pounds 6,000 \text{ m.}) +$$
$$(\quad X \quad - \quad M \quad) = 0$$
$$(\pounds 3,000 \text{ m.} - \pounds 4,000 \text{ m.}) = 0$$

If we can return to Table A.3 we are able to examine how the various sectors 'solved' the problem of their surpluses and deficits, in the sense used earlier (Section 1.5). If a sector is not in balance (i.e. $Y \neq E$) it has either to accumulate assets (the surplus sector) or attempt to sell additional liabilities (the deficit sector) In this illustration the personal sector channelled its surplus of £500 million to the financial sector (banks, insurance companies, building societies, etc.)[2] and the remaining funds originated from the foreign sector which lent its £1,000 million surplus derived from the excess of its exports over imports. The total funds were then used to purchase £1,500 million of government securities, thus allowing the public sector to cover its deficit.

---

[1] $(I - S)$ incorporates the two sectors since I represents the investment spending of the industrial and commercial sector, and S the savings of the personal sector.
[2] Composition of the financial sector is dealt with in Chapter 4.

Additional reading

The reader who wishes to pursue topics in more depth should find the following references useful.

The London Clearing Banks, Evidence by the Committee of London Clearing Bankers to the Committee to Review the Functioning of Financial Institutions, published by the Committee of the London Clearing Bankers, 1978, distributed by Longman Group Ltd.

The British Financial System, J. Revell, Macmillan Press Ltd., 1973

The Economics of Money and Banking, L. V. Chandler & S. M. Goldfeld, 7th edn., Harper International Edition, 1977.

The Failure of World Monetary Reform, 1971–74, J. Williamson, Nelson, 1977

The Evolution of the International Monetary System 1945–77, B. Tew, Hutchinson, 1977.

The Economic System in the U.K., D. Morris (ed.), Oxford University Press, 1976.

Bank reviews and bulletins:

Bank of England *Quarterly Bulletin*

The bank reviews published by the London Clearing Banks

Financial Statement and Budget Report, (H.M.S.O).

Glossary

Arbitrage The opportunities for arbitrage arise when there are differences in the prices or yields on similar assets in different markets. An arbitrage operation would consist of the buying of such assets in the 'cheaper' market and selling in the 'dearer' market. As a result of such activity the difference in prices or yields in the markets would thus narrow or disappear. Arbitrage occurs in such markets as the foreign currency and securities markets.

Adjustable Peg System A system in which exchange rates are fixed but are subject to periodic revaluations/devaluations. Such a system was set up at Bretton Woods in 1944 and operated in the international monetary system during the period 1945–73.

Aggregate Demand The total money demand for goods and services produced in the economy which arises from consumption of domestic products, government expenditure, investment, and exports.

Bank for International Settlements (B.I.S.) An international institution set up in 1930 with the intention of providing banking facilities for central banks. The so-called Group of Ten countries are represented on the Board of Directors, along with Switzerland, and the Board meets regularly at Basle.

Bank Rate The rate of interest which the Bank of England charged for its lending to the discount houses. Bank rate was operational until October 1972 when it was replaced by the Minimum Lending Rate. Bank rate was an administratively determined rate and not a market determined rate.

Bill of Exchange The bill of exchange (or commercial bill) used to be the most important method of financing international trade. The bill of exchange is rather similar to a post-dated cheque except that the bill is drawn by the trader providing the goods (and therefore in effect credit to say, a foreign importer) and 'accepted' by the recipient of the goods by writing his name on the bill. The exporter thus has a promise to pay – an I.O.U. – which may be for three months ahead. The exporter may choose to wait for payment from the importer, or he may arrange with the importer for the bill to be 'accepted' by a London accepting house, or clearing bank. Once such a bill has been accepted, the exporter is able to sell the bill to a discount house or even his own bank, at a discount of course. The bank or discount house may then hold the bill until maturity and finally take payment from the importer. Bills which have been accepted by an acceptance house or bank are termed 'bank bills' and 'fine bank bills' are those which have been accepted by banks or accepting houses of the highest reputation and probity. A 'trade bill' is a bill of exchange which has simply been accepted by a trader. With the growth of international banking links the bill of exchange has become much less important as a means of international finance.

Business Cycle Periodic fluctuations in economic activity which give rise to variations in output and employment.

Call Money Loans to the discount houses which are available to the lending bank on demand and are secured, the security usually being *Treasury bills, commercial bills,* or *certificates of deposit.*

Capital is a stock of goods which have been produced and then used to produce more goods (or services). Capital thus refers to such things as machines, tools, buildings.

Cash Ratio Prior to September 1971 and the introduction of *Competition and Credit Control,* the clearing banks were obliged to hold 8 per cent of their deposits in the form of cash held as notes and coin and balances with the Bank of England. This figure of 8 per cent was known as the cash ratio. Since September 1971 the 'old' cash ratio has been abolished but the London clearing banks, and only they, are obliged to hold 1½ per cent of their eligible liabilities as balances at the Bank of England. In addition, the clearing banks hold around 2 per cent of their liabilities in the form of notes and coin (till money) but this does not count as part of the banks' reserve assets.

Consolidated Fund The central government's cash account which includes all revenue and expenditure items.

Consortium Banks These are banks which are owned by other banks, but no one bank has a majority shareholding. The Bank of England's classification includes the proviso that at least one of the shareholders is an overseas bank. The Midland Bank, for example, has interests in twelve consortium banks. The bulk of the business undertaken by such banks is in foreign currencies (85 per cent, July 1978) i.e. part of the Euro-currency market. Their business tends to be specialised both geographically as well as in kind.

Corset See Supplementary Special Deposits.

Cross-Elasticity of Demand The degree of responsiveness of the demand for a product. For example, a 10 per cent rise in the price of butter may result in a 5 per cent rise in the quantity of margarine demanded. The relationship may be expressed by calculating:

$$\frac{\text{Proportionate change in quantity demanded (good X)}}{\text{Proportionate change in price (good Y)}}$$

Domestic Credit Expansion D.C.E. was introduced in 1968 in the U.K. and is a measure of the change in the money supply which takes into account changes in the balance of payments position. (See chapter 6)

Effective Exchange Rate A measure of the exchange value of a currency under the system of floating exchange rates. The Effective Exchange Rate of a currency is a weighted average of changes in its exchange value against all other currencies.

Equity Capital An expression often used in the context of the provision of new funds for a company by the purchase of ordinary shares issued by the company. Ordinary shares are frequently called 'equities'.

Equity Capital for Industry Equity Capital for Industry (E.C.I.) was set up in May 1976 on initiative from 'the City' and support from the Bank of England. Part of the initial capital of E.C.I. was provided by F.F.I.

Euro-Bond Market A general term which refers to the international market which raises long-term funds in various capital markets and in different currencies. The development of the Euro-bond market is associated with the Euro-dollar and Euro-currency markets. International banks are involved in the issue of Euro-bonds, and about three-quarters of such bonds are in U.S. dollars.

Euro-Dollar Deposit A Euro-dollar deposit is a U.S. dollar bank deposit which is owned by a non-resident of the U.S.A. Such deposits may arise through trade, e.g. sales of goods in the U.S.A. by, say, a German firm, or by the sale of U.S.A. securities held by a non-resident of the U.S.A. Since such dollar deposits are held by non-Europeans as well as Europeans, the term 'Euro-dollar' is a slight misnomer. The main dealers in Euro-dollars (as well as other foreign currencies) are the U.K. banks (mainly the secondary banks) as well as foreign banks based in London. The Euro-dollar and Euro-currency markets are involved with the bidding and the lending of such deposits either to another bank or the final user, e.g. a U.K. firm wishing to purchase capital equipment in the U.S.A.

European Investment Bank (E.I.B.) An E.E.C. institution set up in 1958 to act as a source of project finance primarily within the E.E.C. The main source of funds is bonds and loans raised on international capital markets, supported by capital subscribed by members of the E.E.C.

European Monetary Cooperation Fund (E.M.C.F.) An E.E.C. institution formed in 1973 to supervise the snake arrangements, i.e. to record the currency transactions between the central banks of the participating countries and to administer the financing arrangements.

European Monetary System (E.M.S.) The proposals originally made at Bremen in July 1978 for a system of fixed exchange rates within the E.E.C. supported by a joint fund for intervention in foreign exchange markets.

European Monetary Union (E.M.U.) The proposal that a common currency, supported by a new central bank, should be introduced within the E.E.C.

Exchange Equalisation Account A Treasury account established in 1932 to hold the U.K.'s official reserves of gold and foreign currency. The Exchange Equalisation Account is used by the Bank of England to intervene in foreign exchange markets.

Finance Corporation for Industry (F.C.I.) F.C.I. was established in 1945 by the Bank of England and the London and Scottish Clearing Banks. In contrast to the I.C.F.C., the F.C.I. is intended to provide term loans to finance large-scale industrial projects.

Finance for Industry Finance for Industry (F.F.I.) is a holding company for the *Industrial and Commercial Finance Corporation* (I.C.F.C.) and the *Finance Corporation for Industry* (F.C.I.). It was set up in 1973 and is jointly owned by the Bank of England (15 per cent) and the London and Scottish Clearing Banks (85 per cent).

Fixed Exchange Rate System A system whereby the exchange value of currencies is fixed in terms of some common standard such as gold.

Free-Floating Exchange Rate System A system whereby the exchange value of currencies is determined by market forces and one in which monetary authorities do not intervene to influence exchange rates.

Funding Funding operations by the Bank of England involve the selling of longer dated securities to the non-government sector and the buying of shorter dated assets – usually Treasury bills. One effect of a funding operation is to make the average maturity of the national debt greater, as well as the non-government sector 'less liquid'. Funding operations have, in the past, often been intended to reduce the liquidity of the banking system and its capacity to lend.

General Agreements to Borrow (G.A.B.) An arrangement whereby the Group of Ten (and later Switzerland) provide supplementary resources to the I.M.F. for drawings by members of the Group of Ten. The G.A.B. were established in 1961 and the facilities provided were used extensively by the U.K. and the U.S.A. under the prevailing adjustable peg system.

General Government Expenditure Central and local government expenditure.

Gilt-Edged Securities A common term used to describe British Government fixed interest securities.

Gross Domestic Product (G.D.P.) A measure of the value of the output of goods and services produced in the domestic economy.

Group of Ten: Belgium, Canada, France, Germany, Holland, Italy, Japan, U.K., U.S.A. and Sweden. Switzerland subsequently became an honorary member, making eleven countries in total.

IBELS Interest-bearing eligible liabilities. See Supplementary Special Deposits scheme and chapter 7.

Industrial and Commercial Finance Corporation (I.C.F.C.) This body was set up in 1945 jointly by the Bank of England and London and Scottish clearing banks. The main purpose of the I.C.F.C. is to provide long-term finance to companies unable by virtue of their small size to make use of the new issue market.

Injections Spending arising from government expenditure, investment, and exports which stimulates the level of aggregate demand.

Instruments Variables which the government is able to change in order to influence target variables.

Inter-bank Deposit Bank deposits which form part of the wholesale market, and which are used by banks – mainly the non-clearing banks – to offset the ebbs and flows of inter-bank indebtedness. Inter-bank deposits are denominated in both sterling and foreign currencies. Such deposits assist the secondary banks in the business of matching the maturity structure of their assets and liabilities.

International Development Association: An international institution established in 1960 to assist the World Bank in its lending activities. It has granted loans on more favourable terms (e.g. for longer periods and at lower interest rates) to less-developed countries, i.e. it is a soft loan fund.

International Finance Corporation An international institution established in 1956 to assist the World Bank in its lending activities. The International Finance Corporation supplements the World Bank's activities by making available assistance on a commercial basis to private enterprises within less-developed countries.

International Liquidity Assets which are internationally acceptable in the settlement of debts.

International Monetary Fund (I.M.F.) An institution set up at the Bretton Woods Conference in 1944 to supervise the international monetary system.

Investment A commonly used word which has a precise meaning in economics. The term refers to the purchase of new *capital*, e.g. the buying of a machine. 'Investment' in stocks and shares is simply the purchase of financial assets and need not relate to the production of new capital goods.

Jobber A dealer in securities in the Stock Exchange. The buying and selling activities of jobbers are usually specialised and they deal only with stockbrokers and not directly with the public.

Key Currency A currency which is an important medium of international exchange and is held widely as official reserves by domestic monetary authorities. The U.S.A. dollar became the key currency under the adjustable peg system of exchange rates during the period 1945–73.

Leakages Flows of taxation, saving, and imports spending which are not immediately passed on in the circular flow of income.

Legal Tender This is a property which money possesses if the money-substance must by law be accepted as a means of settling a debt. In the U.K., Bank of England notes are legal tender but the coins issued by the Royal Mint are legal tender only up to limited amounts. It is clear from this definition of legal tender that bank deposits do not have this property even though such deposits are the most important means for settling debt in the U.K.

Lifeboat Operation Following a confidence crisis in respect of a number of secondary banks in 1973 and 1974, the Bank of England and the London and Scottish clearing banks established a committee under the chairmanship of the Deputy Governor of the Bank of England which would consider requests for financial support from such secondary banks who were experiencing rapid withdrawals of deposits. (See Chapter 4, Section 4.6)

Managed Floating A system whereby the exchange value of currencies is determined by market forces but in which domestic monetary authorities use their reserves of domestic and foreign currencies to influence exchange rates.

Minimum Lending Rate The M.L.R. replaced Bank rate as the lending rate for assistance to the discount houses. Until May 1978 the M.L.R. was a market-determined rate which was calculated according to the formula: average rate of discount on Treasury bills + 0.5 percentage point and rounded up to the nearest 0·25 per cent. On May 25 1978 the Bank of England announced that M.L.R. would be set administratively, in effect the 'old' Bank rate arrangement.

Multiplier The ratio of the increase in income to the increase in injections which brought it forth.

National Debt The accumulated debt of central government which increases when there is a central government borrowing requirement.

National Debt Commissioners A government body which has been traditionally responsible for investing the National Insurance Funds and the Ordinary deposit accounts of the National and Trustee Savings Banks. Until 1973 all these funds were automatically invested in central government debt, but since then the Commissioners have been granted wider investment powers.

National Income Accounts The accounts which record the value of transactions within the domestic economy.

National Insurance Funds A central government account into which are paid the National Insurance contributions made by employers and employees and out of which National Insurance benefits are financed.

National Loans Funds The central government account which records transactions involving changes in its financial assets and liabilities.

Near-Money Near-money (sometimes referred to as 'quasi-money') assets refers to those assets which, whilst not performing the means-of-payment function of money, have some of the other characteristics of money, e.g. store of value, medium of exchange. Thus, for example, building society deposits, trade credit, bills of exchange, could be regarded as near-money assets.

Objectives The ends to which economic policies are directed e.g. a certain level of employment.

Open Market Operations The buying and selling of securities (government securities) with the intention of influencing the cash and liquidity base of the banking system and in turn the capacity to lend by the banks. Open market operations are also likely to influence both the level and structure of interest rates.

Organisation of Petroleum Exporting Countries (O.P.E.C.) Oil producing and exporting countries which have experienced massive balance of payments surpluses since the four-fold increase in oil prices in 1973.

Parallel Money Markets This broad term refers to the borrowing and lending (short-term) – largely between the banks – arising from the ebb and flow of funds between the banks. The claims which are associated with these parallel (or complementary) markets are certificates of deposit, inter-bank deposits, short-term loans to local authorities, Euro-currencies, finance house deposits. (See Chapter 5).

Price-Elasticity of Demand The degree of responsiveness of the demand for a product to a change in its price. For example a 10 per cent rise in the price of milk may result in a 2 per cent fall in the quantity demanded. A convenient way of expressing the relationship is to calculate:

$$\frac{\text{Proportionate change in quantity demanded}}{\text{Proportionate change in price}}$$

Thus in the illustration used above, the numerical value of the price-elasticity of demand would be

$$\frac{2}{10} = 0\cdot2$$

Prudential Controls As a result of the secondary banking crisis of 1973–74 the Bank of England together with the London and Scottish clearing banks prepared a joint paper (published in the Bank of England *Quarterly Bulletin*, September 1975, volume 15, No. 3) which set out the broad principles for the assessment of banks' balance sheets. To date, banking supervision and the ensuring of 'banking prudence' by the Bank of England is on an informal basis, i.e. non-statutory, but since the secondary banking crisis of 1973–74 the Bank of England has established a Banking and Money Market Supervision Section which requires all banks registered in the U.K. to submit quarterly returns revealing the main components of their business and to attend interviews at the Bank.

Public Expenditure The expenditure of central government, local authorities, and public corporations which has to be financed by borrowing or taxation.

Public Sector Central government, local authorities, and public corporations.

Public Sector Borrowing Requirement (P.S.B.R.) The amount that the public sector has to borrow to finance its activities.

Quantity Theory of Money A theory which states that changes in the quantity of money bring about variations in the price level.

Retail Deposits Usually regarded as the sum of current accounts and deposit accounts. The use of the expression 'retail' implies that the size of such accounts is relatively small and that the term of the deposit is short. (see *wholesale deposits*)

Retail Price Index An index designed to indicate the general level of prices of goods and services in the U.K. economy. Changes in the Retail Price Index are often used as a measure of the rate of inflation.

Sight Deposits Deposits which are transferable or withdrawable on demand without interest penalty (or interest indemnity). Thus, for example, an individual's current account would represent a sight deposit.

Snake Arrangements which restrict the degree of fluctuation between the exchange values of some European countries, even though these currencies float as a group against all other currencies.

Special Deposits The Special Deposit scheme was announced in 1958. The device involved the mandatory depositing of additional cash with the Bank of England by the London and Scottish Clearing Banks as a percentage of their total deposits. The banks received interest on such deposits in line with the current Treasury bill rate, but these Special Deposits did not count as part of the banks cash and liquidity ratios. Changes in the call for Special Deposits were intended to influence the capacity of the banks to lend. After 1971 and the introduction of *Competition and Credit Control* the Special Deposit scheme applied to all banks.

Special Drawing Rights (S.D.R.s) An additional source of international liquidity introduced by the I.M.F. in 1970. The S.D.R. is a book-keeping entry in the Special Drawing Account of the I.M.F. which, when activated, can be utilised by member countries seeking to finance payments imbalances.

Sterling Balances Sterling bank deposits, money market liabilities, British government stocks, and Treasury bills held by overseas residents.

Supplementary Special Deposits This scheme was introduced in December 1973 and became known as the 'corset'. The target of this scheme was not the assets of the banks but their interest-bearing eligible liabilities; a device which aimed at directly influencing the size of these liabilities. (see Chapter 7)

Tap Stocks These are gilt-edged stocks which are held by the Issue Department of the Bank of England and are known, by the Stock Market, to be available for sale by the Government Broker on behalf of the Bank of England. The tap stocks will vary over time as new issues of stock are made by the Bank, most of this stock being absorbed by the Issue Department and then used as the next tap stock. The Bank usually has a medium-dated and long-dated tap stock available. The prices at which such stocks are sold by the Bank are taken as important market indicators.

Targets The variables which governments hope to influence through the instruments at their disposal e.g. a certain growth in the money supply may be the target to which monetary instruments are directed.

Term Lending This usually refers to medium and long-term lending by banks to, say, companies. The secondary banks in the U.K. were vigorous in the development of this form of lending, but in the 1970s the clearing banks have expanded this form of business – particularly loans of between five and seven years.

Time Deposits Deposits which usually may not be transferred or withdrawn without notice or interest penalty. An individual's deposit account represents such a deposit but in the U.K. the notice of withdrawal may be waived with a consequent loss of interest for the period of notice which has been waived.

Unfunding Unfunding involves the Bank of England selling shorter dated assets – especially Treasury bills – and buying longer dated securities. Such an operation reduces the average maturity of the national debt, and makes the non-government sector 'more liquid'. Unfunding operations are usually intended to raise the liquidity of the banking system and raise its capacity to lend.

Wholesale Deposits These refer to deposits of relatively large denomination placed with banks by large firms and financial intermediaries. The term of the deposit varies, as does the rate of interest on such deposits. Such deposits not only include deposits in excess of £10,000 obtained through bank branches but also deposits obtained through the issue of *certificates of deposit*.

Wilson Committee This is the abbreviated name for the 'Committe to Review the Functioning of Financial Institutions' which was set up in January 1977 under the chairmanship of Sir Harold Wilson.

World Bank (The International Bank for Reconstruction and Development) The sister institution of the I.M.F. which began operations in 1946. The World Bank assists economic development in the poorer countries of the world through making commercial loans to governments and governmental agencies.

Postscript

The new European Monetary System (E.M.S.) first began operations in March 1979, but without the participation of the U.K. Under the scheme, central banks are required to undertake action according to *two* sets of criteria:

1. *A 'parity grid' arrangement* whereby upper and lower intervention rates are established for each currency against all others. No member's currency can move by more than 2¼ per cent against any other member currency, although initially the Italian lira was allowed to move by up to 6 per cent either way.

2. *The European Currency Unit divergence indicator.* The European Currency Unit (E.C.U.) is used as a basis for calculating a central rate for each member's currency. (The E.C.U. is based on a 'basket' of E.E.C. currencies, including sterling, weighted according to their relative importance in E.E.C. output.) Each currency is allocated a maximum percentage deviation against its E.C.U. central rate and when it has reached this limit there is the presumption (but not an obligation) that the domestic government concerned will undertake remedial action.

The reader will recognize that the parity grid arrangement is to operate in a similar way to the snake. But the potentially weaker members of the E.M.S. felt that the parity grid arrangement on its own would put too much of the burden of adjustment on their economies, as did the snake scheme. The inclusion of the E.C.U. divergence indicator represents a compromise since the method of calculation of the E.C.U. results in a decline in its value as weaker E.E.C. currencies depreciate. As a result, the stronger countries will need to take action to ensure that their currencies do not breach the upper values set for them against the E.C.U. By this arrangement it is hoped that adjustment will be to some extent shared.

Index

accepting, 73
accepting houses, 73-4, 159
administration lag, 343
advances, 57, 95, 97, 72-3, 103, 107, 109
aggregate demand, 309
assets
  demand for, 5, 6, 18
  financial, 5, 6, 19, 20, 28, 33
  money, 21, 23-4, 27, 33
  of financial intermediaries, 38, 44-6
  real, 6, 19, 20
  supply of, 6, 18
  see also Clearing banks

balance of payments
  accounts, 245-51
  adjustment between countries, 261-3
  adjustment between regions, 259-61
  adjustment problem, 255-64
  and government borrowing, 139
  and macroeconomic
    management, 331-5, 338, 339-40
  and the money stock, 134-42, 163
  automatic *v.* discretionary
    adjustment, 255-6, 260-1, 262
  capital account, 259-61
  current account, 245, 256-9, 259-61
  elasticity of demand for imports
    and exports, 256-9
  global considerations, 263-4
  investment and other capital
    flows, 248-9
  invisibles, 245-6
  official financing, 250-1
  visibles, 245-6
  U.K. experience under floating, 291-4

Bank Charter Act 1844, 157
Bankers' deposits, 57, 58, 59, 60, 61, 62, 158
bank failure, 84-9, 92
bank financial intermediaries, 43-6, 47, 52, 53
Bank for International Settlements, 254
bank mergers, 93
Bank of England
  and the money market, 154-7
  balance sheets, 157-8
  Bankers' deposits, 58, 59
  Banking department, 57-60
  Banking department liabilities, 57
  bank supervision, 87-8
  control of the banking system, 162-5, 175
  direct controls, 164-5
  establishment, 91
  functions, 147-57
    banking services, 148
    issue of securities, 148
    market management 148-54
    note issue, 148
  government's banker, 122, 123
  Issue department, 149, 150
  lender of last resort, 154
  public deposits, 58, 128
  qualitative controls, 164
  quantitative controls, 164, 167
Bank rate, 110, 161, 163, 174
bank supervision, 84-9
  123 banks, 87
  classification of banks, 86-7
  fringe banks, 87
  insolvency, 85
  'lifeboat', 88
  U.S.A., 190
  White Paper 1976, 87
barter, 22-3, 24-6
base rate, 110
'benign neglect', 279

bill of exchange, 73, 90, 100
branch banking, 93
Bretton Woods Conference, 269
Bretton Woods system
　adjustment, 269-70
　breakdown in the 1970s, 279-80
　co-operation, 273-4
　liquidity, 270-2
　operation in the 1940s and 1950s
　　274-5
　strains of the 1960s, 275-8
Budget, 212, 336
building societies, 16, 45, 48, 50, 53,
　55, 74-6, 111, 174
　and deposit creation, 123-4
　balance sheet, 74
　liquidity ration, 76

capital, 4, 6, 8, 37, 43
cash, 21
　as an asset, 22
　cash shortage, 154-6
　London Clearing Bank holdings,
　　60, 99, 105, 108
　public's demand, 59, 122, 145, 157
cash ratio, 99, 105
　and deposit creation, 114, 128,
　　130, 131, 132, 145
　and the E.E.A., 136, 137
central bank discount rate, 349-50
central government accounts, 216-20
central government borrowing
　requirement
　and the national debt, 216, 227,
　　238
　derivation, 220
certificates of deposit, 57, 73, 101,
　108, 112, 160, 172, 173
circular flow model, 2-5
　and the flow of funds, 7-13
　circular flow, 308-12
Clearing banks, 49, 50, 52, 53, 55-7,
　159, 160, 165, 166
　advances, 57, 95, 97, 103, 107, 109,
　　169
　assets, 96, 97, 99-112
　Bankers' deposits, 57, 58-9
　clearing system, 58-9
　deposits, 98, 110-12

lending policy, 125-6
residual financing role, 133, 151
sight deposits, 56, 115
subsidiaries, 72
clearing house, 58, 93
commercial bills, 73, 90, 100, 105,
　106, 107
Committee of Twenty, 284
Companies Act, 1948, 86
Competition and Credit Control,
　109, 162, 165-76, 236, 238, 346,
　347, 349
　competition, 166-7
　credit control 167
　effectiveness, 168, 170-2, 175, 176
　gilt-edged market, 149, 166
　reserve assets, 107
complementary markets, 104
Consolidated Fund, 217-20
Consumer Credit Act 1974, 87
consumption function, 310
'crawling peg' (or sliding parities)
　system, 302
credit, 44
　and spending, 2
　trade, 27
credit unions (U.S.A.), 178-9
cross-elasticity of demand, 28

deposit banks
　early history, 90-3
　economic basis, 38, 41
　U.K., 48, 90-112
deposit creation
　and advances, 116
　and government borrowing,
　　129-34
　and government receipts, 128-9
　and government spending, 127-8
　and the stock of money, 113-21,
　　145
　deposit-multiplier, 117, 121
　limits, 119, 121-6
deposit multiplier, 117, 127
direct investment, 249
directives, 349
discount houses, 60-2, 72, 99, 100,
　106, 133, 154-7, 159, 173
discounting, 73, 102

dollar
  and the Bretton Woods system,
    270, 271, 277, 279-80, 285
  dollar area, 274, 275
Domestic Credit Expansion
  calculation, 139-40
  definition, 138
  use of the concept, 140-2, 346

E.E.C. and monetary union,
    199-204, 205, 294, 297, 305
  differences between financial
    systems, 202-3
  monetary union implications, 200
  problems for individual countries,
    201-2
  unified central banking, 201-2,
    204
  Werner report, 200
Effective Exchange Rate, 286-91
eligible liabilities, 108, 170
employment objective, 315, 331 see
  also Macroeconomic
  management
equation of exchange, 320
Euro-bond market, 74
Euro-currency market, 74, 104, 112,
    160, 161, 172
  and the oil crisis, 288
  restrictions on loans, 289
European Investment Bank, 303-5
European Monetary Co-operation
  Fund, 296
European Monetary System, 297-8,
    365
European Payments Union, 274-5
European Unit of Account, 304-5
Exchange Control Act 1947, 86
Exchange Equalisation Account,
    135, 155, 252
  and a balance of payments deficit,
    135-6
  and a balance of payments
    surplus, 136-7
Exchange rates,
  and the E.E.A., 135, 136, 137
  and Official Reserves, 136, 137
  determination of, 266-7
exchange rate systems,

adjustable peg, 269-80
  fixed, 268
  fixed v. floating exchange rates,
    298-301
  free-floating, 267
  managed floating, 268-9
expenditure reducing, 262, 263-4,
    276, 332, 338
expenditure-switching, 262
Export Credit Guarantee
  Department, 100, 103

factoring, 79
Federal Deposit Insurance
  Corporation (F.D.I.C.), 180,
    190
Federal Reserve System, 179, 180,
    184-9, 204
  Bankers' bank, 186
  banker to the Federal government,
    187
  discount rate, 189
  Federal Open Market Committee,
    185, 187
  Federal Reserve Districts, 185
  lender of last resort, 186-7, 188
  reserve requirements, 188-9
finance,
  and sectors of the economy, 7-15
  and the circular flow, 2
  and the financial sector, 1, 17
  and the financial system, 1, 6, 17,
    33
  and the government sector, 147
Finance for Industry Ltd., 102

finance houses, 50, 52, 78-80, 159,
    166, 168
financial intermediaries,
  and investment, 43, 46
  assets of U.K. intermediaries, 48,
    51-4
  bank and non-bank, 43-46
  classification, 48-9, 89
  deposit liabilities (sterling), 50
  deposit liabilities (sterling and
    foreign currency), 52
  function, 34, 46
  numbers in the U.K., 48

financial intermediation,
  and lenders, 35-6, 38, 39
  and borrowers, 36-7, 38, 39-40
  and risk, 42
  benefits, 39, 40, 42, 43
  economic basis, 40-2, 46, 68
  nature, 34-42
  process of intermediation, 38-40,
    46
fine-tuning, 344
fiscal policy, 315-8, 328; see also
  Macroeconomic management
floating exchange rates, 267-9,
  284-306
flows,
  flow-of-funds accounts, 7-13, 312,
    354
  sector flows, 7-13
  spending, 6, 7
Friedman, M., 324, 325, 328
'fundamental disequilibrium', 270,
  272, 274, 275
funding, 106, 240

General Agreements to Borrow, 272
General government expenditure see
  public expenditure
gilt-edged market
  and the Government broker, 150
  bank holdings of gilt-edged, 102,
    106, 107
  expectations, 153
  gilt-edged securities, 229-31
  official management, 149, 151,
    163, 166, 175
  redemptions, 152
gold
  and the Bretton Woods system,
    270, 271, 277-8, 279-80
  demonetization, 289-90, 302
  suspension of official
    convertibility, 280, 284
Goldsmith-bankers, 91
gold standard, 268
government accounts, 206-26
Government broker, 150, 152, 240
government securities classifications
  of, 229-30
Gross Domestic Product, 311

Group of Ten, 272

hire purchase, 2
horizontal equity, 222

I.B.E.L.s, 170
import controls, 340
income-expenditure model, 307-19
incomes policies, 339
inflation
  and currency depreciation, 293-4
  and exchange rate systems, 299,
    300
  and international liquidity, 270
  and the money supply, 320-30,
    339, 344, 346
  and the Phillips curve, 333-5
  control via fiscal policy, 315-7,
    331, 338
  control via incomes policy, 335,
    339
  control via monetary policy, 335,
    339, 344, 346
  dangers of hyperinflation, 334
  injections (into the circular flow),
    309-15
  instruments, 336-7, 340-2, 344
insurance companies, 40, 53, 80-2, 111
inter-bank deposits, 71, 160, 172
interbank indebtedness, 59, 61, 122,
  160
inter-bank market, 74, 104, 108, 111,
  160
interest-bearing eligible liabilities see
  I.B.E.L.s
interest rates, 17, 37, 40, 110, 163,
  169-70, 172, 173, 174, 175
  control of, 341, 345, 348
  gilt-edged, 150, 152, 153
  interest rate v. money supply
    control, 153, 162, 239, 240,
    341, 348
  level and structure of, 238-9
  money market, 85, 154-7, 160
  on the national debt, 228
International Development
  Association, 282
International Finance Corporation,
  281-2

international liquidity, 270-2
International Monetary Fund,
    1976 standby facility to the U.K.,
        289, 293
    Articles of Agreement, 269-70, 278
    First Amendment to Articles of
        Agreement, 285
    formation, 269
    General Account, 271
    institutional arrangements, 273-4
    quota system, 271-2, 290
    Second Amendment to Articles of
        Agreement, 285, 289-90, 301,
        302
    Special Drawing Account, 278
    supplementary facilities, 272
investment, 1, 5, 10
    and financial intermediaries, 43
investments
    clearing banks, 102, 106
investment trusts, 30, 83

'J curve' effect, 258, 263, 291
joint stock banks, 55, 91-3

Kaldor, N., 328
Keynes, J.M., 322
Keynesian view, 320, 322-4, 326-30,
    339, 345

lags (in macroeconomic
    management), 342-4
leakages (from the circular flow),
    308-15
'leaning into the wind', 240
leasing, 79
liquid assets ratio, 105, 106, 108, 109,
    163-4, 176
local authorities,
    bills, 100, 108
    borrowing, 73, 83, 101, 159
London and County Securities, 84
London and Scottish Clearing
    Banks, see clearing banks,
    deposit banks

Macroeconomic management,
    331-50
macroeconomic model, 307-19

macroeconomic objectives, 315-16,
    331-5, 336-7, 337-40, 344
managed floating,
    adjustment process, 286-8
    and international co-operation,
        290-1
    defined, 268-9
    historical background, 284-6
    liquidity arrangements, 288-90
    prospects for the future, 301-3
    U.K. experience, 291-4
marginal propensity to consume, 310
marginal propensity to import, 260,
    310
market loans, 71, 100
medium of exchange, 22-3
Minimum Lending Rate, 110, 173-4,
    175, 189, 238-9, 349-50
monetarism, 320, 324-5, 326-30, 339,
    345-7
monetary instruments (techniques),
    344-50
monetary policy,
    and the P.S.B.R., 346-7
    role of, 326-9
    see also Macroeconomic
        management
Monetary union (E.E.C.), 294-8
money,
    M_1, 30-2
    M_2, 30-2
    M_3, 30-2, 134, 173
    and debt management, 239, 240
    and economic activity, 320-30
    and inflation, 23, 24, 26
    and liquidity, 24, 33
    and the balance of payments,
        134-8
    and the government sector, 126-34
    as an asset, 21
    definition, 29, 30, 143
    demand for, 322-6
    deposit creation, 113-21
    functions, 22-7
        medium of exchange, 22-3, 115
        standard for deferred payments,
            26-7
        store of value, 23-4
        unit of account, 24-6

influences on the stock of money,
142-3, 163-4
means of payment, 7, 27, 90, 92,
115
money stock data, 29-32, 33
narrow definition, 30
broad definition, 30
money-substitutes, 27-9, 33
money supply v. interest rate
control, 239, 240, 341, 348
payments mechanism, 90
precautionary demand, 323-4
regulation of the stock of money,
143-4, 169, 341, 344, 345-7,
348
requirements for control of the
stock of money, 144-5
speculative demand, 323-4
sterling M_3, 134, 140, 169
supply of notes and coin, 59
transactions demand, 322-3
money at call, 57, 61, 62, 99, 105,
106, 107, 109, 159, 164
Money Lenders Act 1900, 86
money markets, 154-7, 158-62, 175
moral suasion, 164
multiplier, 312-5
mutual savings banks, 178

national debt, 20
and Competition and Credit
Control, 236
burden of, 241-3
debt management, 237-41
external debt, 237
floating debt, 232
growth of, 227-8
holders of, 232-7
internal v. external debt, 240
productive v. deadweight debt, 242
servicing the debt, 228, 241
types of debt, 229-32
National Debt Commissioners, 233
National Giro, 62-6, 111
net deposits, 64
submission to the 'Wilson
Committee', 64-5
National Income Accounts, 311

national income determination,
307-19
National Loans Fund, 217-20
National Savings Bank, 78
National Savings securities, 232
new issue market, 73, 82
non-bank financial intermediaries,
43-6, 47, 49-51, 52, 53, 89
Northern Ireland banks, see clearing
banks; deposit banks
note issue, 91, 92, 93

official financing, 250-1, 289, 292
official reserves, 136, 137, 250-1, 252,
293, 299, 340, 342
Oil Crisis, 287
Oil Facility, 272, 288
O.P.E.C. surpluses, 287-8
open market operations, 122-3, 348
U.S.A., 187, 188
West Germany, 198-9
operation lag, 343

parallel markets, 104, 158-62, 173,
175
par value, 270
pension funds, 53, 80-2
Phillips curve, 333-5
portfolio investment, 249
price-elasticity of demand, 28
price ratios, 24, 25
primary banking, 54, 55-66, 158,
160, 161, 172
balance sheets, 95-9
Bank of England Banking
department, 57-60
clearing banks, 55-7, 95-112
discount houses, 60-2
operation in the U.K., 94-5
Protection of Depositors Act 1963,
86, 166
Public deposits, 58, 60
public expenditure,
by economic category, 211
by spending authority, 211
by programme, 211-12
definition of, 206-7
goods and services expenditure,
209-10

growth of, 207-10
transfer payments and loans, 209-10
Public Expenditure White Paper, 211, 212, 336
public sector,
  accounts, 213-16
  definition, 206-7
public sector borrowing requirement,
  and domestic credit expansion, 139-40
  derivation, 213-15
  growth, 215
  financing, 225-6
  forecasting the size of, 216
public sector financial deficit,
  derivation, 215

Quantity Theory, 320-2, 324

Radcliffe Report, 163, 329, 345
recognition lag, 343
recycling problem, 288
reserve assets ratio, 68, 70, 71, 107, 108, 109, 166, 168, 169, 173, 176
reserve requirements, 347-8
round-tripping, 173

saving,
  and circular flow, 4, 9, 10
  reasons for, 3, 4
savings and loan associations, 178
'scarce-currency clause', 276
secondary banks, 55, 66-74, 89, 109, 111, 159, 160, 172, 175
  accepting houses, 73
  assets, 71
  definition, 66
  deposits, 67, 71
  method of operation, 68-70
  reserve ratio, 70
sectors,
  behaviour, 9-11, 13-15, 16
  deficit, 13, 14
  definition, 7
  surpluses, 13, 15
  U.K., 12
sight deposits, 30, 56, 72, 109

Slater, Walker Ltd., 84, 88
Smithsonian Conference, 280, 295
snake, 294-8
Special Buyer, 154
Special Deposits, 103, 158, 164, 166, 167, 348-9
Special Drawing Right,
  and the 'Link', 303
  description, 277-8
  future role, 289, 302
sterling area, 274
sterling balances,
  and the balance of payments, 252, 293
  Basle facilities, 253-5
  definition, 251
  ownership, 237, 252
'stop–go', 332, 335
Supplementary Deposit Scheme, 104, 158, 166, 170-1, 174

tap stocks, 150, 240
targets, 336-7, 337-40, 340-2
taxes,
  buoyancy of yield, 224
  costs of collection/compliance, 224
  equity, 222
  incentives, 223
  incidence, 223
  methods of taxation, 220-2
  on capital, 221
  on expenditure, 221
  on income, 220-1
  principles, 222-4
  progressive, proportional, regressive, 222-3
  resource allocation, 223-4
terms of trade, 259
trade-offs (between macroeconomic objectives), 331-5
Treasury bills, 100, 105, 106, 107, 108, 109, 133, 134, 136, 137, 151, 152, 154-5, 156, 163, 164, 173, 232
'tap' issue, 232
Triffin, R., 277
Trustee Savings Banks, 50, 76-7, 89, 111

unit of account, 24-6
unit trusts, 39, 50, 83
U.S.A. commercial banking, 177,
    178, 179, 204
  balance sheets, 182-4
  branch banking, 180
  chain banking, 180-1
  charters, 179, 180
  correspondent banking, 181, 182
  federal funds, 189
  group banking, 180-1
  inter-bank deposit, 181, 182
  national banks, 179-80
  number, 180
  reserve requirements, 188-9
  state banks, 180
  tax and loan accounts, 188
  unit banking, 180

variable rate bonds (or stocks), 231
velocity of circulation, 320-2
vertical equity, 222-3

Ways and Means Advances, 158,
    232, 233
wealth, 7
  composition, 6, 18
  estimates, 19
  growth, 19-20, 33
Werner Report, 200, 294-5
West German banking, 190-9

commercial banks, 191-3, 205
  contrast with the U.K., 194
  credit co-operatives, 193
  discount rate, 197-8
  inter-bank lending, 193, 194
  major financial intermediaries,
    191-4
  mortgage banks, 194
  reserve requirements, 196-7
  savings banks and central giro
    institutions, 193
West German central banking, 191,
    205
  bankers' bank, 195
  banking supervision, 202
  Deutsche Bundesbank operation,
    195-9
  discount rate, 197-8
  lender of last resort, 195, 199
  lombard rate, 198
  monetary policy, 196
  open market operations, 198-9
  reserve requirements, 196
  structure, 195
World Bank (International Bank for
    Reconstruction and
    Development), 280-2, 303

yield
  calculation on a government
    security, 230-1; See also
    interest rates